Haberm:
on Praxis and Modernity

KEY ISSUES IN MODERN SOCIOLOGY

The **Key Issues in Modern Sociology** series publishes scholarly texts that give an accessible exposition of the major structural changes in modern societies. These volumes address an academic audience through their relevance and scholarly quality, and connect sociological thought to public issues. The series covers both substantive and theoretical topics as well as addresses the works of major modern sociologists. The series emphasis is on modern developments in sociology with relevance to contemporary issues such as globalization, warfare, citizenship, human rights, environmental crises, demographic change, religion, postsecularism and civil conflict.

Habermas and Giddens on Praxis and Modernity

A Constructive Comparison

Craig Browne

ANTHEM PRESS

Anthem Press
An imprint of Wimbledon Publishing Company
www.anthempress.com

This edition first published in UK and USA 2018
by ANTHEM PRESS
75–76 Blackfriars Road, London SE1 8HA, UK
or PO Box 9779, London SW19 7ZG, UK
and
244 Madison Ave #116, New York, NY 10016, USA

British Library Cataloguing-in-Publication Data
A catalogue record for this book is available from the British Library.

Library of Congress Cataloging-in-Publication Data
A catalog record for this book has been requested.

ISBN-13: 978-1-78308-862-1 (Pbk)
ISBN-10: 1-78308-862-1 (Pbk)

This title is also available as an e-book.

CONTENTS

ACKNOWLEDGEMENTS

I am quite certain that I would not have been able to complete this book without the support of my family, friends and colleagues. I am most grateful for the work of everyone involved with this project at Anthem Press. I would like to thank the Anthem Press reviewers of a draft of this book for their generosity and most helpful comments. I would particularly like to thank Maria Márkus for her long-standing commitment to my work in social theory. Rob Stones has been enormously significant to the facilitating of this book, and I especially thank him for his interest in my approach to structuration theory. I would like to thank José Maurício Domingues for discussions relating to our shared theoretical interests, as well as for his and Breno Bringel's invitation to participate in the conference on Global Modernity and Social Contestation that they organized. I would like to thank Peter Murphy for his invitation to participate in a conference on Chicago School Sociology – I have learned a great deal from my discussions with him. A number of scholars have contributed to my engagement with the themes of this book, and I would like to mention the contributions of Axel Honneth, Johann P. Arnason, Richard Bernstein and William Outhwaite. I would like to thank Anthony Giddens for discussing his work with me, and Peter Wagner, Hans Joas and Luc Boltanski for the interviews that I conducted with them. My collaborations and discussions with Gilles Verpraet, Simon Susen, Paul Blokker and Colin Cremin have been most valuable. Jocelyn Pixley has been a major source of support, and I have considerably benefited from her advice. I would very much like to thank Phillip Mar for our research collaborations and for his supportive discussions and comments on my work. I would like to thank Daniela Heil most of all for her indefatigable support and incisive perspective.

INTRODUCTION

History is not only an object in front of us, far from us, beyond our reach, it is also our awakening as subjects. (Merleau-Ponty 1973, 30)

Modernity is a sociological category that has both explanatory and normative dimensions. It is commonly used to describe the dominant institutions, patterns of meaning, and modes of living of modern societies. That is, the type of societies that emerged after feudalism, initially in Europe and North America. The category of modernity has always been evaluative, since it is meant to convey some sense of the realization of the modern. The concept of the modern has been consistently used to describe the temporal separation of the present from the past. The modern is not simply a concept or an idea. It is a social imaginary signification, in the sense that Cornelius Castoriadis proposed: the creation of a meaningful outlook on the world and its symbolic representation. Social imaginaries are not just cultural frameworks and representations; they are institution. To be precise, Castoriadis (1987) argues that social imaginaries are instituted and instituting.

The social imaginary of modernity, I argue, concerns the configuring of the relationship between the instituted form of society, in its various dimensions, and the instituting practices of subjects. In its different expressions, modernity involves the view that the existing institution of society is not given and that there is a constant tendency towards transformation inherent in the present. Modernity is a social imaginary in the further sense that this view of the constitution of society and its transformation are only true because of the practices that seek to realize it. For this reason, there is a strong connection between modernity and the ideal of autonomy, since autonomy presupposes that practices are self-determining.

Modernity has to a large extent meant the empowerment of human capabilities. Peter Wagner (1994) observes that modernity is founded on the assumptions that the world is intelligible and shapeable. Of course, the actual institution of modernity has not always been consistent with these principles. Modern institutions have generated new forms of domination and destruction, such as through the market's conditioning of class relations, the power of the apparatuses of the political administrative systems to intensively control individuals and groups, and the destruction of the natural environment as a consequence of industrialization. It is a modernist perspective that assumes that modernity is the condition for transforming modernity's deleterious institutionalization and negative consequences, as well as the transforming of those persisting social relations of domination and the irrational systems of belief that preceded the advent of modernity. This is the modernist standpoint of the two social theorists compared in this work: Jürgen Habermas and Anthony Giddens. Habermas and Giddens have each sought to develop and rethink the modernist vision of the potential constitution of society through the autonomous actions of subjects.

The modernist vision of the autonomous constitution of society is part of a process that emerges from the originally political notion of the constitution of legitimate government. It has a background in the notion that the institution of society originates from the actions of social subjects and that social relations of domination and inequality are amenable to change by the actions of free and equal citizens (Habermas 1996a; Castoriadis 1991). Further, it was at the threshold of modernity that it was recognized that the sphere of political authority did not encompass the broader social preconditions of autonomy. Under pressure from the ensuing political demands and social struggles, this recognition would result in a democratizing of political authority and a protracted process of extending political freedom, eventually to property-less males and subsequently to women. Still, the modernist vision has challenged the sufficiency of political freedom to satisfying the demands for social autonomy, whilst generally considering political freedoms are a progressive development. Further, the unfolding of modernity showed that the 'social' was a realm with its own independent dynamics (Taylor 2004; Honneth 2014). These dynamics have been conceived of in different ways from the outset, such as being viewed as an effect of market exchange or new forms of social association, like those forms generated by the urban metropolis and the concentration of the forces of production.

It was the French Enlightenment, Habermas observes, that incorporated into the concept of modernity the connotations of perfection, improvement and progress; the latter notions drew inspiration from modern science (Habermas 1996a). Modernist perspectives do not derive their justification from prior models or the weight of tradition. Rather, modernism derives its justification from the forms that it gives itself and the linking of the present to the future that it anticipates. In its own formation, the modernist outlook incorporated connotations drawn from the Enlightenment commitment to rationality and the Romantic image of the power of creation. Of course, the Romantic Movement was, in other respects, opposed to the rationalism of the Enlightenment, as well as its individualism. Romanticism evoked as an alternative to rationalization, urbanization and individualism the image of the medieval community's unity with nature. The Romantic Movement, nonetheless, contributed to establishing 'the principle of subjectivity' and the sense of purpose that underlay modernism during the early phase of its inception in the nineteenth century.

> At this juncture, what was considered modern was what assisted the spontaneously self-renewing historical contemporaneity of the *Zeitgeist* to find in itself objective expression. (Habermas 1996a, 39)

Modernity represents not only a major change from the social order of the past, but also a constant tendency towards transformation in the present. In a sense, modernism is precisely the attempt to apply or realize this insight into the changing character of modern society. Modernity involves then a specific cultural outlook and a set of social institutions. Yet, if the modernist vision is one of the autonomous constituting of society by emancipated individuals, the historical development of modernity appears to have institutionalized the dominance of objective social processes over subjectivity. In Marshall Berman's opinion, it is this development that largely shapes the aspirations of modernism: 'I define modernism as any attempt by modern men and women to become subjects as well as objects of modernization, to get a grip on the modern world and make themselves at home in it' (Berman 1988, 6).

The notion of modernity as a social imaginary signification clarifies a significant feature of the comparison that is developed in this work. In the social theories of Habermas and Giddens, modernity is, on the one hand, a topic of interpretation and analysis. Both Habermas and Giddens define the discipline of sociology as distinguished by its concern with the nature of modern societies and the consequences of the unfolding of modernity. According to Habermas, it was the discipline of sociology that 'arose as the theory of bourgeois society; to it fell the task of explaining the course of capitalist modernization of traditional societies and its anomic side effects' (Habermas 1984a, 5). On the other hand, modernity is simultaneously a condition of their theorizing; and their work is animated by the normative intentions connected to modernity, like the aspirations to institute freedom, justice, authenticity, and creativity. Modernity, in effect, informs their perspectives and it is the object of their critical reflections. John Rundell's claim that modernity is constitutive of social relations in a double sense gives significant insight into the reflexive nature of Habermas's and Giddens's respective theoretical projects:

> On the one hand, the category of modernity refers to the historically specific series of complex social formation and institutions that social actors themselves create and inhabit, on the other it is simultaneously a practico-interpretative nexus through which these social forms themselves are constituted. (Rundell 1987, 1–2)

Habermas argues that the core sociological conception of society presumes the modernist vision of the free and equal association of individuals. Sociology seeks to explain the 'tensions, contradictions and ambiguities that arise' from the resistance of reality to the fullest realization of this principle and its normative ideals (Habermas 2001, 59). Giddens similarly considers that modernity is a condition of sociological thought and constitutive of the domain of sociological investigation (Giddens 1990). In his opinion, the sociological conception of society is a product of a specifically modern form of social association and institution (Giddens 1985; 1990). Like Habermas, though on different grounds, Giddens considers that the sociological conception of society is founded on the assumption that the social order is constructed through the actions of associated individuals. Habermas and Giddens develop social theoretical perspectives that reflect what Castoriadis describes as the modern social imaginary of the project of autonomy's exclusion of extra-social explanations of the institution of society or the social order, hence it excludes, for instance, notions of the social structure as divinely ordained (Castoriadis 1991).

In the context of debates over modernity, my decision to explore the possibilities and limitations of the social theories of Habermas and Giddens is not an arbitrary one. There are a myriad of challenges to the modernist project of an autonomous society and these require a constructive response, rather than either simply the reiteration of established positions or the indiscriminate embracing of the rejections of modernity, whether from postmodernist standpoints or the reactionary perspectives that are often defined as religious fundamentalism. On the one hand, rejectionist perspectives are contradictory and necessarily veil the extent to which their positions are actually founded on modernist suppositions. This assessment applies even to fundamentalist discourses and their reactionary mobilizations (see Eisenstadt 1999). On the other hand, these rejections of modernity generally involve some confusion of the part with the whole; and this is a result of analytical deficiencies. There is indisputably considerable validity to critiques of modernity, in that critiques can reference such phenomena as the distortions of the emancipatory intentions of modernist political projects, the destructive environmental consequences of industrialization, and the occlusion of non-Western experiences.

It is likewise correct to claim that critical perspectives on modernity, particularly those of postmodernists, contributed to making modernity a topic of intense debate during the past decades (Lyotard 1984; Beck 1992). There are equally important points of substantive disagreement between various critical and rejectionist positions, especially between those of anti-modernism and postmodernism. Nevertheless, these positions generally share an antipathy towards the presuppositions of the modernist conception, particularly with respect to the notions of rationality and universality. This sets them apart from Habermas and Giddens.

Despite pronounced differences and explicit disagreements, a common defining feature of Habermas's and Giddens's respective programmes is a constructive orientation. That is, the requirements of their projects of renewing social theory guided their critiques of other theoretical perspectives; similarly, when their elaborations appeared unsatisfactory they made revisions. Still, a constructive orientation entails more than continuity and a commitment to an overall purpose. Given the theoretical demands and practical aspirations of Habermas's and Giddens's projects, they each find the further dimensions of originality and innovation unavoidable. A good deal of the value, perhaps ultimately even the validity, of their projects relates to the respective claims they make to have not so much extended established frameworks as to have realized a fundamental transformation of earlier paradigms. It is nevertheless important to stress that their 'abandonments' of earlier paradigms are not based on a rejection of the problems that preceding approaches in social theory addressed. Neither have Habermas and Giddens forsaken the demands of systematic rethinking in favour of discrete arguments and a relativist attitude towards the moral implications of their standpoints – a characteristic of certain postmodern theorists. The explicating of the failings of extant perspectives complemented Habermas's and Giddens's endeavours to develop innovative theoretical perspectives.

For these reasons, Habermas and Giddens are set apart from contemporary perspectives that consider the universalistic value system of the 'modernist project' to have primarily disguised and augmented systematic forms of domination. Although Habermas and Giddens are mainly critics of postmodern approaches, the constructive dimensions of their respective programmes contain synthetic elements that are sometimes assumed to be at odds with the formulation of an internally coherent perspective. Habermas's and Giddens's social theories are assemblages in the two-fold sense of being open to various approaches and incorporating facets of them into their theories, while being explicit that the fabricating process is never finalized. Because of this lack of completion, many of their most developed positions are only provisional.

There is sufficient common ground between Habermas and Giddens to make this critical perspective incisive and the contrast between them reciprocally illuminating. Habermas's theory of communicative action and Giddens's theory of structuration represent two extremely detailed attempts to reconceptualize the action theoretical foundations of sociological theory. Both theorists seek to account for social systems but they largely agree that a conception of social action has an initial precedence in theorizing the constitution of society. These theorists are opposed to a similar range of perspectives and develop their theories from the standpoint of a critique of functionalism. Habermas and Giddens reject a positivist methodology for the social sciences and support some version of a hermeneutically informed method of inquiry. In different ways, they have sought to determine the implications the 'linguistic turn' in philosophy for social theory, yet they refuse any notion of the dissolution of the subject. A notion often associated with structuralist and poststructuralist versions of this transition from consciousness to language in twentieth-century philosophy. At the same time, they consider that subjectivity needs to be rethought from the perspective of its intersubjective constitution and that the modern ideal of autonomy should be redefined in light of this properly social conception.

Habermas's and Giddens's oppositions to the postmodern renunciation of moral universalism and destructive critiques of reason have already been indicated; however, they do suggest that modernity has undergone a significant transformation in the contemporary period. New orientations are required, they believe, to comprehend this development and they have sought to specify the practical-political ramifications of this change for social democracy. In particular, their later writings address the contemporary prospects for a democratizing of late capitalist society and they aim to shape, as well as explain, the new politics of identity and forms of living that have emerged in recent decades. The crisis of the European Union has been a common concern of the most recent works of Habermas and Giddens, as well as something that they have sought to influence through participating in political initiatives and public forums (Habermas 2012; Giddens 2014; 2007).

Similarly, Habermas's and Giddens's explications of the modernist visions have always been combined with explanations of the social structural impediments to the realization of the modernist ideal of the autonomous constitution of society. In one sense, this means that they have each sought to explain prevailing forms of heteronomy and domination. Yet, they consider that modern forms of heteronomy and domination are heavily bound up with the institutional systems, particularly capitalism and the state, that sustain the dynamic character of modernity. In this respect, Habermas's and Giddens's respective approaches to modernity contain a critical diagnostic component.

Habermas sought, above all, to revise the earlier critical theory of the Frankfurt School and its conception of rationalization in modernity as a process of the reification of consciousness. Habermas endeavours to redefine the terms in which this critical diagnosis is framed and offers an alternative approach to the Frankfurt School's vision of rationalization as eventuating in a more pervasive form of domination. Indeed, his critical diagnosis depends on reconfiguring Max Weber's theory of modernity and reinterpreting Weber's theses of modern rationalization's generating a loss of freedom and a loss of meaning (Weber 1958). Broadly, Habermas argues that an original modernizing process of communicative rationalization becomes overtaken by the instrumentally and functionally rationalized systems of the capitalist economy and the bureaucratic state administration. The dominance of markets and bureaucracy results in the erosion and corruption of the communicative infrastructure of social reproduction and this process can generate social pathological consequences, like losses of meaning, legitimacy and identity. Habermas (1984a; 1987a) contends then that modernity is, in its institutional realization and actual developmental trajectory, 'at variance with itself', and that this paradox is manifested in forms of injustice, suffering, and domination, as well as the forms of conflict and resistance to them.

In the case of Giddens's theory, modernity is depicted as inherently 'double-edged'. Giddens claims that modern institutions and ways of living are particularly dynamic compared to premodern conditions and that the heightened reflexivity of modernity involves the active reconstituting of organizations and identities. However, the very same tendencies of modernity, like industrialization and the expansion of information, can have the paradoxical consequences of increasing risk, uncertainty and insecurity. This critical diagnosis is a major feature of Giddens's interventions in relation to contemporary political developments and it underpins his claims for 'utopian realism' in theory and politics (Giddens 1994a). One can readily see that the formats of Habermas's and Giddens's critical diagnoses are concerned with the relationship between the objectivity of the social order and the subjectivity of individuals.

The general themes of history and the subject serve to organize my inquiry into the work of Habermas and Giddens. These two themes were chosen because of their fundamental importance to the modernist vision of the autonomous constitution of society and because the Marxian perspective of a philosophy of praxis developed a particularly salient explication of their intersection. The central place that the subject and history occupy in this perspective is not itself a distinguishing feature of the Marxian philosophy of praxis. Rather, this perspective is distinctive in its assuming that the historical development of society and the constitution of the subject are interdependent processes. Human praxis is conceived to be integral to both of these processes and this conception is founded on the contention that praxis mediates between them. In other words, the distinguishing feature of this perspective is its supposition that the nexus between history and the subject is *practically* constituted and that changing their intersection amounts to a transformation of society.

For this reason, the philosophy of praxis initially derives an image of the *social* from its interpretation of the formative character of human praxis, but the substantive form the social takes is then brought into view through its explicating the historical conditions and consequences of the subject's action. The *social* is conceived to be both the created form and the originating context of the praxis that forges the connection between the subject and history. The praxis philosophy conception of the social represents a specific interpretation and disaggregation of the modernist *problematique* of the relation between the institutionalized order of society and socially instituting practices. It is one that, as my analysis shows, has had a significant bearing on Habermas's and Giddens's perspectives. Given the significance of the philosophy of praxis to the comparison that I develop, it is therefore necessary to explicate some of the background to this approach and its general considerations.

Philosophy of Praxis

The precise meaning of the Marxian perspective of a philosophy of praxis is somewhat elusive. In a sense, praxis philosophy signifies a general orientation with a few distinctive themes rather than a separate theoretical position in its own right. On the one hand, to the extent that Marx remained the common reference point of the philosophy of praxis, there was no need to independently systematize this perspective. On the other hand, the category of praxis philosophy has an elastic quality; it acquired various connotations through its different associations in the history of Marxism. In order to fully appreciate the background to the problem of the intersection of the subject and history, it is necessary to selectively review some of the philosophy of praxis' major developments. Importantly, this will demonstrate that the notion of 'the social' is not a static category and how contemporary theoretical challenges to praxis philosophy are grounded in critiques of the subject and history. The background suppositions of praxis philosophy provide yardsticks for my evaluation of Habermas's and Giddens's respective approaches to modernity. 'Praxis philosophy', Habermas claims, 'hoped to derive the normative content of modernity from the reason embodied in the mediations of social practice' (Habermas 1987b, 343). Habermas's and Giddens's theoretical frameworks seek to modify the praxis philosophy understanding of the social; partly through introducing considerations that are either not found within this tradition or are underdeveloped by it.

At the risk of underestimating significant differences, the opposition to the objectivism of the 'orthodox' Marxist conception of historical materialism is a unifying dimension of the philosophy of praxis tradition. This preliminary, negative definition converges with Western Marxism's original positive retrieval of subjectivity and Lukács, Korsch and Gramsci's complementary, though in each case different, accentuations of the active-practical dimension of social transformation (Lukács 1971; Korsch 1970; Gramsci 1971). Western Marxists criticized the reduction of Marxism's idealist philosophical heritage, they argued that a critical theory differed methodologically from the model of positive science. Marxism did not aim to discover immutable laws but recognized the historical grounds of its critique. In the opinion of Western Marxists, like Lukács and Sartre, Friedrich Engels's extension of the dialectic from the domain of history to the realm of nature gave credence to the scientistic misunderstanding of orthodox Marxism (Engels 1954; Lukács 1971; Sartre 1976). The practical cast of Marx's materialism made it fundamentally different from materialist conceptions derived from the principles of nineteenth-century natural science. Similarly, Marx's critique of idealist notions of the subject did not annul subjectivity; rather the subject was redefined. Marx had, in any case, criticized philosophical materialism for disregarding constituting human practices in the *Theses on Feuerbach* (Marx 1977b). These early Western Marxists were distinguished by their inquiries into the subjective conditions of revolution and the introduction of more complex notions of ideology than the reductionist accounts of consciousness, which some orthodox Marxists considered a materialist outlook required. Since the authority of Communist parties was recognized to be potentially in question, these disputes initiated a reconsideration of the relationship between theory and practice.

Even so, well before the demarcation of a Western Marxist tradition, the designation of Marxism as a philosophy of praxis had gained a certain usage amongst Italian Marxists. This self-definition reflected the substantial influence of Hegelian philosophy over Italian intellectual culture during the late nineteenth and early twentieth centuries (see Piccone 1983). Of course, this usage would later become best known through Gramsci's (1971) *Prison Notebooks*, where the *philosophy of praxis* represented more than a code Gramsci employed to evade the censor; it referred to the Marxist commitment to an 'absolute historicism'. In particular, Gramsci suggested that the evolutionary historical materialist theories ascendant during the Second International were inconsistent with this historicism and that under some circumstances their conception of rigid laws of development were an obstacle to revolutionary social transformation (Gramsci 1994). Yet, this Italian Marxist notion of a philosophy of praxis was itself a product of a specific reading of Hegel. Hegel the phenomenologist of history was unlike Hegel the logician of science – which influenced more objectivist and determinist strands of Marxism (see Jacoby 1981).

The former Hegel (1977) was principally interested in the problem of freedom and the emergence of a consciousness capable of realizing this notion, whereas the latter Hegel (1975; 1967) appeared to subordinate the subject to an overarching system and employed a determinist teleology incommensurate with the standpoint of a philosophy of praxis. It is clear then that not all versions of Hegelian-Marxism constitute a philosophy of praxis, but, generally, Hegelian themes are integral to this orientation. Indeed, a good deal of praxis philosophy would be impossible to comprehend without an appreciation of this Hegelian background and Marx's critical extension of the Young Hegelian programme. In short, the Young Hegelian programme consisted in transforming reality so that it actually conformed to the highest notion that Hegel had shown the modern period contained.

The Young Hegelians' major concern was already the problem of the unification of theory and practice. In their view, Hegel brought philosophy into contact with the historical present and theory to its present conclusion. Despite Hegel's concept of reason having been interpreted as a conservative endorsement of the state, the dialectical principles of Hegel's philosophy incorporated radical change and praxis was demanded to resolve the discrepancy between the reality of the state and its ideal conception. Marx's initial starting point too was a critique of Hegel's resolution of the problem of reconciling the universal and the particular (Marx 1977c). Marx argued that the state did not constitute a real embodiment of the universal and that the citizenship rights connected to this political institution represented only a limited form of emancipation. Socializing the principles of modern freedom was the condition of their becoming real, because the rights of the citizen did not coincide with the social realm of an everyday life practice.

In Marx's analysis, the state was constituted through its abstraction from the social relations of civil society; it created the illusion of an ideal community without actually transcending particular interests. Marx gave the Young Hegelian orientation towards the concrete and finite a more precise sociological determination. He asserted that the problem of unifying theory and practice could not be solved from the side of theory alone, for theory to be realized it had to correspond to the needs of subjects and depended on these subjects capacity to transform the existing social order. For Marx, the working class represented a concrete embodiment of a universal interest in emancipation and the future extension of modern political freedoms corresponded to the needs of this class for radical change. Because labour is the constituting activity of the social realm of everyday life activity, he argued that socialism would be the historical form of the new stage of universal emancipation that would emerge from class struggle and the abolition of private property (Marx 1977a; Marx and Engels 1977).

The unification of theory and practice was probably the aspect of the philosophy of praxis that was under greatest strain from the outset. This difficulty would result in its other dimensions taking on greater prominence. However, for the instigators of the tradition of Western Marxism, the nexus between history and subjectivity in revolutionary practice was constitutive of the social. The revolutionary process represented for them the high water mark of a conscious history making which overturned the old social order and this practice of changing circumstances coincided with the self-transformation of subjects themselves (Marx 1977b). It seemed that the subject and history were fused in the revolution and the belief that such action had a world-historical significance undoubtedly reflected the influence of the French Revolution upon Marxism.

Modern political philosophy had articulated the rational principles of natural law and the notion of political authority based on popular sovereignty, but the French Revolution broke practically with the idea that there is an extra-social source of the social institution (Castoriadis 1990; Habermas 1974a). Marx recognized that this rupture was the precondition for delineating the philosophy of praxis's seminal problem. Marx's understanding of the *social* grounding of critique motivated his analyzing the constitution of society in terms of production. This 'materialism' or 'naturalized humanism' may have distinguished his position from the Young Hegelian programme of critique, yet Marx retained the synthetic interest of Hegelian theory in mediating and transcending many of the traditional philosophical oppositions (Marx 1977a) These antinomies extend beyond those contrasts that have already been mentioned, like the problems of unifying theory and practice, and that of mediating the universal and the particular.

> Communism, as fully developed naturalism equals humanism, and as fully developed humanism equals naturalism; it is the *genuine* resolution of the conflict between man and nature and between man and man – the true resolution of the strife between existence and essence, between objectification and self-confirmation, between freedom and necessity, between the individual and the species. Communism is the riddle of history solved, and knows itself to be this solution. (Marx 1977a, 97)

Marx differed from his contemporaries in locating the condition for the solution to these philosophical antinomies in the transformation of social relations and institutionalizing of a new principle of social organization. He argued that these conceptual oppositions had an actuality that derived from the conditions of their historical genesis and their reproduction through the persistence of unjust social structures. For this reason, the philosophical accounts of these antinomies were true in establishing a set of problems, but mistaken in making them into a permanent condition. In his opinion, such difficulties were inevitable owing to a failure to inquire into the social constitution of these

dualisms and the separation of theory from practice. Marx's criticisms specify two originally unique features of the critical theory of the philosophy of praxis: a reflexive structure based on a notion of the social-historical production of knowledge and an interest
in the social-historical translation of philosophical categories and problems. These set
critical theory apart from the empirical social sciences that are indifferent to the normative implications of knowledge and equally from the idea of critique in transcendental
philosophy, which seeks to supply ahistorical epistemological foundations. It is, however,
worth noting that Kant's privileging of practical over theoretical reason in his critiques
and his activist conception of transcendental consciousness were each significant for the
later development of praxis philosophy (Kant 1997).

This interest in practically transcending conceptual antinomies distinguishes the
praxis philosophy perspective from other approaches that share some similar assumptions. Durkheim recognized the social constitution of the categories of consciousness
to an unparalleled degree, but originally employed various dichotomies to define the
social (see Lukes 1973). Now, these divisions probably reflect the neo-Kantian background to his sociological theory. Moreover, Durkheim's suggestion that 'social facts'
be considered as 'things' contradicts the *process* approach of the philosophy of praxis
and its concern with the constituting activities of the subject (Durkheim 1964a). From
Lukács (1971) onwards, Western Marxists criticized the reification contained in the
equation of social reality with things. Lukács argued that the Marxist dialectical conception of the dynamic relationship between subjectivity and objectivity is superior
to this replication of the immediate experience of capitalism as a reality independent of its social constitution. In the Marxist dialectic, Lukács argued, 'the knowledge that social facts are not objects but relations between men is intensified to the
point where facts are wholly dissolved into processes' (Lukács 1971, 180). Besides its
being basic to the disclosure of the potential for change immanent in the present, an
opposition to static categorizations of society implies a fundamental concern with the
temporal dimension of social action and social structures (Lefebvre 1968; Marcuse
1987; Giddens 1979). This consideration is important to distinction that will be drawn
between Giddens and Habermas, with former more concerned with temporal and
spatial character of society.

Subject and History

Habermas has drawn attention to a further supposition underlying the intention of
overcoming antinomies, that is, that the notion of synthesis depends on a conception
of historical subjectivity (Habermas 1987b; 1978a). In his opinion, this demonstrates
the extent to which Hegel's original diagnosis of the diremptions of modernity shaped
the aspirations of the philosophy of praxis. At the same time, Habermas considers that this continuity decisively determined praxis philosophy's paradigmatic limitations, because Hegel's diagnosis of these modern divisions and his specifying the
means for their resolution were framed within the paradigm of the philosophy of
the subject (Habermas 1987a). Similarly, Marcuse highlighted the intrinsic connection between Hegel's ontological 'principle of subjectivity' and a dialectical emphasis

upon process itself. Marcuse (1967, 63) understands Hegel's attempt to 'bridge' the separations of Kantian philosophy to have resulted in an ontology that posited an identical structure of being:

> The subject that the essence reveals itself to be is not outside the process nor is it its unchangeable substratum; it is the very process itself, and all its characters are dynamic. (Marcuse 1967, 143)

Now, despite the retrieval of subjectivity being a defining feature of Western Marxism, the issues surrounding the subject are associated with fractures within this tradition and the broader disagreements over the exact character of Marx's critique of Hegel's thought. For example, amongst the Frankfurt School circle of critical theory, Adorno (1989) upholds a process approach to society, however, he opposes Hegel's identity thinking on the grounds of its implied suppression of particularity and its subordination of the object to the subject (Adorno 1993; 1979). Adorno's 'negative dialectic' also stresses mediating processes but refuses any abstract accord between the logical concept of identity and the non-identical concrete object. He argues that Hegel's philosophy falsely 'solved' through identity thinking what remains an open questions concerning the constitution of the subject. In so arguing, Adorno sketched a basic dilemma in the history of the notion of the subject:

> 'Subject', for instance, may refer to the particular individual as well to general attributes, to 'consciousness in general' in the language of Kant's *Prolegomena*. The equivocation is not removable simply by terminological clarification, for the two meanings have reciprocal need of each other; one is scarcely to be grasped without the other. The element of individual humanity – what Schelling calls 'egoity' – cannot be thought apart from any concept of the subject; without any remembrance of it, 'subject' would lose all meaning. Conversely, as soon as we reflect upon the human individual as an individual at all, in the form of a general concept – as soon as we cease to mean only the present existence of some particular person – we have already turned it into a universal similar to that which came to be explicit in the idealist concept of the subject. The very term 'particular person' requires a generic concept, lest it be meaningless. (Adorno 1978, 498)

Marx did not entirely eliminate the tensions between these different understandings of the subject, but he established, to be sure, new criteria for conceiving the interconnections between them. Marx's paradigmatic turn to production involved a stress on the concrete and finite individual; the subject is the sensuous human individual, and hence the importance needs have in determining the centrality of production (Markus 1986a; Heller 1976). Yet, Marx's consistent critique of the individualistic standpoint of political economy and liberal philosophy complemented his opposition to idealist notions of a superindividual subject (Marx 1976). Production, Marx argued, is never an activity of isolated individuals; it always implies intersubjective relations and social cooperation. Similarly, in both his historical analyses and political pamphlets, Marx considered association to be constitutive of the political formation of social classes (Marx 1977d; Marx and Engels 1977). And, as such, the revolutionary subject was a collective actor.

Furthermore, Marx retained the Enlightenment perspective in specifying the human species as the subject of historical progress (Marx 1970).

Of particular significance, Marx however went beyond the typical Enlightenment notions of rationality in conceiving the conjunction between these different images of the subject to be a consequence of social relations. A notion of the social underpins each of these images and informs Marx's contention that the attributes of the subject can only be defined historically, rather than through positing an essence that is prior to the historical process and outside of society (Marx 1977b). This social determination of the subject has not precluded subsequent debates over the consistency between Marx's different images of the subject, such as whether it pertains to individual subjects in their social relations, the working class as the collective subject of emancipatory change, or the human species as the subject of the historical process of material production. Even where one alternative among the images of subject has been chosen, it has often meant that the dilemmas have simply been displaced onto another category of the philosophy of praxis. The different rendering of the subject are treated by me as part of the way in which the problem of the modern constitution of society has been addressed; that is, rather than considering the displacement between categories as solely a deficiency. In particular, it enables the complications of Habermas's and Giddens's reformulations of the nexus between the subject and history to be delineated.

Despite the tensions between different understandings of the subject, the anthropological premises of Marx's thought were critical to differentiating the philosophy of praxis perspective from that of orthodox Marxism. Indeed, Marx's *Economic and Philosophical Manuscripts of 1844* are often considered the *locus classicus* of praxis philosophy because of their detailed statement of his anthropology and the way their belated publication confirmed Western Marxists' arguments concerning themes which orthodoxy suppressed (Marx 1977a). In particular, the *Manuscripts'* concept of objectification demonstrated how much richer the philosophical presuppositions of Marx's notion of labour were than those of the dominant evolutionary Marxist theories of human development as deriving from advances in production. The *Manuscripts* similarly disclosed how Marx reworked the normative ideals of the emancipation of the subject in modern thought. Further, they demonstrated the extent to which this reworked conception shaped Marx's entire understanding of the constitution of society. Marx developed in them an expressive account of action that went beyond the Enlightenment notions of the rational subject; he incorporated into his anthropology of labour the ideals of creativity and self-realization that derive from the Romanticist movement (see Joas 1996; Seidman 1983). Marx's romanticism is evident in his view that the created object is an expression and embodiment of the subjectivity of its producer. Similar romantic ideas of subjective creation had influenced the notion of consciousness in German idealist philosophy; however, Marx transformed Hegel and Fichte's respective notions of a world-constituting and creative subjectivity (Hegel 1977; Fichte 1982). Indeed, Marx asserted that the productive activity of labour was the nucleus of Hegel's entire dialectic:

> The outstanding achievement of Hegel's *Phänomenologie* and its final outcome, the dialectic of negativity as the moving and generating principle, is thus first that Hegel conceives of the

self-creation of man as process, conceives objectification as loss of the object, as alienation and the transcendence of this alienation; that he thus grasps the essence of labour and comprehends objective man – true, because real man – as the outcome of man's *own labour*. (Marx 1977a, 140)

This critical insight into Hegel's philosophy was influenced by Feuerbach's method of critique and its 'materialist' attempts to demonstrate inversions of subject and predicate. But since this method was actually compatible with the Hegelian dialectic, Marx was still able to deploy Hegelian categories, like externalization and alienation – the difference being that these categories now disclosed social contradictions grounded in the processes and conditions of material production. It would be hard, from our perspective, to exaggerate the importance of Marx's analysis of objectification and alienation. In the *1844 Manuscripts*, he contends that private property originates from the activity of alienated labour and that the institution of private property subsequently perpetuates the alienation of labour. In this way, the alienation that made the constituting subjects dependent on the things they created served to also disguise the class character of the system of production and ideologically legitimated the capitalist social structure. In this conception, alienation is not solely an individual experience, but a social-structural phenomenon. Merleau-Ponty's commentary on Marx's statement that capital is not a thing but a social relation indicates why the dialectic of subjectivity and objectivity represents the praxis philosophical core of Marx's later systematic critique of political economy (Marx 1976).

> This exchange, by which things become persons and persons things, lays the foundation for the unity of history and philosophy. It makes all problems historical but also all history philosophical, since forces are human projects become institutions. (Merleau-Ponty 1973, 33)

Marx's perception then, that human subjects not only objectify themselves in things but that they are also the *objects* of the historical process delineates a seminal problem: that is, to inquire into praxis is to seek to explain how the creation of a social world can also elude that of its creator. Hence, it is necessary to explain how the social institutions subjects create can determine their activity and thereby deny subjects' autonomy. This basic paradox shaped the analytical approach of the entire tradition of the philosophy of praxis. Marx's opening précis of this problem in *The Eighteenth Brumaire of Louis Napoleon*, remains unsurpassed and is often quoted for this reason:

> Men make their own history, but they do not make it just as they please; they do not make it under circumstances chosen by themselves, but under circumstances directly encountered, given and transmitted from the past. (Marx 1977d, 301)

The twentieth-century history of the philosophy of praxis mirrors the open dialectic implied by the idea of 'making history' and the appreciation of indeterminacy that resulted from it (see Jay 1973; Castoriadis 1987). In a sense, the fortunes of the philosophy of praxis have fluctuated, rather than progressed in a rigid and linear fashion (see Arato and Breines 1979). This history eventuates in the contemporary paradox of the distinctive orientation of the philosophy of praxis being probably more widely recognized than ever before and simultaneously of this perspective being arguably on the wane. The recent stage of praxis philosophy is one in which aspects of its general orientation have become diffuse features of contemporary social theory. Praxis philosophy informs diverse notions of social construction and the different interests of theorists, like Alain Touraine, Pierre Bourdieu, Hans Joas, and José Maurício Dominuges, in analyzing the practical formation of society. In Touraine's terms, this appropriation is concerned with the 'inner workings' of dynamic social processes and it attempts to 'define society according to its historic reality, its historicity, the way it acts on itself – in a word, according to its praxis' (Touraine 1971, 3–4).

According to Giddens, contemporary inquiries into the 'self-production of society' and the practical logic of social reasoning emerged in response to structural-functionalist sociology and the objectivism of positivist methodology in the social sciences perceived limitations (Giddens 1979; 1984). In respect of the underlying themes and the reasoning of the critiques that inspired them, these contemporary reworkings of the intentions of praxis philosophy are responding to problems similar to those found in orthodox Marxism but applying more generally in social thought. At the same time, contemporary theoretical perspectives claiming to represent more advanced and radical approaches have contested the relevance of philosophy of praxis owing to its Marxian background. The philosophy of praxis is seen as implicated in the overall 'crisis of Marxism'. In fact, praxis philosophy has been criticized for its modernist suppositions and figures associated with this perspective, like Agnes Heller and Ferenc Feher, have redefined their perspective in a way that takes some distance from aspects of modernist thought (Heller and Feher1988).

This has meant that the praxis philosophy critique of the subject and history, as well as its synthesis of them, has sometimes been assimilated to modernist perspectives that it originally sought to refine and contest. One of the results of this assimilation has been the contemporary occlusion of the philosophical problems that sociology sought to address and the manner in which this constituted a response to the limitations of the early articulation of the modernist vision of the autonomous constitution of society (see Wagner 2008; Chernilo 2014). For Habermas (1992a, 6–7), a 'reversal of the primacy of theory' over the practical is one of the defining features of twentieth-century thought. Even so, he attributes the prominence of poststructuralist and postmodernist theory to 'the fact that the efforts of praxis philosophy to reformulate the project of modernity along Marxist lines has suffered a loss in credibility' (Habermas 1987b, 327).

Structuralism, Poststructuralism and Postmodernism

The categories of the subject and history have each been the topic of extended critiques by theorists usually associated with the approaches of structuralism, poststructuralism and postmodernism. These movements are connected to the broader 'linguistic turn' in twentieth-century thought and this change to the analysis of language founds a rejection of the paradigm of the philosophy of consciousness. Praxis philosophy was originally defined by its active-practical critique of the philosophy of consciousness and its social critique of the liberal notion of the subject. However, such critiques were a prelude to the presentation of a positive conception of the subject in the philosophy of praxis. By contrast, the structuralist version of the 'linguistic turn' displaces the notion of a constituting subjectivity onto the relation between elements of a language system, and, as Wellmer remarks, with reference also to Wittgenstein's conception of language games, what 'is destroyed by the critique conducted by the philosophy of language is the subject as author and ultimate arbiter of its own intentions' (Wellmer 1991, 65; Honneth 1995b). The linguistic critique of the subject undermines a major conception of reason in modern thought.

Similarly, Freud's psychoanalytic account of the divisions within the psyche has sometimes been seen as paralleling the philosophy of praxis problem of the inversion of the subject into an 'object' of social processes which it does not control (see Habermas 1978a). Yet, the normative model of the emancipation of the subject, deriving from the modern ideal of autonomy, has been placed in question by an appreciation of the fractured nature of the psyche and the dependence of consciousness on the corporeal substrate of the body. Wellmer suggests that a psychological critique of the subject has come to be seen during the twentieth century as complementing and reinforcing the implications of the linguistic critique of the subject (Wellmer 1991, 58–59). These displacements of the notion of constituting subject in epistemology and disputes over the normative-political interpretation of autonomy have substantial consequences for the approach to history of praxis philosophy. Althusser's structuralist critique of Marxist humanism focussed on the intersection of the subject and history. He could not be more explicit in his opposition to the inspiration praxis philosophy drew from Marx's early writings (Althusser 1969). After Lacan, he perceives Freud to have accomplished a scientific rupture analogous to that of Marx. Yet, Althusser's commentary betrays a sense of futility in even envisaging a possible change in the relationship of the subject to history.

> Not in vain did Freud sometimes compare the critical reception of his discovery with the upheavals of the Copernican Revolution. Since Copernicus, we have known that the earth is not the 'centre' of the universe. Since Marx, we have known that the human subject, the economic, political or philosophical ego is not the 'centre' of history – and even, in opposition to the Philosophers of the Enlightenment and to Hegel, that history has no 'centre' except in ideological misrecognition. In turn, Freud has discovered for us that the real subject, the individual in his unique essence, has not the form of an ego, centred on the 'ego', on 'consciousness' or on 'existence' – whether this is the existence of the for-itself, of the body-proper or of 'behaviour' – that the human subject is de-centred, constituted by a structure which has no 'centre' either, except in the imaginary misrecognition of the 'ego', i.e. in the ideological formations in which it 'recognizes' itself. (Althusser 1971, 200–201)

Although the decentering of the subject and history is a common feature of structuralist, poststructuralist and postmodernist theorizing, these themes were developed in various ways and sometimes in opposition to other theorists in these traditions. Despite the modifications in Foucault's thought, his programme included a critical rejection of the synthesis of Marxism and phenomenology that was typical of the postwar praxis philosophy (Foucault 1998). Foucault outlines a number of variant, but overlapping, critiques of the notion of a history constituting subjectivity. He contends that the notion of 'man' is the product of a modern discursive formation that is in the process of being discarded. This image of the subject produces a series of antinomic doublings, like those 'of the empirical and the transcendental, the perpetual relation of the cogito to the unthought, the retreat and return of the origin' (Foucault 1970, 335). These antinomies are all part of the irredeemable project of securing the foundation of knowledge in 'man'.

Foucault likewise endorses Nietzsche's unmasking of the 'monumental history' of development and asserts that notions of historical continuity preserved 'the sovereignty of the subject, and the twin figures of anthropology and humanism' (Foucault 1972, 12; 1977, 161). Foucault contrasts with these his own genealogical approach to history and he utilizes a genealogical method to analyze the normalizing power implicated in the production of subjectivity. The implementation of liberal-humanist ideals, he claims, resulted in new disciplinary mechanisms and the forms of liberal governance which are constitutive of the modern realm of the social (Foucault 1977a; 1980). Foucault's later analyses of the self and the body are part of the renewed poststructuralist interest in alternate subjectivities, yet Foucault's ideas of subjects' resistance to power-knowledge regimes constitutes a too limited account of agency (Foucault 1980; 1982; see Bernstein 1991).

In extending the critical implications of the linguistic turn for the subject and reason, Derrida's deconstruction of logocentrism restores the historicity of meaning that structuralism suppressed (Derrida 1990). The antecedents of Derrida's deconstruction lie in Heidegger's project of 'overcoming metaphysics' and Heidegger's thought has a highly ambivalent relationship to the philosophy of praxis. On the one hand, Heidegger's ontological analysis has consistently influenced theorists in the tradition of praxis philosophy. On the other hand, Heidegger's 'Letter on Humanism' is not only one of the most interesting twentieth-century statements on practice but probably also the most comprehensive critique of the total orientation of praxis philosophy (Heidegger 1993a, 193–242). Bernstein comments that the 'entire thrust of Heidegger's thinking is to displace the question of *praxis* with a far more "fundamental question" – the question of Being *(Seinsfrage)*' (Bernstein 1991, 4).

Postmodernism has acquired diverse meanings through its various associations, but the diversity is compatible with an interest in multiplicity and difference. The postmodernist emphasis on plurality and the 'other' are partly a product of the linguistic and psychological critiques of the subject, and the critique of representation in general. In any case, from its beginnings in architecture and art theory, postmodernism's opposition to certain aspects of modernism has been far more readily discernible than the exact or coherent meaning of postmodernism. Although it is easy to exaggerate the disagreements with the perspective of the philosophy of praxis, the scepticism of postmodern thought towards the Enlightenment conceptions of reason and progress differs from praxis philosophy's endeavour to fully realize these categories. Lyotard's definition of the postmodern incredulity towards metanarratives entails a rejection of any notion of a unified subject of the historical process and a scepticism regarding the universalistic value system of modernity (Lyotard 1984). For Lyotard, the postmodern 'social bond' resides in heterogeneous language games, which do not culminate in an overarching consensual agreement; rather they are composed of 'agonistic' moves and a strategy of paradox replaces the legitimating narratives of modernity.

Whilst Habermas's (1987b) claim that the problems of modernity derive from a deficit and not an excess of reason starkly contrasts with the postmodernist critiques of rationality, his defence of reason depends upon a break with the perspective of the social totality as an expression of the subject and the distinction of communicative rationality from the functionalist reason of social systems. These are substantial revisions, including with respect to Habermas's early original elaboration of the programme of knowledge constitutive interests (Habermas 1978a). Whereas Giddens (1990a) considers that postmodernism is relevant to certain developments in aesthetics and he even accepts that these expressions of postmodernism contain a 'utopian' strain. However, Giddens defends a qualified version of reason against the potential postmodern renunciation of rationality, although he implies that a rethinking of reason is required to confront contemporary developments. In Giddens's opinion, this rethinking should embrace the problems of uncertainty and contingency.

Habermas's and Giddens's refutations of postmodernist interpretations of history are not without sequel and they have serious consequences for their theories. In different ways, Habermas and Giddens combine, on the one hand, claims that the present period is continuous with modernity and not a new postmodern stage, with, on the other hand, extensive arguments about how contemporary changes reflect and realize an altering of some of the basic historical foundations of modernity. Both Habermas and Giddens seek to break with the narrative models of a philosophy of history, even though they disagree considerably about the appropriate means for doing so and the alternative approach to history. Similarly, the modern ideal of the autonomous subject is fundamental to their entire theoretical projects, yet neither claims to defend an unreconstructed notion of the subject. The debates over postmodernism form part of the background to my analysis; and it certainly the case that postmodernism provoked reassessment of modernity, even amongst social theorists opposed to it. In terms of their respective conceptions of modernity, I am interested in the internal cogency of Habermas's and Giddens's positions as well as the relative merits of each theorist's conception compared with the other.

I have briefly commented upon how Habermas and Giddens seek to uphold the values of modernity and denounce the postmodernist rejections of ethical-political universalism. Habermas's and Giddens's theories are undoubtedly important alternatives to postmodernist thought, but the details of their arguments' exhibit certain continuities with structuralism and poststructuralism. Both theorists are concerned with working out the implications of the 'linguistic turn' for social theory, though in different ways. The interest of Habermas and Giddens in the pragmatics of communication is a quite logical extrapolation from the starting point of praxis philosophy in action theory and it is from the intersubjective perspective of pragmatics that they attempt to rethink notions of the subject (Honneth 1991, xxxii). Similarly, despite the contrasts that will be made, Habermas's reconstruction of historical materialism and Giddens's deconstruction of historical materialism are each attempts to incorporate and counter structuralist and poststructuralist perspectives on history. In fact, I argue that the effects that these attempts to simultaneously incorporate and critique have upon their respective standpoints are sometimes unexpected and would appear at times to discord with some of their general positions critical of structuralism, poststructuralism and postmodernism. Giddens is closer to the discontinuous approach to history of Foucault's genealogy, whereas Habermas appropriates a number of the categories and assumptions of the genetic structuralism of Piaget and Kohlberg; indeed, taking them from individual psychological development and applying them to the history of society. A global comparison of Habermas's and Giddens's theories with those of structuralism and poststructuralism is unnecessary and beyond the scope of this work. Nevertheless, there is some value in noting several broad disagreements and specific convergences with the critical positions on the subject and history of structuralism, poststructuralism and postmodernism.

Habermas understands his change to the paradigm of mutual understanding as a 'determinate negation' of the philosophy of the subject. He contrasts this paradigm change with, what he considers to be, the 'parasitic' dependence of postmodernist critiques upon the very notions of the subject and reason that they oppose (Habermas 1987a). Irrespective of whether this argument is correct, the assumptions underlying it concur with my claim that Habermas's and Giddens's works are distinguished by their constructive orientations and attempts to provide new theoretical conceptions that are relevant, in some form, to practices and public policies. Giddens's theory of structuration likewise exhibits such an orientation in commencing from the claim that sociological thought should eliminate any dependence on forms of argumentation borrowed from the natural sciences. He derives much of the justification for his proposals from claims to be modernizing established positions. Beyond any specific criticisms, this approach diverges from postmodernist scepticism about this modernizing perspective's mode of reasoning.

Structure and Comparison

At the outset, I seek to define the unifying feature of Habermas's project and to trace the consequences that this has for his theory. This provides a basis for discerning the continuities and discontinuities of Habermas's theory with the philosophy of praxis. My analysis of Habermas's theory initially takes the form of an immanent critique. I attempt to disclose the themes of the philosophy of praxis that his programme subordinates. The outstanding issues and problems of Habermas's theory influence, in turn, the inflection of my analysis of Giddens's programme. I likewise initially define particular themes organizing Giddens's perspective but these themes do not have the same level of philosophical justification as that of Habermas's unifying consideration. There is, however, a high degree of internal coherence to Giddens's theory of structuration; and explicating its intentions, which have admittedly not always been fully satisfied, is important to this work's comparison. By way of this explication, I demonstrate that Giddens's writings, like those of Habermas, contain important possibilities which remain underdeveloped, although I conclude that the inconsistencies in Giddens's arguments remain unresolved and that the original problems of structuration theory's design have deleterious consequences for his later writings on modernity and the state (Giddens 1994a; 1998a; 2000).

The contrasting understandings of the social and its cognates that emerges from my analysis needs to be seen against the backdrop of a series of other divergences. These differences between Habermas and Giddens range over an array of topics but their respective views of the merits of the Marxian paradigm of production and their assessments of the general implications of Marx's theoretical framework establish some of the key differences concerning such topics as the analysis of history, the relevance of the category of power, the requirements of a theory of social action, the appropriateness of functionalist analysis, the foundations of critique and the knowledgeability, competences and capacities of subjects. There are also important convergences between Habermas's and Giddens's political sociology of late-capitalist societies and a large degree of agreement between them concerning the anchoring of post-traditional social relations in dialogue and democratic procedures. These theorists undoubtedly satisfy a number of the most important considerations of the philosophy of praxis while disregarding others that they consider obsolete. Both theorists originally appropriate some of the features of the general orientation of the philosophy of praxis and endeavour to rethink the nexus between the subject and history, but the untenable facets of their initial proposals leads them to displace the praxis interpretation of the problem of the constitution of the social onto other considerations.

In the case of Habermas, the communicative mediation of social relations is constitutive of forms of individual and collective identity. This notion of identity is basic to his conception of the social but Habermas subordinates some distinctive features of the praxis perspective in developing a more methodologically defendable version of an intersection between the subject and history. For Giddens, the modern tendencies of socialization are the product of the application of reflexivity to shape social arrangements but the increase in the power of social constitution entails a new order of risk and contingency. He has a superior appreciation of the indeterminacy of human praxis, yet this appreciation becomes ultimately a justification for conceptions that are unsatisfactory from the standpoint of critical theory.

For the most part, Giddens's and Habermas's theoretical frameworks successfully develop the implications of their distinctive innovations and they provide new means of approaching the problems that define the programme of the philosophy of praxis. The approaches of Habermas and Giddens contain important possibilities that have not been fully explored and they illuminate the limitations of earlier understandings of the social. Both remain critical of existing social relations of inequality and oppression, but the visions that they ultimately present of a democratic transformation are a peculiar combination of inspiring notions of autonomy and disappointing parameters of change. In fact, it is possible to argue that the latter phases of their work, such as their writings concerned with the European Union, sustain the modernist commitment to change while strongly seeking to preserve elements of the existing institution of society in the face of regressive social developments, like those represented by neoliberalism and neo-nationalist revivals.

For these reasons, my analysis explicates Habermas's and Giddens's theorizing of their approaches to history. These theories of history inform their interpretations of modernity and underpin their normative assessment of modernity's progressive tendencies. In some respects, Habermas's and Giddens's approaches to history are more significant than their actual accounts of historical processes. In particular, the approaches to history express the respective intentions of their social theories. Habermas's contrast between the factual course of rationalization in modernity and the potential contained in the structures of consciousness of cultural modernity, as well as the corresponding modes of interaction deriving from communicative action, depends heavily on the approach to history that he originally developed in the context of his reconstruction of historical materialism (Habermas 1984; 1979). Similarly, Giddens's approach to history was developed under the rubric of his programme of a deconstructive critique of historical materialism (Giddens 1981; 1985).

There is arguably a greater degree of inconsistency between the approach to history that Giddens formulates in terms of the principles of the theory of structuration and the actual substantive content of his historical analyses. This discrepancy is exacerbated in his later works on modernity. Critics, like David Inglis, have highlighted some of the deleterious implications of these later works lacking the long-term historical perspective that characterized Giddens's earlier critiques of historical materialism (Inglis 2013). Inglis claims that Giddens's later works on modernity rely on simplifying and untenable binaries. Further, these accounts of modernity, Inglis argues, reinforce the tendency of current sociology to retreat into the present. The extended treatment in this work of Habermas's and Giddens's accounts of the historical institutionalization of modernity is then a corrective to this tendency of current sociology and the social sciences more generally. My analysis sets out the broader parameters of their theorizing of modernity from an historical perspective. The alternative contemporary theoretical approaches to history of multiple modernities, civilizational analysis and global modernity are considered in the 'Conclusion'. These alternative perspectives develop extended historical sociological interpretations on modernity and its diverse institution. It will be seen that they explore differing configurings of the nexus between history and the subject to that of Habermas and Giddens.

Finally, Habermas and Giddens have distinctively sought to relate their respective social theories to political practice and the capabilities or competences of subjects. In other words, they aim to not just explain social and political developments, but they seek to practically inform and shape developments. The relationship between theory and practice has always been a central consideration of Critical Theory and Habermas has consistently contributed to debates in the public sphere. In the case of Giddens, the elaboration of the political programme of the Third Way is a direct intervention into politics and policy, one closely aligned with the 'new labour' party of Tony Blair and strands of European social democracy. In fact, Habermas and Giddens have both made major contributions to debates over the future of Europe, the prospects of socialism and social democracy, as well as to policy topics, like immigration and cultural diversity, climate change and religion. These practical contributions to political and policy debates are informed by, and, in turn, inform, their social theory interpretations of the contemporary constellation of modernity. My analysis highlights the revisions of earlier positions that underpin their interpretations of contemporary modernity and Habermas's and Giddens's reframing of notions of social transformation.

Part I

NEW PARADIGMS AND SOCIAL
THEORY PERSPECTIVES

Chapter One

HABERMAS'S NEW PARADIGM OF CRITICAL THEORY

In the structures of diffracted intersubjectivity [...] singularization is just as impossible without the inexorable compulsion to universalization as is socialization without concomitant individuation. (Habermas 1991, 218)

Critical Theory and Social Identity: On Habermas's Conceptual Foundations

As I have discussed, the Marxian perspective of the philosophy of praxis derives its conception of the social from an interpretation of the intersection between the subject and history. A distinctive feature of this perspective is its synthetic orientation, generating a concern with the problem of mediation. Starting from Marx's critique of Hegel and Feuerbach, critical theory has sought to transform philosophical concepts through grounding them in social processes. In particular, this Marxian perspective considers that practice constitutes the linkage between the subject and history. This mediation is meant to be a process of transcending many traditional philosophical and political antinomies, like those of the divisions between essence and appearance, subject and object, freedom and necessity. Habermas diverges from several of the praxis perspective's synthetic aspirations, but I argue that he retains a founding interest in the problem of the mediation of the universal and the particular. The intersubjective approach that he develops to this problem of mediation is central to his defence of the continuing relevance of the 'project of modernity' and his claim that 'the rationality structures that *became accessible* in the modern age have *not yet* been exhausted and that they allow for a comprehensive institutional embodiment in the form of extensive processes of democratization' (Habermas 1979a, 129).

Habermas's specification of this mediation of the universal and the particular is based on his demonstrating the rationality intrinsic to communicative action oriented towards mutual understanding. He develops this basic consideration into a theory that is internally organized around the formation of social identity and its moral–practical translations. In Habermas's theory, identity is constitutive of the social, as the intersubjectivity of communication mediates processes of socialization and individuation. The principle of Habermas's discourse ethics exemplifies the normative implications of this mediation of the universal and the particular:

(D) Only those norms can claim to be valid that meet (or could meet) with the approval of all affected in their capacity *as participants in practical discourse*. (Habermas 1990a, 66)

The contention that social identity is the organizing problem of Habermas's theory does not mean that I dispute the accepted view of his discourse theory of morality and justice. That is, the view that Habermas's discourse theory represents a shift towards the more formal perspective of Kant's practical philosophy and a movement somewhat away from the Hegelian vision of morality as grounded in the substantive conditions of ethical life (see Honneth 2014). Rather, the contention that social identity is the organizing problem of Habermas's theory discloses some of the implications of this shift and the tensions that are intrinsic to Habermas's programme. Habermas's discourse theory reformulates the universalistic moral outlook of Kant's categorical imperative – that is, that one should morally 'act only according to that maxim whereby you can, at the same time, will that it should become a universal law' (Kant 1993, 30).

In this chapter, I clarify the seminal connection between Habermas's notion of social identity and his arguments for a change from the paradigm of the subject to the intersubjective paradigm of understanding. Habermas acknowledges that George Herbert Mead anticipated this change in paradigm, and he elaborates important details of his intersubjective conception of social identity through a reconstruction of Mead's analysis. Mead's interpretation of social identity contains additional considerations that Habermas's reconceptualization does not expand upon, and these considerations are briefly recollected in order to highlight some of the limitations of Habermas's theory. In fact, many of these considerations overlap those aspects of the perspective of the philosophy of praxis that Habermas's theory tends to subordinate, such as the dynamic character of social conflict, the temporal content of practices and the linkages between emancipation and creativity. These themes of praxis philosophy will be shown to be relevant to the comparison with Giddens and more recent attempts to rethink the nexus of the subject and history, especially that of Jose Maurício Domingues (Domingues 1995; 2000; 2006).

The philosophical background to Habermas's conception of identity will be traced through a discussion of its parallels with, and divergences from, Hegel's and Adorno's notions of identity. Adorno's critique of the identity thinking is partly accepted by Habermas but principally transformed into a positive appreciation of social identity. Both Adorno and Habermas delimit conceptions of identity that can be traced back to Hegel. Habermas does so, however, in order to define a universalism intrinsic to the mediation of social relations. He replaces Adorno's critique of conceptual thought's formal logic category of identity, as well as the associated dialectical interpretations of subject–object relations, with an explication of the thoroughly social practice of intersubjective communication (Habermas 1984a; 1987b). In my opinion, the accomplishments of Habermas's perspective are profound and undeniable, yet it is more convincing in relation to questions that are proximate to that of social identity than it is to the other topics that it seeks to encompass, especially that of social systems. It will be later shown why Adorno's critique of identity constitutes an attempt to comprehend the deepest sources of instrumental rationality and how from Adorno's standpoint this dominance of identity logic represents the definitive limits to human emancipation in modernity.

Intersubjectivity and Identity

I argue that the axial problem that shapes the 'conceptual strategy' of Habermas's critical social theory is that of the mediation and reconciliation of the universal and the particular. Habermas has sought, above all, to clarify his core intuition concerning the significance of the intersubjective structure of communicative practice in relation to this problem (see Habermas 2008, 9–76). Charles Taylor (1991, 27) elegantly captures this central intuition in describing the discursive 'complementarity' of 'I' and 'We'. 'In discourse', referring to linguistic practices oriented towards mutual understanding, '*we* talk about something. This means, however, that the matter in hand exists not just for me and for you, but for us'. This complementarity is intrinsic to the intersubjective meaning of mutual understanding, because, as Taylor (1991, 27) comments, 'we cannot, however, construe this process to be the attempt to synthesize "I-perspectives" which are completely independent of one another'.

Of particular significance, the mediation of the universal and the particular is conceived to be principally a question *of social identity and its formation* in Habermas's theory. Habermas's intuition concerning the intersubjective structure of understanding leads to a corresponding vision of the potentials for the progressive resolution of the major crisis tendencies of late-capitalist societies, notably, those of the crises of legitimation and the social pathologies of social and individual identity (Habermas 1979; 1987a). Despite the problems ensuing from the subordinating of several other considerations, Habermas's theory of communicative action represents a highly innovative approach to the question of social identity. In my opinion, this intersubjective approach is superior to many alternatives, both on account of the detailed intricacy of its elaboration and its capacity for practical-political illumination.[1] Even so, arguments for its superiority are conditional on social identity being considered a problem that requires the mediating of the universal and particular.

Habermas (1979a, 88; 1990a, 102) believes that the denial of this requirement of mediation cannot be held to consistently. The denial is only really possible from a standpoint external to an identity. In his opinion, an identity that is social not only encounters this problem of mediation, it is *constituted* through the mediating processes of social interaction (Habermas 1974b; 1990a; 1992a). It is worth noting that it is possible to infer from the following remarks of Albrecht Wellmer some of the reasons why Habermas's original attraction to critical theory may be connected to the problem of identity:

> Critical Theory proved to be in a position from which it was possible on the one hand to analyse those aspects of the German cultural tradition that were reactionary, repressive, and hostile to culture, and to do so more precisely than from any other standpoint; and on the other hand to reveal the subversive enlightening, and universalistic features of that same tradition, I would say that Critical Theory was the only theoretical position represented in postwar Germany that made a radical break with fascism conceivable without entailing a similarly radical break with the German cultural tradition, that is, with one's own cultural identity. (Wellmer 1998, 254)

---

1 Jenkins (1996), Craib (1998) and Dunn (1998) provide surveys of some approaches to social identity.

In a similar vein, Richard Bernstein (1985) insightfully explains how Habermas's desire to respond to the twentieth-century German experience was significant for his entire theory. Bernstein finds that the sense of 'rupture' that the aftermath of National Socialism produced led to Habermas's 'strong affinity with the pragmatists' vision and understanding of radical participatory democracy' (Bernstein 1985, 3).

Habermas's explications of this core conviction is not just directed at the problem of individual and social identity in general, rather it is specifically addressed to the questions of a *rational identity* and its *constitution*. Habermas's overall premise is, though conceived differently, the same normative one as that of Hegel's philosophy: that an identity is individuated to the degree to which it is universalistic (Habermas 1987a, 97; 1992a, 148–204). Hegel's account of self-consciousness illustrates this interconnection:

> A self-consciousness exists *for a self-consciousness*. Only so is it in fact self-consciousness; for only in this way does the unity of itself in its otherness become explicit for it[. …] *Spirit* is – this absolute substance which is the unity of the different independent self-consciousnesses which, in their opposition, enjoy perfect freedom and independence: 'I' that is 'We' and 'We' that is 'I'. (Hegel 1977, 110–11)[2]

Hegel's philosophy, Habermas claims, 'is essentially designed to solve' the question of social identity under the conditions of freedom and rationality institutionalized in modernity (1974b, 91). Indeed, Habermas claims that Hegel first formulated his notion of Spirit (*Geist*) in response to this question (1974a, 143–47; 1974b).

Despite the conflict between Hegel's commitment to the philosophy of consciousness and Habermas's formulation of the communicative paradigm of understanding, Habermas's approach exhibits sufficient continuities to be regarded as a rethinking of Hegel's conception of social identity. Habermas's approach is, however, comparatively delimited; he rejects the broader metaphysical grounding of the relationship between the universal and the particular in Hegel's dialectic. This commitment to 'post-metaphysical' thinking does not affect Habermas's consistent opposition to the post-Hegelian 'objectivist' conception of the relationship of the universal and particular (1976a; 1976b; 1992a). That is, objectivist conceptions equate the solution to this problem of the mediation of the universal and particular with the positive knowledge produced by scientific models and their formulating of universally valid law-like statements.

In Habermas's opinion, such conceptions occlude exactly what Hegel had shown to be crucial, that is, that social and individual identity cannot be considered to be like the identification of objects. In these cases, identity is not something that can be externally applied to phenomenon (1974b, 91; 1974a, 146). Social identity and individual identity are types of identity that presuppose a *subject*, and they are posited through the subject's activity. For this reason, Habermas suggests that in 'a certain sense a society achieves or, let me say, produces its identity; and it is by virtue of its own efforts that it does not lose it' (1974b, 91).

---

2   See Matustik (1993, 31–34) for a similar analysis of Hegel's influence on Habermas's conception of identity, and Aboulafia (1995) for an overview of themes similar to mine concerning Habermas's relationship to Mead.

Hegel and Habermas agree that a social identity requires, in principle, some *affirmation*, that is, a consciousness of identity as justified, legitimate and authentic, irrespective of whether this is an individual or collective identity. Of course, this consciousness does not mean that an identity cannot be recognized as something that is conditioned, and of its being alienated, although Habermas is sceptical about the contemporary relevance of Hegel's notion of a 'false identity' (1974b, 91). Nevertheless, this recognition of the heteronomous conditioning of identity includes the possibility of some affirming of transformation; hence, there is an intimate connection between identity and the idea of freedom in the writings of both Hegel and Habermas. Freedom enables the authentic realization of identity, they argue, and Habermas has sought to reconstruct the equivalent moral consciousness of an autonomous subject (1990).

For Hegel, an unfree identity is not a real identity; it merely exists and does not realize the self-determination that is essential to subjectivity (Hegel 1977; 1967). Paradoxically, this determination is probably one of the reasons why Hegel was able to generalize the principle of subjectivity beyond that of the individual subject.[3] Herbert Marcuse explains this in the following terms:

> We must note that the logical category 'subject' does not designate any particular form of subjectivity (such as man) but a general structure that might best be characterized by the concept 'mind'. Subject denotes a universal that individualizes itself, and if we wish to think of a concrete example, we might point to the 'spirit' of a historical epoch. If we have comprehended such an epoch, if we have grasped its notion, we shall see a universal principle that develops, through the self-conscious action of individuals, in all prevailing institutions, facts, and relations. (Marcuse 1967, 155)

Habermas's interpretation of the reciprocity of communication implies a democratic and certainly less potentially repressive rendering of the relationship between the generality of the social and the particularity of the individual. It precludes, in principle, the subordination of the individual to the universal and discloses how this subordination would represent a distortion of the rationality, as well as the participatory democratic implications of communication. This normative content of Habermas's core intuition grants an undoubtedly critical significance to the axial problem that binds together the various different strands of his theory. The following three categorical features illustrate the critical significance of Habermas's approach to social identity: first, a notion of autonomy grounded in the intersubjective conception of the constitution of the subject; second, the idea that actualizing the potential immanent in communication would enlarge the existing institutional embodiment of democracy and justice; and, third, specifying a normative conception of rationality and adumbrating from this processes of social rationalization that would facilitate a reorganization of modern societies. In addition, the model of the communicative mediation of the universal and the particular ties together these

---

3   See also Charles Taylor's (1975, 76–124) chapter titled 'Self-Positing Spirit', in his *Hegel*, and especially pages 77–78 for the segment on Hegel's variant forms of mediation which Habermas's intuition develops.

three features. In so doing, Habermas rethinks the basic sociological problem of the relation of the individual to society from the standpoint of the constitution of identity.

In this rethinking, Habermas critically appropriates George Herbert Mead's conception of *individuation through socialization* so as to delineate the autonomous subject's capacity to participate in discourse and in order to disclose how understanding is anchored in a projection of a 'universal communication community' (Habermas 1992a, 149–204; 1987a 1–47; Mead 1934). Further, Habermas believes that this conception exposes the mistaken complexion of the various antinomies that have been taken to preclude a consistent application of universalistic moral principles and a democratic transformation of society, such as the antinomic juxtaposition of the individual and society that informs liberal notions of freedom and justice (Habermas 1998).

Habermas has worked out the implications of an intersubjective theory of communication to a degree unparalleled in social theory. From the synthetic perspective of praxis philosophy, however, the delimiting aspects of the paradigm of mutual understanding mean it addresses possible alternative dimensions of mediation as though they are derivable from processes of intersubjective identity-formation. That is, a theoretical prioritizing occurs which effectively transforms the dimensions of other problems and, as a result, this 'understanding' based concept of 'rational' identity directs the answers to other questions, such as, as we will see, those pertaining to processes of social action and the dynamics of social change. This prioritizing becomes especially questionable when, as a result of a demand for theoretical coherence, the conception of social identity assumes the role of a model and is implicitly taken to embody the direction for addressing every relation of mediation.[4] The sequels to this delimiting aspect of the communicative paradigm of understanding, though not necessarily the delimitation itself, are highly consequential for the structure of Habermas's theory. In fact, substantial problems are a consequence of Habermas's sustaining positions consistent with his core intuition and defending its integrity. This will become apparent over the course of my overall analysis and these problems will be initially indicated with reference to those themes in Adorno and Mead's work that have a more marginal position in Habermas's theory.

Habermas downgrades various elements found in the early phases of his work that would potentially compromise the paradigmatic version of the mediation of the universal and the particular. This applies to his revising the psychoanalytic perspective of the schema of knowledge constitutive interests, as incorporating psychoanalytic considerations would entail acknowledging greater ambivalence in the relationship between self and other (Habermas 1978a; 1978c). Similarly, the non-symmetrical character of social struggles and class conflict mean that they acquire a more marginal position in his theory. These downgrades coincide with a distancing of his theory from many of the precepts of praxis philosophy. The problem of rationality, for instances, supplants the critique of ideology as the underlying purpose of his theorizing communicative practices. Further, the effects of this defensive conceptual strategy can be seen in the structure of Habermas's

---

4   Without a doubt, this directing also avoids a number of potential difficulties and the inevitability of some prioritizing, of course, means it need not constitute a problem of itself.

diagnosis of contemporary social pathology, that is, its sociological construction of the impinging by the 'external' system 'steering media' of money and power, which function in an instrumentally oriented manner, upon the communicative principle of the lifeworld (Habermas 1987a).

Adorno's Critique of Identity

Adorno's later work bequeathed that the problem of identity would be ineluctable for any future critical theory (Adorno 1979). Even though it is only one among many informants, this bequest is salient to appreciating Habermas's theory's organizing considerations. Habermas consolidated, I argue, the core conviction underlying the design of his theory through a relativizing reinterpretation of Adorno's critique of identity (Habermas 1983, 99–110). For Habermas, the objectivist model of subsuming particular cases under universal laws is a form of mediation practically applicable to the manipulation of objects. In his opinion, it is specifically this 'objectivist' model of conceptual thought that Adorno saw doing violence to the non-identity of the particular. According to Adorno, the historical development of identity thinking in the form of instrumental reason resulted from and entailed a denaturing of human subjectivity (Adorno, 1979; Horkheimer and Adorno 1972). Moreover, Habermas stresses that while Adorno shared with Hegel this critical insight into the undialectical identity of formal logic; Adorno discerned the operations and effects of this damaged subjectivity in even Hegel's philosophy (Habermas 1983, 99–110).

At the level of social theory, Adorno (1993, 87) regarded the 'truth in Hegel's untruth' about the superiority of the totality to consist in its actually revealing the universality bourgeois society possessed through identity. For identity is the 'rational' principle intrinsic to the exchange of commodities, an abstraction produced through the transformation of qualitative differences into similar numerical quantities. This abstract universalism was constitutive of the identity of capitalist society. Adorno could then immanently criticise Hegel's philosophy for its ultimately ignoring the mediating principles of the dialectic and for subordinating the particular to the universal in the notion of identity, without due sensitivity to their margin of difference (Adorno 1978, 16–17; 1979, 313–19; 1993).

While Habermas (1983) acknowledges the perspicuity of Adorno's critique of Hegel's universalism, he pointedly contests its implications and diverges from its 'negative' conclusions. He believes that Adorno's disclosure of Hegel's ultimate neglect of the social totality's power to subjugate was severely compromised. It contained a self-defeating predicament: neither the self-reflection of Adorno's (1979) *Negative Dialectics*, in its stressing the 'primacy of the objective', nor the ceding to art the possibility of evoking a non-instrumental mediation in Adorno's (1984) posthumous *Aesthetic Theory* were capable of the requisite affirmation that critique depended upon. In Habermas's view, critique needs to specify a type of mediation having the normative force of reconciliation in order for it to be based on justified reasons. Habermas considers that Adorno's theory did actually do this intermittently, though usually through recourse to metaphors of reconciled difference and by way of an implicit philosophical universalism grounded in the over-inclusive idea of the subject's reconciliation with the objective realm of nature

(Habermas 1983; 1984a; 1987a). Habermas's acceptance of the appropriateness of control and manipulation to the practical-pragmatic relationship of the subject to objective phenomena means, on the one hand, that he regards the latter idea of reconciliation as largely a utopian postulate (Habermas 1971; 1978a; 1983). On the other hand, although it opens up the possibility for an alternative notion of dialectical mediation, this restrictive reinterpretation of Adorno's critique of identity may be itself criticised for precluding more complex forms of interaction of the subject and object.

Habermas contends that the substance of Adorno's metaphorical allusions to an unforced reconciling that respected the non-identity of the other does have a tangible basis in experience. The practical experience of unimpeded and domination-free communication between subjects anticipates a condition of consensual agreement that does not, at the same time, dissolve the differences between subjects. In fact, Habermas (1983, 107) goes so far as to assert that the idea of reconciliation with nature derives from an unjustified transferring of intersubjective reciprocity onto objective phenomena. If this is accepted, then it is not the case of Habermas's superimposing the communicative notion of intersubjective relations on Adorno's fragmentary allusions to reconciled difference but the opposite.[5] Of course, it can be argued that Habermas's intersubjective paradigm of communication never fully retrieves many of the considerations associated with Adorno's critique of identity, like the relation to nature, the discontinuities of bodily experience, the elements of non-identity in the human psyche, and the nature of aesthetic and social creativity.

Habermas's shift to an intersubjective notion of mediating and reconciling means that social identity defines the parameters of the question of identity in his theory. This redefinition undoubtedly involves a diminution of themes contained in Adorno's philosophical critique and its exacting conditions of the subject's redemption. But the shift underpinning it provides sufficient justification for Habermas to elaborate a 'positive' conception of identity (see Benhabib 1986; Heller 1978). Indeed, it is striking just how much Habermas initially felt compelled to repudiate not only Adorno's reservations regarding philosophical foundations and systematic theorizing, but also those concerning any positive notion of identity. In fact, this repudiation commenced well before Habermas's intuitions concerning communication had sufficiently solidified to constitute the normative grounds of critique.[6] Even if we accept that Habermas's theory does avoid some of the aporias and difficulties of Adorno's position, it is still possible to utilise aspects of Adorno's dialectic to illustrate the parameters of Habermas's delimiting the question of identity and its consequences. For example, Adorno's philosophy points to the problems that the paradigm of understanding encounters with respect to mediating the pre-social and non-social qualities of domains, like nature, the body, the unconscious, and libidinal drives (see McCarthy 1982; 1984; Whitebook 1979; 1984; 1995; Honneth 1991; 1995b; Wellmer 1998, cf. 258–62). Adorno's dialectic preserves the tensions of

---

5   See Coles (1995) for a defence of Adorno's philosophy in relation to some of Habermas's criticisms.
6   'The normative grounds of critique' is partly a paraphrase of the title of Baynes's (1992) work.

mediation and implies that any reconciliation presupposes the radical transcendence of capitalist society.

Communication and Identity

Habermas asserts that the normative justification required for the social affirmation of a rational identity is present in the reciprocity of practical interaction. It is immanent in the symmetrical conditions of speech and the rationality intrinsic to the mutual recognition of validity claims in communicative action, that is, the recognition and agreement over the claims to the truth of statements, the rightness of normative claims, the authenticity of expressions about subjectivity, and the comprehensibility of communication, as well as the consistency of subsequent actions with the position on the validity claim. Habermas considers that the reciprocity and rationality of communication are universal normative supposition of interaction, though they are far from universally fulfilled (Habermas 1984a; 1979a). In other words, he argues that principles of reciprocity and rationality already orient subjects' interactions, in spite of this normative supposition only being a necessary pretence of interaction and their anticipating a circumstance where they are actually fulfilled. The communicative constitution of identity ideally binds together the standpoints of participation and rationality. At the same time, this intersubjective mediating should instantiate a context where any affirmation of social and individual identity is explicitly criticizable on the basis of domination free communication (Habermas 1974b). What this means is that an identity that is constituted through unimpeded communication contains *the possibility of being rationally validated by all the participating subjects*.

According to Habermas, a rational identity is one founded upon universalistic structures of consciousness, yet this presupposes that such an identity has overcome the original determinants of its particularity. The fact that this overcoming of the original conditions of particularity results in a universalism is of important consequence, but it does not in any way dissolve the need for mediating the particular. Habermas contends that the particular, in the form of the individuation of the subjects, increases under these universal conditions, and with this also subjects' differences from one another (Habermas 1992a; 1990a). Even if it is not the only type of identity that can reflectively criticise its past, a universalistic form of identity is the one that is most capable of criticizing a particular identity which was its own. A superiority that is due to the capacity of subjects having a universalistic identity to criticise the identity that they have from the intersubjective standpoint of the other and not only from the 'monological' standpoint of self-interest. The capacity of these subjects to criticise their own identities from the other's standpoint owes to the communicative processes of the constitution of identity (Habermas 1990a; 1998a).

In Habermas's opinion, this specification of identity is not an arbitrary philosophical ideal, but a claim equally satisfying the sociological requirements of critical social theory. He proposes that this communicative constitution of identity represents a development within contemporary society that prefigures a more substantial transformation of existing social relations. At various times, he finds the formal ideal of unimpeded communication to be operative, at least to some degree, in contemporary socialization patterns, aspects of countercultural practices, and, more broadly still, in its represents the 'vanishing point' of the modern rationalised lifeworld (Habermas 1974b; 1976; 1983; 1984a; 1987a; 1987b). He argues that what most distinguishes this type of contemporary identity from those based on 'traditional world images' is its openness to 'counter-arguments and revisions at any time' (Habermas 1974b, 110). However, he claims that this 'post-traditional' identity marries the intersubjective reciprocity of communication with formal procedures. A post-traditional identity implies open and democratic forms of justification and legitimation:

> Collective identity [...] can today only be grounded in the consciousness of universal and equal chances to participate in the kind of communication processes by which identity formation becomes a continuous learning process. Here the individual is no longer confronted by collective identity as a traditional authority, as a fixed objectivity on the basis of which self-identity can be built. Rather, individuals are the participants in the shaping of the collective will underlying the design of a common identity. (Habermas 1974b, 99; see also Habermas 1996a; 2001)

This conception exemplifies why identity constitutes the sociological counterpart and empirical underpinning of Habermas's discourse theory of justice. Further, this restoration of practice as an organizing feature of critical theory enables Habermas to retrieve the idea of socio-historical progress and to demonstrate how progress is a contemporary possibility. In short, Habermas's reinterpretation of identity sought to counteract the critical theory diagnosis of social-historical regression; which had basically constituted an organizing framework of critical theory since the period of the critique of instrumental reason in the 1940s. Horkheimer and Adorno's (1972) *Dialectic of Enlightenment* made the critique of identity central to the explanation of regression, because, as Honneth explains, 'locating the logic of identity at the foundation of rationality' was the 'basic conception by means of which Adorno, together with Horkheimer, draws together the philosophical-historical experience of total reification in bourgeois society' (Honneth 1995b, 99).

In Honneth's opinion, Adorno's post-war writings, composed under the rubric of the framing notion of *an end of mediation*, did not substantially alter the 'definitive repression' of the social that was entailed by this diagnosis of experience (Honneth 1991, 57–96). Adorno remained closed to the potential of the realm of social interaction because his model of late-capitalism envisaged a direct confrontation between administrative systems' techniques of domination and the individual personality. Drawing on psychoanalysis, Adorno assumed that the changes in the structure of capitalism had eroded the social relations that had enabled the formation of the bourgeois individual (Horkheimer and Adorno 1972). By contrast, Habermas's paradigm change necessarily lends itself to sociological analyses intended to discern elements of autonomy in social interaction and the constitution of identity. This potential of communication was first specified in Habermas's early work on the bourgeois public sphere (Habermas 1989). Habermas argued that the public sphere's constitutive normative ideal was that of the formation of public opinion on the basis of rational discussion. In this ideal, public reasoning takes the form of the presentation of arguments in the universal interest, rather than in terms of the particularistic form of self-interest In other respects, Habermas's depiction of the structural transformation that resulted in the 're-feudalization' of the public sphere was in basic agreement with Adorno's perspective on late-capitalism and the culture industry's distortion of the modernist ideal of social autonomy (Habermas 1989).

Habermas (1984a; 1987a) would later make the differences with Adorno clear in *The Theory of Communicative Action*. He considers, first, that Adorno lacked the action theoretical categories necessary for a revised sociological theory. Second, that Adorno remained, ironically, trapped inside the Hegelian logic whose deficiencies he had exposed (Habermas 1987a, 1–2). Third, the paradigm of social mediation remained for Adorno that of the relationship of subject and object. If Habermas is correct about the implications of the paradigm of the subject then this commitment conditions Adorno's failure to develop a theory of action and it could perhaps explains the oscillating characteristic of Adorno's critique of the Hegelian notion of identity (Adorno 1993; 1979). From another perspective, these oscillations may exemplify the power of the dialectical method and Adorno's more demanding expectations concerning the historical transformation of capitalism. Habermas does not dispute, to be sure, the acuity of Adorno's philosophy. In his opinion, Adorno's writings represent the most reflexive and consistent extension of the Western Marxist diagnosis of the logical structure of the capitalist constellation (Habermas 1986, 91–103; 1992b).

Habermas suggests that the dialectical inversions Adorno sketched are endemic to the paradigm of subject and object relations that has dominated modern philosophy and concepts of action in sociological theory. In his opinion, these inversions are never totally eliminable from the philosophy of the subject (Habermas 1987b). One of Habermas's fundamental convictions is that the intersubjective paradigm of mutual understanding is conceptually resistant to the inversions typical of the polarity of subject and object (see Arnason 1979; 1982). Although this resistance is due to the reciprocity intrinsic to the intersubjective structure of communicative action, it does not mean that the normative principles of communicative action are not consistently being overridden and empirically undermined in late-capitalist societies. The final rationale for Habermas's change to the intersubjective paradigm of communication is probably the negative one of contesting the implications of systems theory.

According to Habermas (1987b), Niklas Luhmann's version of systems theory envisages social systems as having the attributes of subjects, like self-reflection and self-determination (Luhmann 1995). Leaving aside the question of the veracity of this interpretation, Habermas considers that systems theory represents the most sophisticated justification of the technocratic ideology that suppresses normative considerations in late capitalist societies and that disregards the processes of public communication. These critical development substantially influenced Habermas's (1984a; 1987a) claim that it is not instrumental reason that is the major source of modern social pathologies but the functionalist reason operating in social systems. It is social systems' identifying, so to speak, themselves with the social totality that give rise to concrete processes dissolving identity.

> Social integration increasingly seems to get substituted by systems integration. And the more this happens, the more identity problems become obsolete. (Habermas 1974b, 98)

Although Adorno's critique of identity logic is supposedly conditioned and limited by its opposition to Hegel's dialectic, the alternate 'genuinely' intersubjective categories of Hegel's theory of the struggle for recognition anticipate Habermas's change of paradigm (Habermas 1974a). At the level of depicting social interaction, Habermas considers that the young Hegel maintained in the idea of *Spirit* an appreciation of the tension between subjects and the practical need for mediating differences (Habermas 1974a). By contrast, Hegel's later ideas of embodying the universal in the constitutional state, and the identity posited as being at the highest stage of consciousness in Hegel's *Phenomenology*, belong to the philosophy of the subject (Hegel 1967; 1977). Now, whilst Kant's (1997) notion of the subject in his practical philosophy already implied that an identity is individuated to the extent that it is universalistic, Hegel's (1967) commitment to the idea of an ethical totality embodied in the community gave expression to a need for an institutional translation of this universalistic identity. Habermas incorporates these two suppositions in his notion of an autonomous subject, that is, that a universalistic outlook is a condition of individuation and that there is a need for an institutional translation of such an identity.

For Habermas, the latter attribute is salient to the subject's exercise of post-conventional structures of moral consciousness and the transformative potential of discourse ethics. That is, a post-conventional consciousness is principled, reflexive, and universalistic. In Habermas's view, a post-conventional consciousness generally endorses a procedural conception of the conditions of validity, justification and legitimacy, although he once entertained the idea of an orientation to 'need satisfaction' as constitutive of an outlook that transcended existing moral conventions – an notion that converges with some of the emphases of earlier Critical Theory on libidinal satisfaction and praxis philosophy's interest in a theory of needs (Habermas 1979). Habermas regards Hegel's critique of Kant's ethical formalism and abstract universalism to have not so much negated the validity of the categorical imperative as disclosed a need for supplementary inquiries into its developmental preconditions and the circumstances of its institutional persistence.

Although Habermas's discourse ethic is located in the tradition of Kant's moral philosophy, he argues that these Hegelian criticisms do not apply to it (Habermas 1990a, 195–215). Discourse theory shares with Hegel's philosophy a genetic conception of the mediating of the universal and the particular. The full realization of an identity occurs at later stages, based on the assumption that identity is the product of a developmental history. Like Hegel, Habermas considers that the later stages of identity formation are comprised of more abstract and universalistic structures of consciousness (Habermas 1990a; 1979a).

The 'heuristic' notion of there being an homology between the phases in the development of individual consciousness and the historical phases of the development of collectively shared cultural meanings and normative structures forms the basis of Habermas's proposed reconstruction of historical materialism (Habermas 1979a). Habermas argues that collective cultural meanings and normative structures have been embodied in myths, worldviews, religions, philosophy, and modern ideologies. Further, that the historical changes in the forms of collective meanings generally represent progressive transitions to higher levels of moral reasoning and more rational modes of justification and legitimation. In this sense, Habermas suggests that there is a broad homology between these collective belief systems and individual consciousness in terms of their development and internal logics. The developmental sequence that Habermas proposes in the forms of cognition and moral judgement is taken from the genetic structuralist psychology of Jean Piaget and Lawrence Kohlberg (Piaget 1985; Kohlberg 1981). In brief, Piaget argued that individual cognition develops over time from an inability to make distinctions between self and world through to an ability as an adult to make cognitive differentiations between the objective world, subjective experience, and the social order. Whereas Kohlberg claimed that the moral consciousness of individuals progresses from a pre-conventional stage through a conventional stage and finally reaches a post-conventional stage, with the attributes of universalistic principles. In the case of both individual and socio-cultural structures of cognition and morality, the stages of the development of consciousness represent, according to Habermas, advances in rationality and justification.

For Habermas, communication is a means of surpassing the particularity of earlier stages of development and for establishing less repressive forms of mediating social interaction. In his view, this latter process reflects the historical acquisition of the universalistic principles that are contained in the pragmatic structures of linguistic communication. It is this derivation of universalism from the mediating processes of communicative action that distinguishes Habermas's conception of identity from that of Hegel. Habermas's communicative version does not posit an encompassing collective subject of the historical process, nor does it suppose that there is a privileged locus for the realization of subjects' autonomy, even though the public sphere of the democratic polity is taken to be particularly significant. Habermas argues that the modern differentiation of social institutions and the 'diffracted' structure of language mean that there can only ever be higher-level intersubjective relations and arrangements. For this reason, Habermas likewise considers that his conception differs from republican political philosophy's notions of a unified collective subject and its view of the political sphere as the locus of its action (Habermas 1996a).

Habermas's conceptualization of an individual's social identity is based on the supposition that its formal structures are almost interchangeable with those of the identity of society.[7] Similarly, the individual's potential for a particular ego-identity depends on the stage of the development of society. These suppositions make individual variations in ego identity, as well as the formations of social identity, a genetic historical process tied to

---

7   The interplay between individual and societal structures of consciousness will be examined in more detail in chapter three, but, in an interview, Habermas (1986, 168) qualifies his position on the homologies between them in the following manner: 'I maintain only (for example, with reference to tribal societies) that individuals can develop structures of which belong to a higher stage than those which are already embodied in the institutions of their society. It is primarily subjects who learn, while societies can take a step forward in the evolutionary learning-process only in a metaphorical sense. New forms of social integration, and new productive forces, are due to the institutionalization and exploitation of forms of knowledge which are individually acquired, but culturally stored and capable of transmission and so, in the long term, accessible to the collective. However, the process of social implementation only takes place as a consequence of political struggles and social movements, of the outsider-role of innovative marginal groups, and so on.'

changes in the structure of society. Habermas accepts that there is an externally describable process of individuation resulting from social differentiation, but, consistent with the positions already outlined, he wants to account for individuation processes resulting from the activity of the subject. In his opinion, the element interlinking these two sources of social individuation, societal differentiation and subjective agency, is the structures of linguistic communication, particularly the pragmatic logic of employing pronouns (Habermas 1979a, 109).

At the same time, Habermas argues that there is a decisive difference between the identity of an autonomous subject and the conventional identity of acquired social roles. To reiterate, an identity that is self-determining in its uniqueness and particularity should not be confused with the fact that any and every form of individual identity is always objectively different from an external standpoint. Further, an autonomous identity not only recognises that the social is part of itself, but it is able to shape the social as well. For this reason, individual and social autonomy are constitutive of each other. However, there is a sense in which Habermas believes that such mutuality and autonomy were not genuine possibilities until modernity, with its universalistic ideal of the autonomous constitution of society by all subjects and the critique of traditional legitimations of heteronomy.

Habermas follows George Herbert Mead's interpretation of how the autonomous individual and social autonomy are reciprocally constituted. He wants to show how the freedom of an individual depends on the freedom of the other. Mead's theory of the intersubjectivity of subjectivity contains, in Habermas's opinion, a suitable sociological conception of mediation and it supplies a paradigmatic account of 'individuation through socialization' (Habermas 1992a, 149–204; 1987a 1–42; Mead 1934).

George Herbert Mead and Intersubjectivity

Mead's notion that self-consciousness emerges from the social context of interaction and the ego's 'taking the standpoint of the other' are incorporated by Habermas into his theory (Mead 1934, 135–226). For Mead, self-consciousness is the outcome of the mediation of symbols, as opposed to the self-relation associated with the objectification of the singular ego. In this way, Mead suggests that the self-understanding that one has in reflection develops out of the understanding between interaction partners. That is, intersubjectivity is the precondition of individual subjectivity. According to Habermas, Mead's key insight concerning consciousness, and which marked a definitive shift to the paradigm of intersubjectivity, was his realization that problem solving of a type requiring innovative learning develops not from the isolated dealing of the subject with 'things and events', but through 'several actors' interactive dealings with each other' (Habermas 1992a, 174).

Mead's perspective is distinctive in its claim that self-consciousness is not the product of introspection but has its origins in the practical processes of social interaction, especially the child's early communication through gestures. In particular, Mead claims that owing to the preceding processes of 'taking the standpoint of the other' in interaction, the identity of the self as the 'me' first enables the development of self-consciousness. This analysis discloses, Habermas argues, the 'intersubjective core' of the ego; it demonstrates that an individual's identity is always inherently social. In Habermas's words, the 'ego, which seems to me to be given in my self-consciousness as what is purely my own, cannot be maintained by me solely through my own power, as it were for me alone – it does not "belong" to me' (Habermas 1992a, 170). This means, in effect, that self-consciousness depends on the reflexive application to oneself of the symbolically generated meanings that were initially external, yet shared with the other partner in interaction. Mead shows how consciousness derives from a common, hence social, interpretation of meaning. Habermas rightly highlights the significance of the participatory-performative dimension of Mead's conception of interaction and how a communicative relation to a 'second person' differs from the objectifying attitude of introspection:

> While introspection requires the objectifying attitude of an observer who confronts himself in the third person, the performative attitude of the speaker and hearer requires the differentiation between 'you', as the alter ego on my level *with whom* I seek to reach an understanding, and the 'something' *about which* I want to reach an understanding with 'you'. As Mead explains it, the actor comes upon himself as a social object in communicative action when he orients himself to the current – you relationship and thereby encounters himself as the alter ego of his alter ego; Mead explicates the self of self-consciousness as this *social* object. (Habermas 1992a, 172)

In *The Theory of Communicative Action*, Habermas (1987a) proposes that the identity of linguistic usage, which presupposes a basic agreement between subjects, constitutes the point of origin of the social. Whilst Mead did present an evolutionary account of the development of communication, Habermas asserts that he did not sufficiently distinguish the more complex mediation associated with linguistic communication from the earlier phase of interaction founded on the 'conversation of gestures' and the simpler communication of general symbolism, like the green light for go. For Mead, the 'vocal gesture' introduces a new dimension of understanding and an 'objectivity' of meaning, which was lacking in the reciprocal recognition of behavioural reactions communicated through prelinguistic gestures. This objectivity is constituted by way of a social agreement about meanings, because the vocal gesture's shared quality, as is explained below, consolidates the individual's 'taking the standpoint of the other' in relation to her or his own actions.

One of the major reasons why Mead's analysis of the intersubjective genesis of self-consciousness coincides with Habermas's core intuition is its practical reinterpretation of the central categories of the philosophy of the subject. Mead argued that the self-relation of reflection was originally acquired performatively, that is, reflection does not originate from an adopting of the 'I' perspective of self-observation, rather it is acquired through applying the perspective of the self as the 'me' for another (Mead 1934). The standpoint of the other was learnt originally through behavioural reactions and such a qualitative transformation is due to the simultaneity of the vocal gesture's expression and perception: 'the actor affects himself at the same time and in the same way as he affects his opposite number' (Habermas 1992a, 176). In effect, this new level of communication makes the actor 'visible to himself as a social object', through the process of adopting the 'objective meaning of his vocal gesture, which stimulates both sides equally' (Habermas 1992a, 177).

Despite the paradigmatic insights contained in Mead's explicating the emergence of identity, Habermas criticizes Mead's neglect of the further distinction between this intersubjective genesis of the self-relation of reflection and the differentiated reflection founded on the reflexivity immanent in language (Habermas 1987a; 1992a). Habermas employs this linguistic extension of reflexivity to clarify Mead's idea of the subjectivity that is not simply bound to that of a 'conventional' role identity. That is, a subjectivity which no longer stands in a subordinate relation to the 'we' of the 'generalised other' (Mead 1934, 152–164). The 'generalised other' previously represented the social collective having power over the subject, but the transition beyond the conventional role stage is marked by a recognition that the *social* is able to be constituted through the common action of autonomous subjects. According to Habermas (1987a, 94–95; 1992a, 182–93), Mead's intersubjective notion of autonomy is bound to the pragmatist image of the self's imaginative projecting its participation in an 'unlimited communication community'. The autonomous subject has learnt to generalise the universalistic normative principles which are founded in communication and that underpin interaction between self and other.

Habermas proposes that such a projection is the logical culmination of the subject's intersubjectively formed structures of consciousness, because the communicative processes of social interaction anticipate this development. In a certain way, the content of communication is less significant to this development than the subject's explicit recognition of the abstract principles that enable linguistic communication and underpin the rationality of the procedures of argumentative discourse. These principles, such as those of mutual respect and equal consideration of all, subsequently facilitate the subject's interaction with a plurality of others, the moral resolution of conflicts and the insight that it has into the specificity of its own identity (Habermas 1990; 1998a, 4–46; 1993, 1–18). Habermas argues that it was through elucidating the formation of the self that Mead worked out another means of conceiving the Hegelian postulate of the 'I' as the universal and the 'I' as the particular.

> Let us imagine individuals being socialized as members of an ideal communication community; they would in the same measure acquire an identity with two complementary aspects: one universalizing, one particularizing. On the one hand, these persons raised under idealized conditions learn to orient themselves within a universalistic framework, that is, to act autonomously. On the other hand, they learn to use this autonomy, which makes them equal to every other morally acting subject, to develop themselves in their subjectivity and singularity. (Habermas 1987a, 97)

At the post-conventional stage of principled reflection, Habermas contends that the subject is conscious of the mechanisms of its historical constitution. Based on this self-consciousness, the subject is able to project an image of its identity into the future. Since the most constitutive structures of consciousness are those acquired through social interaction founded on communication, unsurprisingly the post-conventional subject projects its future participation in an idealised unlimited communication community. However, Habermas claims that the subject does this not only because it has adopted the perspective of moral universalism. The subject projects its participation in such a community for the purpose of maintaining its unique identity and continuing its distinctive life history. In short, Habermas argues that the subject makes a universalistic projection from the standpoint of the particularity of an individual's own self-identity:

> But this moment of idealization no longer concerns only the circle of addresses, which virtually encompasses *everyone*, or the unlimited communication community; rather, it concerns the *claim of individuality itself*, which relates to the guarantee that I consciously give, in light of a considered individual life project, for the continuity of my life history. The idealizing supposition of a universalistic form of life, in which everyone can take up the perspective of everyone else and can count on reciprocal recognition by everybody, makes it possible for individuated beings to exist within a community – individualism as the flipside of universalism. (Habermas 1992a, 196; second emphasis added)

Habermas deepens Mead's elucidation of 'individuation through socialization', but his intersubjective conception of mediation actually reconstructs only one dimension of Mead's understanding of the social. Habermas's reconstruction either leaves out other dimensions found in Mead's writings, or neglects the further considerations that Mead's arguments require. For example, Honneth's (1995a, 71–91) interpretation of Mead's approach as 'naturalizing' Hegel's image of a 'struggle for recognition' initially builds on Habermas's reconstruction (Habermas 1974a; 1978a). However, Honneth gives greater emphasis to the conflictual structure of the development of identity and highlights the significance that struggle has for the learning processes underpinning moral development. Honneth's interpretation arguably retrieves some of the motivational and sensual facets of the constitution of identity that are sidelined, though not ignored, in Habermas's account (Honneth 1995a). The other dimensions of Mead's understanding of the social have likewise been better developed in the work of other contemporary social theorists.

For Mead, the temporal and spatial constitution of society was of fundamental relevance to the social, like the emergence of symbolically anchored agreement between subjects. Indeed, these were intertwined processes of the constitution of the social, or what Mead explicitly called *sociality* (Mead 1932). These temporal and spatial facets of social action were important to the necessitating of intersubjective agreements and to the practical cast of activity giving rise to new contexts. Consequently, it could be argued that Habermas departs from Mead to the extent that the temporal and spatial constitution of the social is relatively peripheral to his theory. These themes have certainly been more energetically pursued by contemporary theorists like Bourdieu (1990; 1977) and, as examined later, Giddens (1984; 1979). Further, in this respect, at least, these two theorists are more consistent with Mead's practical philosophical perspective. Habermas's divergence from Mead extends further in his addressing the themes of the temporal and spatial constitution of the social from the split standpoints of systems theory and cultural consciousness (Habermas 1984a; 1987a; see Joas 1985). In my opinion, Habermas's theory would have been enhanced by taking up this component of Mead's approach to the social.

The third dimension marginalized by Habermas is creativity, Mead associates creativity particularly with the category of the 'I'. Habermas acknowledges the significance of this category, but he circumscribes its potential implications (Habermas 1992; 1987a). Although inexactly specified by Mead (1934, 214–22), the 'I' represents the source of spontaneity and the context transcending capacity of individuals. The 'I' is anchored in the corporeal and psychic dimensions of the self. For this reason, the 'I' is not entirely assimilated to the socially constituted 'me'; yet, Habermas comes close to ascribing an almost complete transformative dominance of the 'me' over the 'I'. He heavily channels the creativity of the 'I' towards projecting what the post-conventional self requires for its actualization. That is, projecting the ideal of participating in an unlimited communication community for purposes of self-expression, but his synthetic concept of identity exhibits a distinct lack of tension between its different elements. Now, there is the possibility that with this lack of tension Habermas is inadvertently admitting an inability to reconcile his notion of social identity with a more open-ended account of social change. In contemporary social theory, the emergence of new forms has been explicated far more by Castoriadis (1987; 1997; 1984) and the creativity of social action has been similarly expanded upon by Hans Joas (1996) and José Maurício Domingues (1996; 2000; 2006). Castoriadis' elucidating the radical imaginary of the psyche is more consistent with the several of the attributes Mead assigns to the 'I'.

Although all of these themes are less developed by Habermas, none of them were peripheral to Mead's thought. Rather, they were components of his perspective that were framed by the political and philosophical aspirations of North American pragmatism. In his conception of social identity, Habermas has most successfully extended those pragmatist arguments for a radical democratizing of complex societies. In so doing, he discloses some of the means by which a form of identity compatible with this aspiration could be brought into being. This significant achievement will be the subject of further analysis and the specific difficulties of Habermas's theory acquire general importance due to the possibilities of a different order of social relations that it anticipates. Nonetheless, the lesser development of these themes is relevant to the comparison that will be made with Giddens's theory of structuration and its attempt to encompass a number of these considerations.

The Paradigm of Understanding and Identity

I have proposed that the attainment of social identity through symbolic understanding is the core of Habermas's theory and that various details are overlain upon this conception of identity. For Habermas, a social identity that is constituted through communicative action mediates between the universal and the particular. This standpoint is the crucible of his notion of rationality; it translates the mutually reinforcing relation of 'individuation through socialization' (Habermas 1991; 1992a). In Habermas's opinion, this process of forming an identity should eventuate in the subject's radical-democratic projection of an 'unlimited communication community'. He believes that the normative content of such a projection is critical of contemporary society (Habermas 1987a; 1992a). However, Habermas does not develop this idea from a normative standpoint alone, he attempts to provide a sociological justification of it. Habermas claims that a rational identity, formed through the processes of communication, is realized in subjects' post-conventional structures of moral consciousness and the autonomous practices that are founded on the social application of universalistic principles of justice (Habermas 1990a; 1979a). The institutionalization of complementary social structures would not only represents an emancipatory-democratic transformation of existing social organization, but would also be the most functional form of coordinating the increasing complexity of modern societies (Habermas 1996a).

All of Habermas's work aims to show that this rational 'identity' is implicit in mutual understanding and that the conditions for a rational organization of society are to some extent already operative in the communicative reproduction of social relations. He claims that the rationality of communication does not need to be chosen against alternatives; rather such choices have been made in the learning processes that determine social and individual development (Habermas 1984a; 1979a). It is naturally difficult to reconcile this claim with the existing conditions of domination and suffering, as well as the systematic distortion of communication. Habermas nevertheless presents this argument on both ontogenetic and phylogenetic levels. The linkage between the two, he implies, is forged through the structures of communication and this connection justifies depicting the individual and society according to a common pattern of development (Habermas 1979a; 1990a). It will be shown later how a pivotal change underpins these contentions. Habermas replaces the praxis philosophy conception of the nexus between the subject and history with the more abstract coordinates of the intersection between individual competences and social evolution (Habermas 1979a; 1984a). A perennial problem in philosophy has been how to integrate a conception of identity with that of the reality of change. Habermas's solution to this problem is to make identity include development, but his elaboration of this claim does not permit much scope for the creative reinvention of social relations and institutions.

The different phases of Habermas's work have been shaped by the consistent problem of the mediation of the universal and the particular. Habermas not only evaluates other perspectives from the standpoint of this problem of mediation, but he has consistently revised those features of his work that appeared inconsistent with the demands of this form of rational mediation. It is the reason why Habermas's early epistemological model privileges Peirce and Dilthey's turn to the symbolic over Marx's paradigm of production (Habermas 1978a). The relationship of subject and object, he believes, logically excludes the reciprocity that underlies the universalism of intersubjective communication. Habermas's *reconstruction of historical materialism* is framed by the same problem and it is broached there primarily in terms of the notion of the logic of development (Habermas 1979a). Like Hegel, Habermas defines developmental progress as the movement towards the universal (Habermas 1979a; 1990a). Further, the intersubjective constitution of identity is integral to Habermas's opposition to systems theory. Indeed, Habermas generalizes a specific criticism of Luhmann's systems theory into the historical trend of the 'internal colonization' of the lifeworld by the system integrating steering media of money and power (Habermas 1976a; 1984a; 1987a). The crisis of identity forms the prototype of the social pathologies ensuing from this displacement of communication by market exchange and administrative power.

Given the analysis presented, it is probably not surprising that Habermas's theory is most convincing in its depiction of the intersubjective-communicative constitution of identity. It is especially original in its clarification of what this mediation of the universal and the particular implies in terms of subjects' moral consciousness. Habermas's theory is much less convincing in its conceptualization of other components of the social – which it overlays upon its approach to identity. This privileging of identity largely determines the limitations of Habermas's perspective on modernity. Notably, this approach's difficulties can be seen in Habermas's various theoretical adjustments and some of these changes culminate in the metaphors of the 'decentred' society (Habermas 1987b; 1996a). In fact, it is actually difficult to see how this decentring can be reconciled with Habermas's notion of identity providing the original framing pattern of modernity, even if it is paradoxically subverted in the actual course of historical modernization.

From this position, Habermas can critically describe those consequences of decentring developments that are at 'variance', in his terms, with modernity's self-definition (Habermas 1987a, 396). This critique takes the form of the argument that the structural modernization of the systems of the capitalist economy and the administrative system come to overtake and subordinate the cultural rationalization of the lifeworld. These criticisms of the substantial imbalances in the rationalization of society are undoubtedly important, but they equally reveal some of the major deficiencies of his approach. Habermas's criticisms depend on a highly functionalist mode of argumentation concerning societal integration and a problematic formulation of a distinction between the spheres of the system and the lifeworld.

In my opinion, it is the changes that Habermas primarily made to his theory during the phase of his 'reconstruction of historical materialism' that result in a subordinating of the philosophy of praxis concern with dynamic processes. The effect is a seriously flawed approach to the nexus between history and the subject (Habermas 1979a; 1979b). In Habermas's reconstruction of historical materialism, there is no real mediation between the evolutionary logic of development and the contingency of history, even though the latter falls under the category of developmental dynamics. The comparison with Giddens's approach to history will make explicit how little historical dynamics are able to alter the direction of social change in Habermas's reconstruction. In large part, this deficiency is carried over into Habermas's major theoretical statement: *The Theory of Communicative Action*, this is in spite of the importance of this work's explication of the dynamics of communicative rationalization and that of the 'inner colonisation of the lifeworld' (Habermas 1984a; 1987b). The disconnection from historical dynamics marks the perimeters in Habermas's theory against the effects of agency, practice and subjectivity.

None of these criticisms actually undermine the validity of Habermas's contention that there is no feasible alternative to communication, especially to the extent that it enables non-violent social coordination (Habermas 1991). At the level of social theory, however, a good deal hinges on how this principle is related to conditions and contexts, history and social structure. Habermas's perspective tends to fall down here. It is not just that his conceptualization of the historical process is weakened by the privileging of the logic of development over developmental dynamics – in a manner that is incompatible with the philosophy of praxis orientation. Habermas's later social theory's elaboration of his basic intuition concerning the mediation of the universal and particular leads to his marginalizing power and conflict (Honneth 1991; Giddens 1982b). Power and conflict are difficult to reconcile with Habermas's notion of communicative action oriented to mutual understanding, except as either external forces that impinge upon it or manifestations of distortions to be overcome.

A theory that centres on the problem of identity, I argue, will privilege the process of coordination, or more broadly those of coordination and distribution, rather than action and process. In particular, Habermas's conception of the 'social' subordinates the practical relationship of action to production, in the normal Marxist sense, and in Touraine's sense of the self-production of society (Touraine 1977; 1988). Ironically, one implication of Habermas's axial conception of identity is precisely that systems will appear superior to actors, because systems emerge to solve the problem of coordination and to relieve action of this function (Habermas 1987b). This connection between identity and coordination is undoubtedly a major reason why law gains greater prominence in Habermas's theory, although this is also influenced by the formal structure of his theory (Habermas 1987b; 1996a). As a consequence, Habermas's theoretical standpoint is one that is not so much 'practical' in itself, in the sense of being transformative and oriented to the action process; rather, it establishes a position of evaluation and justification.

Based on its account of mediation, this evaluative standpoint can ground a critical theory of democracy and modernity, in particular. In *The Theory of Communicative Action*, Habermas assigns critical theory the role of a spotlight, which is consistent with this conjecture (Habermas 1987a, 399–401). More importantly, still, his discourse theory of justice is concerned with evaluating and testing norms, rather than being located in moral action itself (Honneth 1995c). Habermas's (1996a) later discourse theory of democracy regains some of critical theory's practical orientation towards change, yet it does not fully overcome those aspects of Habermas's foundational conception that vitiates its approach to history, power and agency. The discourse theory of justice and democracy anticipates a substantial alteration of late-capitalist society but it would not imply any change in the principles of modernity. Habermas's utopian projection takes the form of actualizing the potential of existing institutions and the normative identity of late-modern societies.

I have argued that the underlying organization of Habermas's theory is determined by his approach to the problem of social identity. In his view, a social identity constituted through communicative action entails a democratic mediation of the universal and the particular. I sketched the background to Habermas's core intuition by noting the parallels that his interpretation of social identity has with that of Hegel's philosophy, examining arguments for a communication theory transformation of Adorno's critique of identity thinking and the positive implications that this change has for critical theory. I then traced its extending Mead's intersubjective analysis of 'individuation through socialization'. I suggested that Habermas overlays various details of his theory upon this conception of social identity and indicated some difficulties that ensue from this conception's ability to deal with a certain range of problems but not others. Even though I have not introduced the manifold issues involved, it should be evident that Habermas's position contrasts with postmodernist 'aversion to the universal'.[8] In Habermas's opinion, the intersubjective reciprocity that underpins universalism enables 'the difference of the other' to be given expression:

> Postmodern suspicion of an indiscriminate assimilating and homogenizing universalism fails to grasp the meaning of this morality and in the heat of controversy obliterates the relational structure of otherness and difference that universalism, properly understood, precisely takes into account. (Habermas 1998a, xxxv)

A stress on particularity and difference is characteristic of recent identity politics, yet the relevance of these developments to the complexion of Habermas's arguments is widely misunderstood. This type of misunderstanding is often a product of resistance to his arguments. Habermas has never obscured the evaluative standpoint of critical theory. The severity of his criticisms of postmodernist thought is partly a result of the method- ological demands of critical theory. That is, critical theory seeks to delineate the progres- sive direction of social change and this requires a methodology that is simultaneously normative and explanatory (see Benhabib 1986; Browne 2008). Despite the substan- tial disagreements with postmodernism, Habermas's central intuition is relevant to the dilemmas of mediating differences. However, the conception of the social that he derives from the change to the intersubjective paradigm of understanding is not typical of the philosophy of praxis and its conception of the connection between the subject and his- tory. My analysis now turns to the reasons that Habermas presented for this departure from the philosophy of praxis and the earlier critical theory of the Frankfurt School in the context of his defending and revising the 'project of modernity' (Habermas 1984a; 1987a; 1987b).

The Determinate Negation of Critical Marxism

Part One: The Frankfurt School's Critique of Instrumental Reason

One could give Habermas's theory of communicative action no higher praise than to say that it successfully makes a case for the continuation of critical theory by means other than those Marx proposed. However much one may disagree with its details, Habermas's theory enlightens the contemporary 'obscurity' and it supplies criteria for discriminating between progressive and regressive tendencies in the present. Habermas is undoubtedly correct to assume that his establishing criteria for distinguishing between progressive from regressive change is continuous with Marx and Western Marxism's modernist perspective. It is equally discontinuous with the indiscriminate critiques of modernity, reason and the subject (Habermas 1987b, 338). Habermas considers that the paradigm of understanding is a 'determinate negation' of the philosophy of the subject:

---

8 This is a paraphrase of Honneth's (1985) title of an article on Lyotard, see also the debates in Benhabib (1995) and Benhabib's (1994) comments on contemporary critics of universalism.

A paradigm only loses its force when it is negated in a determinate manner by a different paradigm, that is when it is devalued in an insightful way; it is certainly resistant to any simple invocation of the extinction of the subject. (Habermas 1987b, 310)

Habermas's theory's encompassing character and comprehensive ambition has never been in dispute. He contends that the theory of communicative action reconciles the supposedly divergent problematics of the critical theory of the Frankfurt School and the Marxist philosophy of praxis. However, he argues that with this shift to the 'paradigm of understanding' the approaches of these streams of critical Marxism have been effectively superseded (Habermas 1987a; 1987b). It supersedes them principally because this paradigm change overcomes the aporias of the philosophy of the subject to which the Marxist tradition remained bound. In Habermas's opinion, founding a theory of society in mutual understanding accomplishes a transition to the standpoint of intersubjectivity; it should be distinguished from those linguistic perspectives that are premised on the relationship of subject and object (Habermas 1991, 233–38; 1992a, 57–73).

Habermas (1987b) argues that the category of labour cannot accomplish this transition to intersubjectivity, whilst the growth in the complexity of social systems has overtaken the explanatory capacity of the action theoretical category of social labour. These assertions can be criticised, of course, and there are strong grounds for considering Marx's notion of labour as intrinsically intersubjective (Markus 1986). However, Habermas's argument is that Marx's adoption of the perspective of labour merely changed the 'accent' of the philosophy of the subject, from that of self-conscious reflection to production (Habermas 1987b, 63). To a certain degree, this claim may appear inconsistent with Habermas's earlier view that Marx developed a transformative critique of the 'knowing subject' with his active pragmatist conception of labour (Habermas 1979a, 133). In Habermas's opinion, the intersubjective standpoint of communication theory is more radical in its consequences. Marx only intimated at the possibility of a properly intersubjective perspective without realizing its full significance. In this respect, according to Habermas, Marx was simply like the other participants in the 'philosophical discourse of modernity' (Habermas 1987b).

Habermas proposal that his theory of communicative action supplants and reconciles the salient differences between the earlier Frankfurt School's critical theory and the postwar philosophy of praxis is equally contentious. Even if it were true, it is in no way the result of a synthesis of these approaches. Despite the fact that such a synthesis was held out as a possibility in Habermas's earlier phenomenological inquiry into the anthropologically founded social practices that shape the constitution of knowledge (Habermas 1978a). He now considers that this earlier attempt to supplement the philosophical anthropology of 'objectification' with that of communicative interaction was an insufficient response to Western Marxism's major limitations. In his opinion, the anthropology of the philosophy of praxis and the Frankfurt School's category of reason share some of the same fundamental deficiencies of the subject-centred philosophy of consciousness (Habermas 1987b). These traditions naturally differ in their manifesting these deficiencies, but they can ultimately be traced back to the intrinsic limitations of Marx's critique of Hegel from the standpoint of social labour and forward to the revelation of these limitations by developments in the alternate paradigm of language and understanding (Habermas 1987b; 1992a). Habermas proposes, instead, that:

> In the theory of communicative action, the feedback process by which lifeworld and everyday communicative practice are intertwined takes over the mediating role that Marx and Western Marxism had reserved to social practice. (Habermas 1987b, 316)

According to Habermas, the linguistic turn of twentieth-century philosophy has proven so significant that it now defines the level of explanation acceptable within this discipline (Habermas 1992a, 7–8, 44–48). He argues that each of the twentieth century's four major philosophical movements – analytical philosophy, phenomenology, Western Marxism, structuralism – has in some way had to confront this turn from consciousness to language and they have all been modified by this change. However, it was only with his theory of communicative action that the movement of Western Marxism found a satisfactory form of elaborating this turn in a way consistent with its own purposes. It was, nevertheless, not only his receptivity to important developments in other theoretical streams that compelled the paradigm change in critical theory. The Western Marxist tradition's internal limitations necessitated this change. In particular, the most serious limitation countenancing this change was already present in Horkheimer and Adorno's shift to the critique of instrumental reason (Horkheimer and Adorno 1972). For Horkheimer and Adorno's account of the dialectic of the enlightenment problematized the connection of subjectivity and reason. This connection had unfolded historically, they argued, in the oppressive form of instrumental reason. In making this critique, they were challenging some of the core emancipatory claims of modernity. The connection of subjectivity and reason had been a cornerstone of endeavours to comprehend the possibility of freedom and emancipation since the rationalist philosophies of the Enlightenment and German Idealism (see Touraine 1995).

Adorno and Horkheimer's (1972) contention reflected their loss of belief in the earlier critical theory programme of an 'interdisciplinary materialism' and a broad disenchantment regarding the prospects and the agency of change (see Dubiel 1984; Wiggershaus 1994). Habermas argues that the disjuncture of the critique of instrumental reason was, however, not simply the result of the historically contingent circumstances of its formulation. These circumstances included the ideological integration of the working class in western democracies, the bureaucratic distortion of socialist ideals in the Soviet Union and Stalinism, and the apparent congruence between capitalism and the Fascist state. Rather, Adorno and Horkheimer's disillusioned critique of instrumental reason was conditioned by the limitations intrinsic to the philosophy of consciousness, particularly because they demonstrated how the philosophy of consciousness did not contain a way out of the bind. The rationality that enabled the liberation of humanity from the constraints of nature was driven by an imperative for self-preservation that extended reification (Habermas 1984a, 386; Horkheimer and Adorno 1972).

Habermas aims to provide a communication theoretical equivalent for the Western Marxist conception of the rationalization of society generating an extensive reification of consciousness. For Western Marxism, reification is where the objective structures of commodity exchange and formal rationality appear to have power over the social relations of the subjects that constitute them. Habermas's theoretical equivalent takes the form of an account of the 'internal colonization of the lifeworld' by the functionalist reason operative in the capitalist economy and political-administrative system, so that the communication processes that are essential to the lifeworld's reproduction are undermined by the intrusion of the instrumental and functional exigencies that organize these systems (Habermas 1984a; 1987b). At the same time, and with the same categories, Habermas contests Horkheimer and Adorno's formulation of the 'dialectic of the enlightenment', as well as their vision of modernity culminating in the 'totally administered society' (Horkheimer and Adorno 1972; Adorno 1974; Horkheimer 1978). In short, the shift to the paradigm of mutual understanding, Habermas argues, makes it possible to demonstrate the internal connection between the rationality of communicative action and the reproduction of the modern lifeworld (Habermas 1984a; 1987a; 1987b).

The development of an intersubjective concept of rationality therefore forms the basis for Habermas's reversing Horkheimer and Adorno's pessimistic social-historical diagnosis. Despite revising their overall account of modernity, Habermas (1984a; 1987a; 1987b) finds their conceptualization highly instructive. The fact of his repeatedly returning to their elucidation of the dialectic of subject-centred reason indicates that he regards it as exemplary. It has the further relevance of attempting to illuminate the anthropological origins of the constitution of the subject in teleological models of action. As I have noted, Habermas's social theory is very much based upon a contrast between the orientation toward mutual understanding of communicative action and the teleological dimensions of strategic and instrumental types of action. What Habermas finds most instructive about the critique of instrumental reason is how it formulates the intractable problems of the dialectic of subject and object. In particular, Horkheimer and Adorno (1972) clarify the genesis of the self through the instrumental relation of the subject to nature (see Browne 2016). This 'primal history of subjectivity' involves the domination of the self in the process of dominating nature, but it is this very history that made subjectivity possible in the first place (Habermas 1983, 99–109). Horkheimer and Adorno present a story of repression in the very process of self-constitution. In their opinion, the ambivalence inherent in overcoming the constraints of nature besets later notions of freedom. The elevation of the subject over nature originates a destructive cycle of rationalization that itself depends on the denial of nature in the subject:

> This very denial, the nucleus of all civilizing rationality, is the germ cell of a proliferating mythic irrationality: with the denial of nature in man not merely the *telos* of the outward control of nature but the *telos* of man's own life is distorted and befogged. As soon as man cuts off his consciousness of himself as nature, all the ends for which he keeps himself alive – social progress, the heightening of all his natural and spiritual powers, even consciousness itself – are nullified; the enthronement of means as ends, which in late capitalism has taken on the character of open madness, is already perceptible. Man's domination over himself, which grounds his selfhood, is virtually always the destruction of the subject in whose service it takes place; for the substance which is dominated, suppressed and undone by self-preservation is none other than that very life for which the accomplishments of self-preservation are supposed to be functional; it is in fact just what is supposed to be preserved. (Horkheimer and Adorno 1972, 54–55)

The subject-centred reason of the 'paradigm' of the philosophy of consciousness has dominated modern thought, appearing in a multitude of guises. In the present context, it is sufficient to simply indicate what Habermas considers to be the minimal features shared by perspectives within this paradigm and those typical suppositions. On his analysis, the first of three interrelated features is that the philosophy of consciousness is tied to the relationship of subject and object. It is fixed to a model of the cognitive representation of things and objects in consciousness. The relation of subject and object has such conceptual priority that other forms of mediation, like that of the communication between subjects, are implicitly reduced to it. The second feature is that the philosophy of consciousness is essentially solipsistic and therefore monological; it posits an initial independence of the subject from the world (Habermas 1987b; 1984a). In so doing, it abstracts from intersubjectivity. The third feature is that the practices of subject-centred reason are derived from the manipulation of objects, manipulation being the practical counterpart of the representation of things in consciousness. Not only does this imply that the subject relates solely to entities in an objectivating attitude; but also that the subject applies this objectivating perspective to itself in reflection. In effect, the subject knows itself as subject through its being equivalent to the objective entities it encounters (Habermas 1984a, 392–396). It is not too difficult to then perceive how Horkheimer and Adorno were able to identify the nucleus of reification in this objectifying self-relation.

In Habermas's opinion, as a consequence of these three features, the philosophy of consciousness is unable to conceptualise the logic of social interaction. Specifically, the normative dimension of the reciprocity between subjects can never be adequately apprehended from the perspective of subject-centred reason. Horkheimer and Adorno (1972) were then correct, in the terms of the philosophy of consciousness, to subsume the rational subject under the problem of self-preservation, because in this paradigm the subject is tied to the manipulation of objects. Horkheimer and Adorno's illumination of the paradigm of subjecting-centred reason's aporias was a substantial achievement; yet it was, in a sense, paradoxically purchased at the cost of exposing the immanent limitations of their own programme and its continuity with the reason they critiqued. Habermas believes that this assessment justifies his replacing critical theory's normative grounding in a philosophy of history with a theory of communication, as well as his theory's diverging somewhat from the former format of immanent critique (Habermas 1984a; 1987a). Of course, the veracity of Habermas's critical assessment does not necessarily mean that his proposed resolution is satisfactory. It has already been indicated how there are some losses as well as gains from this change in paradigm and its sequels, such as the difficulties that Habermas's formulation has with respect to the social dynamics of power and conflict.

In his commentaries on the Frankfurt School and praxis philosophy strands of critical Marxism, Habermas underlines their alleged lack of clarity concerning their normative foundations. He considers that the disintegration of the Frankfurt School's original interdisciplinary research programme brought these difficulties to the fore. However, this breakdown was preceded by a series of highly consequential shifts in the normative grounding of Marxian critical theory. According to Habermas, the Frankfurt School's interdisciplinary inquiry into the capitalist reification of consciousness was made 'after the theory of value had lost its foundational role. With this, of course, also went the normative content of rational natural law theory that was preserved in value theory' (Habermas 1987a, 381). Even at the stage of the critique of instrumental reason, critical theory continued to find its justification in the Marxist philosophy of history. In Habermas's opinion, Horkheimer and Adorno's loss of confidence in the 'rational potential of bourgeois culture' simply exposed the 'fragility' of this justification. In any case, he argues, the Marxist philosophy of history was 'not able to support an empirical research program' because it was based upon a translating arguments about an 'objective teleology in history' into 'pseudo-normative propositions' (Habermas 1987b, 382; 1982, 230–32). The provision of alternative normative foundations for Critical Theory has been a major concern of Habermas's change to the paradigm of communication and his search for an appropriate mediation of the universal and the particular.

Habermas does pick up on a somewhat different, though connected, normative reference point that is implicit in Horkheimer and Adorno's critique of instrumental reason. It is similarly conditioned by their negative philosophy of history, but it derives from their attempt to disclose what was originally damaged by the dominance of instrumental reason. In Habermas's opinion, the concept of *mimesis* occupies, to a certain extent, this place in their discourse and it serves as a yardstick and normative point of reference. By way of the concept of *mimesis* Horkheimer and Adorno were able to insinuate at the possibility of a less repressive mediation, if not the complete reconciliation of the subject and nature, self and other. Now, as we saw in relation to his core intuition, Habermas is interested in the motifs of freedom and reconciliation in Adorno and Horkheimer's work. He believes that these motifs point beyond the perspective of the philosophy of consciousness. However, the category of *mimesis* belongs to the context of their reassessing the relationship of myth and enlightenment. In my opinion, the notion of *mimesis* incorporates a rather different sense of connection and disconnection to modernity than that of Habermas's notion of intersubjective communication's reciprocity and rationality. *Mimesis* is not the opposite of reason, but nor is it identical to instrumental reason (see Browne 2016).

Horkheimer and Adorno (1972, xvi) do not juxtapose *mimesis* to reason, as their central thesis was that 'myth is already enlightenment; and enlightenment reverts to mythology'. Mythical thought pursues its objectives by way of *mimesis*, re-enacting in ritual natural processes so as to control them. In this sense, mythical thought harbours elements of a disposition towards instrumental reason, but the enlightening process of disenchanting nature facilitated the unimpeded expansion and full development of instrumental reason. Horkheimer and Adorno's genealogy of the rational subject took part of its bearings from Max Weber's interpretation of the disenchantment of the world. After Weber, they argued that the dominance of instrumental reason in the 'totally administered society' was destroying the possibility of the autonomous individual. The latter thesis drew part of its inspiration from Weber's diagnoses of industrial capitalism eventuating in a seemingly ineluctable 'Iron Cage' and a 'loss of freedom' – with the dominance of the formal rationality of bureaucracy (Weber 1930; 1958). By way of their negative historical projection, Horkheimer and Adorno (1972) perceived the pattern of instrumental reason to be deeply set in western culture. In effect, they argued that modern capitalism was characterised by a peculiarly more intensive application of instrumental reason. Wellmer suggests that the self-referential dimension of Horkheimer and Adorno's critique of reason actually conflicted with critical social theory's historical orientation.

> A philosophical theory with such a dramatic self-interpretation cannot point any more to traces, elements, or tendencies of historical reality itself to substantiate the emphatic idea of reason which it nevertheless opposes to the perverted rationality of existing social reality. Since Horkheimer and Adorno, in ironical agreement with Weber, see conceptual thinking – geared to domination and self-preservation – as the ultimate root of the perversions of modern rationality, they cannot even trust that the idea of an unperverted rationality could be kept alive in the sphere of discursive thinking; only if conceptual thinking is turned against itself and against its own reifying tendencies can there be any hope that the memory of reconciliation is preserved in philosophical thought. (Wellmer 1985, 48)

This almost complete identification of rationality and reification pushed the normative dimensions of the Frankfurt School's critical theory in an increasingly utopian direction (Benhabib 1986; 1981; Wellmer 1985). Habermas (1984a; 1987a; 1987b; 1983) argues that the Frankfurt School theorists' later normative alternatives, in Adorno's case that of avant-garde artistic forms and Marcuse's postulate of need satisfaction through libidinal happiness, exacerbated the contrast between rationalization and utopian projects of its transfiguration (Adorno 1984; Marcuse 1966; 1969). For this very reason, they were unsuited to the task of practically grounding a critical theory of society, even though they remained significant in their evoking alternatives to the logic of capitalist rationalization. Habermas based this assessment on the rationality criterion of the mediation of the universal and the particular, a criterion that was equally adhered to by the first generation of critical theorists. This may be why Habermas suggests that some of the connotations that Horkheimer and Adorno intended with the category of *mimesis*, like that of a non-violent interaction of subject and object, can be better formulated in the intersubjective format of a theory of communication (Habermas 1984a). In contrast to their conclusions of the dissolution of the subject and the one-dimensional rationalization of modern society, Habermas contends that a theory of communicative rationality is founded on an appreciation of how these ideals are operative within the practice of everyday social interaction.

The notion of communicative rationality could appear quite counterfactual and, indeed, this is part of the reason for this notion's critical potential. In fact, Habermas distinguishes his formal pragmatic depiction of communicative action from the empirical pragmatic description of acts of communication, which are regularly distorted by social relations of power and conditioned by contingent circumstances. Nevertheless, Habermas contends that the rationality of communicative action is a necessary, though not fully realised, part of social reproduction and that modernity is intrinsically bound up with its expansion. The justification of these claims can be discerned from the main features of Habermas's formal-pragmatic theory of communicative action. First, his central argument is that the acquisition of the ability to communicate has a universal core that derives from the basic structures and rules that all subjects master in learning to speak a language. Second, he asserts that all speech is 'oriented toward the idea of truth', including conscious deception. Moreover, communicative action possess a rationally bonding and motivating force, since all action orientations can be rationally vindicated, through (a) the thematizing in speech of their associated criticizable validity claim, and in (b) the process of giving argumentative reasons both for, and against, these validity claims can be rationally redeemed (Habermas 1979a; 1984a).

In a sense, Habermas's notion of the rational redemption of validity claims develops from pragmatist philosophy's original idea that interaction involves both communicating about something in the world and taking up a relationship to another subject. Habermas proposes that the standard 'speech act' has the peculiar 'double-structure' of an illocutionary component and a propositional component (Habermas 1984a). Generally, the illocutionary component determines the sense in which the propositional content is to be understood, for instance, as a request, wish, promise, statement of fact, and so on.[9] The propositional component contains referential and predictive expressions, whereas the illocutionary component is usually specified by the performative sentence in the first person present indicative with a direct object in the second person. For example, the statement that 'I promise that I will come tomorrow' has the illocutionary component of a promise and the propositional content relating to the claim to 'come tomorrow'.

This 'double structure' of speech fixes the two levels which speaker and hearer must simultaneously reach an understanding about in communication: the intersubjective relation and the propositional content communicated. The double structure of speech enables the illocutionary and propositional components to be uncoupled in the production and transformation of speech acts. For example, the propositional component can remain invariant throughout changes in the illocutionary component, so that speech acts are 'propositionally differentiated out' (Habermas 1979a). Similarly, the illocutionary component of a previous speech act may become the propositional component of a new speech act. There is no reason why the embedding of prior speech acts cannot continue indefinitely. The latter is, for Habermas, another way of articulating the linguistic turn's implication that statements pertain to 'states of affairs' and not to things (Habermas 1991; 1992a). Further, the double structure of speech demonstrates how language can be a medium of intersubjective reflection.

The illocutionary component of a speech act usually determines the aspect of validity that the speaker wants an utterance to be understood to be first and foremost about. Habermas distinguishes four 'validity claims' a speaker may raise: truth, rightness, truthfulness and comprehensibility. These validity claims are, he argues, constitutive of the rational structure of communicative action, because a validity claim can be rejected only by way of criticism and defended against this criticism by way of refuting it with reasons

---

9   Habermas's analysis is restricted to the explicit standard form or 'ideal typical' speech act. This standard form generally consists of:

    'I   (verb)   you that   (sentence) ...'

For example: 'I (hereby) promise you that I will come tomorrow.'
        <u>Illocutionary</u> component   <u>Propositional</u> component

or grounds. The acceptance or rejection of a validity claim is then intrinsically connected to the speaker and hearer's provision of reasons or grounds.[10] In fact, Habermas argues that to understand the meaning of a speech act depends on knowing 'what makes it acceptable' and its recognition is therefore inherently intersubjective (Habermas 1984a, 297). A rational bonding is achieved through the reciprocal recognition of validity claims, because the hearer knows the grounds or reasons with which a speaker would be able to redeem the validity claim raised. The 'internal' connection between meaning and validity is implied by the hearer not only responding to a speech act in understanding the meaning of the utterance but in taking a 'yes' or 'no' position in relation to the validity claim the hearer is also in a position to accept or decline the speech act offer.

Habermas believes that the necessary, if not the sufficient, conditions for a theory of rationality are present in everyday communicative action, because the reciprocal recognition of criticizable validity claims reveals the rationality of subjects to the extent that they are able to employ modes of argumentation to support validity claim. In his opinion,

> communicative rationality carries with it connotations based ultimately on the central experience of the unconstrained, unifying, consensus-bringing force of argumentative speech, in which different participants overcome their merely subjective views and, owing to the mutuality of rationally motivated conviction, assure themselves of both the unity of the objective world and the intersubjectivity of their lifeworld. (Habermas 1984a, 10)

Part Two: The Expressive Totality and Ethical Totality of Praxis Philosophy

Despite his view of the critique of instrumental reason resulting in a debilitating of the normative grounding of critical theory, Habermas suggests that the Frankfurt School theorists still posed the problem of the reification of consciousness in a way that retained its tie to reason and rationality (Habermas 1987b, 75). By contrast, the Marxist tradition of praxis philosophy developed from an initial retrieval of the normative conception found in Marx's early notion of labour. Habermas claims however that praxis philosophy let the connection between its key categories of creativity and self-expression and those of reason and rationality become less than perspicacious in the process of elaborating its perspective (Habermas 1987b, 75–76). In Habermas's usage, this criticism of praxis philosophy applies largely to those post-war Marxist theorists who drew major

---

10 'With their illocutionary acts, speaker and hearer raise validity claims and demand they be recognised. But this recognition need not follow irrationally, since the validity claims have a cognitive character and can be checked. In the final analysis, the speaker can illocutionarily influence the hearer and vice versa, because speech-act-typical commitments are connected with cognitively testable validity claims – that is, because the reciprocal bonds have a rational basis. The engaged speaker normally connects the specific sense in which he would like to take up an interpersonal relationship with a thematically stressed validity claim and thereby chooses a specific mode of communication' (Habermas 1979a, 63).

inspiration from Marx's early philosophical anthropology, and many of whom were influenced by twentieth-century phenomenology. Praxis philosophy derives its normative underpinning from an extension of the originally 'Romantic Movement' interpretation of an expressive and self-realizing subjectivity. That is, the subject is constituted through its objectification and objectifications are externalizations of subjectivity. The generative dimension of social constitution is of preeminent importance to praxis philosophy. For this perspective, reification results from objectifications appearing independent of the subject that produced them. In this praxis perspective, notions of self-determination are internally connected to those of the subject's self-realization. Habermas's perceives the following theoretical synthesis to underlie praxis philosophy and its vision of social autonomy:

> The model of the externalization and appropriation of essential powers was derived, on the one hand, from dynamizing Aristotle's concept of form – the individual unfolds his essential powers through his own productive activity – and, on the other hand, form the philosophy of reflection's mediation of the Aristotelian concept of form with an aesthetic one – the objectifications in which subjectivity takes on external shape are at the same time the symbolic expression of both a conscious act of creation and an unconscious process of self-formation. (Habermas 1987b, 77–78)

On this interpretation, Marx's early concepts of labour and alienation form the prototype for the whole praxis philosophy tradition. Drawing on Honneth's analysis, Habermas argues that the rationalization of production overtook the artisan system that partly justified an expressivist conception of labour (Habermas 1982, 225; 1987b; Honneth 1995b, 15–49). He claims that Marx's analyses of the industrial capitalist economy comprehended the implications of this development, unlike some later variations of the philosophy of praxis. Marx 'abandoned the anthropological model of labour as externalization, which still furnished the standard for the critique of alienated labour in the "Paris Manuscripts", and shifted the burden of normatively grounding to the labour theory of value' (Habermas 1982, 225–226). This interpretation is open to dispute. Habermas could be criticised for ignoring the underlying continuities in Marx's thought. In fact, Habermas provides contradictory accounts of Marx's position on the cycle of objectification and appropriation, which is central to the social theory of praxis philosophy. On the one hand, Habermas claims that Marx's shift from the 'romantic' critique of alienated labour to the theory of value was a response to the demands of complexity and recognition of the independent internal logic of the capitalist economic system. On the other hand, Habermas argues that Marx's critique of political economy remained within the philosophy of the subject, which meant that an 'anthropocentric' image of social systems complemented a truncated concept of action (Habermas 1982).

The notion of Marx's abandonment of labour as externalization contradicts Habermas's representations of it as a primary instance of Marx's allegiance to the paradigm of the philosophy of the subject. In the case of the labour theory of value, Habermas (1987a; 1987b) faults Marx for conceiving developments in the capitalist system to be simply an expression of class relations. Before examining the context of this criticism of the subject-centred reasoning of Marx's critique of political economy, it is worth mentioning that Habermas's analysis has been criticised for ignoring the categorical differentiation of the paradigm of production and neglecting the intersubjective perspective of the social division of labour in the production paradigm (Grumley 1991; 1992; Markus 1986a; Giddens 1982b).

Habermas's critique of praxis philosophy principally relies on the change to the intersubjective approach of the paradigm of understanding and the revisions it enables in the action theoretical foundations of social theory. Where originally Habermas conceived of communication as a form of social activity that is separate from, but largely complementary to that of labour, communication later has a coordinating function in relation to all other types of action (Habermas 1984a). Indeed, communicative action is the paradigmatic form of social activity, making understanding constitutive of the social. Hans Joas suggests that Habermas announces the 'end of the philosophy of praxis' in claiming 'not only that his theory of communicative action defines more precisely than ever before a particular type of human praxis, but also that this theory takes the place of the philosophy of praxis as a whole' (Joas 1993, 173). Habermas's claim is based not only on the universal significance of communicative action as a form of practice, but also on the merits of his synthetic model of modernity (Habermas 1987a; 1987b). This means that some of the justifications for replacing the praxis philosophy perspective are those considerations that motivated Habermas's widely disputed incorporating aspects of a systems theory approach. In this respect, his position is quite different to Giddens's attempt to address similar considerations from a reformulated praxis perspective: the theory of structuration.

Habermas argues that praxis philosophy simply underestimates the complexity of late-capitalist society and the significance of the changes in system integration in terms of development. In short, the complexity and developmental advances of capitalist modernity represent, according to Habermas, fundamental restraints on any project to reorganise society. In his opinion, praxis philosophy cannot come to terms with the implications of complexity and development because of its allegiance to the subject-centred perspective of production. This is not a matter of oversight, rather it owes to the basic aspiration of praxis philosophy:

> Praxis philosophy is guided by the intuition that it still makes sense to try to realize the idea of an ethical totality *even* under the functional constraints set by highly complex social systems. (Habermas 1987b, 62)

Habermas appears to suggest that the complexity of a 'decentred' society made the conceptual model of functionalist systems theory superior to the Marxist perspective in terms of the explanation of the social realm of material production.

> If one imagines the metabolism between human beings and nature as a circular process in which production and consumption mutually stimulate and expand each other, this presents two criteria for evaluating social evolution: the increase in the technically useful knowledge, and the differentiation as well as universalization of needs. Both can be subsumed under the functionalist viewpoint of an increase in complexity. (Habermas 1987b, 81)

Arnason importantly notes that Habermas's dialogue with systems theory was from the outset centred on its application to labour (Arnason 1979; 1982). The arguments that Habermas deploys to disclose the limits of praxis philosophy are heavily based on his attempt to integrate the frameworks of system and action theory. Yet, this formulation of a two-dimensional conception of society, as lifeworld and system, is one of the most, if not the most, controversial and heavily criticised facets of his theory (McCarthy 1985; Bohman 1989; Calhoun 1995). This construction will be examined in greater detail later, but what I want to highlight here is how the preceding discussion implies that difficulties would probably arise from Habermas's not sufficiently considering whether functionalist analyses of systems is a means that could be adapted to the ends of a critical theory of society.

In my opinion, there is a fundamental tension between the weight that Habermas places on integrating systems theory and his intended criticism of the predominance of functionalist reason in contemporary capitalist society. In fact, his criticisms of systems theory often seem like an adjunct to his general argument and a type of functionalist reasoning is evident in Habermas's own diagnosis of social pathologies. He argues that these are an effect of an imbalance of rationalization rather than endemic to modernity. In this way, Habermas's criticisms of Parsons's theory of modernity seem to rebound on his own theory (Habermas 1987a). For instance, he comments that Parsons's conceptual harmonizing 'reduce sociopathologies to systemic disequilibria' (Habermas 1987a, 292).

Honneth considers that Habermas's critique of the philosophy of praxis has been a source of confusion (Honneth 1991, xxxi). The arguably legitimate criticism of those praxis philosophy depictions of systems as collective subjects appears to be unjustifiably extended to the basic orientation of the praxis perspective. The praxis philosophy orientation permits alternatives that do not warrant this criticism; hence some of the divisions that Habermas creates between his own theory and the praxis perspective are founded on a misunderstanding. Like the philosophy of praxis, Habermas wants to uphold the priority of action theory, rather than the objectivating and structural perspective of social systems. There are important reasons for integrating a systems theory perspective, but not all of these are identical with the deficiencies that Habermas claims to find in the philosophy of praxis. Rather, in the first instance, his motive for drawing on systems theory is the obvious limitations of a purely communicative or interpretative approach to society. Habermas has consistently distinguished the functional requirement of the material reproduction of society from that of social integration through communication. There is the further need to take into account the objective social processes that may be obscure from the perspective of actors and that occur, so to speak, 'behind the back of social actors'. In Habermas's opinion, the latter processes require an objectifying perspective for their elucidation.

Habermas's turn to systems theory was connected then to his rejection of the Hegelian-Marxist concept of totality, though he emphatically rejects the category of totality on the grounds of communication theory's intersubjective implications. According to Habermas, the complexity and differentiation of modern society makes untenable the expressivist understanding of a social totality that is an objectification of the subject:

> Systems theory and action theory are the *disjecta membra* of a dialectical concept of totality employed by Marx himself and then by Lukács – though they were unable to reconstruct it

in terms that might provide an equivalent of the basic concepts of the Hegelian logic they rejected as idealistic. (Habermas 1984a, 343–44)

This position on the category of totality demonstrates how Habermas's adaptation of systems theory was conditioned by a need to rethink the basic problems of social theory, like the connection between action and social order, structure and agency. Habermas had been criticised for assimilating institutional orders to a single action orientation, but in *The Theory of Communicative Action* he perceives this to be a failing of Weber's account of rationalization and the earlier Frankfurt School critical theory (Habermas 1984a; 1987b; Honneth 1991; McCarthy 1978). The combination of an intersubjective theory of pragmatic communication and a systems theoretical perspective supposedly enable him to rectify this failing, though there are grounds for questioning whether he is consistent in disassociating the rationality of systems from that of purposive-rational. His argument that a systems theoretical perspective is required to account for the unintended consequences of action is similarly questionable. I will later considering whether this alleged limitation of action theory is correct, and whether, even if it is the case, a change to the functionalist perspective of systems theory is warranted by it (see Joas 1993, 141).

For Habermas, the Hegelian logic that Marx incorporated into the labour theory of value enabled a translation between system and action categories. But he argues that this construction is no longer convincing, being insufficiently complex with respect of the different types of interchange between action and systems. Marx's 'error' consisted in failing to satisfactorily separate them. Marx, Habermas claims, did not sufficiently appreciate the independent logic of systems, despite being among the first to recognize it. 'Marx has in view a future state of affairs in which the objective semblance of capital has dissolved' (Habermas 1987a, 340). A corollary of this criticism is that the model of workers self-management cannot serve, in Habermas's opinion, as the foundation of a project of democratizing a highly differentiated society. From the standpoint of system integration, he argues that there are intrinsic limitations to this model and its legitimacy within the philosophy of praxis is partly due to its heritage in the expressivist concept of the subject. By contrast, I have argued that Habermas accentuates instead coordination and distribution, rather than the generative dimension of production. His assessment of workers' self-management is therefore consistent with this point of view and, for this reason, the theoretical foundations of his claims about the limitations of 'workers self-management' and democratizing of the market system are open to counter-criticism.

Habermas's theorizing of the conceptual division between the functionalist perspective of systems and the action theory perspective of the lifeworld is supplemented by an empirical sociological argument that has decisive implications for the utopian project of labour. According to Habermas, changes in patterns of employment and the social organization of late-capitalist societies have largely rendered the paradigm of work obsolete (Habermas 1987b, 79). In retrospect, this empirical assertion appears rather misleading. However, important reasons for Habermas's initial turn to systems theory were the development of the welfare state and the conclusions that he drew from his critique of Marxian political economy. It was no longer feasible, in his view, to conceptualise the capitalist economy as a self-regulating system, its operation are now highly dependent on extensive state intervention. Systems theory appeared originally, to him, as a possibly ideological, but nonetheless important, approach to the interchange between the welfare state and a capitalist economy (Habermas 1976c). Habermas would develop the implications of this contention in his major work (Habermas 1984a; 1987a).

In *The Theory of Communicative Action*, Habermas specifically treats the emergence of systems as a historical problem, but, unlike his original analysis of late-capitalist legitimation problems and early critique of functionalist logic, the critical intentions of this later analysis does not at all mean that he dissents from the functionalist criteria of complexity and adaptation (Habermas 1987a; 1976c; 1988b). Indeed, these criteria disclose, in his opinion, some of the most fundamental deficiencies of Marx's social theory:

> Marx is convinced a priori that in capital he has before him nothing more than the mystified form of a class relation. This interpretation excludes from the start the question of whether the systemic interconnection of the capitalist economy and the modern state administration do not also represent a higher and evolutionarily advantageous level of integration by comparison to traditional societies. Marx conceives of capitalist society so strongly as a totality that he fails to recognize the intrinsic evolutionary value that media-steered subsystems possess. (Habermas 1987b, 339)

Habermas raises a number of other, often familiar, arguments in the context of announcing the 'end of the philosophy of praxis'. The most important of these is the philosophical claim that a normative theory of justice is possible from the intersubjective standpoint of communication, but not so much from the perspective of the paradigm of production. As it has already been stated, Habermas's original interest in communication partly derived from the alternative it potentially constituted to the strategic and technical conjoining of theory and practice during the modern period. He distinguishes his discourse theory of morality, law and democracy from more recent Neo-Aristotelian practical philosophy, but returns to his original motivation in differentiating political praxis from the paradigm of production. 'It is the form of interaction processes that must be altered if one wants to discover practically what the members of a society in any given situation might want and what they should do in their common interest' (Habermas 1987b, 82).

Habermas contends that, unlike the paradigm of production, the principles of democratic procedure are intrinsic to the paradigm of understanding (Habermas 1996a). Indeed, as the next chapter explains, this contention is consistent with the major assumption of his explanation of long-term historical transformations and the democratizing potential of the project of modernity. The notion of normative learning leading first to changing patterns of social interaction and that this development then shapes historical transitions, through being drawn upon in response to crises in the system of material production, constitutes simultaneously a major part of the explanatory framework and emancipatory vision of Habermas's *reconstruction of historical materialism* and *The Theory of Communicative Action* (Habermas 1990a; 1979a; 1984a; 1987a).

Besides the argument that the instrumental orientation of labour means that the production paradigm is unable to specify the *social* mediation between subjects, another contention is advanced in relation to this claim about social mediation. One that appears close to Adorno's position and that might even seem to contain elements of a concession to postmodern critics of reason and the subject, even though it is used against them. Habermas argues that mediation through social labour entails the universalism of the philosophy of the subject. It cannot but result in the oppression of the particular (Habermas 1992a, 149). Habermas asserts that 'the individual' is only conceivable from within the paradigm of mutual understanding; for it has abandoned the metaphysics of subject-centred reason and presupposes instead the 'ineliminable' differences between individual speakers in communicative action. Rather than the doubling of the transcendental subject in the realm of the social, that Foucault had diagnosed as endemic to the modern 'discourses of man', communicative action oriented toward reaching understanding is 'a medium for those formative processes that at once make possible both socialization and individuation' (Habermas 1992a, 48; 1987b). This core contention underpins Habermas's response to postmodern criticisms of reason's exclusionary consequences and 'essentialist' notions of the subject. It is precisely on the basis of this discursive mediation that Habermas defends the universalistic principles of modernity. He argues that it contains the means for overcoming the false antinomies of liberal and communitarian positions in political philosophy (Habermas 1998a; 1996a).

Habermas intervenes in the debates over postmodernism in order to preclude the potential assimilation of the Frankfurt School critical theory to postmodernist positions. He insists that Horkheimer and Adorno never renounced the supposition that emancipation was bound to reason, even in the context of their exposure of the sinister character of reason as domination. Partly under the influence of Nietzsche's thesis of a will to power and nihilistic denial of human progress as articulated by the Hegelian dialectic, Horkheimer and Adorno's critique of instrumental reason sought to expose the imperatives of self-preservation and domination lying behind the ideals of scientific objectivity and the truth claims of positivism as well as implicated in the ascetic ideals and the normative claims of religion and those of a secular universalist morality (Habermas 1987b, 122). In Habermas's opinion, this dimension of their critique was itself a product of the modernist development of a reflexive stage in the critique of ideology. But, given their difficulties in supplying normative foundations for critical theory, it could create the mistaken impression that they shared common ground with the Nietzsche inspired poststructuralist versions of postmodernism. As we have seen, he considers that Horkheimer and Adorno presented an 'oversimplified' image of modernity; they obscured the rationalization of, what Weber termed, the different modern cultural spheres of 'value'.

> The *Dialectic of Enlightenment* does not do justice to the rational content of cultural modernity that was captured in bourgeois ideals (and also instrumentalized along with them). I am thinking here of the specific theoretical dynamic that continually pushes the sciences, and even the self-reflection of the sciences, *beyond* merely engendering technically useful knowledge; I am referring, further, to the universalistic foundations of law and morality that have also been incorporated (in however distorted and incomplete fashion) into the institutions of constitutional government, into the forms of democratic will-formation, and into individualist patterns of identity formation; I have in mind, finally, the productivity and explosive power of basic aesthetic experiences that a subjectivity liberated from the imperatives of purposive activity and from conventions of quotidian perception gains from its own decentring – experiences that are presented in works of avant-garde art, that are articulated in the discourses of

art criticism, and that also achieve a *certain measure* of illuminating effect (or at least contrasts that are instructive) in the innovatively enriched range of values proper to self-realization. (Habermas 1987b, 113)

This differentiation of cultural value spheres is a major evidential premise of Habermas's theory of the communicative rationalization of modernity. In his view, one of the problems of Horkheimer and Adorno's conceptions of reason and domination was that they were closed to the formal and intersubjective procedures of *discourse*. In a sense, Habermas is reworking his earlier argument on the discursive validation of scientific inquiry in proposing that it is the extension of the rationality of action oriented to mutual understanding that enables the progressive developments distinctive to the inner logic of each sphere of value. Further, he claims that the everyday practice of communicative reasoning is the means by which modern subjects mediate modern value syndromes, and hence Weber's view of the irreconcilability of values in modernity is a misdiagnosis of the problems of rationalization (Weber 1958). The actual deficiency, Habermas argues, is that of an effective communicative mediation between the expertise of value spheres and the lay communication in subject's their everyday lifeworld. This can have pathological effects when expertise, such as associated with the state's therapeutic agencies, intervenes in the lifeworld and disempowers social actors of their communicative capacities.

In Habermas's opinion, the solution provided by the separation between communicative rationality and the functionalist reason of social system was not an option available to Horkheimer and Adorno, because they held onto the project of realizing a substantive reason that would be objectified in the total culture (Habermas 1984a, 366–99). Rejecting Weber's Neo-Kantian methodology, whilst affirming Weber's thesis of a loss of meaning only strengthened them in their vision of the improbability of reversing the dialectic of rationalization. This demonstrates, according to Habermas, that the synthetic incorporating of Weber's notion of rationality into the Hegelian-Marxian perspective of historical subjectivity does not permit an adequate distinguishing between different types of action and their rationalization. It produces confusions between action and systems (Habermas 1984a, 145). For this reason, he believes, revizing Weber's typology of action from the perspective of the rationality of communication is central to the task of correcting Horkheimer and Adorno's account of the dialectic of the enlightenment with a different theory of modernity.

The theme of modernity has been a persistent topic of Habermas's writings, but it acquires such importance that it shapes the internal structure of the entire argument of *The Theory of Communicative Action* (Habermas 1984a; 1987b). He argues that Marx, Weber, Horkheimer and Adorno, all have some alternative image of an 'encompassing societal rationality' against which they judge the factual process of the rationalization of society. They are each, however, unable to specify the normative basis of this judgement, owing to their attachment to the philosophy of consciousness and teleological models of action. And, similarly, the rationality encapsulated in the vision of 'either the 'association of free producers', or modelled after 'an ethically rational conduct of life' or 'in the idea of fraternal relations with a resurrected nature' would in each case, according to him, 'have to be confirmed at the same level as forces of production, sub-systems of purposive-rational action, totalitarian carriers of instrumental reason' (Habermas 1984a, 144–45).

However important it may be in the light of Habermas's revisions to his theory, this contention is not entirely convincing and probably illuminates more the restrictions upon his theory. Habermas's claim that there is an 'underlying identity' among these theories could be justified only by underestimating the emancipatory connotations the Marxist theorists incorporated into their images of transformation. It is Habermas who excludes the possibility of a fundamental change in the orientation of material production, not Marx, or Horkheimer and Adorno. He has, to be sure, consistently argued the latter but the rigidity resulting from his separation of the logics of rationalization tends to exclude any reconstitution of action orientations. Even though Habermas does acknowledge certain differences amongst Marx, Weber, Horkheimer and Adorno in the context of diagnosing the failures of their critical accounts of modernity, for example, he notes that unlike Weber's critical theses, Horkheimer's pessimistic judgement on rationalization was grounded in psychological categories, the means by which Habermas intends to over-come their failures does not differ (Habermas 1984a). In his opinion, *the theory of communicative action* overcomes the 'action-theoretical bottlenecks' which prohibited Marx, Weber, Horkheimer and Adorno, from each developing a sufficiently differentiated appreciation of the rationalization of modernity. He argues, especially against Weber's conception, that linking action to the validity basis of speech discloses how rationalization transpires not so much in conscious action orientations but in the background horizon of subjects' lifeworld (Habermas 1984a, 144–45).

Habermas is convinced that by stressing the difference between the logics of the rationalization of action and the developments in the complexity of social systems, he precludes any vision of an underlying similitude between these two domains. It is worth mentioning again, that many critics have seen this latter argument as a concession to Luhmann's critique of the action theoretical foundations of Weber's model of bureau-cracy (Luhmann 1982; Joas 1993; Misgeld 1985; McCarthy 1985). In this respect, it is not the limitations of the Hegelian-Marxist notion of an ethical totality and an 'expressivist' notion of historical subjectivity which motivates Habermas's attempt to define the limits of the rationalization of action for the functional reproduction of formally organized systems, but a need to rectify his previous assimilation of institutional orders to a single action type, a reduction no doubted influenced by his earlier interpretation of Weber (Habermas 1971; 1991; Joas 1983; Honneth 1991; McCarthy 1984b; 1985).

Conclusion

In this chapter, it has been argued that Habermas's theory's overall organizing problem is that of the mediation of the universal and the particular. Habermas's central intuition is that this mediation is immanent in intersubjective communication and that overcoming restrictions on communication enables the formation of a rational social identity. These founding suppositions inform Habermas's arguments for a change to the paradigm of intersubjective communication and they are central to his theory of modernity. It was shown how Habermas developed this perspective through a reformulation of the critical theory problematic of the critique of identity. Habermas's divergence from Adorno's dialectical approach to identity opens the way for his alternate conception of capitalist modernity, one that distinguishes processes of communicative rationalization from the predominant instrumental rationality of modern capitalism and administrative systems.

Habermas's interpretation of the intersubjective constitution of identity through the communication between self and other was profoundly influenced by the perspective of George Herbert Mead and its vision of individualization through socialization. Habermas substantially develops the democratic implications of Mead's theory and its notion of how the moral consciousness of subjects is formed through practical interaction. At the same time, it was shown how Habermas somewhat subordinates a number of themes in Mead's theory that overlap with the distinctive orientation of the philosophy of praxis, such as the themes of creativity and temporality. As will be explored in greater detail, the lesser significance of these themes in Habermas's theory results in some of its limitations. Further, Habermas's critical distancing from the philosophy of praxis justifies an interest in Giddens's theory of structuration, since it endeavours to reformulate aspects of the praxis perspective and directly engages with themes like those of temporality, power and conflict.

Habermas argues that the discourse of modernity has been dominated by the philosophy of the subject and that the project of modernity requires a change to the intersubjective paradigm of communication in order to overcome the aporias of 'subject-centred reason' (Habermas 1987b). While the Frankfurt School's critical theory exposed the continuities between subject-centred reason and heteronomous social relations, it ultimately reached a theoretical and practical impasse owing to its lacking a compelling alternative. Habermas argues that the philosophy of praxis is similarly deficient. Despite Habermas's valid intention of constructively responding to the problems that he identifies in the philosophy of praxis, the form and content of his response is open to serious question, especially given it involves not just a turn to intersubjective communication but also a dependence on system theory in its theory of modernity.

The later explications of Habermas's theoretical approach to history and the institutionalization of modernity in Part II of this work enable a fuller assessment of the merits of these assertions and their implications. Similarly, Habermas's argument that the philosophy of praxis does not adequately appreciate the limits to the potential democratization of the social systems of the capitalist market economy and the bureaucratic-administrative state will be assessed in that context. The fact that Giddens's theory of structuration is founded on some quite different suppositions, as well as sharing a commitment to the modernist vision, does imply that there may be alternative ways of approaching modern social systems and understanding the trajectory of modernization. In this regard, the next chapter will be show how Giddens's attempt to reformulate elements of the praxis philosophy approach contrasts with Habermas's displacement of the praxis perspective and its conception of the social as derived from the intersection of the subject and history.

Chapter Two

GIDDENS'S THEORY OF STRUCTURATION – AN ONTOLOGY OF THE SOCIAL

The Contrasting Suppositions of Giddens's Theory of Structuration

> Human history is created by intentional activities but is not an intended project; it persistently eludes efforts to bring it under conscious direction. However, such attempts are continually made by human beings, who operate under the threat and the promise of the circumstance that they are the only creatures who make their 'history' in cognisance of that fact. (Giddens 1984, 270)

Giddens's programme of a theory of structuration aims to develop an original perspective that constructively reformulates some of the central assumptions of social theory. This project results in a series of innovative propositions and it has elucidated the basic social theory problem of the relationship between structure and action. Giddens's starting point is, then, the problem of the sociological dichotomies that Habermas tackles in the guise of distinguishing between lifeworld and system. The inherent problems of Habermas's attempt to simultaneously distinguish and connect these two categories give some indication of the difficulty of the problem Giddens confronted and underlines why his theory of structuration warrants serious consideration. Held and Thompson (1989) distinguish between the strand of Giddens's writings concerned with the provision of a substantive account of modern societies from those whose focus is the resolution of more general problems of social theory. Yet, the interlacing of these strands is probably the location of some of Giddens's core insights. One of the major intentions of the theory of structuration is to pare back sociological concepts to their elementary meaning. At the same time, this intention coincides with Giddens's aspiration of introducing, as Tucker observes, 'a conceptual vocabulary which can illuminate contemporary social changes in late modernity' (Tucker 1998, 3).

The theory of structuration has been pursued through the synthesis of a multitude of perspectives, which has certain parallels with Habermas's theory. In Habermas's case, the epistemic requirements of theoretical synthesis have been the subject of more systematic reflection and justification (Habermas 1984a). Like Habermas's theory, Giddens's work has been criticized as eclectic, however, he argues that such a critical perception ignores the systematic intent of his distillation of significant insights from different approaches and the structuration theory reformulation of them (see Hirst 1982; Therborn 1971).

Structuration theory is orientated towards disclosing the elemental processes involved in the constitution and reproduction of social practices and institutions. Giddens (1990b) defines its programme as that of the provision of an 'overall ontology of social life', through the clarification of the recursive social practices that simultaneously constitute society and individuals as subjects.

The ontological focus of Giddens's theory places it in the tradition of dialectics concerned with the finitude and contingency of the human condition. Habermas's theory of communicative action, by contrasts, represents a reconstruction of the 'Socratic' sense of dialectics as dialogue (see Bernstein 1985). As we have seen, Habermas derives the normative and epistemological grounding of critical theory from the principles and procedures of intersubjective communication. Whether from the perspective of an ideal speech situation or a decolonized lifeworld, Habermas argues that the rationality of communicative action enables the discursive validation of social norms and the development of the subjects' competences for autonomous action. The rationality of communicative action provides, in effect, the basis for the political and cultural project of a social transformation (Habermas 1984a; 1987a). In a general sense, Giddens accepts these normative principles as ideals, but considers that Habermas's elaboration of them is generally too distant from the actual problems confronting any transformation of society. This position derives from a principal difference between these two theorists. The ontological perspective of Giddens's theory determines his claim that 'there is no more elemental concept than that of power', but power is understood here as the generative achievements of practice (Giddens 1984, 283).

In the theory of structuration, there is an integral connection between the account of human agency and this notion of power. Agency is defined as the transformative capacity of the subject; the practical basis of agency is the possibility of choosing between alternatives and pursuing different courses of action. From this insight into Giddens's suppositions, thematic continuities can be discerned which link his early work on suicide and power to his later analyses of risk and trust (Giddens 1977; 1990a; 1991a). While Giddens recognizes that risk and trust necessarily involve ethics and morality, these normative considerations do not have the same organizing significance for his theory as that of power. This contrast with Habermas can likewise be seen in how similar insights into the experience of finitude and contingency lead Habermas to draw conclusions about the normative character of human forms of living and the intersubective constitution of identity.

> Moral intuitions are intuitions that instruct us on how best to behave in situations where it is in our power to counteract the extreme vulnerability of others by being thoughtful and considerate. In anthropological terms, morality is a safety device compensating for a vulnerability built into the socio-cultural form of life. The basic facts are the following: creatures that are individuated only through socialization are vulnerable and morally in need of consideration. (Habermas 1990a, 199)

A major component of Giddens's theoretical programme is his 'contemporary critique of historical materialism' (Giddens 1981a; 1985a; 1994a). In contrast to Habermas's

(1979a) 'reconstruction of historical materialism', Giddens's critique is a 'deconstruction'. While it does not conform to all of Derrida's meanings of deconstruction, Giddens's critique aims to show how Marx's intentions were undermined in the elaboration of 'historical materialism' and how marginalized features of Marx's writings should be seen as important to the whole which appears to exclude them (Derrida 1982; Giddens 1981a). In these critiques, Giddens interprets the problem of presence and absence, a theme that is critical to Derrida's philosophy and preceding him Heidegger's thought, from the standpoint of the question of the historical constitution of the social. The changes in the relationship between presence and absence, he argues, should be understood in terms of power. This interpretation of the historical significance of power constitutes a major axis of his critique of Marx's theory and the evolutionary conception of the 'orthodox' Marxist theory of 'historical materialism'. Still, the negative connotations of this critical deconstruction does not convey the positive impact that Marx's theory had on Giddens's original formulation of the theory of structuration. He considers that Marx's writings contain the most detailed and apposite conception of the problem that his theory seeks to address. In fact, Marx's dialectical interpretation of the relationship between structure and action serves as something of a model. Giddens seeks to reconstruct the notion of praxis, but delineates it from the substantive content of the Marxist theory of history:

> Only if historical materialism is regarded as embodying the more abstract elements of a theory of human *Praxis*, snippets of which can be gleaned from the diversity of Marx's writings, does it remain an indispensable contribution to social theory today. (Giddens 1981a, 2)

The theory of structuration sustains and transforms Marx's conception of praxis, but, in accordance with theorists influenced by structuralism, Giddens speaks of practices rather than the praxis of a constituting transcendental subject (see Descombes 1980). Giddens's reconstruction of the category of praxis is based on an initial separating of the notion of production from its identification with social labour. The notion of production is thereby broadened to encompass other practices. Giddens considers that all practices are to varying degrees constitutive of the social, because structure only exists in its instantiation and its reproduction is brought about by the very practices that it enables or constrains. In effect, praxis is now understood in connection to Giddens's generative notion of power and material production is conceptualized as one of the modalities of power. This notion of power does not mean that subjects are viewed as capable of reconstituting society at will, rather the extension of power translates into the social systems which traverse time and space.

> Human societies, or social systems would plainly not exist without human agency. But it is not the case that actors create social systems: they reproduce or transform them, remaking what is already made in the continuity of *praxis*. (Giddens 1984, 171)

Despite the importance of the theoretical suppositions linking power and ontology, I will argue that there are some serious inconsistencies between Giddens's general theoretical conceptions and his historical analyses of how social systems transcend individuals and institutionalize social relations of domination. Indeed, these discrepancies are apparent in his early work's descriptions of the constitution of modern institutions and they are arguably compounded in some of his later public policy prescriptions, which tend to underplay power and domination (Giddens 1998a; 2000). Nevertheless, Giddens proposes that the transformative potential of agency persists no matter how much agency is circumscribed. This is because social relations always involve some 'dialectic of control' and the recurrence of practices is a condition of the reproduction of social systems. The inspiration of this process approach to social systems would appear to be primarily Marx's analysis of structure of capitalist production and the transformation of labour-power into surplus-value, although, as we have seen, the theory of structuration generalizes the implications of such a perspective beyond material production (Marx 1976). Further, Marx's account of the dynamic character of the capitalist mode of production provides the prototype for accounting for the unceasing transformations of modernity. Yet Giddens's 'critique' claims that Marx actually underestimated the discontinuity of capitalist society. Indeed, Giddens's later works contend that the economic theory of socialism is obsolete (Giddens 1990a; 1981a; 1994a; 1998a).

Although it will be explored in more detail later, it is worth noting a few features of the contrast between Giddens's deconstruction and Habermas's reconstruction of historical materialism from the standpoint of the paradigm of communication. On the question of historical change, Giddens rejects evolutionary arguments altogether, whereas Habermas reconstructs a theory of evolution by distinguishing between the logic of development and the dynamics of historical change. Giddens's emphasis upon power contrasts with Habermas's primarily cultural supplementation of historical materialism, as well as the latter's attempt to renew the normative foundations of critical theory through a theory of communicative action (Arnason 1984). If Habermas is the second attempt to draw on Weber in the tradition of critical theory then Giddens's reworking of Weber's interest in domination is a potentially illuminating alternative that might be seen as challenging Habermas's theory of modernity's organizing problem of cultural rationalization. The implications of cultural rationalization might appear quite different from the angle of domination. In particular, such a perspective on rationality may be critical of the universalistic claims about modernity that Habermas endeavours to uphold (see Benhabib 1986; Arnason 1991b). These differences concerning the substantive features of social development are probably relevant to the contrast between the perspective on history that Giddens develops and Habermas's view of a developmental logic of historical learning processes and their institutionalization. In an extended note to a major statement of his theory, Giddens distinguishes his approach to Weber from that of Habermas:

> Habermas's Weber (surprisingly perhaps) tends to be a Parsonian style Weber concerned above all with the rationalization of values and with 'social differentiation', portrayed as generalized processes of development. Social life is not depicted here through the lenses I would prefer to borrow from Weber, as concerned with the multifarious practices and struggles of concretely located actors; with conflict and the clash of sectional interests; and with the territoriality and surveillance of political formations or states. (Giddens 1984, xxxvi)

Due to the comprehensiveness of their writings, the conflicting claims of Habermas and Giddens extend over a range of topics and issues. It would be misleading then to reduce these contrasts to an extrapolation of the differences in their respective approaches to Marx and Weber. In fact, the points of agreement between Giddens and Habermas are quite extensive and differences arise from the alternative elaboration of similar intentions. In particular, both theorists are decisively influenced by modern hermeneutics and they are critics of functionalist reason. However, my analysis suggests that Habermas's critique of functionalist reason is undermined by the implicit functionalism of his overall conception of the social. This functionalist orientation is discernible in his adapting the categories of differentiation and complexity in theorizing modernity and, more generally, in the congruence Habermas seeks to establish between different dimensions of historical development, like the normative principles of justice and modes of production, which is in other respects insightful and relevant to the critique of ideology. In my opinion, Giddens's critique of functionalism is more consistent and thoroughgoing.

Of particular interest is the way in which Giddens utilizes Marx's conception of the real abstraction of the capitalist system of production to conceptualize modern social systems. This has parallels with Habermas's critique of the reifying tendencies of late-capitalism, but equally significant differences. Giddens gives prominence to aspects of Marx's original proposition that Habermas subordinates, like the process approach of dialectical reasoning and the relationship between the social and natural. The distinction between the social and the natural is understood by Giddens as a social process that is constitutive of the dynamic quality of modern systems. He seeks to elucidate the historicity of social structure by relating Heidegger's phenomenological reflections on time to Marx's theory of value (Heidegger 1962). This is by no means the first attempt at such a synthesis in the history of the philosophy of praxis (see Marcuse 1987; Kosik 1976; Goldmann 1977).

In my opinion, Giddens's pursuit of this line of analysis is not an unequivocal success, but the underlying intention is that of developing his critique of functionalist accounts of social systems. This makes it an important contrast to Habermas's theory. Habermas's *The Theory of Communicative Action* implies that there is little scope for the critique of social systems from a perspective internal to their operations. At the same time, he argues that Luhmann's 'hierarchy of action systems' neglects the limits that the cultural pattern of the lifeworld imposes on the differentiation of systems (Habermas 1987a, 155). By contrast, Giddens is much more interested in the internal constitution of systems. For the reasons indicated, Giddens's critique of functionalism could be extended to the logic of Habermas's account of the course of rationalization. Although there is some common ground in respect to the deleterious consequences they perceive, Giddens conceives this development somewhat differently. Despite the revisions in his position on modernity, I suggest that Giddens's initial attempt to rethink the constitution of the *social* forms the background to the later categories concerned with explicating contemporary changes.

One of the reasons why Habermas is interested in Weber's theory of the rationalization is because it constitutes an alternative to the discredited perspective of the philosophy of history (Habermas 1984a). Habermas's reinterpretation of Weber contributes to his reconstruction of the formal structures of the competences of modern subjects, such as the competences that enable individuals' action, cognition and moral judgements. The development of the characteristics attributed to these competences, like universalistic and principled notions of justice, is integral to Habermas's defending and upholding of the Enlightenment ideal of progress. Giddens purports to incorporate into his standpoint the implications of the contemporary period's radical break with the 'progressivism' that underpinned the view that socialism is the next stage of social development and guided movements for a radical transformation of capitalist society (Giddens 1994a; 1998a). The break with 'progressivism' does not alter the fact that Giddens himself argues from the perspective of social progress, as evident from his editing a collection titled *The Progressive Manifesto*, and he readily deploys the notion of progress or modernization to critique existing positions that he feels need to be superseded (Giddens 2003).

Nevertheless, Giddens's supposed rupture with 'progressivism' has manifold implications for the problems of conceiving the intersection between the subject and history. These implications need to be located in the context of a shift from his earlier historical analyses' emphasis on power to his later assaying the implications of risk in late-modernity. The different emphases should not be seen as entirely juxtaposed, since a similar conception of change underlies both of them. Vico's notion that history is knowable because it is the product of human activity has often been considered the instigator of the modern philosophy of history and containing the key supposition of the philosophy of praxis (see Jay 1984; Habermas 1974a). Giddens does not contest this hermeneutic background, but contends that the paradoxical consequences of the reflexive application of knowledge in the present has unravelled the equation Enlightenment thought made between greater understanding and control over the direction of history. He asserts that the criterion of agency is actually associated with modern subjects' experience of disorientation and that the principle of agency, that is, that things could be otherwise, coincides with modern scientific inquiry's notion of systematic doubt. In practical terms, this means that scientific knowledge claims are implicated in renewing the dynamism of modernity and the reflexive reorganizing of practices, yet Giddens considers that this rationalization has reached a point of problematizing the notion of rationality (Giddens 1990a; 1994a).

On the one hand, this development promotes counterfactual thinking and anticipatory practices that seek, in his terms, to 'colonize' the future. On the other hand, the tendency of the dynamic of modernity to extend the consequences of action far beyond the immediate contexts of interaction and the related increasing awareness of the 'unpredictable' outcomes of human intervention promote a sense of dislocation on the part of subjects and the experience of a 'runaway world' (Giddens 1990a; 1991a; 1994a). For Giddens, the appreciation of human constitution undermines the 'providential' view of history, but this was not fully recognized until changes in the contemporary period, like the 'the end of nature', the rise of 'post-traditional lifestyle' and the ecological critique of 'productivism' (Giddens 1994a; 1991a). In a sense, Giddens was articulating similar claims concerning the intersection of the subject and history in his earlier critiques of evolutionary theory and functionalism.

> I accept that 'history has no subject' in a Hegelian sense of the progressive overcoming of
> self-alienation of humanity, or in any sense that might be discerned in evolutionary theories,

but I do not at all accept a 'subjectless history' – if that term means that the events that govern human social affairs are determined by forces of which those involved are wholly unaware. It is precisely to counter such a view of history or the social sciences that I elaborated some of the main tenets of the theory of structuration [...] Foucault defines his 'genealogical method' as 'a form of history which accounts for the constitution of knowledges, discourses, domains of objects, etc., without reference to a subject, whether it be transcendental in relation to the field of events or whether it chases its empty identity throughout history'. This view exemplifies the confusion which structuralism helped to introduce into French thought, between history without a transcendental subject and history without knowledgeable human subjects (on the levels of practical and discursive consciousness). The disavowal of the first must be kept quite distinct from an acknowledgment of the cardinal significance of the second. History is not retrievable as a human project; but neither is it comprehensible except as the outcome of human projects. (Giddens 1981a, 171)

Giddens believes that Marx's (1970, 21) contention that humanity only solves such problems as it sets for itself is an updated version of the providential understanding of history. He specifically rejects the teleological reasoning of historical materialism and asserts that critical theory is today 'without guarantees'. 'A critical theory without guarantees must confront the situation that, just as history has no inherent teleology, neither are there privileged agents of the realization of the processes of social reform' (Giddens 1984, 338).

In his critiques of historical materialism and analyses of late-modernity, Giddens explores the contours of a more open-ended conception of history. His approach is very much organized around the problem of the historicity ensuing from the social constitution of time and the orientation to the future that this gives to social practices in modernity. The synthetic perspective of the philosophy of praxis is continued in respect of his attempt to overcome the sociological dichotomy of structure and action, but there is another sense of mediation that his writings explore. This is the mediation ensuing from the intersection of social processes that originate from different contexts and involve differing layers of temporality. These types of social processes range from the historical origins of the city to contemporary globalization. In such cases, the intersecting processes can give rise to transformations (Giddens 1981a; 1985a; 1994a). In Giddens's opinion, this consideration implies a discontinuous notion of historical change and he introduces a novel array of theoretical categories to theorize its implications. In addition, he believes that this idea of transformation highlights the contingency intrinsic to social reproduction and it indicates why the recurrence of practices has to be explained, rather than presumed on the basis of the supposed functional needs of social systems and the requirements of social adaptation (Giddens 1979; 1981a; 1984).

Giddens originally used the term structuration in a less technical sense to refer to the relationship between the mediate and 'proximate' structuration of class (Giddens 1973). His point was to enable the investigation into '*the modes in which* "economic" relationships become translated into "non-economic" social structures' and to demonstrate how the indirect effects of class become conditions that influence the direct reproduction of class relations (Giddens 1973, 105). He would recognize that revealing the linkages between the moments of any process of structuration requires a more complex explication of the

temporal and spatial arrangement of social relations than found in his original explication of class structure. In the first full-length study on structuration theory, Ira Cohen
(1989, 4) comments that Giddens is not 'obsessed by a single *idée fixe*'. Now, while subsequent developments in Giddens's programme reinforce the validity of this observation,
there are still key intuitions that determine the construction of his theory and its 'conceptual strategy'. The most important intuition is that practices contain structure and
that systems require practice for their reproduction. It means that action is never entirely
independent of structure. However, tied to this intuition is the supposition that structuration does not simply happen in time and space, but that time and space are intrinsic to
the very shape of social relations and that this is a process that is constitutive of social
systems.

This conception associates the organization of social systems with a great deal of
power, even if the ultimate outcome of structuration is a reproduction of an existing
pattern. It is in this sense that Giddens suggests that 'the fundamental question of social
theory, as I see it – the "problem of order" conceived of in a way quite alien to Parsons's
formulation when he coined the phrase – is to explicate how the limitations of individual "presence" are transcended by the "stretching" of social relations across time
and space' (Giddens 1984, 35). This reinterpretation of the problem of social order
stresses the persistence of society against the transience of the individual, but the disparity between these histories should not, in Giddens's opinion, lead to an underestimation
of the importance of individuals' knowledge for social reproduction and an exaggeration
of the constraining dimension of society. From this perspective on time-space distanciation, Giddens would seem to suggest that the idea of history changes its social meaning,
and therefore the meaning of the social, in the course of history.

For Giddens, there is a division between traditional cultures and modern society.
The practices typical of the former have some affinity with the recursive character of
everyday modern action, but social conditions have changed so much that in a post-
traditional society recursive practices can take the pathological form of compulsions,
rather than simply routines and practices of social reproduction (Giddens 1984, 202;
1994b). Moreover, Giddens adopts Levi-Strauss's account of tribal societies' instantiation of 'reversible time' and anchoring of practices in oral traditions, whereas he claims
that the mediating practices typical of modern institutions instantiate the 'historicity'
typical of organizations and associations. These reflexively monitor their operations in
order to initiate change and this reflexivity entails practices that attempt to anticipate
the future.

The socialist programme of overcoming the inequality and alienation of capitalist
society originally drew on this historicity and found its justification in the claim that the
transformation that would enable subjects to determine the direction of change would
lead to socialism (Giddens 1981a, 224). Giddens claims, however, that the historicity of
the contemporary phase of modernization generates forms of socialization that have
largely undermined socialism as a programme of economic organization. In fact, he
argues that contemporary socialization brought to the surface the tensions between the
egalitarian objectives of socialism and the claim of socialism to institute a higher level of
rationality in economic coordination (Giddens 1994a, 62).

In this introductory overview, I have outlined a set of suppositions that contrast with those of Habermas and highlighted those themes in Giddens's analyses of modernity that are salient to this comparison, as well as to several pertinent changes or additions in his interpretation of modernity. A fuller appreciation of Giddens's perspective presupposes an explication of its assumptions about practice and the major categories of the theory of structuration. I have pointed to the interlacing of structuration theory categories and the interpretation of modernity, but equally alluded to assumptions that eventual produce discordances between them.

The Dialectics of Practice

> Every process of action is a production of something new, a fresh act; but at the same time all action exists in continuity with the past, which supplies the means of its initiation [...] The most disruptive modes of social change, like the most rigidly stable forms, involve structuration. (Giddens 1979, 106)

Giddens's turn to the theory of praxis was part of a renewal of interest in Marx's writings, particularly those of the young Marx. This coincided with the social upheaval during the 1960s that contributed to the dissolution of the orthodox consensus in sociology. While the perceptions of Marx's position in the history of sociological theory altered, Giddens's assessment was indicative of how interpretations of Weber and Durkheim changed. Their dialogue and debate with the Marxism of their time took on greater importance. In addition, the divergences between Marx and Marxism's orthodoxy were accentuated. In this context, Marx's category of praxis provided the meaningful grounds for the critique of orthodox Marxism. Bernstein comments that the 'most interesting and important' aspect of the revival of interest in Marx was its 'explosive political significance. In countries such as Poland, Czechoslovakia, and Yugoslavia, the rediscovery of "authentic" Marxism has been the primary intellectual weapon for the criticism of the totalitarian and bureaucratic tendencies of existing Communist regimes. Implicitly – and sometimes explicitly – the basic argument emerging is that Communist societies do not represent the historical realization of Marxism but its betrayal' (Bernstein 1971, 78).

Giddens's (1976; 1979) critique of Parsons and functionalism drew on some of the impulses that had always inspired the standpoint of praxis in the Marxian tradition. This is apparent in his denial of the closure that he perceived in the concept of function and his understanding of how historical determinism undermines agency. These impulses equally influence Giddens's critique of the developmental perspective of historical materialism, but I will concentrate here on Giddens's continuities with Marx's critique of the apparent solidifying of conditions into a seeming 'second nature' that are historically produced (Marx 1976). Giddens aims to open up the possibility of conceiving society as produced, as well as historically conditioning. But, as Marx's analysis of capitalist accumulation disclosed, the historically conditioning dimension of society is itself produced. A thesis that broadens the scope and possibilities for social change, it implies that social structures and relations are neither inevitable nor natural. In the case of Giddens, this outlook is not so much founded in the activity of labour and the struggles of social movements, but in a general appreciation of the constitutive and transformative capacities of everyday practices.

Despite this divergence from Marx's perspective, these arguments provide criteria for distinguishing between theories of praxis and the more limited concerns of sociological theories of action. The intention of the perspective of praxis is one originally orientating a theory, that is, praxis is not one aspect of a theory that only becomes relevant according to the theme under consideration. These precepts are recalled in order to indicate the approach of a praxis orientation, because these considerations will be applied to Giddens's theory, rather than to the critiques and sources that inspired it. For instance, Giddens's critical evaluation of those approaches that drew selectively upon Marx, as well as Weber, to correct Parsons's 'consensual' version of functionalism, like the conflict theories of Dahrendorf, Lockwood and Rex, was informed by the generative considerations of a praxis philosophy perspective (Giddens 1973, 14; 1976, 98–99). Of the facets of Marx's thought neglected in these syntheses, he argues that the philosophical anthropology of praxis was most significant; it implied a different and incommensurate understanding of social change. One based on Marx's 'ontological emphasis' 'upon man as producer, as creator, an emphasis which stands in stark and dramatic contrast to Parsons's fascination with the "problem of order"' (Giddens 1976, 99).

The sketch so far in this section of the orientation of the Marxian perspective of praxis philosophy is obviously insufficient as a characterization of this tradition. It served the more modest purpose of establishing the influence that this tradition had on the framing of Giddens's theory of structuration. Giddens's project can be distinguished among the competing paradigms of contemporary social theory by its aspiring to translate the praxis perspective into a comprehensive social theory relevant to contemporary circumstances (Joas 1993, 172–73). In pursuing this programme, he naturally amends this perspective in accordance with the selectivity of his appreciation. The result is a tension between Giddens's recognition that the praxis perspective is an overall orientation and the limited appropriation of themes drawn from it (see Kilminster 1991). For this reason, the claim that Giddens's general outlook reflects a liberal understanding of freedom does not contradict the assertion that structuration theory reformulates the praxis conception to the extent that it might otherwise (see Loyal 2003: Smith 1998). The selectivity of Giddens's reformulation can be seen in his lesser concern with elaborating upon the epistemological implications of a praxis perspective. This contrasts with Habermas's (1978a; 1978b) programme of knowledge constitutive interests, which sought to develop the epistemological proposals incipient in Marx's (1977) *Theses on Feuerbach*. Giddens's overriding interest lies in the 'ontological' connotations of praxis philosophy, which he describes in the following terms:

> I take *Praxis* to be an ontological term, expressing a fundamental trait of human social existence. To speak of human social activity as *Praxis* is to reject every conception of human beings as 'determined objects' and as unambiguously 'free subjects'. (Giddens 1981a, 53–54)

Of course, rejecting these false alternatives requires surmounting many of the traditional antinomies that lie behind them. Praxis philosophy does not seek to overcome these antinomies in the abstract form of scientific truth; rather, it distinctively considers that these problems are grounded in the historical development of society. In this way, the stress placed upon the constitutive accomplishments of subjects must be mediated by the recognition that the constituted social world precedes and exceeds the intentions of agents. Now, this means that history is intrinsic to the ontological conception of praxis, as the mediation between inherited circumstances and anticipated – as well as unanticipated – developments is a creation of subjects' praxis. Indeed, Feenberg claims the 'idea that history, properly understood, has ontological significance is the main philosophical claim of the philosophy of praxis' (Feenberg 1981, 10). Giddens largely accepts these philosophical presuppositions in attempting to surmount the antonymic interpretations of structure and action in sociological theory. However, he does not accept the thesis that material production is the decisive factor determining historical development and social change. Structuration theory proposes the primacy of production asserted by historical materialism be considered a historically contingent development and not the ontological foundation of a theory of history (Giddens 1981a; 1985a).

Despite the apparent opposition of structural and action perspectives, Giddens believes that at a deeper level they share a common conception of structure as external to practice. As a consequence, these perspectives represent, to varying degrees, the mistaken alternatives of depicting subjects as either entirely free from structure, or fully determined by structure. Without sacrificing the element of truth contained in both these opposed sociological perspectives, a transformation of the concept of structure was thus required to solve this antinomy. Giddens argues that structure should also be conceived of as internal to practice (Giddens 1979; 1984; Stones 2005). That is, structure constitutes both a facilitating and limiting condition of action. Yet, in the theory of structuration, even these conditions are understood to be constructed through practice and are not given. Structuration theory's initial innovation is its conceiving structure to possess only a 'virtual existence', Giddens's argument is that it is through recurrent social practices that structure is instantiated; and this proposition accords precedence to neither the individual or society. Instead, *practice* is the basic element from which an account of society and the individual are to be developed. For this reason, he replaces the dualism of structure and action with a concept of the *duality of structure*. Structure is both a *medium* that is reproduced in being drawn upon in social action and the *outcome* of these practices (Giddens 1979, 1984).

In twentieth-century social theory, Bourdieu (1977; 1990) and Sartre (1976; 1963) developed formulations intended to similarly solve the dichotomy of structure and action from praxis perspectives. Giddens acknowledges the influence of these theorists upon his own perspective, but suggests that a condensed statement by Marx exactly expresses the standpoint that he seeks to elaborate:

> Everything that has a fixed form [...] appears as merely a moment, a vanishing moment, in this movement [...] The conditions and objectifications of the process are themselves equally moments of it, and its only subjects are the individuals, but individuals in mutual relationships, which they equally reproduce and produce anew. (Marx as quoted in Giddens 1979, 53)

The general standpoint that structuration theory shares with Marx is precisely this perception that social structures should be conceived and analyzed in terms of *process*. There is a certain agreement that this is necessary for a convincing social explanation, as distinct from more limited forms of analysis, and despite other important epistemological differences. Giddens's criticisms of functionalism partly turn on his perception that the concept of function often served to preclude the depiction of processes of reproduction and social change. By contrast, Marx in the preceding quotation emphasizes social processes are continuous, ongoing and, for Giddens, more importantly still, contingent. In order to clarify this movement, he proposes that it is necessary to apprehend the temporality intrinsic to all social practices. In my opinion, Giddens's development of the implications of this proposal is potentially his most important contribution to the philosophy of praxis perspective.

It could be argued, however, that the essential principle of the praxis perspective is its specific interpretation of the genesis and reproduction of processes of material and social reproduction. That is, in Marx's categories, it explains *social objectivations* in terms of the constitutive activity and the conditions incorporated into this process of *objectification* (see Bernstein 1971; Avineri 1968). This principle determines labour's importance in Marx's dialectic and Marx's opposition to approaches that separate the consequences from the genesis of social structure (Marx 1973, 89–111; Lukács 1971). It is the latter interconnection that Giddens aims to develop independently of its background in Hegel's logic, because the praxis perspective considers consequences and genesis different moments of structuration, rather than distinct processes.

Habermas, as we saw, criticized this philosophical background and its notion of totality, yet, the different moments of this whole process can be stressed in relation to one another. For instance, Marx's *Economic and Philosophical Manuscripts of 1844* assert that the systematic conflicts associated with capitalist production and private property originate in and are reproduced through the alienating relation of the labourer to his or her own activity of labour (Marx 1977; Markus 1982, 141–44). Whereas Marx's later economic writings postulate that labour is a unique commodity, capable of producing greater value than the cost of its reproduction, similarly traces the dynamic development of the capitalist economic system to the process of production, or, in general terms, to the constituting human activity (Marx 1976). In other respects, the later economic writings concern the production process as a whole and the capitalist system; labour is accordingly situated within these broader frameworks (see Postone 1993; Sayer 1987). Marx's interest in the *social totality* is indicated by the sentence preceding the above quotation from the *Gundrisse* that Giddens drew upon to illustrate the standpoint that structuration theory seeks to develop.

> When we consider bourgeois society in the long view and as a whole, then the final result of the process of social production always appears as society itself, that is, the human being itself in its social relations. (Marx 1973, 712)

Labour as praxis retains its centrality in both these illustrations from different stages in Marx's writings. Giddens's (1981a, 53–56) terminology of the 'mediating' and 'transforming' features of practices implies a change in content. It is not an innocent shift in meaning; for it is precisely the 'elision of labour and Praxis' that he does not accept (Giddens 1981a, 53). In the theory of structuration, Giddens proposes that praxis 'be treated as the universal basis of social life' (Giddens 1982b, 157). The generic category of praxis should account for social labour without being reducible to it. In order to clarify this conception, he distinguishes between two meanings of labour in Marx, which obviously cannot be absolutely separated. One is a more encompassing, primarily philosophical notion of labour. Marx suggests, particularly in his early writings, that, as a form of practice, the activity of labour constituted the solution to the questions his philosophical predecessors and contemporaries posed but were unable to resolve (Marx 1977a). Through this interpretation of labour, Marx sought to overcome: on the one hand, the contemplative standpoint of philosophies of consciousness and reflection. And, on the other hand, the traditional materialist philosophies, which considered nature to be distinct from the activity and intervention of humanity. For Marx, nature was transformed through human labour and became knowable through this activity.

In Giddens's opinion, Marx's notion of labour is—at one and the same time—critical of Hegelian philosophy and considerably influenced by Hegel's theory of the self-creation of humanity. He describes this version of labour as referring to the 'interplay of human activity and material nature: an interplay at the root of the "historical" character of human culture when contrasted to the "fixed" or instinctive life of the animals. Labour here shades into Praxis, as the generic production and reproduction of human social life' (Giddens 1979, 151).

These remarks are sufficient to recall a few of the familiar, but distinctive, philosophical tenets Marx incorporated into the notion of labour. From the discussion of the premises of structuration theory, it is evident that Marx's disclosure of the active and practical constitution of social life has enduring ontological and epistemological significance. Giddens believes that it represents a radical transformation of perspective; one which would be paralleled in other fields, like the philosophy of language (Giddens 1979; 1987). However, Giddens argues that incorporating into the concept of praxis insights drawn from such alternative traditions of philosophy and social theory can avoid its elision with labour. There is some justification to this generic approach, because, as Arnason remarks: 'the most fundamental weakness' of the Marxist tradition has been 'the tendency to understand praxis as labour writ large' (Arnason 1991a, 78). Habermas, as we saw, argues that Marx's philosophical anthropology of the subject was the major source of this enlarging of labour into an activity of a transcendental subject (Habermas 1978a; 1987b).

Leaving aside the difficulties of Habermas's interpretation, he correctly notes that in Marx's early writings the activity of labour was conceived as simultaneously a process of the objectification of the self and of self-formation. In this notion of labour, Marx fused together motifs from the romantic view of the expressive realization of the subject in its creations and the Aristotelian understanding of praxis as those forms of activity which contained their ends within themselves (Aristotle 1976). Marx thereby effectively subsumed in this notion of labour the original Aristotelian meaning of *praxis* under that of *poiesis* (Markus 1986b). This notion of labour implied the normative model of an autonomous conscious self-realization in work and the critical alternative of alienation eventuating from a deformation of the relationship of the subject to their work activity.

Giddens emphasizes how Marx's concept of alienated labour was not just psychological or subjective, but integral to his structural analysis of the capitalist system (Giddens 1971). Even when the inclusive meaning of labour has been restricted, its presuppositions continued to serve as a model drawn upon in the construction of theories of praxis. In order to delineate a generic conception of praxis from this notion of labour, Giddens breaks with Marx's anthropological foundations whilst retaining the participatory-practical intentions that informed Marx's conception of labour. Giddens disavows the central principle of this framework: the dialectical relation of subject and object as the constitutive model of all human practice. In the case of the theory of structuration, a decentring is accomplished through treating the relation of subject and object as one dimension of a series comprising social practices. In my opinion, this break then modifies the anthropology of labour rather than dissolves it entirely.

Giddens considers that the second meaning of labour in Marx is rather more 'limited'. Social labour is simply part of the process of production. This interpretation circumscribes labour to a concrete activity pertaining to production and its delimited form is specific to the social system of an economy. Labour, in this sense, can without difficulty be reformulated in the terms of structuration theory; with praxis serving as the more inclusive concept. Giddens regards 'social labour: as the socially organized productive activities whereby human beings interact creatively with material nature. Labour then remains an intrinsically social activity, among other types of activity or forms of institution' (Giddens 1982b, 157).

Despite these arguments, the conceptual orientation of structuration theory parallels in other respects the differentiated configuration of elements comprised in the Marxian paradigm of production (see Markus 1986a). Even though they are meant to underpin a critical deconstruction of historical materialism, many of the initial theoretical innovations of the theory of structuration appear to merely reformulate aspects of Marx's production paradigm. Indeed, Giddens criticizes Habermas's failure to sufficiently differentiate between the concept of labour and the range of categories Marx developed in his analysis of production (Giddens 1982b). And, as well as salient to his criticisms of Habermas's distinction between labour and interaction, Giddens's generic conception of praxis reflects a recognition of how production in Marx's theory was concerned with a complex process of structuration.

Although there is no direct equivalent to the production paradigm's distinction between material content and social form in structuration theory, this is an important theme connecting the arguments Giddens develops in his critiques of historical materialism to the conceptual reformulations of his perspective (Markus 1986; Grumley 1991; 1992). Marx's analyses influenced Giddens's defining structure as possessing only a virtual existence and his distinguishing social categories from the substantive institutional forms they assume in a definite society. Giddens describes how in *Capital*: 'the whole weight of' Marx's 'theory is towards setting out the principles which underlie the operation of the capitalist economy. Marx's analysis moves upon the level of an attempt to undercut the influence which physical categories such as prices, rents or rates of interest have in the theory of political economy, in order to expose the social relationships which lie at the root of them' (Giddens 1971, 52). Giddens directly follows this assertion with a quotation from Marx explicating capitalist production as a process of reification and this may suggest that originally structuration theory was meant to serve a quite critical conception and that the point was to show the 'virtual existence' of structure relative to the constitutive activities of subjects. At least, this is clearly the meaning of the statement from Marx that:

> The social character of activity, the social form of the product, and of the participation of the individual in production, appear as alienated, reified (*sachlich*) in relation to the individual [...] Universal exchange of activities and products, which has become the condition of existence of, and the mutual connection between, particular individuals, take the form of a thing, alienated from and independent of themselves. (Marx as quoted in Giddens 1971, 52)

Marx's interpretation of commodification, as entailing a duality of both substance and form, is a prominent part of Giddens's argument regarding the historically distinctive nature of the capitalist transformation (Giddens 1981a). With this reference to commodification, Giddens is seeking to answer the question of what were the historical preconditions for capitalist production to constitute an institutional system that is internally organized toward its own reproduction? This transformation corresponds to class becoming the defining structural principle of social organization and in some respects 'institutional reflexivity' differentiates capitalist production from all preceding forms of production. After Giddens's (1981a) first volume of his critique of historical materialism, there is a broadening of this focus beyond the institution of capitalism. He rather contends that this reflexivity is a defining dynamic of modern social systems in general (Giddens 1990a, 1991a). However, even from the fairly oblique manner in which the premises of this question of the historical preconditions of capitalism are outlined at this point, it is evident that the capitalist economy is only one of the historical forms of the broader production of society that Marx's paradigm conceptualized (Grumley 1992; Markus 1986a).

Although Giddens describes his critiques of historical materialism as 'deconstructions', they are not primarily 'textual or philological' analyses (Giddens 1982c). Perhaps, this lack of attention to Marx's texts explains why his critiques of historical materialism sometimes reduce the broader version of the Marxian paradigm of production to the narrower institutional forms of labour. Ironically, this occurs in spite of the fact that Marx's conception of praxis, as the production and reproduction of material life, originally served as something of a model for the structuration perspective. But probably a more significant reason for this reduction is the nature of the modifications specific to the structuration perspective, rather than any oversight. According to Markus's (1986a) exposition rather than Habermas's (1987a) critique, Marx's paradigm of production and Giddens's theory of structuration common conceptual orientation includes their opposing the extension of concepts from the philosophy of the subject, but, rather than rejecting these categories entirely, they reinterpret them in different ways on the basis of a theory of social constitution. Consequently, it is the interpretation of production as a social process, rather than the category of labour itself, which represents the feature of Marx's work that influenced the structuration approach. With the basic idea of social praxis extracted from Marx serving to organize Giddens's incorporating insights drawn from a multitude of different perspectives. This organizing does not impose a similitude of content, as it would be apposite to invert the above proposition into the production of the social as a process to intimate at Marx's influence. In sum, this suggests an appropriate designation of structuration theory's linkage to the Marxian version of social praxis is that of a shared general orientation and not that of a theoretical foundation.

There are essentially two theoretical innovations of the theory of structuration that make a distinctive, if not entirely original, contribution to the perspective of praxis philosophy, and which will be the subject of further discussion. The first is the exploration of the temporal and spatial aspects of all social practices; and through this connections are forged with some otherwise quite distant areas of substantive research, like time-geography and Goffman's analyses (Giddens 1984; 1981a). The second contribution is the unusual conjoining of practice to a notion of power. Giddens's elucidating of the temporal and spatial dimensions of practice continues Marx's original emphasis on human finitude and the production paradigm's radical historicism (Grumley 1991). However, it is also a reinterpretation, as Giddens's conceptualizing human finitude and time was significantly influenced by Heidegger's ontology (Heidegger 1962). In part, this sociological recasting of these ontological presuppositions inspired the structuration distinction between the 'virtual existence', in being instantiated in practice, of structure and social systems binding of time and space. Rather than commencing from a distinction between material content and social form, this proposal implies that systems are the social form as it possesses or, more accurately incorporating, its material content (Giddens 1979, 64; 1981a). In other words, a radical constructionist approach to social systems appears the counterpart to Giddens's accent on the historicity of practice. Given these ontological presuppositions, Giddens intends to eliminate all naturalistic assumptions regarding the constitution of society. Structuration theory aims to make explicit the most elemental factors and conditions of this processes of social constitution.

The imprecision of these remarks is not entirely unintended at this point. I will argue that in these proposals, which concern more than novel definitions of structure and system, are found some of the most serious tensions and deficiencies of the structuration approach to society. But, paradoxically, they also constitute the constructive possibilities of Giddens's perspective on history and social change. Many of these arguments are made in his deconstruction of historical materialism, but they would need to be developed beyond the limiting framework of the theory of structuration. And these conclusions are particularly justified when Giddens's project is evaluated from the practical-political standpoint of critical theory. In relation to the second innovative contribution to praxis philosophy, it is through conjoining practice to a notion of power that Giddens initially distinguishes his understanding of practice from Marx's identifying the production of society with the activity of social labour. In the theory of structuration, power is one of the principal means for conceptualizing the generation of social processes, power is considered intrinsic to the very meaning of agency. Indeed, the 'transformative capacity' of agents' practices is not so much defined by its opposition to power, but, instead, consists in the actualizing and altering manifestations of power (Giddens 1984). Power is generated both through individual freedom and the social relations of domination and exploitation. This suggestion implies that power precedes the 'systems' of relations of domination and it is probably the fundamental element of the constitution of society. But precedence here refers not to the temporality of the actual processes of structuration, but to the generative properties of structure in forming 'systems' of social relations which 'materialize' and embody' power (Giddens 1979, 66).

The need to explicate the meaning of precedence results from the ambiguities of Giddens's structuration ontology, but this conception is directed towards grasping power as the means as well as the outcome of the production, reproduction and transformation of relations of domination. According to Giddens (1979), it differs from the majority of interpretations of power; they have privileged the nature of the results and outcomes in defining power. He implies that rather than perceiving power as a precondition for domination, power is depicted as a consequence of domination. This depiction is not wrong, of course, but it often occludes the process questions of constitution and reproduction. In this way, power is simplified to its most typical manifest forms and often involves an 'undialectical' notion of domination, because it presumes that power is operative without explaining its operation. In the terms of the philosophy of praxis, these discussions have neglected how reproduction is always itself production. For Giddens, the consequences of a specific form of domination are themselves to be explained in terms of the historical genesis and processes of structuration. Manifest types of domination recreate the conditions of this process, but, he argues, power is 'not itself a resource', in the sense of a static property of structure (Giddens 1984, 16; 1979, 91). Power is the generative capacity to mobilize the resources comprising structure and through this process systems of domination are reproduced. This outlines how the power implied by domination is exercised and this process conception supposedly, as we will see in more detail, avoids the antinomic representations of structure and action that have pervaded theories of power.

Giddens treats the social organization of the fabrication and 'allocation' of material resources as a dimension of the generation and distribution of power. Given the delineation of Marx's influence upon structuration theory, this proposal pursues a task Arnason considered to be still outstanding in social theory. That is, 'of integrating Marx's analysis of economic structures into a more comprehensive and diversified theory of power' (Aranson 1991a, 66). At the same time, Giddens's interpretation of power as central to the constitution of society is employed against Marx, being fundamental to his deconstructive critique of historical materialism (Giddens 1984; 1985a). This perspective is opposed to any the notion of a unified species-subject. Habermas's reconstruction of historical materialism is similarly concerned to break away from this notion of a unified species-subject on the basis of the intersubjectivity of linguistic theory and the differentiations of a systems theory perspective. By contrast, the connection between Giddens's two praxis-philosophical innovations: power and time-space are critical to his critique of the historical materialist interpretation of class-divided precapitalist social formations. The historical grounding of this connection can somewhat, though not entirely I claim later, explain why he is able to overlay the notion of risk upon the basic theses of conception of social constitution. In my opinion, risk does not exactly fit the format of Giddens's

analysis of contradiction, but it is associated with the process that underpins the historical instantiating of social forms of contradiction.

> Human life is contradictory in the sense that the human being, as *Dasein*, originates and
> disappears into the world of Being, the world of nature, yet as conscious reflective agent is
> the negation of the organic. The mediator of the contradictory character of human exis-
> tence is society itself, for only in and through membership of society does the human being
> acquire 'second nature'. In all societies which remain closely involved with the modalities and
> rhythms of nature in day-to-day life, the institutions that mediate and express such contradic-
> tion are centred upon religion, magic and myth [...] Existential contradiction, in virtue of
> its very character, remains fundamental in all types of society. But in class-divided societies it
> becomes partly 'externalised' rather than remaining directly incorporated within the sphere
> of day-to-day life. *This externalisation is the state.* I want to propose the following thesis: *in all
> except tribal societies the state is the focus of the contradictory character of human societal organisation.*
> (Giddens 1981, 237; 1979, 160–162)

The Structure of Social Action and the Historicity of Social Structure

Like Habermas, Giddens draws upon many of the divergent and sometimes opposed
traditions of social theory and twentieth-century philosophy. He does this to supplement the Marxist perspective's insights into social constitution. This procedure aims to
modify the category of praxis, based on a revised understanding of the characteristic
features common to all human practices. Giddens's revisions are presented as an 'ontology', because it concerns the structure that enables specific forms of practices and the
different conditions they express. What he appears to imply by this is that the analytical
distinction between forms of human action are ancillary. That is, typological distinctions appear in the structuration perspective as derivations drawn from the elemental
components of practice. These are unified at the level of ontology. The construction of
action types involves separating and emphasizing one moment as predominating in relation to the others. For this reason, types of social action are the specific content that the
abstract general dimensions of practice acquire through the institutional patterning that
focus agents' action and interactions. Similarly, dependent on this proposal's ontological framework is the task of evaluating the relative significance of types of substantive
action. Giddens's thesis of the duality of structure suggests that this task depends on
interpretations of the mediation and transformation of social systems. Systems constitute
the concrete institutional organization of a society.

It would be a mistake to assume from the generic nature of this ontological postulate that it is intended to be a transcendental theoretical construct. Giddens strenuously
underlines the concrete and situated nature of all practices. Indeed, he argues that it is
through explicating the ontological suppositions of practice that its situated quality can
best be appreciated. In the theory of structuration, situated refers not only to those contexts within which practices occur, but more to the incorporating of contexts as an inevitable part of the constitution of practices. This notion of incorporating means that the
binding of circumstances of presence and absence has a profound influence on action
and interaction (Giddens 1984; 1990a). Social practices may transform the relating of

presence and absence, hence the generation of contexts needs to be explained and it should not be taken as given. The explanation of contexts on the basis of the ontological disclosure of how time and space are intrinsic to structuration processes distinguishes this approach from some other versions of epistemological and cultural contextualism (see Seidman 1998; Stones 2005).

In order to clarify this supposition, Giddens refers to Heidegger's ontology and the latter may have influenced his claim that the epistemological requirements of grounding have often misled theories of action and obscured the basic features of practice. It is not only approaches influenced by transcendental philosophy that are open to this criticism, in Giddens's opinion, a large number of theories commence from highly intentional and elaborated forms of action. These are often actually concerned with the moments of reflection upon action, rather than the reflexivity internal to the processes of acting (Giddens 1976; 1979). Although this contention is one of the underlying justifications of the ontological approach of structuration theory, Giddens is open to reproach for his evanescent formulation of it. In fact, the ontological format of structuration theory was not based on detailed prior argument regarding its justification; it has rather been an implicit part of its elaboration (see Cohen 1989, 1–32; 279–88). The theory of structuration is founded on a conception of action as a process of the subject's continuous practical involvement. This activity is initially that of the *duree* of everyday interaction and action's original characteristic is never a superseded phase (Giddens 1979, 53–59). It persists in a mediated relation with the other moments and forms of action, like those of the subject's realizing reflected plans and explicitly reasoned action.

According to Giddens, the intrinsically practical cast of the knowledge contained in unfocussed action is of a different order to that exhibited in reflexive and reasoned action. It is the latter that many other approaches to action, like analytical philosophies of action and Parsons's 'action frame of reference', have tended to focus upon. These conceptions often reflect a transposing of epistemological considerations onto action, such as in the case of some analytical approaches treating intentions as equivalent to causes. This transposing is not surprising given their underestimating the transformative potential and knowledgeable features of the routine conduct of everyday practices (Giddens 1979, 245–59). Indeed, by neglecting the intertwining of unfocussed practical involvements with ensuing forms action, these approaches produce a distorted view of the relationship between practice and the constitution of the subject. These difficulties are rather diffuse and they are not limited to particular frameworks; Giddens criticizes Parsons's theory for being concerned with the conditions for action rather than action itself, as well as post-structuralism for misrepresenting the practicality of language use (Giddens 1979, 28–48; 1987, 73–108).

There are, of course, approaches to action and subjectivity that are more proximate to the structuration conceptualization of practice. Giddens (1984; 1979; 1976) acknowledges that phenomenologists, like Schutz and Merleau-Ponty, elucidated everyday action's principally pre-reflexive stocks of knowledge, grasping the essentially practical character of bodily involvements and subjects' perceptions. Giddens claims that phenomenological theories are, however, deficient with regard to the nature of social practice, as well as limited in their ability to explain long-term developments and large-scale social processes. Namely, he contends that they lack an adequate theoretical formulation, as opposed to empirical appreciation, of the inherently recursive nature of social practices. No doubt this criticism can be readily contested and the regularity of practices is implied by the concept of lifeworld, Giddens argues, though, that an adequate theoretical formulation requires a suspension of the 'subjectivist' premises of the phenomenological tradition in favour of a concept of structure (Giddens 1984; 1979; Schutz 1967). In his opinion, it is equally necessary to reformulate the concept of structure in order to avoid the 'objectivist' connotations it has held in social theory. In other words, explicating recurrent social practices supposes a conception of the duality of structure and this conceptualization supposedly supplants the dichotomy between subject and object. In this duality the constitutive character of subjects' knowledge and those capacities realized in practices retain their significance, but structure is the means for the reproduction of these practices, hence subjects presupposes structure. The duality of structure means that recurrent social practices are the condition and medium of the reproduction of structure. In particular, this regularity of practices derives from the instantiation of rules, and it is rules, along with the other dimension of resources, that comprise structure.

Structuration theory conceives of rules as procedures for the continuation of the practices. In this sense, rules neither need to be formally codified or institutionally sanctioned, nor are agents' explicit knowledge and capacity to account for rules a condition for following them. In Giddens's opinion, rules can be of this type but the more overt forms of rules do not always coincide with those of the greatest significance for the general conduct of everyday life (Giddens 1984, 22). He believes that the opposite is probably the case, with those rules that most regularly 'structure' action tacitly grasped by actors and informally sanctioned. According to Giddens, the fact that the rules orientating action are not always at the explicit disposition of subjects does not amount to a justification for the dissolution of the subject by the notion of structure. This mistake is made in the case of discussions of rules within the structuralist traditions of linguistics and social theory (Giddens 1979). Rules should be related to the practical character of subjects' capacities and their knowledge to 'go on'. He claims that often the subordination of these features of action is due to analyses of action privileging the question of 'action as meaning', but discounting those meanings that are not given explicit form in being articulated by agents. In addition, as suggested, 'meaning' is mostly understood in a way that is basically consonant with various schools of social inquiry's notions of theoretical knowledge. This is detrimental, Giddens believes, to understanding the everyday *duree* of acting, where this sort of explicit knowledge is unnecessary (Giddens 1976, 53). On his analysis, everyday conduct contains a logic that is not identical to the discursive giving of reasons, but which enables distinctive processes of rationalization and reflection.

In my opinion, this view of everyday action differs little at the level of description from Schutz's social phenomenology and basically Giddens's position similarly reiterates the implications of ethnomethodological research into lay knowledge (Schutz 1967; Garfinkel 1967). His arguments are, however, really directed against certain versions of analytical philosophy and the shadow cast by epistemology. According to Giddens, structuration theory's starting point makes it possible to perceive that the explicit verbal or institutional expression of a rule is already an interpretation of it (Giddens 1984, 23). He believes that this conception avoids the confusions in the usage of rules in analytical philosophy of action, while clarifying an important factor in altering their application. In any event, Giddens accepts that agents can generally provide accounts and reasons when required for their mundane practices. Yet, explicating the practical knowledge of their rule following is often only a result of the very disruption of these practices. Ethnomethodological investigations, for example, have clarified the extent to which accountability depends on disrupting unproblematic understandings and the distinctive reasoning of everyday interactions (Garfinkel 1967; Heritage 1984). Given this, Giddens proposes that when analyzing agents' reasons the situation-specific requirements and motives for giving reasons needs to be taken into account, as well as the nature of their reasoning clarified (Giddens 1984).

Giddens suggests that four perspectives have investigated the 'practical consciousness' exhibited in the *duree* of everyday practices: psychoanalysis, ethnomethodology, phenomenology and ordinary language philosophy. Thompson notes that ordinary language philosophy emerged through the critique of logical atomism and Vienna Circle positivist philosophy, it 'may be regarded as the second stage in the development of the contemporary analytical school' (Thompson 1981, 9). More broadly, as Habermas's analysis of the pragmatics of communication highlighted, it constituted a philosophical rejection of introspective consciousness as the grounds of meaning and action (Habermas 1984). Giddens accords ordinary language philosophy importance because it 'has been responsible for making clear the shortcomings' of the previous objectivism of orthodox scientific theories (Giddens 1984, 7). But he is especially interested in this development in analytical philosophy because it includes Wittgenstein's philosophy, which is a seminal influence on the theory of structuration. Just how significant Wittgenstein is for structuration theory can be gauged from Giddens wanting 'to propose that there is a direct continuity between Marx and Wittgenstein in respect of the production and reproduction of society as *Praxis*' (Giddens 1979, 4).

In light of the importance of Wittgenstein's philosophy to Giddens's conceptual strategy, the distance between the theory of structuration and analytical approaches may be exaggerated. Indeed, the distance between them seems less significant than the somewhat analogous form of reasoning employed when the purpose of the theory of structuration is presented by Giddens as a tool that focuses social analysis and emphasis is placed more on the procedural implications of its approach to research (Giddens 1984). This is not meant to imply that the differences are unimportant and a case could be made that Giddens's notion of practice has more similarities with the pragmatism's 'process' interpretation of action (Joas 1993). The influence of pragmatist philosophy appears mediated through the investigations pursued by subsequent strands of North American sociology (Sica 1991). However, the point I am making is that in the absence of detailed epistemological reflection upon its procedure of conceptualization, the theory of structuration may be open to being interpreted as similar to that of analytical philosophy. This conjecture finds support in the problem of defining a plausible way of reconciling Giddens's (1991b, 204) assertion that structuration theory is 'not intended to be a theory of anything, in the sense of advancing general-izations about social reality' and his assertion that it is simultaneously concerned with the provision of an overall ontology of social life (Giddens 1991b, 204). For either its ontological premises are grounds for differentiating structuration theory and the basis of its critique of analytical philosophy of action; or considerations somewhat analo-gous to those of analytical philosophy, like the analytical distinguishing of the basic elements of social action and system reproduction, precede and guide the formulating of this ontology. A sharp differentiation of these alternatives is probably undesirable from the standpoint of structuration theory and inconsistent with the procedure of having one inform the other.

This could be still regarded as merely an important shift in perspective to the other dimensions of action, a move that is in itself not really a departure from the analytical approach with respect to the generation of knowledge. On the one hand, this places greater strain on the general presuppositions of its conception of action, rather than upon the empirical analysis of action, and it especially puts additional weight upon the connections that this conception of action has to Giddens's differentiated model of the subject, which will be outlined in a later chapter. On the other hand, it raises the ques-tion that Habermas posed in distinguishing the system from the lifeworld. That is, what is the structuration explanation of the means by which the social comes to possess the character of a system organized by 'structural principals', for which reformulating action is an important but incomplete contribution. The illumination of these two very different queries and mediating between them are fundamental requirement for transcending the limits of action theory without renouncing the need to rectify the problem that 'ortho-dox sociology lacked a theory of action' (Giddens 1979, 253). This was the commencing problem of the theory of structuration.

The Theory of Structuration: Action and Structure; Rules and Resources

> I came to see that an 'ontology of social life' must supply a detailed understanding of the nature of action, together with what in post-structuralism is described as a 'theory of the sub-ject'; and that, likewise the notion of 'structure' itself is a complicated and difficult one. The pre-existing debate about the relation between 'the individual' and 'society', which overlapped with the controversy between methodological individualists and their opponents seemed to me misleading in its terms of reference. According to the structurationist approach, social theory does not 'begin' either with the individual or with society, both of which are notions that need to be reconstructed through other concepts. In structuration theory, the core con-cern of the social sciences is with recurrent practices and their transformations. (Giddens 1991b, 203)

The theory of structuration represents a sustained attempt to overcome the traditional opposition of structural and action approaches in social theory. Giddens seeks to incor-porate the respective insights of the established sociological paradigms without being subject to the weaknesses that derive from their opposed emphases. On the one hand, structural perspectives, particularly those influenced by Durkheim, have tended to clarify structure in relation to constraint.[1] This understanding of structure has often been combined, Giddens argues, with an underestimation of the knowledgeability and practical capacities of agents. Where these two premises coincide, they result in a neglect not only of the constitution of structure through action, but also the enabling aspects of structure which may be as fundamental to its reproduction as constraint is. On the other hand, interpretative approaches have stressed the practical accomplishments of subjects, but have largely avoided analyzing institutions and tend to represent the practices of social actors as occurring independently of structure. This often results in an obscuring of the dependence of action upon structure and of how it is that action is limited by structure. The inadequacies of interpretative sociologies have been the obverse of those in structural perspectives. The stress of the theory of structuration upon generative processes means that structure is, controversially, conceived as 'always both constraining and enabling' (Giddens 1984, 45). Fundamental to this reconciliation of the dualism of structure and action is the formulation of the concept of the 'duality of structure'. This concept enables Giddens to define structure as 'both the medium and outcome of the reproduction of practices,' consisting of those generic and elemental rules and resources drawn upon and reproduced by social practices (Giddens 1979, 5). Structure is not intended to describe features of social life, because this formulation seeks to capture the general recursiveness of social practices without defining apriori the specific, substantive content of structuration. The reasoning behind this apparently abstract definition rests on Giddens's argument that structure has only a 'virtual existence' in relation to the instantiation of practice and as 'memory traces' orienting the conduct of agents (Giddens 1979; 1984).

Rules are generalized procedures that coordinate the constitution and reproduction of social conduct and interaction. In this way, rules serve to obviate but not eliminate the degree of contingency associated with all social practices, through enabling the agent to continue and 'go on' while limiting the transformative options of practice. Structure does not exist separately from practice, nor do agents have to be capable of formulating the underlying principles of rules to realize them in practice. Giddens draws an analogy with language, as one of a series of illustrations of this meaning of rules. The structure of a language is reproduced in every sentence we use and is at the same time the medium for the production of these sentences. This linguistic illustration is connected to only one of the two 'modalities' of rules, that is, signifying or meaning constituting – which also entails constraint in the form of prescribing the conditions of intelligibility. The second modality is that of normative sanctions. Normative sanctions focus upon the rights and obligations of participants in interaction but also express the asymmetries of domination involved in social relations (Giddens 1979, 85–88). Normative sanctions are in the

---

1   Durkheim's position is, of course, more complex than a one-sided focus on constraint, the influence here seems to originate from the defining in *The Rules of Sociological Method*, of social facts in relation to constraint; but *The Elementary Forms of Religious Life*, for instance, presents an account of enablement and constraint in the context of a highly original theory of social constitution (Durkheim 1964a; 1976; see Frisby and Sayer 1986).

majority of circumstances of interaction not formalized in institutions, nor are institutional sanctions usually the predominant reason for agents compliance. One of the major points Giddens seeks to draw out is that the rules instantiated in social action do not necessarily reflect deeply internalized societal norms, belief systems and motivational commitments. Adherence to rules can often only involve actors' awareness and conditional pragmatic acceptance of these as the constraint and means for continuing interaction.

This conceptualization of rules forms part of a series of associated categories that constitute an alternative to neo-Parsonian versions of sociological role theory. As is well known, the category of role was intended in its Parsonian formulation to provide a 'direct articulation' of the connection between the structural features of systems and the individual (Giddens 1979, 115). In Parsonian theory, roles served as a means of bridging the potential disjuncture between processes of system integration and social integration, by establishing a complementarity between internalization and institutionalization. In a somewhat similar vein to the contemporaneous critical proposals of Touraine (1988; 1977), Giddens (1979; 1976) argues that this structural-functionalist understanding of social roles results in a fallacious conception of agency, which, in turn, originates from its debilitative notion of action. Broadly, each of his arguments criticizing the suppositions of Parsons's social theory are redeployed, like those critical of its privileging the moment of normative integration, its view of consensus as the basis of social order, with order being conceived principally as the resolving of a conflict between the individual and society. Giddens contends that Parsons's reliance on commensurate orientations enabled the conditions of system reproduction to be anchored in the individual's 'personality', rather than conceived as produced through action.

Parsons's theory remained important to Giddens because the empirical analyses of roles tended to give the appearance of being detached from an encompassing theoretical model of society. This reflected, in his opinion, a tacit acceptance of a sort of division of labour in sociological thought during the 'orthodox consensus' of functionalist theory and postivist methodology (Giddens 1979). Still, Giddens's recognition of Mead's richer original insights and other elaborations of social roles, including even revisions of the concept of roles within functionalist thought, modulate his conversion of this category in structuration theory. Giddens's notion of the duality of structure incorporated considerations incipient in the literature contesting functionalist models of roles (see Joas 1993). In particular, the consideration that the normative prescriptions of social roles should not be conceived in a determining sense of directions underlying interaction performances, but, rather, as actualized in the processes of their practical intersubjective negotiation concurs with several of the precepts of Giddens's own approach. For instance, its explicating rules in their practical instantiating as modalities of structuration and his analytical concern with grasping the intersecting of the transformative capacities of agency with the obligatory facets of role-identity.

Despite incorporating of these types of considerations into the basic concepts of the theory of structuration, the problem Giddens's formulations are directed towards still largely overlaps that of Parsonian theory. That is, in theorizing the composition of society, he appears most interested in explicating these modalities of rules as institution 'positioning' interaction and how the 'structural properties' of social relations form a set of regular practices which are constitutive for the structuration of systems (Giddens 1984). This interest is brought out clearly in his conceptualizing structure as also composed of 'resources'. It means that rules are not only always part of a combination but that their substantive instantiating in practice is intrinsically related to the capacities of actors and the structural components of systems. Even though as facets of systems these structural components are not reducible to specific circumstances of individual's interactions, they are constitutive of the capacities which agents deploy in their practices. They are not objective and logically separate from the subjective capacities of agents. Practices are conditioned by systems which are actually social relations of autonomy and dependence. This is an instance of Giddens's proximity to Marx's analysis of the reproduction of capital and labour, the resources drawn upon facilitate in the regular recurrence of practices their reproduction. Hence, Giddens's generative interpretation of power fundamentally informs the concept of resources. Although both components of structure are entwined in the reproduction of relations of domination, the mode in which resources facilitate the structuration of social systems diverged analytically from the mode of rules (Giddens 1984, 28–34). Resources, having only a virtual existence as structure, are the abstract means for deciphering institutional alignments. He analytically distinguishes between two primary forms of resource mobilization.

> Allocative resources refer to capabilities [...] generating command over objects, goods or material phenomena. Authoritative resources refer to types of transformative capacity generating command over persons or actors. (Giddens 1984, 33)

This distinction between allocative and authoritative resources is the central axis of Giddens's deconstructive critique of historical materialism. Basically, the alternative dimensions of the expansion of domination and power that they represent provide a framework for reconceptualizing social change from the perspective of long-term historical processes (Giddens 1981a; 1985a). This suggests a different dynamic to that of the reproduction of lifeworld and system, the notion of a congruence between the social integration and system integration seems to fit Giddens's view of the tautological, and therefore redundant, arguments of functionalism (Giddens 1981a). Since the two forms of resources are general features of structure, central to Giddens's (1981a; 1985a) historical analyses is the relationship between them. Systematic forms of domination are most apparent where allocative and authoritative resources intersect.

Although Giddens's analytical interest is notably in how one type of resource translates into the other, the distinction between the two resources and his conception of their mutual translation appears tailored towards a significant socio-political problem of the twentieth century: that of Marx's potential inconsistencies and the practical lacunae of 'official Marxism' concerning the possibility of a purely technical distinction between the 'management of things' and the management of people. As G. Markus (1986b; 1986a) suggests, this idea of a technical administration which does not constitute an independent locus of power is not only theoretically questionable in the light of the production paradigm's distinction between material content and social form, but this oversight concerning the accrual of power is a major source of a political legacy of bureaucratization and authoritarianism. It is in part a desire to account for the modern context of totalitarian social organization which led Giddens to reflect upon the problem of the limited consideration of administration in Marx's image of socialism, and this stimulated a turn to the category of surveillance under the influence of Foucault (Giddens 1979; 1981a; 1985a). At the same time, Giddens's understanding of social structure draws attention to the significant insights comprised in Marx's account of the translation in capitalist processes of production between property and authority, and especially insights into the systematic domination intrinsic to the 'real subsumption' of labour under capital (Marx 1976; see Rundell 1987; Postone 1993).

The central thesis of Giddens's critiques of historical materialism is that allocative and authoritative 'resources interlace differently in different types of society' and that 'in non-capitalist societies coordination of authoritative resources forms the determining axis of societal integration and change' (Giddens 1981a, 4). Based on his generative conception of power, he defines authoritative resources as 'capabilities of controlling the humanly created world of society itself' (Giddens 1981a, 51). Historical materialism gives primacy instead to allocative resources, but Giddens argues that this primacy is only applicable to capitalist society and not to the enormous range of non- or pre-capitalist societies. This is hardly a novel criticism, given that the early Lukács (1971) had stressed this basic difference of capitalist society against the an ascendant Marxist orthodoxy which projected the primacy of the economic system of production backwards in history. Giddens further argues that Marx underestimated the extent to which this change in the relationship between resources is a crucial aspect of the radical discontinuity of capitalism (Giddens 1981a). This later argument could similarly be simply rejected as a superficial misunderstanding, its merits largely depending, as we will see in the next chapter, on how Giddens's framework disaggregates what Marx and Marxists describe as those direct precapitalist relations of domination and servitude.

Time and Space: The Elemental Constituents of the Social

In Giddens's opinion, his approach is the opposite of the 'consequence explanations' of structural-functionalist interpretations of institutions. Structuration theory highlights instead the mechanisms of human interaction that sustain institutions (Giddens 1981a, 41–56). The institutional typology of signification, domination and legitimation explicates the social systems' ordering of the two modalities of rules and the forms of resource mobilization implicated in structure. This explicatition, in combination with the analysis of enduring structures, defined as 'structural properties', then enables the classification of this 'clustering' of institutions that form the 'structural principles' of social systems. The structuration theory concept of social systems incorporates what has been traditionally associated with structure in sociology, that is, the patterning of social relations and social interaction across and binding time and space. Yet this notion of system differs somewhat in its intention to effect a problematizing of a number of assumptions about society and permit a wide range of variation in the degree of systemness. Rather than conceiving of society as analogous to 'organic' self-sustaining entities, Giddens maintains that societies should be conceived as traversed by systems of intersocietal relations. He argues that societies are also social systems, which having distinctive structural principles, ' "stand out" in bas-relief from a background of a range of other systemic relationships in which they are embedded' (Giddens 1984, 164). These formulations reflect Giddens's contention that the sociological representations of society, as based upon clearly demarcated territorial boundaries that circumscribe social relations, are derived from the historically unique features institutionalized in the system of modern nation-states (Giddens 1985a).

The theory of structuration's definition of social systems is circular but less tautological than it may at first appear, because it is premised upon Giddens's break with the predominant understanding of time and space in social theory (Giddens 1981a, 26–48; 1979, 198–233; 1987, 140–65). According to him, both the functionalist differentiation of statics from dynamics, and the structuralist distinction between synchrony and diachrony, share a common tendency to analytically abstract from time. Where temporality enters into these approaches, it is based upon a prior theoretical identification of history with change. Giddens considers that this separating of social processes from time is methodologically dubious and ontologically implausible. Social life is irremediably historical, because time is basic to the very meaning of both continuity and change. The claim that the problem of order is the core dilemma confronting all analyses of society is closely related to this assimilation of history with change. From the functionalist perspective of adaptation and control, order is represented as society's solution for avoiding collapse and disintegration. While this conception of society has often been criticized for its static and harmonist assumptions, Giddens develops these arguments further into virtually a complete rejection of functionalist perspectives and explanations. Structuration theory dispenses not only with the metaphorical contrast between order and disintegration, but also replaces the problem of order with that of the provision and maintenance of *form* by social practices. This approach transforms the basic question of social analysis into the process of ordering or patterning which social practices acquire through the duality of structure. Form is then constituted through and by social systems' binding of time and space.

There is an intrinsic connection between these proposals for reconceptualizing time and space and Giddens's formulation of structure as 'internal' to practice rather than 'external'. Together these represent the most innovative dimensions of structuration theory. This attempt at redefining sociological categories and assumptions in a manner that renders time and space intrinsic to their very meaning draws its inspiration from Heidegger's reflections on time as the 'horizon of all being'. These ideas are sociologically translated into the theory of structuration through the proposition that time and space are not the frameworks of social practices but are essential elements of the constitution of action and social reproduction. Giddens also refers to the relevance of Bergson's critique of the tendency in modern thought towards the spatialization of time and James and Mead's pragmatist conceptions of time as general informants of the structuration perspective. However, his basic aspiration seems to be that of transforming what were, in the ontology of Heidegger's (1962) *Being and Time*, the existential attributes of *Dasein* into those elemental constituents of praxis, as the production and reproduction of social life (Giddens 1979, 3–4).

For Giddens, a full appreciation of the significance of time and space in social theory has to some extent been inhibited by a tacit incorporation of the basic tenets of modern western conceptions of time and space. This resulted in a failure to appreciate the distinctiveness and implications of this conception. It is important to delineate the characteristics of modern western understanding of time and space, so as to not confuse these with their definitive form and to underline the possible variations in their socio-cultural imposition. Time and space are conceived in modern western thought as dimensions separable from action and cognition, as the parameters or frameworks within which these occur. Kant's philosophy gave the most sophisticated articulation of the suppositions of this conception. The full complexity of the transcendental aesthetic of the first critique will not be sketched here, but, for Kant, time and space are 'pure forms of sensory intuition' and *a priori* presuppositions of the perception of phenomena. In this way, there is a prior ordering of the indeterminate array of the experiences of the subject through locating things in time and space. However, for Kant (1997), time and space are not categories derived from the empirical experience of them in their own right, even though there can be no apprehension of phenomena without the fixing and delimiting of them in time and space. As Roberts puts it: 'We do not see the space; we only see what is occupying it. Nor do we experience time; we only experience events *in* time' (Roberts 1988, 14–15; Kant 1997, B 38; B46). In particular, Giddens suggests that compared to the classical world, the modern conception, partly illustrated in the transcendental procedure of Kant, depends on a notion of time and subsequently space as empty. Importantly, this notion makes time and space amenable to quantification. This argument is of profound importance to Giddens's historical account of the radical discontinuity of capitalist society and his analyses of modernity (Giddens 1981a; 1990a).

Heidegger's thesis that the nature of being is inherently temporal challenges the assumptions of modern Western depictions of beings existing within the separate dimensions of time and space. In Heidegger's opinion, this depiction was connected to the limitations of Western thought that derive from its displacing an ontological concern with being by a preoccupation with epistemology (Giddens 1981a, 31). On the one hand, Giddens's critique of the implicit epistemological complexion of many theories of action is consistent with these assertions. On the other hand, his purpose in appropriating insights from Heidegger's (1962) ontology for constructing an anti-functionalist conception of social institutions is quite distinctive. It differs from those perspectives that made the linguistic turn the basis for overcoming the limitations of the philosophy of consciousness, however, it is not an entirely unprecedented appropriation in terms of the history of Western Marxism. Giddens's sociological translation of aspects of Heidegger's theorizing was framed by the continuities that the structuration perspective has to the radical historicism of the philosophy of praxis (see Marcuse 1987; Kosik 1976).

The translation of Heidegger's ontology informs the structuration theory understanding of practices as a continuous flow, as well as its critique of the philosophical grounds of other models of action.[2] Giddens (1987, 140–65) criticizes the potential

---

2   Although there are loose affinities between facets of Giddens's understanding of structure and Husserl's (1970) conception of the lifeworld, Heidegger's (1962) emphasis upon the priority of 'being-in-the-world', including a priority over the epistemological considerations determining Husserl's (1960; 1964) early phenomenological investigations, appears to influence a basic presupposition of the structuration perspective: its commencing from practices in their character of being-in-the-world. Of course, the theme of historicity can be traced back to Husserl's analyses of internal time consciousness.

cultural ethnocentrism of Heidegger's notion of the individual's consciousness of finitude, which is an integral part of Heidegger's hermeneutic interpretation of the facticity of being-in-the-world. Yet, there is a certain irony involved in his making this criticism, given Giddens's analysis relies so much on a global contrast between traditional and modern conceptions of time. In any case, this criticism is particularly feint and countermanded in the process of his translating Heidegger's reflections on time and being. The apprehension of finitude is fundamental to Giddens's own theoretical model of the constitution of the subject and his reformulating of the theme of finitude is likewise central to his theorizing time and space as elemental constituents of the social. These proposals provide some of the philosophical underpinning, even though the basic motivation was that of the problems of social analysis, for Giddens's rejection of all static theoretical conceptions of society and social relations. The contrast between statics and dynamics has been a common feature of functionalist social theory and he claims that a similar conception is implicit in such structuralist distinctions as those between code and usage, synchronic and diachronic (Giddens 1979). These distinctions are sometimes defended on methodological grounds, for instance, with reference to the synchronic character of anthropological investigations. Giddens criticisms are, however, cast in ontological terms. He argues that patterns 'of social relationships exist only in so far as the latter are organized as systems' (Giddens 1979, 61–62) and 'social systems exist as systems only in and through' their reproduction over time (Giddens 1981a, 17).

Giddens (1979) accepts the interpretation of Heidegger's analytics of the temporality of *Dasein* constituting an ontology of the possible. This ontology can be defined in its distinctiveness as disclosing the actuality of the possible. At a general level, this disclosure is supposed to be sociologically translated into the theory of structuration. Now, that some propinquity persists is suggested by one commentator describing the 'basic status' of the project of the theory of structuration as an '*ontology of potentials*' (Cohen 1989, 11). However, propinquity is not identity, Heidegger's (1993) *Letter on Humanism*, sharply distinguishes a hermeneutic interpretation of the being of the possible for *Dasein* from the category of *potential*. For Heidegger, potential belongs to the traditional metaphysical determination of being. For the present, it will be sufficient to note that these sorts of elision may be essential to the reframing inherent in the procedure of translation. Indeed, the antinomic structure intrinsic to translating Heidegger's ontology was ostensible from the first conversion associating it with the structuration category of practice.[3]

---

3   It is worth remarking in respect of this consideration, though tangential to the purpose of the present exposition, that the conclusion which Castoriadis draws from his reflections upon the philosophy of Heidegger is diametrically opposed to the understanding that Giddens and others hold of it as constituting an ontology of the possible (Castoriadis 1984; 1991). This is in spite of Castoriadis's own elucidating of the social imaginary as the institution of a world horizon, as commentators like Habermas (1987b) have suggested, exhibiting some pronounced similarities with the later philosophy of Heidegger. Similarities, that is, with specifically those features of the later philosophy with which Giddens does not seriously engage, but then Giddens could have dwelled longer on the implications of a sociological appropriation of Heidegger's thought in general.

Giddens is most interested in developing Heidegger's notion of 'presencing', as a 'fourth dimensional' processual constituting of the relation between past, present and future. He seeks to reconcile this notion of presencing with his understanding of practice, so as to transform the apprehension of intervals from that of their identification with quantified instances. By presencing he is intending to underline the practical instantiating of differences separating all dimensions of temporality. He argues the ontological structure of presencing has been concealed by constituted forms of the perception of time, like that of time as an externally apprehended succession of temporal presents and the representation of time as the marking of a sequence of instants that are supposedly strictly divisible from one another. Of course, this constitution of time, as we will see later, is significant in its own right for the coordination of social processes. 'Presencing' entails a parallel reconceptualizing of space, so that temporal and spatial intervals 'are not instants, and neither is time-space "composed" of them. Rather, intervals are *structured differences* that give form to content, whether this be hours on a clock, notes in a musical rhythm, or centimetres on a ruler. To say this, in other words, is to reaffirm time-space as "presencing" rather than as contentless form in which objects exist' (Giddens 1981a, 33–34).

The patterning of time and space is not a phenomenon external to social practices, even though these dimensions are the elemental constituents of them. That is, time and space are constitutive of the shape of any pattern of practices and the processes organizing these generating *form* are temporally and spatially situated processes. Form is realized continuously through practices instantiating structure and the concrete organization of social processes that transform and reproduce systems. This means form is not, as in logic, juxtaposed to content. Patterns only exist over time and space; no pattern is comprised within the singular temporal-spatial instance, but nor are they strictly derivable from the analysis of an aggregate combination of such instances. A seminal determinant of their shape is the capacity and means by which social systems 'stretch' and 'bind' time and space. With these arguments, Giddens's purpose is not simply that of augmenting traditional conceptions of social reproduction and change; he aims to transform the basic understanding of these processes. Social systems exist through their binding of time and space; due to the persistent and regular reproduction of their institutional structures, systems constitute the enduring 'concrete' forms of social relations. Institutional structures, in turn, situate social practices, but in the specific constitutive sense of 'presencing'. The most deeply embedded structural principles are distinguished by their duration and extension over time and space. Of most interest to the structuration perspective is utilizing this distinction to analyze processes of the intersection and transformation between structure and system. The conditions and content of structuration can be traced through the practices mobilizing and converting the set of institutionalized structures that facilitate time-space distanciation. These latter processes of time-space distanciation can mediate 'presence' in the reproduction and transformation of social systems, such mediation facilitates social relations extending beyond the immediate contexts of action.

The notion of presencing provides another means by which Giddens can articulate his conception of social order as the provision and maintenance of form. This conception is intended to contrast with the Parsonian formulation of social order as a problem of normative integration. Giddens suggests that the relating of presence and absence is a more basic 'ontological' trait of social life. The form of their relating sets the parameters of the distanciation underlying processes like normative integration, as well as reproducing the recursive ordering of practices. From this interpretation of the notion of presence, structuration theory draws a distinction between different types of integration and the forms of the reciprocal patterning of relations of autonomy and dependence these entail, for both individuals and larger collectivities. *Social integration* is defined as relations between actors conducted on the basis of co-presence, and concerns those immediate temporal and spatial contexts of interaction, whereas *system integration* is defined as relations sustained between actors and collectivities which are physically absent and concerns interconnections that extend over larger spans of time and space. 'The mechanisms of system integration certainly presuppose those of social integration, but such mechanisms are also distinct in some key respects from those involved in relations of co-presence' (Giddens 1984, 28). This distinction between social and system integration is draws attention to the mechanisms and media of overcoming presence. Mechanisms set the parameters of distanciation through processes relating presence and absence. These conceptualizations of the constitutive significance of time and space are meant to assist the theory of structuration in its programmatic intention of transcending the fissure between the so-called micro and macro approaches. The distinction between these two approaches reinforced the traditional antinomic conceptions of action and structure, in social theory by way of associating each almost exclusively one of the poles of the antinomy between structure and action.

The theory of structuration proposes that 'every moment of social reproduction' involves three layers of temporality and their interpenetration (Giddens 1981a, 19–20). The first is the temporality of day-to-day activity specified within the generic concept of practice. It has been elucidated how this conception endeavours to break with some of those suppositions of the philosophy of consciousness which conditioned theories of action. The second layer is the temporality of the lifecycle of the human organism; and this is closely associated with the human, *Dasein* in its perception of finitude. According to Giddens, this temporality of the individual's 'first nature' always exists in a form which is socially acquired and reconstituted as a 'second nature' through the transformative power of practice and the socializing mediation of structure. In relation to mediation, structure is implicated in the reproduction of systems transcending the individual. These existential reflections bear upon the interpretative horizon of the arguments at the foreground of Giddens's theorizing the contingent processes of the production of subjectivity. Finally, there is then, the '*longue durée* of institutional time: the long term sedimentation or development of social institutions' (Giddens 1981a, 19–20). From the analysis of this 'longest' layer of temporality, the 'deepest' structural principles of social systems can be discerned. However, he rejects the notion that any logical primacy should be attributed to any one of these three layers. The contingent conditions of social reproduction mean each presupposes the other and is implicated in its structuration.

Giddens's substantive accounts of historical change initially centre on the different time-space constitutions of social systems. Different historical formations of allocative and authoritative resources are defined by the extent to which they are the means of the temporal and spatial extension of a society. Giddens proposes that there are highly general, but also very elemental senses in which the constraints of time and geography are always overcome (Giddens 1981a). He argues that transcending these 'natural' barriers is always a process of *social* constitution, rather than simply one of adaptation to the environment. In a similar vein, as we will see, he wants to avoid the evolutionary narrative of a general historical transition from simple to complex societal structures. Instead of universally employing the notion of differentiation, he considers that this change is one of type of transition, which needs to be recognized as always a specific, contingent occurrence rather than a general, necessary development (Giddens 1981a, 90). From his perspective what is more important than classifying the level of the structural differentiation of the historical social formations is the apprehending of the *social processes* of their change and reproduction.

Giddens's understanding of modernity as radically discontinuous is, therefore, not based on the usual contrasts of societal complexity and structural differentiation, since these contrasts can, in his opinion, occlude the dynamic nature of distinctively modern institutions. Even so, Giddens's argument that Marx underestimated the discontinuity of capitalist modernity is highly contentious and possibly draws its strongest justification from the twentieth-century experience of the problems of superseding capitalism. He does not, as would be plainly idiosyncratic, suggest that Marx obscured the dynamics of capitalism, but claims that Marx's contention that 'the potential for the construction of a socialist society' 'is from the beginning an immanent negative principle of the continued reproduction of capitalism itself' underestimated the capacity of capitalism for renewal and presents an erroneous image of historical closure when the dialectic of change is determined by a teleological pattern of development (Giddens 1981a, 233; 230–39).

A Structuration Theory of the Subject

The argument that it is necessary to unpack a number of the assumptions surrounding the concept of society has similar implications for the notion of the subject. Giddens largely accepts the post-structuralist demand for a decentring of the subject, but argues that this does not dispense with the necessity of an account of agency so much as it calls for its reformulation (Giddens 1984, 1–110; 1979, 9–130; 1987 73–108). The decentring of the subject is reinterpreted in the theory of structuration from the perspective of practice. Rather than deriving practice from subjectivity, Giddens suggests that practice precedes subjectivity, being the very means of the constitution of the subject. This constitution of the subject is inseparable from the duality of structure and connected through this to the system patterning of social relations and social interaction. On the one hand, this involves a consideration of the consequences of action which extend in time and space beyond the contexts of interaction and are not intended by the agent. On the other hand, the agent's knowledge, necessary for practically accomplishing the requirements of action, may in other respects be limited and these represent the 'unacknowledged conditions' of action'. For instance, the agent's unconscious sources of motivation and the dependence of action upon the results of previously unintended consequences.

These 'unacknowledged conditions' and 'unintended consequences' of action form the perimeters of a 'stratification model of the agent'. Action is conceived, as examined earlier, to be a *continuous flow of conduct and interaction* and, as such, is neither an accumulation of discrete acts, nor is its analysis identical with the philosophical interpretation of the intentionality of the subject. Accordingly, reflexive monitoring, rationalization and motivation which comprise the three stratification layers of the acting self are treated as 'embedded sets of processes'. Agents continuously reflexively monitor themselves and others with whom they interact, while maintaining a general awareness of the social and physical contexts of action. These contexts are not subsidiary to action, as Giddens's (1984, 34–47, 64–93, 110–139) extended discussion of regionalization, positioning and the body seeks to underline their constitutive significance. Rationalization consists of those reasons or grounds that individuals have about their activity. Reflexive monitoring and rationalization do not presuppose, nor should they be confused with, the capacity for discursively articulating reasons. Discursive articulation is an unusual form of action to the extent that it is often a consequence of the interrupting or problematizing of the flow of conduct. For the most part action consists of habitual doings which are only indirectly motivated. Exceptions to this usually derive from the nature of a particular situation and the explicit requirements of an action performance. This is where the motivational components of agency are likely to intrude upon action. Motivation then differs significantly, as it is considered to lie behind action and refers to the individual's potential for action and the wants that prompt action. There appear in this account two differing dimensions of motivation. The first is agents' overall plans, which have the character of long-term projects, and in their generality are distinguished from the particular reasons and capacities realized in conduct. Second, there are agents' unconscious sources of motivation which are impermeable to consciousness and discursive articulation.

Giddens stresses the *routinized* capacity to 'go on' displaying what is defined as 'practical consciousness'. The concept of practical consciousness is intended to capture the above range of skills and knowledge that are constantly involved in action, irrespective of whether the subject is capable of discursively articulating them. Despite acknowledged affinities with the Freudian concept of the preconscious, Giddens argues that the Freudian account of psychic structures too readily transposes those aspects of consciousness that are not amenable to discursive articulation into the domain of the unconscious. The praxiological premises of the stratification model of agency require an alternative demarcation of practical consciousness from the unconscious. The opacity of practical consciousness is precisely associated with the habituated familiarity of routines and the latter's role in diminishing the personality system's unconscious sources of anxiety. Practical consciousness is not restricted to individuals' self-consciousness, as it includes those expectations and assumptions mutually held and realized by agents in interaction. The third domain of psychic organization is the consciousness of social conditions and actions that the subject can discursively formulate. Between discursive and practical consciousness there is not the rigid barrier of repression that differentiates the unconscious.

These three dimensions of the psychic organization of the individual are specified through a selective incorporation of the insights of Freudian and ego psychology. Yet, what is most distinctive about Giddens's assimilation of these approaches is that their interpretations of the personality system of the subject are clarified in relation to the writings of ethno-methodologists and Goffman on the theme of the dissonance associated with the unsettling of the routine continuities of mundane practices (Garfinkel 1967; Goffman 1971). This clarification leads him to integrate the account of agency with the proposed model of psychic organization on the basis of an interpretation of the *self as a basic security system*, revealing also the importance of routinized practices. Routine practices provide the subject with ontological security, through the containment and diminution of unconscious sources of anxiety, and the reduction of the degree of contingency that would otherwise intolerably pervade all action. This stratification model of agency is then complemented by the connections Giddens makes between the individual's acquisition of an integrated self and its psychogenetic development. Based upon the analytical investigations of early childhood in the writings of Erikson and Winnicott, he finds that one crucial aspect of this development is the capacity to deal with the anxiety associated with circumstances of non-presence from, or absence of, significant others. Giddens's reinterpretation of social order, founded upon the ontological supposition that time and space are elemental constituents of social life, and the reproduction of systems mediating presence and absence which generate social form, then finds a certain resonance in the manner he sought to theorize ontogeny.

The infant's earliest experience of absence congeals, in an obviously inchoate form, something like the subsequent insecurities the individual confronts in its practical involvement in a decentred world. For this reason, the psychic capacities of emotionally defusing anxieties at this early stage represents the nucleus of those aspects of practical consciousness which make possible and renew the individual's feelings of ontological security. Giddens strongly underlines the capacity of practical consciousness to 'bracket' the range of potentially infinite facets of a decentred reality that could disrupt even the most trivial everyday action. By labelling this capacity 'bracketing', he sought in effect to extend a methodological principle of Husserl's phenomenological inquiry into an operative feature of all behaviour. He justifies this modification on the grounds that anxiety is intimately related to the principle constitutive of agency: that things could be otherwise. Bracketing is imperceptibly enacted in the routine continuity of practice, its major source of support being the very regularity of social reproduction, but anxiety is never completely stilled. Anxiety derives from action always also involving the individual's taken for granted 'capacity – and, indeed, necessity – for' projecting possibilities 'ahead' of the present and to anticipate these future potentialities counterfactually in thought (Giddens 1991a, 147).[4]

---

4   I have already mentioned the philosophical influence of Heidegger and Husserl upon Giddens's conceptualization of action, but it is also worth remarking upon how much of this analysis was anticipated by Schutz (1967) in his *The Phenomenology of the Social World*. In this context, see especially section 9 of chapter 2: 'The Concept of Action. Project and Protention' and the concluding paragraph of this section begins: 'We have traced back the analysis of action to the projection of the act in the future perfect tense. From this can be deduced with complete necessity the concept of the unity of the action. The unity of the action is constituted by the fact that the act already exists "in project", which will be realized step by step through the action. *The unity of the act is a function of the span or breadth of the project'* (Schutz 1967; 62).

This connection explicates how practice intersects with the generic existential uncertainties of the human condition. Given that Giddens usually views these uncertainties as addressed 'fundamentally on the level of behaviour', unhinging this epoché would have appreciable consequences (Giddens 1991a, 48). It poses existential questions of the type he surveys under the headings of: the individual's concern with the world of being in general, the finitude of one's own life, relations to other persons, and finally that of self-identity (Giddens 1991a). In each case, being explicitly fixated upon indefinite distressing potential eventualities, can ultimately lead to anxieties that paralyze action. Existential uncertainties can here take a form that is psychologically debilitating for the individual. Giddens finds Laing's (1965) interpretation of schizophrenia relevant to this analysis; he employs Laing's account of ontological insecurity quite broadly, for instance, to illuminate the sources of nationalism in the modern world (Giddens 1991a; 1981a). He argues that the disabling of the creative transformative capacity of action is fairly clearly shown by certain features typical of neuroses, like the compulsion to repeat fixed routines and the collapsing of the agent's own horizon of action. These behavioural patterns have a far smaller compass than that of everyday action, but the affinities that they exhibit to it, in their being highly repetitive, suggest symptom formation can be a way by which individuals seek to restore in another form their lost sense of the ontological reality of the world. In this sense, by mediating their experience of anxiety, symptoms are for these individuals an equivalent to the bracketing generally instaurated by practical consciousness. Consequently, this interpretation of psychic conflict suggests that symptoms are not necessarily the result of prior repression, but, in line with Giddens's stratification proposal, originate as defensive substitutes for an initially unconscious anxiety. According to him, anxiety 'is essentially fear which has lost its object through unconsciously formed emotive tensions that express "internal dangers" rather than externalized threats' (Giddens 1991a, 44). In his view, the model of the modality of psychic agency that derives anxiety from repression should be reversed. It is unconscious anxiety that creates 'repression, and the behavioural symptoms associated with it' (Giddens 1991a, 44).

The capacity of practical consciousness for bracketing anxiety, however, depends upon the prior formation of *basic trust*. Trust is founded upon the infant's 'sense of confidence' in the reliability of the other and its 'awakening of a sense that absence does not signify desertion' (Giddens 1984, 34; 1991a). Basic trust is originally unconscious, but the sort of 'emotional inoculation' that it provides against the strain and tension of absence cannot be produced by the individual monad alone. Rather, basic trust derives from the 'unconscious', implicit sociality contained within the intersubjective relationship between the infant and its caretaker. Not only does this sociality chronologically precede the child's recognizing the differentiation between the other and its own self but it gives initial shape to the relationship even before this recognition becomes self-conscious. By blending togetherness and separation through the time-space structuring of interaction, this relationship between infant and caretaker creates the 'virtual' in-between and 'unconscious' space filled by basic trust. In particular, it shapes the originally corporeal and affective sources of the infant's later distinctively cognitive construction of differentiations. First, this is due to the infant's relationship to its caretaker being heavily mediated through the demands and pleasures of its body. At this initial stage, cognition is in no sense independent of 'bodily' experience, but, at the same stage, the infant does not yet possess a conscious outline of its body and an awareness of the substantive contours of its own boundaries. Second, Giddens proposes, after Winnicott (1971), that the 'potential space' between the child and its caretaker comes to be bridged by 'transitional objects'. These objects first enable the infant to apprehend in a mediated fashion entities that are apart from its own being. Significantly, the tension and uncertainty generated by separations are ameliorated to a degree by these objects and the 'routinized' or 'ritualized' contexts of the experience of uncertainty.

This containing of anxiety, however, depends on the infant's having partially transferred some of the affective qualities associated with basic trust onto external objects it can manipulate without being able to control at will. Grafted upon its earliest trust and quite unlike conscious certainty, the child acquires 'faith' in the ontological stability and depth of what has still to be subject to 'reality testing' proper in the Freudian sense (Freud 1984). This attenuated surety constitutes the psychical underpinnings for the infant to have sufficient confidence to 'go on', and by proceeding qualitative developmental changes occur in the infant. It will lead later to the child's recognizing differentiations in the world, but, above all, this early form of affective trust forms the basis of the infant's capacity to cope with the sense of fragility this recognition entails. The child's confidence in its later cognitive achievements remains psychodynamically conditional upon trust and the underlying diffuse experience of ontological security.

This stress on the practical constituting of subjectivity and the internal structure of interaction results in an inversion of two basic psychological assumptions of developmental progression deriving from the philosophy of consciousness. Neither of these revisions is particularly distinctive, nor original to Giddens's perspective, both are widely represented in recent literature. On the one hand, because self-consciousness emerges through bodily differentiations, the child does not first learn that she has a body from self-conscious reflection. Experiences of bodily differentiation largely emerge out 'of its practical engagement with the object-world and other people' (Giddens 1991a, 56). On the other hand, self-consciousness 'has no primacy over the awareness of others, since language – which is intrinsically public – is the means of access to both. Intersubjectivity does not derive from subjectivity, but the other way around' (Giddens 1991a, 51). In agreement with Habermas, this means the emergence of the self-identity of subjectivity is dependent upon the child's acquisition of a social identity. For it is anchored in the capacity to use personal pronouns, and this occurs by way of differentiating persons and things other than herself. The discursive employment of I and Me over time and circumstances 'is the most elemental feature of reflexive conceptions of personhood' (Giddens 1991a, 53). If this process is taken to be completely infra-linguistic then it does not fully define, in Giddens's opinion, the sense and experience of the self-awareness of the initial emergence of self-identity, or all conditions of its persistence over time. This initiating process itself depends upon the, prior to language, unsocialized part of the individual attaching itself to the linguistic signification of an I. In order to distinguish his own account centred on practical consciousness, Giddens comes close to mistakenly ascribing to Mead a view of linguistic competence as exhaustively defining self-identity and unjustifiably criticizing him for ignoring the unsocialized segments of the psyche (Giddens

1991a, 53). This very criticism can be turned around and rebounds on Giddens's own model of the subject.

The notion of an autonomous subject in Giddens's writings consists of individuals' increasing control over the *constitution of their identity*. It is realized through the full range of the agent's practices and interactions. This presupposes the subject's reflexive awareness of the overall motivational projects that lie behind concrete instances of practice and a certain degree of control over the unconscious sources of anxiety necessary for the securing of an integrated self. However, autonomy is not confined to the internal dimensions of subjectivity, which would be a meaningless distinction from the perspective of the theory of structuration. Beside very exceptional circumstances, agency means there are always alternative courses of action and that a 'dialectic of control' is operative in all social interaction. Autonomy then requires altering the balance between the constraining and enabling aspects of structure. This proposition supplies the lines along which the emancipatory transformation of enduring systems of social relations of domination and exploitation would, according to Giddens, be pursued as a process of structuration. For instance, he contends, that a programme of 'positive welfare' today would seek to foster *the autotelic self.*

> The autotelic self is one with an inner confidence which comes from self-respect, and one where a sense of ontological security, originating in basic trust, allows for the positive appreciation of social difference. It refers to a person able to translate potential threats into rewarding challenges, someone who is able to turn entropy into a consistent flow of experience. The autotelic self does not seek to neutralize risk or to suppose that 'someone else will take care of the problem'; risk is confronted as the active challenge which generates self-actualization. (Giddens 1994a, 192)

Conclusion

It has been argued that Giddens's theory of structuration has sought to overcome a number of traditional sociological dichotomies and that the category of practice is integral to this theory's perspective and synthetic orientation. In fact, this practical standpoint is originally formulated as a social ontology that is intended to clarify the elemental conditions of the constitution and reproduction of social life. Even though there are many highly significant overlaps in their social theories, Giddens's intention of reworking the perspective of the philosophy of praxis contrasts with Habermas's assessment of the exhaustion of praxis philosophy. Like Habermas, Giddens opposes Marx's conceptions of the primacy of material production, but he seeks to develop the more general sense of the productive character of practice. It leads to his ontological notion of the integrity of agency and power, as well as to his attempt to explicate the dynamic character of the processes of structuration. This explication focuses on the enactment of practices and the temporal and spatial configuring of social processes. Similarly, this perspective on social life informs the structuration theory notion of the individual subject and its foregrounding of its practical formation. Notably, the theory of structuration highlights the role of practical consciousness relative to the more specific conditions of applying discursive consciousness. Giddens argues that a sense of security is provided by routine and regularized action. Yet, he later argues that the risks and accelerated character of contemporary modernization intensifies individuals' experience of potential ontological insecurity.

The various concepts that comprise the theory of structuration constitute a distinctive means of approaching the nexus between the subject and history. Giddens contends that processes of structuration generate radically different constitutions of the social. As a consequence, historical projects are not framed in relation to an invariant problem. While Giddens's proposed ontology of social life is meant to have general application and is, so to speak, open to different substantiations, it does appear heavily tailored to the dynamic character of modern societies, particularly the sense of change in the process of reproduction. In large part, as the later analysis shows, Giddens's perspective on historical processes centres on clarifying the transition to the reflexive character of modern social systems and the acceleration of change that results from it. Similarly, Giddens defines agency in terms of transformative capacity. However, his notion that structure is always simultaneously constraining and enabling has been subject to extensive criticism (see Thompson 2001; Stones 2005). In some contexts, this claim may appear misleading, since the labour market is hardly enabling to those excluded from it. Still, this criticism may overlook how differentials in enablement generate modifications in practices and the dialectic of control that is present in contexts of social interaction.

The centrality of power to Giddens's perspective contrasts with Habermas's accentuation of the normative quality of the intersubjective formation of identity and the significance of cultural rationalization to modernity and historical evolution in general. The next section on these respective critical theories of history and their accounts of the institutionalization of modernity explores the implications of these contrasting orientations and the ensuing redefinitions of their programmes.

Part II

INSTITUTIONALIZING MODERNITY: DEVELOPMENT AND DISCONTINUITY

Chapter Three

HABERMAS ON THE INSTITUTIONALIZING OF MODERNITY: COMMUNICATIVE RATIONALITY, LIFEWORLD AND SYSTEM

Introduction

Habermas defines modernity as a project that is incomplete, rather than as a phase of development that has been superseded by postmodernity (Habermas 1996d; 1984; 1987b). The project of modernity seeks to realize the ideals of universal emancipation, autonomy, authenticity and social progress. In his opinion, the project of modernity is based on rationality and it finds expression in different spheres of society. It is not limited to the instrumental and functionalist rationalization of the capitalist economy and the state's bureaucratic administrative system, rather it also occurs by way of communicative rationality in the spheres of science, art, and morality, as well as the broader interpersonal relations and social interaction of individuals' lifeworld. Habermas's change to the paradigm of communication is then supposed to both enable a proper appreciation of the potential of modernity's cultural rationalization and overcome the difficulties that he believes bedevilled the Frankfurt School's critique of instrumental reason. The project of modernity derives from the critique of religious and metaphysical belief system's totalizing character, while at the same time depending on individual and collective learning processes that integrate the rationalization of the differentiated spheres of value:

> The project of modernity as it was formulated by the philosophers of the Enlightenment in the eighteenth century consists in the relentless development of the objectivating sciences, of the universalistic foundations of morality and law, and of autonomous art, all in accord with their own immanent logic. But it at the same time also results in releasing the cognitive potentials accumulated in the processes from their esoteric high forms and attempting to apply them in the sphere of praxis, that is, to encourage the rational organization of social relations. (Habermas 1996d, 45)

One of the things to state about the project of modernity is that a loss of commitment to the project means the end of it. Habermas's intention is precisely to demonstrate that the project of modernity is binding upon modern individuals and that the price of renouncing the normative commitments of the modernist project is regression, both at the level of the modern individual and the social collective. In this sense, he seeks to show that postmodernist ambivalence is a symptom of a decline in the project of modernity and a position that fails to appreciate the full implications of wavering. Habermas perceived parallels between postmodernism and the counter-enlightenment positions that developed in Germany between the twentieth century's two world wars. He similarly remarked on the dangers of renouncing the value of rationality and the institutions of liberal democracy that had, however inadequately, sought to realize elements of the project of modernity. Notably, he pointed to West German anticapitalist terrorism in the 1970s and the state's reaction to it as part of the background motivations for his complex defence of rationality in *The Theory of Communicative Action* (Habermas 1986; 1984a; 1987a). Habermas believes that the delineation of communicative reason counters the totalizing critiques of reason to be found in segments of the ecological and counter-cultural movements. The 'Preface' to *The Theory of Communicative Action* explains this in the following terms:

> When this opposition sharpens into a demand for de-differentiation at whatever price, an important distinction is lost. Restricting the growth of monetary-administrative complexity is by no means synonamous with surrendering modern forms of life. In structurally differentiated lifeworlds a potential for reason is marked out that cannot be conceptualized as a heightening of system complexity. (Habermas 1984, xlii)

Giddens's position on the project of modernity is more equivocal. He certainly endorses the values of the project of modernity but for a number of reasons he does not accept the notion of an overarching project. Giddens rejects a teleological view of history and the notion of project can imply too strong a sense of direction. It has parallels with Marx's comment about humanity setting itself problems that it solves, which Giddens regularly refers to in order to illustrate the approach to history that he contests (Giddens 1979; 1981 Marx 1970). He argues that projects are an inevitable and necessary feature of human agency, as well as something that characterizes modern social movements and organizations. In this sense, it is possible for the project of modernity to be consciously assumed by dimensions of society. Modernity entails, in Giddens's view, a much greater consciousness of historicity; the use of history to make history is pervasive in modernity. In particular, Giddens contends that modernity is shaped by the view that future history is open rather than bound to repeat the past. Nevertheless, his position is that modernity is 'double-edged'; modernity generates opportunities and threats, forms of emancipation and domination (Giddens 1990, see Wagner 1994).

The unfolding of modernity, Giddens argues, has created a greater sense of contingency and the current phase of modernization has led to the undermining of some of former assumptions about the trajectory of modernity. The most conspicuous features of this change in outlooks with the radicalizing of modernity are, according to him, 'the *dissolution of evolutionism*, the *disappearance of historical teleology*, the recognition of *thoroughgoing, constitutive reflexivity*, together with the *evaporating of the privileged position of the West*' (Giddens 1990, 52–53). This assessment represents an extrapolation from the themes of Giddens's general approach to historical change. It certainly contrasts with some of the connotations of Habermas's position, yet the implication that Habermas may neglect some of the trends that underlie these considerations is contentious. Habermas, rather, seeks to think-through some of these considerations in a manner that upholds the project of modernity.

Habermas's endorsement of the project of modernity reflected a shift away from substantive images of social-historical transition and emancipation, such as that of socialism as defined by collective ownership of private property. With some exceptions, this tendency of not formulating a substantive image of a just social order would become even more pronounced in Habermas's work. This partly owes to the immanent logic of Habermas's discourse theory and the complications of substantive changes in modern societies, from the collapse of state socialism to the growth in cultural diversity. One of the justifications that Habermas gave for proposing a theory of social evolution was that it enables practical discourses to adjudicate between scenarios about progressive transitions. It does this primarily through evolutionary theory's disclosure of the logic of development.

It has been noted already that Habermas's and Giddens's general theoretical approaches to history are more significant than their reconstructions of substantive history, since many of the developments associated with the institution of modernity that they detail are broadly accepted, like the greater separation of the market from political authority with the consolidation capitalism and the tendencies that Max Weber defined as the disenchantment of religious and metaphysical belief systems with the expansion of scientific and technical rationality (Weber 1958a; 1958b; 1958c). For this reason, this chapter equally explores the underpinning suppositions of Habermas's conception of modernization. These suppositions derive from earlier theoretical revisions and those positions outlined in his 'reconstruction of historical materialism' (Habermas 1979a). Similarly, Habermas sought to incorporate into his theory advances in philosophy and the social sciences, one of the implications of which is a critical distancing from praxis philosophy. Moreover, Habermas's theory of modernity is intended to enable a diagnosis of the contemporary social pathologies of capitalist societies and the emerging conflicts of welfare state mass democracies. All of these considerations make Habermas's theory enormously significant and a point of reference for any discussion about the prospects of modernity, irrespective of the specific deficiencies and limitations that can be identified in its formulation.

Habermas's Theorizing of History: Competences and Development

Almost from the outset, Habermas's appreciation of the significance of intersubjective communication moderated his version of Hegelian-Marxist social theory. He considers that an intersubjective notion of the historical subject can be derived from Hegel's *Jena* sketches of the struggle for recognition (Habermas 1974a). These *Jena* sketches of labour and interaction intimate at a possible 'materialist phenomenology of mind', as Spirit was conceived as constituted through the practical media serving to interrelate subjects. Habermas (1974a, 161–66), however, criticizes Hegel for superimposing the conceptual figures of alienation and appropriation, drawn from the externalization and objectification model of the subject, upon the genuinely intersubjective categories of the *Jena* system of separation and reconciliation. Habermas ultimately considers that the tensions between the intersubjective structure of language and the 'idealistic' motif of the reflection of a unitary collective subject are irreconcilable. He resolved these tensions in favour of the former, a conclusion with considerable consequences for his theory of modernity.

Although Habermas delimited the Hegelian conception in rejecting any reconciliation with nature, he had previously, as Honneth and Joas state, 'understood history as a universal process in which the human species constitutes itself as the subject of world history in instrumental and interactive education processes' (Honneth and Joas 1988, 158). The critique of the idea of unitary collective subject is decisive for his criticisms of praxis philosophy and it applies to aspects of his earlier theory of knowledge constitutive interests (Habermas 1987b; 1978a). Despite various retractions, Habermas (1979a; 1984a) seeks to formulate a conceptual intersection that is equivalent to that between the subject and history. In his theory, a linkage between individual competences and social development is meant to supersede the earlier praxis philosophical understanding of the social nexus. This alternate linkage involves a substantial change in the categories of the subject and history. It potentially diminishes distinctive features of the praxis philosophy approach to the autonomous constitution of society. Moreover, it lays the groundwork for a different approach to the 'project of modernity' and its justification.

The change Habermas makes to the combination of individuals' competences and social development challenges the position of the subject and history as key organizing categories of Critical Theory. The two primary frameworks Habermas draws upon in reformulating the nexus of the subject and history are the formal pragmatic theory of linguistic communication and systems theory. Each of them involves a decentring of the subject and history, both separately and in their interconnection.

There is a long-standing tension within the Marxist tradition between determinist theories of social evolution and accounts of the transformative power of subjects. These typical contrasts may not apply to Habermas's approach to history and social change, yet neither are this contrast's issues entirely irrelevant to it. Habermas's reconstruction of historical materialism has been subjected to detailed and sustained criticism, but these critiques are not always centred on his core problem of the mediation of the universal and the particular (see Strydom1992; Schmidt 1982; Giddens 1982b; Rockmore 1989). Habermas's explication of long-term social change is largely consistent with Hegel's contention that a universalistic stage of consciousness is achieved through the surpassing of preceding stages (Hegel 1977; Habermas 1979a). Unlike his earlier retention of Hegel's dynamic phenomenological sense of the historical process in the programme of 'knowledge constitutive interests', Habermas's reconstruction of historical materialism entailed a rather rigid and inflexible conception of social evolution. The dynamic quality of historical change is restored in his theory of communicative rationalization and the differentiation of 'systems' from the lifeworld (Habermas 1984; 1987a). However, the basic pattern and direction of change remain the same and it defines the 'project of modernity'.

This is a quite different perspective to the praxis philosophical vision of the contestation that originally enabled the modernist vision of an autonomous constitution of society and that is a condition of its further realization. The social conflicts of the struggles opposing domination have a more ancillary status in Habermas's conceptions of communicative rationalization and social evolution (see Honneth 1991; Honneth and Joas 1988; Arnason 1991b). This difference from praxis philosophy is apparent in Habermas's elaboration of a theory of communicative competence taking precedence over the formerly central methodology of the critique of ideology (Habermas 1970b; 1979a; McCarthy 1978). The critique of ideology contests domination and ideological denials of conflict, whereas a theory of communicative competence is closer to the format of 'traditional theory'. It establishes a general truth that is not conditional on future transformative practices (see Jay 1984, 481, 494–97). Habermas argues that the normative foundations of critique need to be revised and this formed part of the justification for the construction of a theory of communicative competence (Habermas 1970b; 1979a). Habermas was explicitly moving away from the Hegelian-Marxist model of 'immanent critique', with its residual ties to the suppositions of the philosophy of history (see Browne 2008).

Habermas claims that the 'cynicism' of current bourgeois consciousness undermines the contrast that the immanent critique of ideology drew between 'what men and things could be and what they actually are' (Habermas 1982, 231). He argues that the labour theory of value incorporated the 'normative core' of the natural law tradition's ideal of a fair exchange of equivalents. Its critique of exploitation was less dependent on a philosophy of history. The problem was that Marx had insufficiently explicated this normative derivation and, owing to the state's intervention into the market and developments in capitalist organization, the conditions that enable the labour theory of value to found a critical political economy no longer apply (Habermas 1982, 230–31). For these reasons, Habermas considers that critical theory needs to revise its normative foundations and he believes that this could be achieved through explicating the rational structure of communicative action.

From the standpoint of social theory, giving precedence to the problem of normative grounding is not without potential problems and drawbacks. In short, it means that the other theoretical revisions should be consistent with the normative principles that Habermas derives from processes of reaching mutual understanding (see Thompson 1981; 1982). Notably, this is evident in how the concepts of social action in Habermas's theory are tailored to the normative model of consensual agreement. The limitations of Habermas's later account of domination's can be partly traced to how this normative tailoring excludes a more nuanced conception of power. Habermas places social processes inconsistent with the normative principles of understanding in the realm of the system (Honneth 1991; Giddens 1982b). Similarly, this tailoring's effects can be seen in how his definition of social action excludes a range of practices and experiences, like those of creative and expressive forms of action (see Joas 1993; Habermas 1991; McCarthy 1984b). It leads to an elision of the difference between the process of action and the coordination of action (Joas 1993). Habermas naturally does not see it this way. He considers that such tailoring is a metatheoretical decision; it is not a choice at the disposition of subjects. Rather, the orientation of communicative action towards agreement is built into the structure of language (Habermas 1982, 227; 1979a, 177; 1994, 111).

The notion of the collective subject's formation had provided a sense of the continuity and direction of the historical processes. Similarly, the divisions of the subject could represent the conflicts in the historical constitution of potentials for autonomy. As a consequence, Habermas's break with this conception alters the place of history in his theory. He argues that the shift to the intersubjective structure of communication entails an opposition to the equation of the social with a singular subject and the totalizing conception of history that results from it, such as those of the philosophy of history. Habermas's employing systems theory categories to explicate supra-individual social developments is a more controversial change:

> Since the collective subject of a meaning-constituted lifeworld, which is borrowed from transcendental philosophy, proves to be misleading at least in sociology, the concept of system recommends itself to us. Social systems are units that can solve objectively problems by means of suprasubjective learning processes. (Habermas as quoted in Honneth and Joas 1988, 159)

Of particular significance, this theoretical modification can be attributed to the conclusions that Habermas drew in the course of his debate with the systems theorist Niklas Luhmann (Habermas 1976c; see Sixel 1976; Holub 1991; McCarthy 1978). In fact, his entire theory of modernity is heavily conditioned by the perceived need to respond to Luhmann's systems theory; yet, the manner in which this is undertaken undermines its intended purpose of a critique of functionalist reason and its institutional, as well as systems theory, expression. One can readily perceive, however, how Habermas's critique of praxis philosophy conception of the nexus of history and the subject was conditioned by some of the implications of Luhmann's theoretical revision of the preceding structural-functionalist conception of social systems and its rupture with action theory (Luhmann 1982; 1989; 1995).

The notion of differentiation has been central to structural-functionalist interpretations of historical change and modernity. Luhmann's reformulating of this notion accentuates how the development of social systems is a self-regulating process (Luhmann 1982; 1995). Social differentiation is not reducible to the originating activity of a constituting subject, rather the differentiation of social systems is conditioned by the interchange that they have with their environment. Systems may even be constitutive of subjects in some spheres, though systems are not at the disposition of subjects. Luhmann proposes that systems reduce the 'interchange' problem of complexity by regulating their internal composition. This involves processes of differentiating between inside and outside. There is no unifying centre to society that a collective subject could occupy and the problem of complexity overarches subjects. Habermas accepts the force of this systems theory critique of the subject. He rather contests what he takes to be the implications of Luhmann's version of this critique. In fact, his critical appropriation of systems theory overlooks some of the arguments of his original critique of systems theory, such as that it replicates the explanatory deficiencies of functionalism (see Habermas 1976c; 1988a; 1984a; 1987a). Now, this oversight is one of the reasons for exploring Giddens's theory of structuration and its objective of a more consistently anti-functionalist theory. As noted already, Habermas believed that Luhmann's systems theory articulated the technocratic ideology of contemporary capitalism in much the same way that Marx considered that nineteenth-century political economy did at that time.

Axel Honneth (1991) argues that the Habermas's early work contains two competing versions of critique. One founded on the idea of moral development being driven by the struggle of subordinate groups against social relations of domination. Hegel's (1979; 1986) concept of the struggle for recognition inspired this version of critique and it is the one that Honneth (1995) has subsequently sought to develop. Habermas's supplementing labour with the intersubjective dimension of moral interaction parallels Hegel's theory (Habermas 1978a; 1978b). The second version of critique derives from the critique of technocracy and it is this version that prevails. Habermas's readiness to incorporate systems theory categories owes to his acceptance of the social-historical diagnosis of the technocracy thesis. His position differs from systems theory's proponents in its considering that it represents an emergent technocratic domination. Honneth claims that the contention that systems of purposive-rational action are increasingly self-determining conditions Habermas's theorizing social conflicts and conceptualizing the pathologies of 'sub-system's' colonization of the lifeworld (Habermas 1987a).

> Thus the same process that the technocracy thesis describes affirmatively is presented as a process of the draining off of communicatively achieved relations of life through purposive-rationally determined action accomplishments, through a 'dominance of technology'. Habermas' theory is so deeply shaped by this experience that it appears in the background of all other crisis phenomena and current problems. (Honneth 1991, 266)

In Habermas's opinion, the intersubjective formation of identity through language constitutes a social process that cannot be adequately explained by systems theory. His increasing appreciation of the intersubjective structure of language influenced his critical movement away from notions of a collective subject and the substituting of the intersection of individual competences and historical development for the praxis philosophy conception of the social nexus. This reformulation presupposes a precise delineation of the contrast between systematic inquiries into linguistic competences and the hermeneutic concern with communicative experience (Habermas 1988b). Further, this contrast basically overlaps the distinction between reconstruction and the reflection of the subject on of its formation that Habermas only became properly aware of after his early programme of the practical interests guiding forms of knowledge (Habermas 1978a). A reconstruction of linguistic competences is not limited to the hermeneutic explication of meaning; it is a type of inquiry that is instead concerned with the underlying rules of linguistic communication. These rules are universal in being followed by all linguistically competent subjects. The methodology of rational reconstruction is therefore somewhat similar to a transcendental analysis of universal and necessary presuppositions. A rational reconstruction explicates the necessary and general requirements of communication, rather that the contingent and circumstantial conditions of acts of communication.

Despite rational reconstruction's significant and innovative qualities, Habermas's attempt to make claims equivalent to a transcendental analysis is one source of the problems that his approach has with respect to history and the unfolding of modernity. It is by these means that Habermas seeks to demonstrate the mutually reinforcing processes of historical development and the formation of individual competences. This conception of interconnection is constitutive of a social nexus that can only be rationalized. The 'social' can be reconfigured but not fundamentally reconstituted with respect to its underlying logic. Habermas depicts a process of historical development that eventuates in the communicative constitution of social relations becoming increasingly transparent and subject to the universalistic principles of discourse in modernity. This is really the only sense in which his later theory can conceive of the social nexus becoming open to the possibility of being creatively redefined. In fact, Habermas's privileging of the logic of historical development, derived from rational reconstruction, over the dynamics of historical development reinforces this tendency to limit possible alternatives.

The reconstruction of the connection between individual competences and social development amounts to a change from the praxis philosophy problem of conceiving the social as arising from the intersection of history and the subject to something equivalent to, what Hennis describes, as Max Weber's methodological tenet of interrelating 'personality and life orders' (Hennis 1988). There are far reaching implications of a Weber-inspired formulation displacing the praxis philosophy approach to the social, besides simply the difference between the interests in the classification of types rather than a concern with the dynamic processes of social constitution. In my opinion, three specific implications of this position are consistent with deficiencies that have been recognized by critics.

First, according to Strydom (1993; 1992), it leads to the problem Klaus Eder illuminates of the learning processes that lead to social rationalization appearing individualistic, despite learning being generated in the communicative practices of social interaction. Eder puts forward the intrinsically social alternative of the forms of collective learning processes engendered by association and cooperation, and such learning occurs in connection with the struggles of social movements (Strydom 1993; Eder 1992). This alternative approach, which sustains a greater continuity with the praxis philosophy problem of the nexus between the subject and history, has been expanded upon in the work of Jose Maurício Domingues on modernity and collective subjectivity (Domingues 1996; 2000; 2006; 2012).

Second, an almost inevitable outcome of Habermas's approach is that the weight of the category of the social shifts from collective forms to the interactions of individual subjects. In *The Theory of Communicative Action*, Habermas (1987b, 43–152) does indeed depict a general historical movement from supra-individual symbolic and ritualistic modes of social integration to those taking the properly intersubjective form of communicative action. Ironically, despite Habermas's later grounding of his theory in the reciprocal relationship of the lifeworld and communicative action, this formulation effectively extends the sociological scope of systems theoretical analysis. The outcome of this development is an increase in the contingency of interaction and greater effort is necessary to overcome the probability of disagreement. In other words, it exposes the limitations of communicative action as a mechanism of coordination and implies that media of system integration are by definition appropriate for complex social relations.

Third, according to Arnason (1979; 1991b), the trajectory of Habermas's project is one of increasing historical closure; it results in the depiction of a rather rigid and inflexible pattern of rationalization. This social-historical closure is finalized in the theory of communicative action's reworking of Weber's theory of the rationalization of modern society (Habermas 1984a). Arnason argues that Habermas's theory of evolution already precludes alternative developments: 'The internal history of the mind is devoid of creativity. It is restricted to the clarification and rationalization of its original context, i.e., the natural and social correlates of action' (Arnason 1979, 217). Arnason proposes that modernity should be conceived of less as a project and more as a 'field of tensions' (Arnason 1991b). The openness this implies to the different trajectories of modernization and how conflicts condition their institution leads to Arnason's subsequent development, along with S. N. Eisenstadt, of the approach of multiple modernities. It is worth noting that these proposals concerning the multiplication of modernity derive from different interpretations of the implications of Weber's comparative historical sociology to that of Habermas. The sense in which the multiple modernities perspective constitutes a reconsideration of the forms of the relation of the subject and history will be returned to in the 'Conclusion'.

This assessment of the problems underlying Habermas's theory of modernity needs to be counterbalanced by an appreciation of the considerable accomplishments of his account of the communicative rationalization of the lifeworld (Habermas 1984a; 1987a). His theory of communicative action presupposes the historical occurrence of this process of rationalization, since this enables its basic features to be discerned. Habermas argues that it is the contemporary threat to communication, in the form of the 'inner colonization of the lifeworld', that promotes a genuine recognition of communicative action. Habermas compares this aspect of his theory to Marx's claim that it is the 'abstraction' of capitalist production that made historically 'true in practice' the supposition that labour is a universal feature of the reproduction of the species and that this abstraction enabled Adam Smith to perceive that labour is the source of the creation of value (Habermas 1987a, 402–3).

Despite the failings of Habermas's explication of the thesis of the colonization of the lifeworld, it is without a doubt a substantial explanation of critical developments that take the form of a threat to identity (Habermas 1987a, 355). Indeed, if the colonization thesis is situated alongside the undoubtedly brilliant and compellingly elaborated thesis of the communicative rationalization of the lifeworld then it is clear why Habermas's critical theory is the only real alternative of comparable stature to Marx's original. And yet, the paradigm differences are perhaps less significant than the incommensurate approaches to history. In the case of Habermas's theory, a quasi-functionalist notion of pathologies resulting from a diversion from the normal pattern of development replaces the dialectical reasoning of Marx's critique of the social contradictions of capitalist production. Habermas's entire argument depends upon the modernization of society eventuating in a historical shift from the progressive 'mediatization' of the lifeworld by law and the system coordinating media of money and power to that of its 'inner colonization' by these media, with destructive consequences for the communicative infrastructure of society (Habermas 1987a). This development is presented as paradoxical, because the communicative rationalization of the lifeworld first makes possible the differentiation and increasing independence of social systems. The autonomy of systems is the source of the 'abstraction' that gives rise to contemporary pathologies, through systemic steering media encroaching into domains of the symbolic reproduction of the lifeworld.

This dialectic of system and lifeworld not only contains substantial analytical problems, but it is broadly situated within a theory of evolution that is open to criticisms. Basically, a number of the questionable features of Habermas's *reconstruction of historical materialism* are retained in the theory of communicative action, like the distinction between the logic of development and developmental dynamics, the basic assumption of a correspondence between individual competences and social evolution, the distinction between formal structures and concrete forms of life. These are modified through their application to questions that had been less prominent. Habermas aims to show that cultural rationalization was the 'pacemaker' in the process of rationalization leading to 'modernity'. In the theory of communicative action, this argument proceeds through an explication of Weber's interpretation of the role that ethical conduct played in the development of capitalism (Habermas 1984a; 1987a). In other words, social modernization was dependent upon an initial process of cultural modernization. Habermas contrasts the broader potential of cultural modernity to that of the one-dimensional course of social modernization. He uses this argument as the basis of a critique of contemporary society for not making full use of the learning potential already available. Nevertheless, the difference from Marx cannot be more explicitly stated by Habermas than in his comment that the theory of communicative action's reconstruction of rationality is initially 'unhistorical' (Habermas 1987a, 383; 1982; see Best 1995).

Communicative Rationalization

Habermas's reconstruction of the process of social-historical rationalization depends on his reinterpretation of action theory. In his opinion, Weber (1930; 1958a; 1958b; 1958c) failed to adequately conceptualize the breadth of the process of cultural rationalization that he outlined. Weber's analysis of rationality focussed on the solitary, monological subject and purposive-rational action orientated to success. Habermas believes that Weber's account of the ethical conduct that facilitated rationalization contains a basis for revising Weber's interpretation of modernity. In other words, Weber's analysis of cultural rationalization is more complex than the typology of action that informed his theory of rationality and evaluation of modernity. Habermas's account of the rationality of communicative action seeks to challenge Weber's assumption that 'at the level of the subsystems of economics, politics and law, interestingly enough, only the rationality aspects of purposive-rational, not of value-rational action is supposed to have structure forming effects' (Habermas 1979c, 191). According to Habermas, a reinterpretation of ethical conduct from the perspective of intersubjective communication reveals that the actual course of capitalist modernization, predominantly confined to the purposive rationalization of the subsystems of the economy and state-administration, was only one of the possible courses that modernity could have taken (Habermas 1984a).

Habermas effectively elucidates Weber's complex framework of cultural analysis, though this may be more fluid than Habermas's formal depiction of value-spheres of science, art and morality. Habermas's typology of action and account of rationalization are less convincing in their specification of how alternatives could have been realized as part of the historical process than in their detailing the exact opposite. That is, rationalization appears to demonstrate the historical restricting of alternatives and the displacing of the transformative dimension of action (see Arnason 1991b; Joas 1993; Alexander 1991). One of the basic dilemmas of Habermas's reinterpretation of the institutionalization of modernity is outlined in his comment that Weber's theory of action 'depicted the global process of rationalization as a tendency toward replacing communal social action *(Gemeinschaftshandeln)* with rationally regulated action *(Gesellschaftshandeln)*. But only if we differentiate *Gesellschaftshandeln* into action oriented to reaching understanding and action oriented to success can we conceive the communicative rationalization of everyday action and the formation of subsystems of purposive-rational economic action as *complementary* developments. Both reflect, it is true, the institutional embodiment of rationality complexes; but in other respects they are *counteracting* tendencies' (Habermas 1984a, 341).

According to Habermas, Weber's conception of rationally regulated action lacked the intersubjective perspective of communicative action. The sequels of this deficiency are found in Weber's value scepticism, legal positivism and general ambivalence concerning rationalization. By contrast, Habermas suggests that if Weber had traced rational agreement 'back to the moral-practical foundations of discursive will-formation' then 'it would have become clear in this context that action in society (*Gesellschaftshandeln*) is distinguished from action in community (*Gemeinschaftshandeln*) not through the purposive-rational action orientations of the participants, but through the higher, namely postconventional stage of moral-practical rationality' (Habermas 1984a, 284). Habermas attempts to justify, then, a complex and differentiated concept of communicative rationality. He proposes that the argumentative redemption of validity claims is the basis for innovative social learning and it represents a rationality and emancipatory potential set in the very structures of the reproduction of the human species. This theory of rationality functions as a normative basis for a critique that seeks to illuminate the selectivity and deformations characteristic of capitalist modernization (Habermas 1984a; 1987a).

Habermas's analysis of the pragmatics of communication is continuous with the perspective of praxis philosophy in its focus on the performative dimension, but his account of the actual processes of acting tends to be defined by other considerations. He is more interested in the implications of the constitution of action-types in relation to the distinction between three formal worlds: objective, social and subjective, the capacity of subjects to reflect upon the different structure of each action-type, and to, accordingly, coordinate their actions through the pragmatics of communication. In other words, his primary interest is in demonstrating that underlying each type of action is an aspect of communication that reflexively specifies it. Communication provides acting subjects with an initial unifying framework within which to act. The strength of this approach is its capacity to clarify the rationalizable potential of each type of action through the mode of argumentation associated with each of the three formal worlds. Its weakness is that in focussing on the differentiated structure of communication and the adoption of the appropriate attitude to the objective, subjective and social worlds, Habermas assimilates the actual acting process to its prerequisites, especially to the competences of individuals. It is these indirect determinants of action that tend to be foregrounded in his theory, rather than practical processes of action.

These dimensions of action underline how subjects' communicative competence involves utilizing capacities that extend beyond the ability to form grammatically correct speech acts. It presupposes the speaker's ability to successfully embed the relevant type of speech-act in relation to the world and the hearer's competence to adopt the appropriate attitude to the validity claim in order to decide whether to accept or reject it. From the formal-pragmatic reconstruction of communicative action, Habermas considers that 'non-naturalistic standards of normal, that is, undisturbed communication' can be obtained (Habermas 1984a, 139). For instance, the inability to consistently separate out these formal worlds and to adopt the appropriate attitude may indicate a foreshortened stage of maturational development and communication pathology. Habermas believes that the explication of the rational structure of communicative action can be utilized to identify an individual's speech pathology and serve as a counterfactual yardstick for recognizing the social deceptions ensuing from systematically distorted communication (Habermas 1979a; 1984a). The widespread capacity to differentiate these formal worlds is a result of the historical learning processes associated with the communicative rationalization of the lifeworld and not simply a matter of individuals' natural learning. This argument is fundamental to Habermas's attempt to correct Weber's theory of the rationalization of modern society and Weber's pessimistic conclusions about its future prospects (Habermas 1984a).

The concept of 'lifeworld' is intended to complement and supplement the notion of communicative action. Action oriented to understanding bonds subjects and coordinates subjects' actions through the reciprocal recognition of criticizable validity claims; it is internally connected to the reproduction of the lifeworld. Habermas's sociological analysis transforms the original phenomenological conception of the lifeworld by introducing the structural components of social institutions, culture and personality. Yet, he claims that his formal-pragmatics analysis leads to a distinct, though related, transcendental understanding of the lifeworld (Habermas 1991, 233). That is, consistent with the phenomenological notion, Habermas conceives of the lifeworld as the naively understood background horizon of consciousness, which is comprised of more or less diffuse unproblematic convictions. A subject's own lifeworld is invisible to herself, except as a particular horizon of relevance determined by the shifting definitions of concrete situations. It may become explicit as a need for agreement or criticism of suppositions arises. The lifeworld is simultaneously unreflectively known, yet beyond the compass of the formal attributes of explicit knowledge.

Habermas diverges from the philosophy of consciousness in asserting that the 'lifeworld owes this certainty to a social a.priori built into the intersubjectivity of mutual understanding in language' (Habermas 1987a, 131). A lifeworld contains both normative convictions and empathetic identifications with the feelings of others, whilst the rational bonding of communicatively achieved agreement assures subjects of the intersubjectivity of their lifeworld. The lifeworld is a substantial reservoir and 'bulwark' against the contingent possibility of disagreement and misunderstanding in everyday practices. A subject's lifeworld is a pretheoretical background of taken-for-granted assumptions that self-evidently represent the world as always already interpreted and implicitly understood (Habermas 1984a; 1987a).

The fundamental background knowledge that must tacitly supplement our knowledge of the acceptability conditions of linguistically standardised expressions if hearers are able to understand their literal meanings, has remarkable features. It is an implicit knowledge that cannot be represented in a finite number of propositions, it is a holistically structured knowledge, the basic elements of which intrinsically define one another; and it is a knowledge that does not stand at our disposition, in as much as we cannot make it conscious and place it in doubt as we please. (Habermas 1984a, 336)

Habermas's typology of action is partly organized by the lifeworld's framework of interpretation and the reflective structure of linguistic communication. He initially aims to correct Weber's interpretation of action through the paradigm change to the intersubjective perspective of communicative action oriented to mutual understanding (Habermas 1984a; Weber 1978). This change from the perspective of the individual actor enables Habermas to incorporate into his variegated model of action the implications of his formal-pragmatic analysis of communication and to redefine the category of rationality. There are two significant innovations that are made possible by the intersubjective paradigm of understanding: first, the complementary relationship of the lifeworld and communicative action transforms the phenomenological conception of the former and avoids the monological standpoint of most action theory. In a sense, the lifeworld is 'internal' to the subject but decentred in respect of the individual actor. It implies a notion of the social which is not anchored in the standpoint of the philosophy of the subject, but which does not deny the constituting activities of subjectivity:

A circular process comes into play between the lifeworld as the resource from which communicative action draws, and the lifeworld as the product of this action, in this process, no gap is left by the disappearance of the transcendental subject. (Habermas 1992a, 43)

The second innovation in relation to theories of action is connected to the different validity claims and the enumeration of the three 'world' model of the subjective, social and objective domains. Like the lifeworld, but distinct from it, the three worlds represent a 'system of reference' for communicative action and correspond to the adult subject's decentred cognition. Habermas claims that other theories of action either operate with a single objective world model, or the different world-relations remain implicit in their accounts of action without recognizing their constitutive significance. Habermas argues that the action concepts of social-scientific theories can be reduced to four analytically distinct types: teleological, dramaturgical, normative, and communicative. Teleological action most conforms to the orientation to success, even though two of the other three types of action may be connected to this orientation (Habermas 1984a, 84–102).

Instrumental action is teleological because the subject seeks to attain an end or bring about the occurrence of a desired state of affairs in the objective world by choosing means that appear likely to succeed in a given situation and applies them in an effective manner. The teleological type of action is expanded into the category of strategic action when the subject's calculations of success involve anticipating the choices made by at least one additional goal-directed actor. Habermas contends that both types of teleological action, however, presuppose only one objective world, though in strategic action the subject deals with other decision-making systems as well as physical objects. Dramaturgical action is oriented to the subjective world and refers to social interactions where participants encounter one another through constituting a visible public for one another. In presenting herself to a public, the actor seeks to evoke a certain impression and, in so doing, discloses a certain part of her subjectivity, such as through stylizing the expression of experience and by interacting in a way that steers access to subjectivities, conveying one's desires, feelings, thoughts, intentions and so on (Habermas 1984a, 86).

In the case of normatively regulated action, subjects are oriented to fulfilling or deviating from collectively shared norms that are recognized as valid. In complying with such generalized normative expectations of behaviour, subjects refer to the common social world. Habermas contends that valid norms represent an agreement that regulates the action of the members of a social group to whom it obtains (Habermas 1984a, 85). In his model, there is a closer affinity between normatively regulated action and communicative action than the other types. But communicative action is the broader category; it facilitates discourses over the norms that are applied and assesses their claim to validity. Communicative action refers to when at least two subjects capable of speech and action establish interpersonal relations through verbal or extra-verbal communication. It is through communicative action that subjects arrive at a common situation definition that admits of consensus and coordinate their plans of action by way of this intersubjective understanding. Communicative action has a more encompassing system of reference than the other three types of action.

> Only the communicative model of action presupposes language as a medium of uncurtailed communication whereby speakers and hearers, out of the context of their preinterpreted lifeworld, refer simultaneously to things in the objective, social and subjective worlds in order to negotiate common definitions of the situations. (Habermas 1984a, 95)

Habermas's reconstruction of communicative action is the starting point for a theory of communicative rationality. Like Weber's concepts of action, but from a different angle, Habermas's conception of action is strongly tailored to discerning the rationalization of modern society (Habermas 1984a, xli). Habermas's tendency to argue that communicative action has a coordinating function in relation to other orientations and his claim that the rationality of understanding is not a value-choice but intrinsic to communication seem to preclude alternatives based on the criteria of rationality. Further, it correlates rationality with the formal procedures that serve to coordinate social interaction (Habermas 1982, 227–28). These are some of the reasons why Arnason argues that the theory of communicative rationality eventuates in a closed and restricted understanding of action:

> To sum up, Habermas' specific approach to the problematic of social action begins with a far-reaching and emphatic reference to the constitutive role of meaning. The socially relevant patterns of meaning are not reducible to values and norms; rather, they must (as the concept of communicative action is meant to show) be analyzed as totalizing horizons of interpretation – not simply ways of making sense of society and its environment, but as differentiated world-perspectives. However, this broadened view of meaning is not used to underline the

diversity and openness of action. Instead, the argument shifts towards the construction of principles which impose limits and directions upon the variation of meaning as well as upon the corresponding patterns of action. These principles are then grounded in the reconstructive analysis of language. (Aranason 1991a, 73)

Habermas's notion that the social is split between the principles of sociation associated with the system and the lifeworld significantly contributes to this limiting view of action. Habermas accepts that the problems of coordination is a central concern of a theory of action, but proposes that the intersubjectivity of communicative action represents a properly social conception of action. It provides the grounds for a consistent and justified critique of strategic and monological models of action, as well as what Parsons's referred to as the 'voluntarist' interpretations of action (Parsons 1949). Habermas aims to extend and rectify Parsons's attempt to join the system and action paradigms in social theory. Parsons's delineation of the problem of order is the starting point of Habermas's determining the possibilities and limitations of coordination through communicative action: 'An interaction may be understood as the solution to the problem of how the action plans of several actors can be coordinated in such a way that the actions of Alter can be connected up with those of Ego' (Habermas 1998b, 221). In this respect, the intersubjectivity of the paradigm of understanding introduces a properly social definition of interaction and marks out the difference between it and the exchange that occurs when subjects only encounters an object. It represents a perspective, as Taylor (1991, 24) observes, that is opposed to any 'atomistic conception of society'.

This emphasis on the coordinating capacity of communication converges with Habermas's seminal intuition regarding the intersubjective constitution of social identity. In his opinion, communicative action is capable of coordinating interaction, because it is both an action type and an interpretation of action. However, the difficulty with this position is specified in Joas's comment that 'Habermas identifies in a misleading fashion a typology of action with the distinction among types of coordination of action' (Joas 1993, 133). Habermas's attempt to establish a linkage between the orientation to validity claims and argumentative discourses reinforces the merits of this criticism. Despite detrimentally affecting the distinction between system and lifeworld, the linkage between discourses and communicative action underpins what is probably the most compelling aspect of Habermas's reconceptualization of the philosophy of praxis problem of the intersection of the subject and history: the notion of the communicative rationalization of the lifeworld.

Habermas seeks to elaborate a comprehensive and differentiated concept of rationality. He wants to overcome the cognitive instrumentalist restriction of rationality to only either true propositions about states of affair or effective instrumental interventions in the (objective) world. He develops the concept of communicative rationality by way of a formal examination of the modes of argumentation that apply to different validity claims. The grounds or types of reasons involved changes in accordance with whether the validity claim relates to the objective, social, or subjective world. Habermas argues that the principles of argumentation enable innovative learning in the spheres of science, morality and art (Habermas 1984a). In other words, Habermas considers that there are four modes of argumentation and each is appropriate for treating one of the four problematic validity claims (Habermas 1984a, 8–42). Unlike the 'totalizing' conception of reason as emanating from a subject, Habermas does not seek to assimilate and unify these separate dimensions of reason. Rather, he defends the idea of balance and equilibrium between these formal determinants of rationality. The formal character of argumentative procedures alters the problem of rationality in such a way that it concerns whether one may systematically expect that subjects

> have good reasons for their expressions and that these expressions are correct or successful in the cognitive dimension, reliable or insightful in the moral-practical dimension, discerning or illuminating in the evaluative dimension, or candid or self-critical in the expressive dimension, that they exhibit understanding in the hermeneutic dimension; or 'indeed' whether they are 'reasonable' in all these dimensions. When there appears a systematic effect in these respects, across various domains of interaction and over long periods perhaps even over the space of a lifetime, we also speak of the rationality of a conduct of life. And in the socio-cultural conditions for such a life there is reflected perhaps the rationality of a lifeworld shared not only by individuals but by collectives as well. (Habermas 1984a, 43)

Due to the foundation of the learning potential of modern science, morality and art in communicative action, Habermas believes that these differentiated spheres of reason potentially represents a self-correcting principle that could be utilized against the selective course of capitalist rationalization. However, the justification for this contention precludes the substantive evaluation of rationality, which is typical of the philosophy of praxis. It is the formal procedures of argumentation and communicative practice that Habermas uses to evaluates rationalization, rather than its substantive content. He terms this an abstract determinant of rationalization, which is distinct from an assessment of concrete forms of life as a totality (Habermas 1984a, 73–74). He maintains, particularly against Weber, that rationalization transpires less in the explicit orientations for action but instead in the context-forming horizon of the lifeworld that underlies communicative practice. In broad terms, the historical transformation embodied in the communicative rationalization of the lifeworld led to the emergence in modernity of post-conventional universalistic norms of interaction and an expansion in reflexivity, as well as an extended scope for autonomous action. These are all reflected in the competences of modern socialized subjects.

Based on the intersection between competences and development in his phylogenetic reconstruction of sociocultural evolution, Habermas aims to demonstrate that the transition to modernity meant that the encompassing hold of sacred traditions and ritualized practice over all spheres of life is broken. As the authority of traditional interpretations and understandings diminish, the need for maintaining consensus and coordinating action is increasingly met by the interpretive achievements of subjects' communicative action. Modernization as rationalization meant that interactions were no longer restricted by traditionally given, normatively ascribed understandings, but conducted on the basis of the communicatively achieved agreement between subjects. This process leads to the restructuring of the lifeworld into the three structural components of 'culture', 'society' and 'personality'. In effect, the three structural components of the lifeworld become differentiated from one another and each component's reproduction derives from communicative action oriented to understanding (Habermas 1984a; 1987a).

Habermas clarifies the structural differentiation of the lifeworld by drawing homologies between the ontogenetic stages of the development of moral consciousness and the phylogenetic development of collectively held normative structures, legal and moral representations, and the types of ethics of stages of social integration (Habermas 1984a). He finds parallels between the system of demarcations drawn by the ego and the development of world-views, leading to the decentred modern understanding of the world that differentiates between the three formal worlds of 'world', 'society' and 'self'. Both the decentring of world-views and the development of post-conventional structures of law and morality render the background knowledge of the lifeworld dependent on the validity basis of speech and communicative action (Habermas 1984a). The integrity of an individuals' lifeworld and identity come to depend on the acceptance or rejection of the validity claims made by alter to ego on the basis of the provision of argumentative reasons.

Habermas claims that the transition to the modern understanding of the world is marked by the categorical demarcation enabling the communicative validity claim referring to each 'world' to be differentiated. He justifies this claim through a rather global comparison of mythical and modern modes of thought, finding mythical thought is often based on an assimilating structure that excludes the differentiation of a decentred understanding of the world. Alongside the unifying power of myth, this means that there is a tendency for premodern systems of thought to be closed rather than open to critical revision (Habermas 1984a, 61–66). The modern decentred understanding of the world permits cultural traditions to be temporalized and self-reflective, opening them up to critique and continuous reinterpretation and re-evaluation. All of these claims are critical to Habermas's exposition and 'defense' of the project of modernity.

Habermas argues that the progressive modernization resulting from the `communicative rationalization of the lifeworld' entails the emergence of specialized institutions for the reproduction of traditions, solidarities and identities. Following from this, the methodical examination of cultural traditions through the procedures of argumentation facilitates learning achievements in the now differentiated spheres of objectivating thought, moral-practical insight and aesthetic perception. This differentiation, between the once unified cultural value spheres of science, morality and art, leads to the institutionalization of discourses concerned with working out the internal logic of each of them.[1] In this way, Habermas aims to establish how communicative action has driven the process of the rationalization in different value spheres and how the standards of justification have been enhanced, which is reflected in the corresponding institutionalization of more advanced forms of reasoning and superior knowledge.

---

1   There has been an extended debate on Habermas's depiction of cultural rationalization and the separation between the spheres of value; amongst these are the contributions of McCarthy (1984b); Seel (1991); Warnke (1995); and Habermas's response and concessions are contained in Habermas (1984b; 1991).

Significantly, Habermas argues that it is the universally regulated formal procedures of justification to which modern systems of institutions owe their legitimating force. Discourse theory's conception legitimacy as deriving from procedures is a major contribution to discussions of democracy. Habermas maintains that there is one other decisive component of the rationalization and differentiation of the lifeworld. It makes possible the historical uncoupling of system from the lifeworld. The system is the formally organized spheres of the economy and state administration that follow non-normative functional imperatives. In these spheres of system integration, action is not oriented to understanding but coordinated through the functional interconnection of action consequences. Modern systems obey the logic of purposive-rationality rather than communicative reason. This development is critical to Habermas's entire explanation of the institutionalizing of modernity and the rationalization of cultural understandings, as well the depiction of the corresponding individual competences. These cultural understandings and competences represent the original preconditions for the separation and consolidation of the system.

Lifeworld and System

Conceptual Presuppositions

Habermas's major historical assertion is that the transition from traditional to modern societies involved the 'uncoupling' of the formally organized subsystems of the economy and the administrative system from the lifeworld (Habermas 1984a; 1987a). From the functionalist perspective of the maintenance of social order, this uncoupling of systems occurred partly because the rationalization of the lifeworld eventuates in an increasing dependence upon communicatively achieved understanding and consensus for the coordination of action. The 'delinguistified' steering media of money and power uncouple action from processes of reaching understanding and coordinate it through generalized instrumental values. In this way, the potentially excessive demands upon communicative action are lessened and capitalist modernization entails the extensive rationalization of the economic and political systems.

Habermas likewise revises his earlier analysis of identity crises, proposing that contemporary social pathologies are due to the systemic steering media of money and power displacing communicative action in the reproduction of the lifeworld's structural components of culture, society and personality (Habermas 1984a; 1987a). It is through the delinguistified steering media of money and power that the functional dynamic of system integration infiltrates the lifeworld and threatens to replace social integration. In this later account, the disturbances which result from the competition between these two mechanisms of societal integration are better clarified than in his earlier theory of late-capitalist crisis tendencies, though critics have questioned whether the categories of social integration and system integration can be juxtaposed in the manner that Habermas's critical diagnosis presupposes (see Mouzelis 1992; 1997; Giddens 1987; Bohman 1989). Some of these critics refer to Lockwood's intention that social integration and system integration apply to any situation and others have suggest that the money and power have always been implicated in the structuring of the lifeworld (Lockwood 1964). My later analysis supports many of these critics' arguments, but often criticisms of Habermas's distinction between system and lifeworld are founded on inaccurate depictions of his approach and a failure to take into account how he addresses the issues they raise.

What is not in dispute is that the distinction between system and lifeworld points to a central problem in social theory. Indeed, much of Habermas's use of this distinction is illuminating. His analyses are often intuitively correct, but much of the construction of his argument needs to be restructured, rather than rejected entirely. He has subsequently made some important amendments to his interpretation of contemporary capitalist societies. In so doing, he has demonstrated possibilities contained in his approach that were not originally explored, although these modifications do not rectify many of the failings of its historical perspective and the problems that it has in respect of the themes that have been identified, such as the influence of the technocratic thesis upon it and the limitations with respect to the internal dynamics of social systems (Habermas 1991; 1996a).

The manner in which Habermas initially formulates the difference between system and lifeworld is not in itself an empirical distinction between two separate institutional domains of society, but, rather, of two mechanisms of integration that each in their own way create social order through coordinating action (Habermas 1987a; 1985c; 1991). It follows then that for Habermas social integration and system integration represent two different but interdependent perspectives for analyzing society. On the one hand, system integration represents a manner of coordinating action through the non-normative functional interconnection of action consequences. On the other hand, social integration refers to actor's consciously harmonizing action orientations on the basis of commonly shared norms and values within their lifeworld. The analysis of the lifeworld paradigm of social integration is bound to the internal performative perspective of participants and thus seeks to reconstruct the intuitively held meanings of actors' symbolically structured lifeworld. This knowledge enables 'alter' and 'ego' to consciously arrive at a normative consensus about their action orientations. Social integration results from this 'circular' process of drawing on the lifeworld background and extending it by way of this communicative agreement.

By contrast, the paradigm of system integration is grasped through the external perspective of an observer who seeks to comprehend the 'counterintuitive regularities of action processes' (Habermas 1985c, 176). The observer perspective is necessitated by the fact that with system integration the consequences of social action may proceed 'behind the back of individuals' or may be 'beyond the conscious horizon of the action orientation of actors involved'. Habermas has been convincingly criticized for running together different theoretical problems in equating the unintended consequences of action with that of the requirement of a systems theoretical perspective (see Joas 1993). The general claim he is making about the integration of complex social organizations is clear, however, action theoretical perspectives are relevant even in the case of 'the market'. Habermas rather claims that the market 'is one of those systemic mechanisms that stabilize non-intended interconnections of action by way of functionally intermeshing action consequence' (Habermas 1987a, 150). Yet, this definition overlooks how in other contexts the unintended consequences may be inconsequential for the integration of social systems

Habermas believes that the inadequacies of the major traditions of social theory are in part due to their one-sided reliance upon either the systems-theoretic objectivating perspective or the action-theoretic perspective of participants. In his opinion, a genuine integration of system and action paradigms in social theory actually requires 'transforming each into the other' (Habermas 1987a, 155). According to Habermas, even the major attempt in twentieth-century social theory to integrate the two paradigms failed. Parsons rightly recognized the priority of action theory but ultimately subordinated action theory to the system perspective (Habermas 1987a, 200–01). Despite this evaluation, Habermas finds Parsons's failed attempt to reconcile the two paradigms instructive; his own approach to the joining system and lifeworld seeks to build upon it. The problem is that it is difficult to perceive how this approach can serve the purpose of critical theory and the result is a tension between Habermas's intentions and his social theory. Habermas criticizes Parsons's too 'harmonious' conception of modernity, but appropriates aspects of systems theory to criticize the philosophy of praxis. He admits that the problem of the translation or exchange between the system and action paradigms has its antecedents in Marx's theory and its notion of the objectification of the subject. However, he argues that there is an overwhelming need to revise this approach:

> Marx brought in the theory of value so as to be able to connect economic statements about a system's anonymous interdependence with historical statements about the lifeworld contexts of actors, individual or collective. These strategies have since lost their plausibility. Thus systems theory and action theory can be viewed as the *disjecta membra* of this Hegelian-Marxist heritage. (Habermas 1987a, 202)

The functionalist understanding of social differentiation is integral to this evaluation of Marx's critique of political economy. I shall argue that Habermas's utilizing aspects of Parsons's approach to correct Marx's version of the connection between system and action theory is fraught with difficulties. Habermas proposes that, in fixing on the exchange between wage-labour and capital, Marx's theory of value is limited to only one case of a series of interchanges between system and lifeworld. He also understands himself to be breaking with the limitations of the labour theory of value in considering the conflict between system and lifeworld to be one between 'principles of sociation' rather than action orientations (Habermas 1987a, 318). 'The theory of value', he argues, 'provides no basis for a concept of reification, enabling us to identify syndromes of alienation relative to the degree of rationalization attained in the lifeworld' (Habermas 1987a, 341). This problem is critical to the historical perspective of Habermas's theory; but, unlike the labour theory of value's supposition of a constituting subject, he proposes that while the lifeworld is reproduced through the action of subjects it embodies formal structures of knowledge and competences that are decentred in relation to them.

Despite the impression created by the colonization of the lifeworld thesis regarding contemporary reification, the inner logic of communicative rationalization determines the transformation to modernity. The differentiation of the system can be traced back to the changes in the lifeworld (Habermas 1987a, 173). Habermas's position that the lifeworld has a type of programming function and originally lays down the direction of the normal pattern of modernization is closer to Parsons's perspective than his criticisms convey. This proximity to Parsons is basic to his critique of Luhmann's version of systems theory. It leads Habermas to anchor the principles organizing the distinction between system and lifeworld deep in the historical process and in a way that is conceptually rather rigid, giving rise to a somewhat inflexible functionalist view of development. This is apparent his comments that from the systems' perspective the lifeworld 'gets cut down more and more to one subsystem among others' but that 'the lifeworld remains the subsystem that defines the pattern of the social system as a whole' (Habermas 1987a, 154). This contrast underpins Habermas's critique of the paradoxical course of modern rationalization.

Development and Differentiation

Habermas elaborates the distinction between system and lifeworld from the standpoint of methodology and he then situates these categories in an evolutionary perspective. In the process of social development, lifeworld and system become separated from one another, and within each there occurs increasing differentiation. In the first instance, the internal differentiation of the lifeworld owing to its rationalization facilitates the differentiation of the system. This analysis overlays another categorization of the social upon the intersection between competences and development, as Habermas contends that his account addresses the problem that Durkheim (1964b) identified of connecting changes in system differentiation and changes in patterns of social integration (Habermas 1987a, 117–18; see Alexander 1992).

The historical stages of social differentiation that he presents largely correspond to the broader evolutionary framework of the intersection of competences and development, but the lifeworld is originally coextensive with society and rationalization breaks into two the requirements of social reproduction. Habermas understands 'social evolution as a second-order process of differentiation: system and lifeworld are differentiated in the sense that the complexity of the one and rationality of the other grows' (Habermas 1987a, 153). The expansion of purposive-rationality within the economy and the administrative system represents an increased capacity for material reproduction and heightened complexity. At each developmental phase, the complexity of the system becomes increasingly distinct from the rationalization of the lifeworld based on learning achievements in the sphere of communicative action.

Uncoupling renders the lifeworld dependent on the system for material reproduction from the economy and organization and steering-performance from the state's bureaucratic apparatuses. Whilst the lifeworld becomes, alternatively, specialized in the symbolic reproduction of cultural traditions, personal identities, and social integration. This ties its symbolic reproduction to communicative action. The lifeworld's structures are further rationalized as the constraints of material reproduction are lessened.

> Under the functional aspect of mutual understanding, communicative action serves the transmission and renewal of cultural knowledge; under the aspect of coordinating action, it serves social integration and the establishment of solidarity; under the aspect of socialization it

serves the formation of personal identities. The symbolic structures of the lifeworld are reproduced by way of the continuation of valid knowledge, the stabilisation of group solidarity,
and the socialization of responsible actors. (Habermas 1987a, 137)

In the opinion of critics, the notion of the detachment of the system from the lifeworld and
Habermas's definition of power as a systemic steering medium produce an image of the lifeworld as a 'power-free sphere of communication' and 'a level of symbolic self-communication
that is set off from the real pursuit of interests' (Honneth 1991, 300; Dux 1991, 95). In spite
of Habermas's (1991, 245–46) rejecting this criticism as misrepresenting his approach, it
appears justified in relation to his theory's emphases. The contrast between the orientations
to success and understanding reinforces the impression that conflicts arise only from the
external systemic steering media impinging on communicative action. Habermas is correct,
though, in arguing that the lifeworld cannot be reduced to the domain of cultural reproduction alone. Still, this does not alter the fact that each of the three structural components of
the lifeworld are directly related to the formation of identity and that this facet of social
integration is basic to the congruence of culture, society and personality.

What I wish to emphasize at this point is Habermas's insistence that the symbolic
reproduction of the lifeworld's components has to be understood as a dynamic process in
which the structures of all three components undergo change. This aspect of his account
of the communicative reproduction of the lifeworld is especially insightful. In fact, the
'vanishing points' that Habermas (1987a, 146; 1987b, 344–45) projects for each structural component of the lifeworld on this basis of processes of communicative rationalization establishes post-traditional normative standards of interaction and procedures for
democratization.

> The vanishing points of these evolutionary trends are: for culture, a state in which traditions
> that have become reflective and then set aflow undergo continuous revision, for society, a state
> in which legitimate orders are dependent upon formal procedures for positing and justifying
> norms, and for personality, a state in which a highly abstract ego-identity is continuously
> stabilized through self-steering. (Habermas 1987a, 146)

In the case of historical evolution, the distinction between system and lifeworld is a 'second order' differentiation that presupposes a preceding series of structural changes in
the process of social development. The separation can be explained with reference to
Habermas's 'historical materialist' theory of evolution. Namely, the transformation of
patterns of social integration led to the alteration of the institutional core of society. This
development first made possible the uncoupling of the formally organized subsystems
of the economy and state-administration from the lifeworld. This explanation attributes
particular significance to moral development and especially the institution of law. It is an
interpretation of development that is largely in agreement with Parsons's conception of
evolution. Indeed, the institution of law is the most substantive means Habermas proposes for historically ascertaining the boundaries between the lifeworld and the political-
administrative and economic systems. Law is central not only to the classification of the
stages of development but also to the process of social change itself. For Habermas's
thesis is that 'higher levels of integration cannot be established in social evolution until

legal institutions develop in which moral consciousness on the conventional, and then postconventional, levels is embodied' (Habermas 1987a, 174–75).

Law occupies a privileged position in the classification of societies because of the requirement of 'anchoring' the coordinating mechanisms of 'systematically integrated domains of action' in the lifeworld. Significantly, the developmental stage of legal consciousness circumscribes these systematically integrated domains level of complexity. In the form just presented, the latter is a fairly typical functionalist argument concerning the congruence of social structures. In my view, this conception of social change is ultimately an impediment to adequately satisfying Habermas's intended critique of functionalist reason. The general historical trend that the theory of communicative action seeks to document is that of an increasing pervasiveness of the law in modernity. The thesis that Habermas advances in *The Theory of Communicative Action* is that the deleterious repercussions of the legal regulation of the lifeworld are working themselves out in the contemporary period (Habermas 1984a; 1987a). A more positive estimation of law prevails in Habermas's later discourse theory of law volume: *Between Facts and Norms* (Habermas 1996a). My analysis of the institution of modernity therefore gives prominence to Habermas's account of law and it will become apparent how this organizing theme supplements the logic of the historical development of normative structures and technical-organizational knowledge.

The contrast sketched between the institutionalization of post-conventional structures of moral consciousness and the deleterious effects of legal regulation demonstrates that the position law occupies in the theory of communicative action is open to opposed readings. This potential ambiguity is a consequence of a substantial tension between Habermas's explanation of the contemporary problematizing of the welfare-state compromise and his overall account of the rationalization of modernity. He argues, on the one hand, that the rationalization of the lifeworld leads to the institutional differentiation of law and to the legal institutionalizing of postconventional structures of consciousness that are principled, reflexive and universalistic. When considered from this developmental standpoint, the theory of communicative action cannot but present an overwhelmingly favourable interpretation of law. On the other hand, the contemporary tendency towards legal regulation or 'juridification' is the primary and only really detailed illustration that Habermas provides of the process of the colonization of the lifeworld by the economic and administrative systems. This exemplar is not by chance. Law is implicated in the constitution of distinction between system and lifeworld (Habermas 1987a). This tension may, however, be regarded as one that is not so much between Habermas's alternative interpretations of the same phenomena, but as one reflecting the paradoxical course that he believes modernization has taken.

The appreciation of this very paradox is meant to facilitate a rational and discriminating critique of modernity. The problem is that Habermas's aim of defending the normative potential of modernity, specifically through the explication of the rational structures of the communicative reproduction of the lifeworld, is at the same time linked by him to an acceptance of the logical difference of the social systems in such a guise that seems to preclude any internal democratizing and reorganization of them. The character of this argument is unsatisfactory from the perspective of critical theory. Habermas's later volume *Between Facts and Norms* somewhat reverses the logic of excluding any reconstitution of systems. It illuminates the potential for democratizing systems that are contained, but occluded, in the theory of communicative action (Habermas 1996a; 1987a). These two works cannot be juxtaposed in a global fashion, as the same normative principles are conceived in both to be already operative without being fully realized. The positive dimension of the tension between 'facts' and 'norms' is marginalized at that point in *The Theory of Communicative Action* where the argument moves in the opposite direction of considering the degree of the legal systems detachment from the lifeworld and its role in the undermining of communicative action in social integration (Habermas 1987a, 356–73).

Habermas's interest in law is influenced by a need to overcome the 'monism' of the orthodox Marxist theory of capitalist modernization. However, there are deep-seated conceptual reasons for the significant place that law acquires in his theory. These reasons are connected to those that led to his subordinating types of action to the problem of action coordination. I contend that any approach that posits the problem of 'coordination' as the preliminary question of social theory will tend to gravitate towards the institution of law. This is almost inevitable in Habermas's case, due to the normative complexion of his seminal intuition regarding social identity. The decisiveness of this intuition is evident in the manner in which Habermas superimposes law upon a pattern of understanding framed by communicative action (Habermas 1991; 1996a; 1987a). Law, he argues, facilitates the coordination of action under those conditions where a basic consensus and processes of communication have either broken down or are institutionally predetermined. Whilst the choice of coordination as social theory's basic problem may lead to the institution of law, the specific features of Habermas's evolutionary theory involves a certain conception of what law is, or should be. For Habermas, the legal 'anchoring' of the system in the lifeworld is critical to rationalization. It determines the degree of variation possible at each historical stage and it is to this reconstruction of historical development that I now turn.

Historical Change

There are historically different leading mechanisms of system differentiation. But in the early societies, which are systematically integrated through kinship, these mechanisms, such as that of prestige, essentially overlap those of social integration (Habermas 1987a, 165). The transition from the segmental differentiation of tribal societies to the stratification systems founded upon political domination entails a significant change in the conditions of legitimation. The fact that the lifeworld is 'coextensive' with tribal society is reflected in tribal society being 'reproduced in every interaction' and the institution of kinship fuses the mechanisms of social integration and system integration (Habermas 1987a, 157). Given that the institutional core of tribal society is kinship, Habermas suggests that the first mechanism of system integration is the exchange of women. The exchange of women facilitates the segmental differentiation of the combination of similar groups in a larger social unit and this produces a basically egalitarian horizontal structure.

According to Habermas (1987a, 162), it 'is only with the *vertical stratification* of unilinear descent groups that power differentials arise that can be used for the authoritative combination of specialized activities, that is for *organization*'. But this hierarchy does not constitute a distinct institutional sphere of political power. Both types of tribal society are founded on mythological legitimation and Habermas contends that Durkheim's conception of a *conscience collective* discloses how sacred authority derives from a normative projection of the general community (Habermas 1987a; Durkheim 1964b; 1976). In this way, he proposes that Durkheim's conception of an 'ideal' projection of the social overlaps Mead's notion of the 'generalized other'. Habermas traces out a similar process of collective evolution deriving from the differentiations language makes possible. In agreement with his earlier argument concerning the rationalization of worldviews, he describes this development as the 'linguistification of the sacred' (Habermas 1987a, 77–111).

Habermas reformulates Durkheim's account of change from mechanical solidarity to organic solidarity as a process of disenchantment and communicative rationalization (Durkheim 1964b). He claims that the differentiation of institutions becomes incompatible with social integration through ritual practices. Linguistification undermines certain characteristics of the sacred that are critical to mythical modes of thought's lack of differentiation, like the 'spellbinding power of the holy', the subjective attraction that is combined with a renunciation of the self, and the non-discursive introjection of moral authority. In the long-term, the erosion of the sacred foundations of morality and social solidarity makes possible the *internal* rationalization of myths and religions, the generalization of moral and legal norms, and progressive individuation. These changes are all connected by Habermas to the initial shift from normatively ascribed consensus to communicative achieved agreement, so that actors' contingent accomplishments increasingly displace tradition. It is only when the formal worlds, that are the referent of validity claims, are 'constituted, or at least have begun to be differentiated, does language function as a mechanism of coordination' (Habermas 1987a, 27). Of particular significance, the ideal projection of the community overhangs this development and it is the original precondition for the critique of sacred authority. In line with his basic intuition, Habermas attributes such projections to the communicative constitution of identity.

The transition from ritual action to communicative action means that the scope of areas of social life covered by the existing sacred interpretations declines. This change in the condition of legitimating institutions is, above all, reflected in the location of law in politically stratified societies and the 'conventional' stage of moral consciousness that informs it. The institutional 'nucleus' of these societies is the state, which gains its legitimacy from the administration of law and possesses the power to sanction. However, at this conventional stage of moral consciousness, the law is recognized as an order giving legitimacy to the ruler's 'factual power' to sanction. Habermas (1987a, 177) argues that because '*judicial office is itself a source of legitimate power, political domination can first crystallize around this office*'. The role of judge, which is assumed by the holder of political power, is to 'protect the integrity of the legal order'. The notion of subjects' moral responsibility in relation to the norms of civil conduct complements this recognition of the validity of the legal institution.

Habermas's sketch of the changes associated with the transition to politically organized class-divided societies is basically a variation on Durkheim's (1964b) account of social differentiation involving the growth of restitutive law in relation to an original system of repressive law. Law does not yet have the constitutive significance for mechanisms of system integration that it acquires at the stage of modernity. It does nevertheless enable a level of differentiation that was not permitted by the 'institutional core' of kinship and it represents a more advanced type of conflict regulation. The latter is necessitated by the legitimation problems created by class domination that emerge in politically stratified societies. Habermas considers that the logically higher level of justification that politically organized societies require is associated with developments in communication and moral consciousness, like the 'linguistification of the sacred':

> The political order as a whole is constituted as a legal order, but it is laid like a shell around a society whose core domains are by no means legally organised throughout. Social intercourse is institutionalised much more in forms of traditional mores than through law. (Habermas 1987a, 178, 177–79)

The media that coordinate the integration of social systems separate from the social integration of the lifeworld are only fully institutionalized at the stage of modernity. The separation of the economic subsystem that is coordinated through the medium of money from that of political power is a decisive step in this process. Habermas argues that this separation into subsystems depends on the norms of civil law institutionalizing exchange as an 'ethically neutralized' sphere of action that is thereby amenable to being regulated through the strategic pursuit of private interests. 'In the framework of societies organized around a state, markets for goods arise that are steered by relations of exchange, that is, by the medium of money' (Habermas 1987a, 165).

Habermas has market exchange in mind in describing systems as 'sheering off' from the lifeworld and constituting 'spheres of norm free sociality'. His account of these developments fits the model sketched previously. The changes in moral consciousness that precede them led to a principled normative orientation and patterns of action based on distinctions that cannot be completely realized in social orders of political domination. At the postconventional level, there is the profoundly significant separation between law and morality. Morality is now based upon a principled cognitive orientation and it is 'deinstitutionalized to such an extent that it is now anchored only in the personality system as an *internal* control on behaviour' (Habermas 1987a, 174). This differentiation moves the law in the opposite direction; law becomes an '*external force*' requiring only 'abstract obedience' to the sanctions that the legal system can invoke; it is less dependent on legal subjects' ethical motivations. The tendency for law to become more abstract and formal, as a result of the communicative rationalization of the lifeworld, makes it an exemplar of 'value generalization' in Durkheim and Parsons's terms (Habermas 1987a, 83–87).

> The universalization of law and morality noted by Durkheim can be explained in its structural aspect by the gradual shifting of problems of justifying and applying norms over to processes of consensus formation in language. Once a community of believers has been securalized into a community of cooperation, only a universalistic morality can retain its obligatory character. And only a formal law based on abstract principles creates a divide between legality and morality such that the domains of action, in which the responsibility for settling disputed

questions of applying norms is institutionally lifted from participants, gets sharply separated from those in which it is radically demanded of them. (Habermas 1987a, 90)

For Habermas, this process underlies the historical uncoupling of system and lifeworld, because the functional needs that the steering media supposedly satisfy expand as a consequence of it. On the one hand, the rationalization of lifeworld leads to a decline in the range and dimensions of action that are coordinated on the basis of a predetermined normative agreement. It eventuates in the coordination of action increasingly depending upon the far more contingent processes of a communicatively arrived at consensus. On the other hand, the separation between the compliance required by formal law and that of an internalized morality creates the circumstances required for detaching those actions that are oriented to success from the more exacting legitimation requirements of those that are oriented to understanding. The difference between these action orientations becomes 'plainer', Habermas claims, in the context of an institutional 'polarization' of social integration and system integration.

> This polarization reflects an uncoupling of system integration from social integration which presupposes a differentiation on the plane of interaction not only between action oriented to success and to mutual understanding, but between the corresponding mechanisms of action coordination – the ways in which ego brings alter to continue interaction and the bases upon which alter forms generalized action orientations. (Habermas 1987a, 181)

The contrast between 'formal' organizations constituted in law and the lifeworld enables Habermas to establish a correlation between type of integration and coordinating media. The functional need for media arises precisely from the potential overburdening and other associated risks of the reliance upon mutual understanding for action coordination and the integration of society (Habermas 1987a, 183). For these reasons, media function as 'relief mechanisms', they either serve to 'condense' communication while still being oriented to the formation of consensus, or they replace mutual understanding through language and are indifferent to the achievement of agreement. Prestige and influence are the instances of the former communication media, while money and power are two normatively 'neutral' steering media. By their detachment from the normative content of understanding, money and power make possible an unparalleled increase in the complexity of subsystems and their purposive rationalization. Steering media switch social action over to a success or purposive-rational orientation that is stabilized through functional interconnections, rather than communicatively derived agreement, in the formally organized and quasi-autonomous systems. Money and power accomplish this by encoding generalized forms of obligations and expectations. These supposedly neutralize and render the systems of the economy and state-administration independent of their members' normative value-orientations and the motivations formed within the lifeworld.

   Money and power relieve these subsystems from the burden of actors' need to negotiate consensus. In formal organizations, superiors need to act towards understanding only 'with reservation' and the validity basis of speech is suspended (Habermas 1987a, 310–11). Given these claims, it is easy to see from why critics, like McCarthy (1985) argue that Habermas was 'seduced' into exaggerating the autonomy of systems and consequently ignored the 'negotiated' structure of actual organizations. Habermas claims about the purposive-rationality of systems is based on the assumption that

> the transfer of action coordination from language over to steering media means an uncoupling of interaction from lifeworld contexts. Media such as money and power attach to empirical ties; they encode a purposive-rational attitude toward calculable amounts of value and make it possible to exert generalized, strategic influence on the decisions of other participants while *bypassing* processes of consensus-oriented communication. Inasmuch as they do not merely simplify linguistic communication, but *replaces* it with a symbolic generalization of rewards and punishments, the lifeworld contexts in which processes of reaching understanding are always embedded are devalued in favour of media-steered interactions; the lifeworld is no longer needed for the coordination of action. (Habermas 1987a, 183)

The generalized media like influence and prestige do not, in Habermas's opinion, have the same system-forming aspects of money and power, because they never entirely loose their connection to the lifeworld. Ultimately, prestige and influence depend on criteria of normative validity and cultural values based in the lifeworld of a particular collective (Habermas 1987a, 272–75). In the process of development, the earlier historical anchorage of system mechanisms in the lifeworld, provided in egalitarian tribal societies 'by sex and generation roles; in hierarchical tribal societies by status descent groups; in politically stratified class society by political office' are superseded (Brand 1990, 41). In opposition to the functionalist reasoning of systems theory, Habermas claims that the 'social is not absorbed as such by organized action systems; rather, it is split up into spheres of action constituted as the lifeworld and spheres neutralized against the lifeworld' (Habermas 1987a, 309). However, it is by no means clear that the difference in principle here does not actually resolve the possibility that he has already conceded too much ground to systems theory and that this too undermines the possibility which his approach may contain for reversing the very trends he diagnoses of a colonization of the lifeworld. In fact, the design of his diagnosis of these 'reifying' tendencies presupposes the basic validity of the systems theory argument of complexity and its characterization of formal organizations' structure and operating conditions.

For Habermas, it is civil law in 'economically constituted class societies' that institutionally anchors the steering media in the lifeworld. In this sense, law retains a link to informal everyday 'communicative practice' and the interchange between the lifeworld and the subsystems of the economy and bureaucratic power are mediated through it (Habermas 1987a, 185). The law being subject to more direct normative justification, Habermas would have to otherwise probably accept a systems theoretical conception of law.[2] He claims that the developmental significance of law as a coordinating mechanism

---

2   If not a systems theory conception of law then it would seem the 'legal positivism' of Weber, since Habermas regards the self-regulating legal proceduralism of Luhmann's systems theory as a modernized version of Weber's legal positivism (Weber 1978; Luhmann 1985). My point, again, is that in juxtaposing his theory of communicative action to these approaches, Habermas seems to undermine his own critical aspirations.

can be fully seen only when its historical system integrating function of mediating between the two subsystems is taken into account.

> It is only with the expansion and consolidation of the market economy within the territorial state that capitalist society entered upon the stage of a self-sufficient reproduction steered by its own driving mechanisms. And only when legal domination developed into the bourgeois legal and constitutional order did the relationship of functional complementarity and reciprocal stabilization between a capitalist economy and an unproductive state get established. (Habermas 1987a, 316)

From the fact of a historical uncoupling of the domains of system integration and social integration one 'cannot directly infer', Habermas (1987a, 185) argues that there need be a 'linear dependency in one direction or the other.' Rather, the institutions which anchor the system in the lifeworld, and given his account this must refer particularly to the law, could serve as a 'channel' in either direction. By institutionalizing or normatively anchoring the systemic steering media in the lifeworld, law provides the means for the 'second order', so to speak, coordinating of the two competing principles of 'sociation'. This development is critical to Habermas's argument that Marx's model of capitalism underestimates the complexity of modern society. From the inception of modernized society, bourgeois civil law establishes a series of interchange relations between the private and public domains of social integration and system integration. He argues that there is as well as that interchange between labour power and income which intersects with the relationship between demand and the provision of goods and services, the interchange between taxes and organizational accomplishments, which is coordinated with that between political decision and mass loyalty (Habermas 1987a, 320).

These interchanges overlap in other ways than those traversing the private sphere and the economic systems and the public sphere and the administrative system, but corresponding to these distinctions are a set of actors' legally institutionalized social roles, like those of bureaucrat and client, consumer and employee. I will come back to these roles in the context of examining the contemporary reification of the lifeworld, however, these processes of differentiation undoubtedly contribute to evolutionary progress. Habermas admits that 'viewed historically, the monetarization and bureaucratization of labour power and government performance is by no means a painless process; its price is the destruction of traditional forms of life' (Habermas 1987a, 321). Still, the balance of his historical account is heavily weighted in favour of these developments and, in seeking to mark out a perspective of critique that is not regressive in relation to them, he seems to uncritically adopt a functionalist perspective. He appears to dispute only their external effects.

> In spite of the destructive side effects of the violent processes of capital accumulation and state formation, the new organizational forms gained wide acceptance and considerable permanency on the strength of their greater effectiveness and superior level of integration. The capitalist mode of production and bureaucratic-legal domination can better fulfill the tasks of materially reproducing the lifeworld – in Parsons' terms, the functions of adaptation and goal attainment – than could the institutions of the feudal order that preceded them. This is the

functionalist 'rationality' of organizationally structured private enterprises and public institutions, which Weber never tired of calling to our attention. (Habermas 1987a, 321)

According to Habermas, the disturbances and crises of capitalist modernization are neither due to the purposive-rationalization of the system uncoupled from the lifeworld,
nor to the lifeworld's mediatization owing to its dependence upon the system for material
reproduction.

For Habermas's theory to constitute a convincing alternative to strands of critical
Marxism, it is not sufficient to highlight their perceived limitations in relation to the
asserted superiority of its own framework. It needs to reformulate their explanations of
the origins and nature of contemporary forms of domination, particularly because critical theorists understood the suffering and conflicts generated by these forms of oppression to contain tendencies prefiguring an emancipatory transformation (see Benhabib
1986). Habermas retains these concerns in his 'diagnosis' of the pathologies of contemporary society, but he argues that the effects of 'reification' in late-capitalist society are
'non-class specific'.

The categories of system and lifeworld are integral to his rethinking Marx's conceptions of the 'real abstraction' of capitalist production, and its extension from Lukács
through to Adorno, in the Weber influenced, theory of rationalization as a process of the
reification of consciousness. He detaches this conception of reification from its integrity
with the paradigm of production and translates it into the format of his theory of the
series of interchanges between system and lifeworld. The archetype of contemporary
reification is not the subsumption of labour under the commodity form but the situation
of the client of a welfare bureaucracy (Habermas 1987a, 322). This exemplar derives
from Habermas's estimation of the 'illuminating power' of Weber's thesis of a 'loss of
freedom'. He claims it 'can best be appreciated if we understand the bureaucratization
of spheres of action as the model for a technicizing of the lifeworld that robs actors of
the meaning of their own actions' (Habermas 1987a, 302).

The prelude to this analysis of contemporary reification is an account of the structural
violence of historical 'forms of understanding'. This is meant to replace Lukács's notion
of the 'forms of objectivity', which constitute the cognitive a.priori of a social totality
and expresses the dominant experience of subjectivity. 'A form of mutual understanding represents a compromise between the general structures of communicative action
and reproductive constraints unavailable as themes within a given lifeworld' (Habermas
1987a, 187). Since this analysis overlaps his account of the development of worldviews,
the crux of his argument can be summarized in the contention that the formal structures of communicative action, like the 'propositionally differentiated double structure'
of speech acts and the world relations of validity claims are not completely differentiated
in premodern societies due to the constraints imposed by the 'violence' of structures
of domination. These systematic restrictions immunize, to varying degrees, premodern
modes of legitimation, like the authority of the sacred, from critical interrogation.

The logic of progress underlying his argument about the connection between rationalization and the uncoupling of system and lifeworld leads Habermas to suggest that
this type of 'structural violence' is superseded in modernity. The modern form of

understanding is 'too transparent to provide a niche for this structural violence by means of inconspicuous restrictions on communication' (Habermas 1987a, 196, 354). Since Habermas's critique is heavily conditioned by these rationality considerations, he discerns contemporary social pathologies in the deformations of the structure of communication, rather than directly in the experience of subjects and the dynamics of conflict. In this way, the explication of the formal structures of communicative action replaces the critique of ideology and supplies a more epistemologically secure means for recognizing distortions. Even so, Habermas contends that the transparency of modern forms of understanding means that late-capitalist societies had to find a 'functional equivalent' for ideology-formation in the fragmentation of consciousness. Fragmentation results from 'everyday consciousness' being 'robbed of its power to synthesize' (Habermas 1987a, 355).

> In place of 'false consciousness' we today have a 'fragmented consciousness' that blocks enlightenment by the mechanisms of reification. It is only with this that conditions for a colonization of the lifeworld are met. (Habermas 1987a, 355)

Habermas seeks to reinterpret Weber's thesis of a 'loss of meaning' along these lines. Weber (1958) maintained that modern consciousness' 'disenchantment of the world' led to a strict demarcation of culture from nature and a subjectivizing of belief systems. Whilst the loss of a global interpretation of the world facilitates the differentiation of the value spheres of science, morality and art, the cultural values they encapsulate are incommensurate and irreconcilable. By contrast, Habermas claims rationalization is not the cause of a loss of meaning but the 'cultural impoverishment' of the lifeworld that occurs when professionalized expert cultures are cut off from the communicative infrastructure of everyday practice. A chasm between expert-specialist knowledge and the everyday culture is established when there is no means of communication facilitating translation into lay discourses and enabling public access to the full spectrum of cultural transmission. Under these circumstances, there is a draining of the lifeworld's interpretative resources. This cultural impoverishment reinforces the 'systemically induced reification' and undermines effective resistance to it (Habermas 1987a, 327).

The paradox of modernity is that the cultural rationalization of the lifeworld first made possible the development of the systems of the economy and state-administration that threaten the social integrative principle of the symbolic reproduction of the lifeworld. However, this paradox does not arise from an inversion equivalent to the alienation of the subject from the products of its constituting activity, the systemic steering media of money and power produce 'complex networks that no one has to comprehend or be responsible for' (Habermas 1987a, 184). Mediatization only leads to pathology when it extends beyond linking system integration and social integration and turns into a colonization threatening the lifeworld's symbolic reproduction. Colonization occurs when the 'delinguistified' systemic steering media of money and power replace communication oriented to understanding precisely where the symbolic reproduction of lifeworld's structural components is at stake. The communicative infrastructure of the lifeworld, Habermas argues, cannot be subordinated to functional system-imperatives and their purposive-rational action orientations without the pathological consequences of mutually reinforcing pathologies in each of the lifeworld's structural components.

> The pathologies of the lifeworld arise in three domains: in the sphere of cultural repro-
> duction, the consequence is a loss of meaning; in the sphere of social integration, anomie
> emerges; and as regards personality, we are faced with psychopathologies. Since each of these
> spheres contributes to the reproduction of the other two, the crisis phenomena are in fact
> more complex: the loss of meaning in the cultural domain can lead to the withdrawal of
> legitimation in the sphere of social integration, and to a crisis of education and orientation in
> the person. Anomie can imply increasing instability of collective identities, and for the indi-
> vidual growing alienation. Psychopathologies bring with them the rupture of traditions, and
> in the social sphere a withdrawal of motivation. (Benhabib 1986, 249–50)

Habermas's formulation of the uncoupling and intersection between the system and the lifeworld needs to be understood in the light of the 'class compromise' of the welfare state and his attempt to explain the contemporary breakdown in the social consensus that underpinned it. In fact, he seems to believe that, given the material achievements of capitalist modernization and the 'success' of the welfare state, it could appear inexplicable that 'there should be any conflicts breaking out at all' (Habermas 1987a, 350). In a sense, he attempts to incorporate these successes and achievements into his answer to the basic question: of why the systemic steering media should extend at all beyond mediatization to a colonization of the lifeworld. This basic question highlights the difficulties of his attempt to critique functionalist reason while utilizing a model of functionally organized social systems. The general subordination of dynamics in his theory means that it is the imbalance between the domains of system integration and social integration which appears the source of pathologies; even though Habermas knows the explanatory weakness of Parsons's too harmonious image of modernity and that Marx, by contrast, aimed to show in the labour theory of value that the class conflict of capitalist production manifested itself in system problems. He opposes Marx's premise, but basically returns to his earlier legitimation crisis argument of the displacement of the conflicts of capitalist economic system (Habermas 1976c; see Ingram 1987). This conflictual background is otherwise fairly difficult to discern in Habermas's theory of rationalization. There is actually a considerable imbalance between the extensive revisions being proposed and the analysis Habermas provides of the generation of system problems. The position Habermas proposes is summarized in the following terms:

> *Mediatization* assumes the sociopathological form of an *internal colonization* when critical dis-
> equilibria in material reproduction – that is, systemic crises amenable to systems-theoretic
> analysis – can be avoided only at the cost of disturbances in the symbolic reproduction of
> the lifeworld – that is, of 'subjectively' experienced, identity-threatening crises or pathologies.
> (Habermas 1987a, 305)

This 'guiding idea' still seems to depend on a type of 'consequence explanation', which has been associated in sociology with functionalism. Likewise, there is the problem of the limited analysis of the internal logic of system reproduction, which can be traced to

Habermas's treatment of systems from the standpoint of output, rather than the inner dynamics. McCarthy (1985) and Berger (1991), argue that Habermas's notion that the systems are 'constituted in positive law' tends to preclude detailed analysis of system dynamics. This does not mean that his analysis of the colonization of the lifeworld is not illuminating and original but that the larger evolutionary context of his argument cuts across its critical intention. It has solicited criticisms from commentators attuned to the orientation of the philosophy of praxis. Postone (1993) considers that it presents a trajectory of development that is actually external to history:

> It is important to note that, within the framework of Habermas' reconstruction, the possibilities resulting from the process of disenchantment are present at the *beginning* of capitalism. This implies that capitalism represents a *deformation* of what had become possible as a result of a universal inner logic of historical development. The standpoint of critique, in other words, is *outside* of capitalism, in what Habermas earlier termed 'the sphere of interaction,' now interpreted as a universal social potential. Similarly, capitalism is implicitly understood in terms of cognitive-instrumental reason alone (what Habermas had considered the sphere of labour in his earlier works) – that is, as one-dimensional. (Postone 1993, 246)

Despite the deficiencies indicated by these criticisms, Habermas's thesis of the colonization of the lifeworld provides a perceptive but flawed account for the new forms of protest. These protests do not fit the pattern of the conflict between labour and capital, but converge around the themes of cultural identity and 'the grammar of forms of life' (Habermas 1987a, 392). He suggests that these new conflicts arise at the 'seam between system and lifeworld' and that the protests of the new social movements, like the ecological movement, the women's movement, and urban resistance, are not so much focussed on the problems of security and economic distribution. The latter were the themes of the welfare-state compromise and, in Habermas's opinion, many of the new social movements' demands cannot be ameliorated through the types of compensations and rewards at the disposal of the system, especially because it is the intervention of the system into the lifeworld that is the source of discontent.

This interpretation overlaps Habermas's earlier account of the ambivalent consequences of welfare-state activity to sustain the conditions of capital accumulation and reproduce labour power. That is, the increased burden of the state's operation, through such action as the bureaucratic regulating of key areas of socialization as the family and school, rendered it susceptible to crises of legitimation and motivation. However, the dilemma specified in the thesis of the colonization of the lifeworld is that the direction for overcoming the class inequalities of capitalist society historically came from the lifeworld, yet the changes that this initiated are indirectly giving rise to the non-class specific experiences of the reification of communication. Although the 'welfare-state compromise' provides a range of rights, securities and compensations, contemporary consciousness has become increasingly aware of the price exacted by the steering media of administrative power, for example, of the social-psychological disturbances resulting paradoxically from the therapeutic operations of 'normalization' and the bureaucratic disempowering of citizens owing to centralized control over resources and the 'expert' administration of programmes (Habermas 1987a). Habermas described the background motivation to his entire theory of the rationalization of modernity as that of enabling a position which could overcome the impasse of the welfare state and the shifting of problems that gave rise to crises of legitimation between either the state's medium of power and the monetary exchange medium of the market. The latter turn to the market had emerged with the rise of neoliberalism and the notion of communicative rationality was intended to contest the quantifying and instrumental conceptions of reason that underlie arguments for market solutions to social questions (Habermas 1986).

Conclusion

In this chapter, the diversity of considerations that inform Habermas's conception of modernity's institutionalization has been reviewed. The complexity of Habermas's conception is partly a result of his theory proposing an interpretation of both the potentials inherent in modernity for future progress and the current forms of social pathology that derive from an imbalance in modernity's institutionalization. Further, Habermas's formulation of modernity's double-sided institution is not grounded in the Hegelian logic that had enabled an interconnection between contradictory tendencies to be formulated. Instead, he replaces the praxis philosophy nexus of history and the subject with the interrelationship of individual competences and historical development. Praxis philosophy's dynamic sense of the contesting of the relationship that the heteronomous institution of society has to instituting practices is rather qualified in Habermas's theory's alternative synthesis of historical development and competences. These differences from praxis philosophy are equally manifest in Habermas's comparative relegating of notions of innovation and creativity, although it could be argued that elements of these notions are inherent in his conception of rationality and rationalization. Habermas's thesis of the communicative rationalization of the lifeworld depicts a substantial dynamic of cultural change and this process constitutes an important practical application of critical reason. Nevertheless, the extent to which the logic of historical development has priority over developmental dynamics in Habermas's approach to history will become even clearer after the explication of Giddens's framework of historical analysis.

Habermas's core proposition that the institution of modernity involves the differentiation of the systemically integrated domains of the capitalist economy and the administrative state from the socially integrated domain of the lifeworld was explored. It was argued that, while this conception is convincing in a general sense, it is often at cross-purposes with Habermas's theory's intentions, for instance, it relies on a type of functionalist explanation in the context of an overall critique of functionalist reason. In Habermas's account of modernity, the logic of systems theory is deployed in opposition to demands for the internal democratization of social systems, yet the penetration of the lifeworld by the instrumental and functionalist logic organizing subsystems is depicted by him as the major source of contemporary discontent. By contrast, the explication of the lifeworld's communicative rationalization effectively discloses how the expectations of democratic legitimacy have been enhanced in the public sphere. Similarly, Habermas shows how communication has played a significant role in the democratic reorganization of the private sphere.

In Habermas's opinion, the discrepancy between the tendencies of communicative rationalization and the expansion of system integration at the expense of it constitutes the paradox of modernity. The notion of the internal colonization of the lifeworld captures some of the conflicts relating to this disparity. However, its analysis remains conditioned more by the alleged logical differences between social spheres and less by the dynamics of structuration. Habermas refers to the displacement of the contradictions of capitalist accumulation as the source of the erosion of the lifeworld's communicative infrastructure but his theory is limited in its explanation of these dynamics of the capitalist system.

The preceding discussion focussed on the more abstract conditions that underlie the institutionalization of modernity, rather than the substantive historical sociological conditions of modernity's institutionalization in particular contexts, like Europe, North America or East Asia. Habermas's accounts of substantive processes does not depart from the familiar details of the formation of European modernity, but it should be clear that his analysis of modernity tends to focus on developments within the nation-state formation. It was only later that Habermas would give sustained attention to globalization and the transnational dimensions of modernity. In some respects, the fact that these developments are of such consequence that, as we will see, he subsequently responds to them may be indicative of how the theory of communicative action's depiction of welfare state mass democracies was being somewhat overtaken and needed to be modified. The suppositions of Giddens's theory of history are more attuned to the effects of the interconnections between social formations and it offers a somewhat different, though related, interpretation of the reflexivity of modern social systems. Despite the weaknesses of Habermas's theory of modernity, the significance and originality of its interpretation of cultural modernization should be underlined. This interpretation clarifies, to be sure, how the democraticizing implications of unrestrained communication are present, though impeded and distorted, in modern subjects' practices of social reproduction.

Chapter Four

GIDDENS ON INSTITUTIONALIZING MODERNITY: POWER AND DISCONTINUITY

Introduction

Like Habermas, Giddens sought to develop a theoretical perspective on history that could inform analyses of the tensions and contradictions of contemporary capitalist society. Giddens's theoretical arguments about the historical formation of modernity were originally shaped by questions that related to the prospects of a transition to socialism and whether socialism is an immanent tendency within capitalist society (Giddens 1981a). He would later contend that the current phase of modernization has undermined and overtaken the conditions that had been used to formerly justify socialism. Rather than Habermas's proposed reconstruction of historical materialism, Giddens elaborated a critical deconstruction of Marx's theory of history (Giddens 1981; 1985). The project of a contemporary critique of historical materialism expanded on the structuration theory conception of practice that Giddens partly derived from Marx, but its 'deconstruction' of historical materialism's underlying assumptions contrasts with Habermas's endeavour to reconstruct them (Giddens 1981a).

Giddens's critique of historical materialism presents power as the linchpin of historical process, rather than material production or culture. Power is conceived to be constitutive of social relations of domination and power is expressed historically in the differing alignments of authoritative resources and allocative resources, as well as being articulated in the structuring of time-space relations. According to Giddens, the centrality of production, or allocative resources, to capitalism is one of the major reasons why modernity is radically discontinuous with preceding social formations. This historical change explains why, he argues that, class relations are integral to the reproduction of capitalism in a way that was not the case for prior social formations. At the same time, Giddens increasingly emphasizes that the principal institutions of modernity extend beyond capitalism and that the institution of authoritative resources, especially in the organization of military violence and surveillance, have substantially shaped modernity.

The separation between sociology and history is one of the binaries that Giddens has sought to overcome with the theory of structuration (Giddens 1984). This intention is evident in structuration theory's process approach and the importance that Giddens attributes to the temporal, as well as the spatial, constitution of society. These considerations are evident in Giddens's analysis of precapitalist social formations and his attempt to formulate categories that takes into account the significance of exogenous and endogenous social process for historical change, as well as the intersections between them.

Giddens's perspective on the institutionalization of modernity not only contrasts with Habermas's theory in its framing and some of its historical details; it also contrasts with aspects of Giddens's later work on the contemporary phase of modernization. My analysis notes how this shift is anticipated in the changes that occur over the course of Giddens's volumes of 'a contemporary critique of historical materialism' (Giddens 1981; 1985; 1994). Notably, I suggest that the original structuration theory focus on generative processes implies a somewhat different perspective on historical change and social organization than Giddens's later emphasis on modernizing developments' consequences. Similarly, weaknesses are detected in Giddens's formulation of the category of structural principles, which had been critical to his classification of social formations. These inconsistencies concerning structural principles – and which probably reflect difficulties in reconciling the general framework of the theory of structuration and the analyses of historical processes – may explain Giddens's subsequent accentuation of the institutional diversity of modernity. This latter perspective could be considered to either change the parameters of the praxis philosophy question of the nexus of the subject and history, or restrict it in a way that means that it can never be properly resolved, and hence that it can be dispensed with in its original form.

Functionalism and Evolutionary Theory

The theory of structuration's premises serve to differentiate Giddens's framework of historical analysis from influential competing paradigms. These contrasts were initially specified through his critical deconstruction of evolutionism in its various manifestations and the more latent continuation of its influence in social theory (Giddens 1979; 1981a). Similar arguments are advanced against evolutionism as those which pertain to functionalism. Common to both are biological analogies and a reliance upon the notion of adaptation. These biological analogies and the alternative suggestion of homologies with individual development, such as that proposed by Habermas, have been central for the representation of history as a teleological process of growth. This enables the equation of temporally successive stages with progress in history and it is one of the sources of the 'normative illusion' that Giddens critically associates with many evolutionary theories. He claims that the investigation and analysis of the contingent conditions of social change and reproduction are occluded by the notion of adaptation and similar concepts, like that of the functionalist notion of the 'needs' of social systems (Giddens 1979; 1981a).

For Giddens, these assumptions are reflected in the tendency to superimpose upon history a set of requirements or mechanisms universally determining processes of development. As a consequence, history is reduced to a process of social change through the forms where these developments appear as progressive elaborations. Evolutionary thinkers, he states, often 'compress general into specific evolution' (Giddens 1984, 239). The limitations of such an explanatory orientation have been concealed by the conception of society that it presupposes and which structuration theory has sought to reformulate.

Giddens argues that detailed consideration of intersocietal relations must complement the elucidation of endogenous developments in analyses of social change, since the conditions that made this analytical-explanatory distinction perceptible are not universal features of human societies but have been historically established. Giddens deploys concepts like those of 'time-space edges' and 'world-time' in order to indicate that these intersections and the processes facilitating social change vary according to contexts (Giddens 1984, 244–56; 1979; 1981a).

This focus upon the conjunctural facets of social change facilitates a recognition of what the formulation of universal laws of development generally has occluded and down played. That is, that the relationship of history to temporality is not uniformly linear, rather it is segmented in line with geographical regionalization. The concept of 'episodic transformations', derived from Ernst Gellner and modified by Giddens, theoretically characterizes these conjunctural social transformations and makes generalizations about them possible. Episodes mark 'the opening' and instantiation of a sequence of changes which transforms the institutional organization and even the structural principle of a societal totality. The central concern of structuration theory with process necessitates an explanation of the mechanisms or dynamics of an episode. These dynamics determine the intensity of change exacted and the momentum of its occurrence, and similarly the extensional scope and range it has in time and space. Accordingly, the assumption that there is a continuum of developmental stages is replaced by that of *social systems having time-space paths*, which are often inconsistent and incommensurate (see Giddens 1981a, 69–89, 180–262).

Given these arguments it is clear that Giddens rejects Habermas's claim that the purpose of evolutionary theory is to contribute to practical discourses about future alternative developmental possibilities and to thereby clarify the direction of social progress. However, it would be difficult to determine the relevance of a theory of history that did not contribute in some way to such practical discourses. In a sense, Giddens appears to be opposed primarily to the sense of determinism that is typical of evolutionary theories. He accepts that there are discrete lines of progressive development in different fields, but argues that these are not constitutive of a social totality in themselves and major change involves greater discontinuities than is implied by evolutionary social theory. Habermas argues that social theories generally contain implicit assumptions about social evolution and it is not surprising that critics have suggested that Giddens's theory still presents some discrete phases of social evolution and developmental tendencies (Wright 1989).

Precapitalist Forms and Time-Space Distanciation

Giddens's historical analyses do not just explore the supposedly irremediable problems of historical materialism; his critique aims to reinforce the claimed merits of structuration theory's alternate conceptual framework. He dismisses at the outset theses representative of historical materialist explanations (Giddens 1981a, 1–2). Giddens rejects as simply mistaken Marx and Engels's (1977) view that history is the product of class struggle. He likewise argues that Marx's (1970) famous thesis of the contradiction between the development of the forces of production and that of the social relations of production cannot be justified as a universally valid mechanism of epochal social change. Giddens comes close to rejecting the possibility of a general schematic ordering of the developmental levels of societies, although he admits that this approach to history has hardly been exclusive to historical materialism. In actual fact, Giddens (1981) proposes a highly conventional categorization of tribal-band, agrarian class-divided, and capitalist, social formations, with a number of sub-types in the class-divided category. The generality of this categorization reflects Giddens's intention of distancing his perspective on history from some of the typical assumptions concerning development in explanations of historical change. For instance, he argues that many theories of historical development obscure the co-existence of different types of social formations at the same point of time.

Furthermore, Giddens criticizes the 'ethnocentric' bias of Marx's historical schema and asserts that subsequent research has demonstrated that there is no universal dynamic of expanding the forces of production (Giddens 1981a, 153; see Arnason 1984). These general critical formulations are supplemented by specific criticisms of Marxist arguments. Giddens opposes, what he terms, the 'felicitous conjunction' of class and contradiction in Marx's theory (Giddens 1981, 235). It was supposed to bring together the dynamic of history and the subject that would overcome class subordination and exploitation, owing to its structural location in capitalist production (Lukács 1971). The problem of explaining why this conjunction did not lead to the abolition of capitalism resulted in later Marxist investigations into class-consciousness and the mechanisms modifying the crises of capitalist production. Although he disputes aspects of the Marxist framing of this problem, Giddens stresses in response to it the institutional significance of the nation-state to modern society and the mediating of everyday consciousness in nationalism (Giddens 1981a, 191–196; 1985a). He argues that it was national consciousness and the welfare state that blocked the potential for radical revolutionary change. The state and national identification diverted the crisis tendencies intrinsic to the capitalist mode of production because they were always far more fundamental to modernity than the Marxist perspective presumed. Giddens suggests that the state's origins are far more deeply infrastructural than historical materialism comprehends. This criticism expresses his main thesis: that *power has never been adequately theorized by historical materialism* (Giddens 1981a; 1985a).

> It will be my argument here that Marx was right to have reservations about the significance of class as a structural feature of the Asiatic societies, on the grounds that apply also to the ancient civilizations of the Near East and to those of Meso-America and Peru. But he was wrong, I think, to suppose that Greece and Rome, or European feudalism, were distinctly different in this respect: that is, they were 'class societies' whereas the others were not. In none of these societies was control of private property the most significant basis of power, nor indeed was the distribution of allocative resources more generally. (Giddens 1981, 107)

The tenor of these observations is somewhat misleading with respect to other dimensions of Giddens's critique. He uses aspects of Marx's theory as both a point of departure and a guide. However, he does not investigate the subsequent traditions of Marx interpretation; nor, as he himself admits, are his critiques philological (Giddens 1982c, 1982b; Arnason 1991a). These limitations have significant implications. In my opinion, they undermine the general applicability of his critiques to the Marxian tradition as a whole. Neo-Marxist commentators rightly suggest that Giddens does not consider the full extent to which his arguments overlap those of critical and revisionist Marxist perspectives (Wright 1989; Sayer 1990). Giddens's critique's object is the fairly orthodox versions of historical materialism, but he seems to believes that revisionist Marxist approaches to history are unable to sufficiently distance themselves from the orthodoxy's flaws and intentions. For this reason, he argues that as thoroughgoing critique as he intends to pursue could only be elaborated in the manner of a deconstruction of the Marxist theory of history.

This deconstruction involves reading segments of Marx's work against the programme of historical materialism. It discloses the fabrication of a unified historical materialist perspective out of variegated different theoretical elements. It does this by playing off one aspect or interpretation of the original against another. Giddens's critique is directed to discerning the distinctive features of the Marxian proposition that can be opposed to functionalist forms of explanation and evolutionary interpretations of history (Giddens 1981a; 1982c, 1982d; 1984) Unlike Habermas's (1979a) reconstruction, Giddens's deconstruction delimits in order to initiate a standpoint distinct from these social theory perspectives, including elements of them contained in other social theory approaches.

Based on his distinctive conception of structure as internal to practice, the time-space 'distanciating' or extension of social relations is the key to Giddens's understanding of the social structures of historical formations. He considers that social systems' 'stretching', or 'binding', time and space supplies form to interactions by coordinating relations of presence and absence (see Gregory 1989). In other words, this coordination defines the historical relationships between social integration and system integration. Giddens's distinction between structure and system was influenced by Marx's distinction between labour and labour-power, so that this line of inquiry represents another attempt to elucidate processes like those Marx defined as the 'real abstraction' characteristic of capitalist production (Marx 1976). The notion of structure having only a virtual existence, in so far as it is instantiated through being drawn upon in the practical processes of action and is reproduced by these practices, has strong analogies with the assumptions of Marx's theory of value. Given this inspiration, it is not surprising that Giddens endorses much of Marx's analysis of the labour process and capital accumulation.

Giddens somewhat unconvincingly argues that capitalist modernity is historically much more different from earlier social formations than Marx acknowledged. He is more convincing in claiming that modernity is more institutionally differentiated than Marx appreciated, although this is not really a matter of recognition but of the relative weighting attributed to different institutions (Giddens 1981a, 1982b). Besides capitalism, the institutional clusters of modernity include industrialism, surveillance and the military violence of the nation-state (Giddens 1985a). The notion of the institutional diversity of modernity marks a shift from the perspective of Giddens's first volume of his critique of historical materialism (Giddens 1981a). There he argued that capitalism is a distinctively class society, because class is the overall structural principle of this social formation; unlike precapitalist class-divided societies where classes exist but are not the structural principle of societal organization. The subsequent claim that capitalism constitutes only one of modernity's four institutional dimensions presages later changes in Giddens's perspective and it opens the way for the 'structural pluralism of his political program of The Third Way' (Giddens 1998; 2000).

The differences between Giddens's standpoints on industrialism demonstrate some of the consequences of this change from the original position on structural principles of capitalist modernity and how Giddens applies contrasting arguments to the same phenomenon (Giddens 1981a, 123). Even in arguing that industrialism constitutes an independent institutional cluster of modernity, Giddens accepts that industrialism originally developed under the auspices of capitalism. This precedence was originally interpreted to mean that capitalism is the generative principle of industrialism, that is, capital accumulation in the context of a competitive market and conflicts over the control of production stimulate and determine the direction of industrialism. The transformation of nature and the creation of a manufactured environment are not organized according to principles different from those of capitalism. Giddens originally opposed this analysis of the mechanics of capitalist production to theories of industrial society and the arguments of a transition to a post-industrial society (Giddens 1981a).

> For the theory of industrial society (and its latter-day affiliate, linked to a conception of a supposedly 'post-industrial' world) has no account of the mechanism generating the changes it diagnoses: technology appears as its own prime-mover. (Giddens 1981, 122)

Giddens later places greater stress on the claim that modernity is not reducible to capitalism. This results in the separating of industrialism as a distinct institutional sphere (Giddens 1985a; 1990a). Besides opposing Marx's 'class reductionism', the major justification of this shift is industrialism's significant consequences. These changes in Giddens's model produce a more flexible account that is less convincing in its explanation of 'inner dynamics'. A model that permits one institutional dimensions of modernity and then another to be prioritized replaces the explicating of the principle form of sociality that capitalism generated.

Giddens rejects Marxist understandings of historical transitions that are based on the projection backwards of the dialectic of the forces of production and the relations of production. He proposes, instead, that the dynamic of precapitalist social formations is related to the distinction between allocative and authoritative resources, as this distinction concerns the intersections and workings of the media of the historical formation and transformation of societies. These resources are critical to Giddens's elucidating how the structural principles of social systems are composed out of the 'virtually' existent structure; thereby constituting societies as systems of time-space distanciation. According to Giddens, resources may constrain and enable practices, yet they 'are not possessed by individual social actors but are features of the societal totality' (Giddens 1981a, 52). The abstract level of structural principles is the basis for historical categorization and classification. Giddens's critical theory of history's axial problem is summarized in the claim that 'analysing structural principles involved in domination we are hence concerned with studying over-all interconnections between property and authority in the long-term reproduction of societies' (Giddens 1981a, 55).

Between concrete practices and structural principles are the 'structural sets' which link and mediate the translation between them (Giddens 1981a, 54–55). For Giddens, Marx's (1976) account of the circuits of capital is an exemplar of this mutual convertibility of rules and resources. However, the conversion of different phenomena that is made possible by the exchanges of the symbolic token of money is an even more general example of forming structural sets (Giddens 1981a, 55; Giddens 1984). By their linking different levels and mutually interrelating rules and resources, structural sets contain the nucleus for the reflexivity of social systems. These different layers of social structure clarify the degree of the, to use Alain Touraine's (1977) term, 'self-production of society', or the reflexive self-organization of institutions. This is one of the ways in which Giddens's generative conception of power represents a different framework for defining the facilitating conditions and permissible limits of historical types of social transformation, one certainly closer in its orientation to the Marxist approach than functionalist theory.

Despite the ambiguities of the category of structural principle examined later, Giddens's conceptualization of resources does not leave any doubts about the axial dimension of his reinterpretation of social systems. Power is the practical capacity to mobilize resources and it conditions systems of domination. The supposition that power is more fundamental than domination implies that power produces domination. Power being the means of its reproduction. Giddens connects a generative conception of power to the structural principles of social organization, so that he contends that taken 'together, the allocative and authoritative resources' are 'constitutive of the societal totality as a structured system of domination' (Giddens 1981a, 52). From this perspective, he argues that authoritative resources coincide with the structural principle of non-capitalist social formations, because their coordination is 'the more fundamental lever of change'. In other words, 'authoritative resources are the prime carriers of time-space distanciation' in pre-capitalist and non-capitalist societies (Giddens 1981a, 92). To be precise, authoritative forms of domination shape the mobilizing of allocative resources, rather than the other way around. Authoritative resources regulate the relation between the political-administrative centre and the agrarian periphery in class-divided societies.

Like Habermas, but on quite different grounds, Giddens contends that anthropological and ethnological research contradicts the standard historical materialist interpretations of pre-capitalist and non-capitalist societies. He employs the concept of time-space distanciation to suggest that it is *presence* that above all characterizes the social organization of tribal or band societies. These societies exhibited a low degree of time-space distanciation and their 'most distinctive feature' was the merging of the structure of social relations with interaction contexts of 'high presence availability' (Giddens 1981a, 160).

Giddens's decision not to provide a substantive institutional definition of resources is logically connected to his theory's basic aim of observing how the substance and content of resources change as medium and outcomes of historical processes of structuration. The most important historical exemplar of this change is probably property. Its alienability enables property to become a media of increasing time-space distanciation. The intensive alienability of property originally occurred in connection with the commodification of the means of production and this alienability contrasts with precapitalist agrarian property. The latter constituted an impediment to distanciation, due to the limited

possibilities of its conversion through exchange, the relatively fixed structures of agricul-
tural reproduction, and, presumably, its conditioning by the modality of authoritative
resources that structure precapitalist relations of domination. In *A Contemporary Critique
of Historical Materialism*, Giddens's (1981a) analysis of the limited alienability of agrarian
forms of property draws substantially on Marx's (1973, 471–510) account of precapitalist social formations in the *Grundrisse*. Marx stressed there the significance of ecological
factors and the communal character of precapitalist social relations. These constitute
a far more complex interconnection of the social and natural than is conceivable from
Habermas's perspective of production as a system of technical appropriation and control
of the material environment.

Marx (1973) argued that the limited alienability of property was conditioned by the
forms of social cooperation embodied in the 'communal character' of these precapitalist societies. The process of production is itself mediated by precapitalist forms of social
relations and Marx implies that their social mediation of property has not completely
severed the ties of humans to the organic realm of nature. According to Giddens, Marx
suggests that 'production is subordinated to the social relations connecting nature, the
individual and the social community' in precapitalist social formations (Giddens 1981a,
80). Giddens adopts Lefort's (1978) contention that the *'forms which precede capitalist production' (Formen)*, section of the *Grundrisse* contains a 'different vision of history' to Marx's
sketches of the 'materialist conception of history' (Marx 1973, 471–514; Marx 1970;
Marx and Engels 1976). The *Formen* diverges from the social evolutionary idea of the
continuity in the stages of the development of productive forces. Rather than detailing
a sequence of universal development, it presents instead a 'discontinuous' conception of
history and outlines alternative paths of change.

Capitalism is depicted in the *Formen* as a radically discontinuous system of production
and not as the 'summation' of preceding history (Marx 1973, Giddens 1981a). In this
analysis, it is the *dissolution* of features common to all earlier modes of production that
is critical to the constitution of the capitalist system of production. Notably, the origins
of capitalism lie in the dissolution of the precapitalist subsumption of production under
relations of authority and the forms of landed community mediating the appropriating
of nature. Giddens argues that this discontinuity of capitalist social relations enables
the structures of material production to acquire an independent internal logic and the
properties of a fully *reflexive* system. The processes of dissolution are the condition of
property becoming a medium of distanciation and a consequence of the extension of
mediation. Giddens claims that only this structure creates the dynamic for a continuous
expansion of the forces of production. It is on account of the centrality of production
that class relations become the structural principle determining the organization of capitalist society.

In sum, Giddens suggests that the implications of Marx's *Formen* analysis are that
there is no single trajectory of historical development, nor mechanism of social change.
He proposes that capitalist production is a radically and qualitatively different form of
social organization to those of all prior formations. This interpretation provides the prototype for Giddens's later general conception of institutional reflexivity. Capitalism instan-
tiates a structure which is distinctively *social* by way of dissolving those continuities with

the natural environment that were integral to the organizing principles and mediating processes of precapitalist societies (Giddens 1981a; 1985a). For Giddens, the institutionalizing of the division between the social and the natural is a defining feature of modernity, however, the emergence of capitalism as a system of production that is 'insulated' against political modes of domination resulted from a broad conjunction of changes that undermined the structural principle of class-divided societies. Notably, the changes in the other institutional dimension of modernity were significant to the consolidating of capitalism, but they equally constitute independent sources of power.

Before considering these dimensions of Giddens's interpretation of the institutionalizing of modernity in more detail, it is worth noting a conceptual ambiguity that may have precipitated the greater accentuation of the various institutional clusters and which, to my mind, has general implications for the theory of structuration. These ambiguities appear to coalesce around the seemingly pivotal concept of structural principles and the contrasting explanations that are provided of this category. First, structural principles are explicitly defined as the aspect of social systems most deeply embedded in time and space. In this sense, they have a greater persistence than the more contingent social structures. Second, they are considered the most abstract means of classifying societies. Yet, the emphasis here on the methodological problem of classification implies a subtle difference from substantive systems. Structural principles are abstract in the sense of their not having a 'real' existence in the sense of concrete phenomena, but of supplying a theoretical approach to social reality. At best, it would seem paradoxical to suggest that such abstract classificatory principles are enduring. Third, at other times, Giddens argues that such structural principles exist as they are produced and reproduced, being anchored in actors' knowledgeability (Giddens 1981a, 64). Fourth, while this conception could be made compatible with either of the above versions of principles, it is more difficult to reconcile it with Giddens's notion of methodologically bracketing agents' perspective in some cases of institutional analysis. Moreover, this anchoring in subjects conflicts with the version of structural principles presented in *The Constitution of Society*, where they are defined as properties of social systems (Giddens 1984). Fifth, some of these interpretative dilemmas originate in the difficulties structuration theory has in reconciling its ontological orientation with Giddens's historical conceptualization (see Cohen 1989). The effects of these problems are articulated in the different answers that Giddens gives at various times to the crucial question of the social and its constitution. I argue that these difficulties surrounding the notion of structural principles are neither resolved conceptually, nor dissolved by the weight of historical analysis. Instead, such problems can be traced back to the tensions contained in the original design and aspirations of Giddens's project. Furthermore, they persist into his later writings on modernity and its reflexivity, even though there they are partially obscured by his reworkings of earlier arguments.

The State and Capitalism

The understanding of modernity inherited from the philosophers of the Enlightenment and the social theorists of the nineteenth and early twentieth centuries contain profound and enduring insights. Giddens (1990a; 1994a) contends that these interpretations are based, however, on assumptions about history and social change that are in need of substantial revision. He initially revised the teleological arguments of functionalism and social evolutionism, and sought to discern the effects of these arguments on the perspective of historical materialism. In his opinion, Marx failed to adequately theorize the logic of power and this critical analysis constituted the background to many of the theory of structuration's conceptual formulations and Gidden's account of precapitalist formations.

Giddens relates the general limitations of Marx's conception of modernity to the problems of power, although the reasons are different from those applying to the deficiencies he perceived in Marx's interpretation of class-divided societies. Marxism's inadequate appreciation of power conditioned its supposed underestimation of the significance of the modern state and this led to the inadequacies of historical materialist explanations of nationalism (Giddens 1981a; 1985a). Even though there are important developments in his theory, the critical deconstruction of historical materialism frames Giddens's later writings on the trajectory of the social transformation associated with modernity. It is clear from the perspective of these later work's incipient sociological critique of contemporary society that the balance of Giddens's historical perspective and its leading theme changes: broadly, from the analysis of domination to coming to terms with the implications of risk at the stage of reflexive modernization.

The idea of the interplay between contingency and power has always been a distinctive feature of Giddens's approach, but I will argue that his dialectical understanding of social processes receives different applications. There is a sense in which this is a justified outcome of an approach that stresses the interplay of systems that have different points of origin and their conjuncture gives rise to different effects depending on the historical and spatial circumstances. In this respect, this conclusion regarding social transformation was already implicit in his critique of notions of the intersection between history and the subject, but he considers that his recent writings seek to uphold a participatory conception of politics that owes something to praxis philosophy's generative interpretation of the conditions of democratization and social constitution (Giddens 1994a).

Giddens believes that his approach diverges significantly from the assumptions of the developmental models of earlier modernization theory (Giddens 1990a). His central and sustained proposition is that modernity is radically discontinuous in its nature from all preceding social orders and that the fundamental contrasts between premodernity and modernity are more significant than the continuities. Hence, he asserts that the dynamic and institutional features of modernity are inexplicable if they are conceived of as an accentuation of premodern trends and tendencies. In general terms, this appears as merely a restatement of the dominant sociological conception of the substantial difference of modern society. One that has largely defined the self-understanding of this discipline, whether it derives from Durkheim's (1964) distinction between mechanical and organic solidarity or Weber's (1930; 1958) notions of rationalization and the disenchantment of the world.

For Giddens, the specific character of the discontinuity of modernity and its facilitating processes has been largely misrepresented. Sociological theories of change have emphasized endogenous processes and tended to regard exogenous factors and intersocietal relations as less important. He claims that these limitations are reflected in many sociological theories neglect of some of the most profound aspects of twentieth-century history, like war, nationalism and the degradation of the environment (Giddens 1990a). However, the omission of these topics was constitutive for much sociological thought, precisely because it was only through such neglect that a number of explanations of modernity could be sustained and normative integration considered the foundation of the social. Similarly, he claims that a simplified conception of change resulted from the classical sociologists' attempts to define a single dynamic determining the development of modernity (Giddens 1990). Although the contrast between the traditional and modern has been formulated in a diverse manner, these arguments reflect his view that a renewed appreciation of the dynamic character that marks out the discontinuity of modernity cannot be achieved through a reinvigorating of the established paradigms of social theory. I will not assess the merits of each of these arguments here, because it is Giddens's proposed replacement that is being assessed and ultimately it determines the validity of these claims.

Given the centrality of power to his critique of historical materialism, it is not surprising that Giddens considers the state was critical to institutionalizing the capitalist system of production and the discontinuity of modernity more generally. In his opinion, Marxist explanations of historical change tend to underestimate how significant the state was to facilitating and embedding capitalism. Of course, this assertion could be contested. However, he argues that the state was itself changed in this historical transformation. The systematic arrangements integral to class-divided social organization were reconstituted. Giddens elucidates a critical discontinuity that is similar to Marx's description of the precondition of capitalism's real abstraction.

> Capitalism is distinctively a 'class society': the capital/wage-labour relation is predicated upon the dissolution of the ties between nature, community and the individual characteristic of other societal forms. From the side of wage-labour, this involves the eradication of the 'relation to the earth – land and soil – as natural conditions of production', and concomitantly of the 'real community' within which such production is ordered. From the side of capital, what is involved is the commodification of property (the full alienability of property) and its circulation through the medium of money. (Giddens 1981a, 81)

The processes of commodification radically alters property. Giddens accepts that Marx's conceptualizing of this aspect of capitalism remains of enduring significance. He suggests that there were two successive phases of commodification, each corresponding to a phase in the development of the modern state. The widespread commodification of land and products occurred during the period of the Absolutist state, whilst the commodification of labour power happened extensively during the later phase of the nation-state (Giddens 1985a, 140). In Giddens's opinion, Marxist perspectives tend to underestimate the significance of the centralizing of administrative control in the Absolutist state. Similarly, he considers that the concentration in the state of the means of violence had a constitutive significance for the emergence of modern institutions in general.

Despite increasing centralized authority enabling the fixing of definite borders, the structural principles of class-divided societies persisted in the European Absolutist state.

Indeed, Giddens has difficulties reconciling the discrepancy between those key features of the Absolutist state tying it to class-divided societies and its historical consequence in promoting the transition to modernity. No doubt this discrepancy reflects tensions intrinsic to the transformation from class-divided to modern capitalist society. But Giddens's project is marked by more substantial problems, as indicated by revisions in its historical perspective. The elaboration of the notion of sovereignty during the Absolutist period was of wider significance than the political transformation of the forms of authoritative resources. Sovereignty expressed the actual centralized possession of military force and represented a new conception justifying a coercive system of law. Not only was it associated with the development in Europe of an international system of states but sovereignty was integral to consolidating the qualitative change in the character of property.

> Where most property was in land, ownership rights were usually guaranteed by a mixture of custom and law, bolstered very often by the direct possession of the means of violence by those laying claim to those rights. But where property becomes capital, even landed property, ownership cannot be defended primarily as a 'sitting claim of possession'. (Giddens 1985a, 152)

During the Absolutist period, the dominant class remained the land owning minority; however, in line with Perry Anderson's (1974b) analysis, Giddens (1985a, 97) suggests that the movement of authority 'upward' to the monarchy reflected the impact of those economic and political processes that undermined the autonomy of the local peasant community. Giddens's understanding of power informs his view that these changes in the dynamic of class relations proved the most consequential effect of the 'alliance' of Absolute authority with the rising bourgeois class (Giddens 1981, 180). The creation of a propertyless mass of free labour was the most structurally significant change for the development and embedding of capitalism. Of course, this conclusion is consistent with the main theses of Marx's (1976) account of 'primitive accumulation' and the creation of the labour market is equally integral to Weber's conception of capitalism. The connection to the latter's perspective is evident in Giddens (1985a, 152) contention that '(w)ithout the centralization of a coercive apparatus of law, it is doubtful either that this process could have been accomplished, or that the rights of property as capital could have become firmly embedded'. This is the case even though the commodification of labour power occurred extensively later during the period of the nation-state.

European absolutism was not only the precursor to the modern system of states, but changes during this period facilitated the other institutions of modernity, as well as capitalism. For example, changes in state administration initiated more intensive regulation of social practices and facilitated the extensive coordination of social systems, through such measures as the state securing legal contracts and enacting of a unified system of measurement. Likewise, the sovereignty of the state underpins the system of taxation 'underwriting' its expenses and activities, 'since productive enterprise is largely carried outside the scope of its direct control' (Giddens 1985a, 157). Giddens contends that the state's legal authority and taxation arrangements refined the distinction between public and private property. The commodification of property and the expansion of the monetary system actually enabled the greater intensive reach of state administration into the everyday life of the population. These changes were initiated during the period of the absolutist state but their full implications were only realized in the nation-state. Giddens draws attention to how endogenous and exogenous changes reciprocally reinforced each other. On the one hand, he points to how the nation-state emerged in a system of international state relations and this system had historically taken shape in European Absolutism. On the other had, he argues the nation-state replaced the city as the chief 'power container'. The internal pacification of social relations due to the sovereignty of the nation-state and administrative control had a symbiotic relationship to the capitalist system.

> The process of internal pacification, I shall argue, is only possible because of the heightened administrative unity that distinguishes the nation-state from previous state forms. On the other hand, the very administrative unity depends upon the 'infrastructural' transformations brought into play by the development of industrial capitalism, which help finally to dissolve the segmental character of class-divided societies. (Giddens 1985a, 160)

Given the significance of this thesis to Giddens's conception of the institutionalizing of modernity, it is worthwhile clarifying the overall historical change from precapitalist social formations that it involved. Despite the media and institutions of authoritative sources of power distinguishing class-divided from tribal societies, the extensive spread and intensive reach of administrative control and surveillance into routine practices were considerably limited. Giddens relates this to their low degree of reflexivity and limited organizational capacity, but he argues against attributing these limitations to the level of development of the forces of production in class-divided societies. In Giddens's opinion, later Marxists largely overlooked the significance of Marx's assertion that the division of labour in precapitalist societies was largely equivalent to the division between town and country (Marx and Engels 1976, 38). The city is the primary 'storage container' of power in class-divided societies, being basic to these societies' administrative and political integration. Giddens equates the emergence of the state with the origins of the city and the city structures. Cities formed centres binding together political, cultural, religious, and economic structures. It is through this concentrating of structures that the city was able to constitute a new systemic principle organizing institutions and for its division from the countryside to become the structural principle of class-divided societies.

In precapitalist societies, the relationship of the city to the country was the most important determinant of the overall distanciation. This 'spatial' formation of social relations was at source of the contradiction between two forms of organization, one located in the city and the other in the agrarian community. City and countryside were two social forms loosely dependent upon each other, without determining the inner organization of each other. The contradiction between them results from the dialectic of control between the centre and the periphery, which has its origins in precapitalist societies' segmental character and those limitations intrinsic to their means of system integration. Underlying this conflict was the persistence in the country periphery of 'localized communities' and 'the modes of organization of kinship and tradition that characterized them' (Giddens 1981a, 103; 1985a).

The structural principle of class-divided societies is most clearly brought out in the case of empires, since they exhibited the greatest degree of time-space distanciation prior to capitalist modernity. Although empires were originally the product of the combination of cities, the dialectic between the centre and periphery, or the division between city and countryside, took its most explicit form in imperial social orders. Reflecting the fact that pre-capitalist social systems had *frontiers* rather than definite *boundaries*, there were even in the case of empires decided limits to the scope of domination and the power to sanction. The boundaries that did exist were basically the physical walls of cities and the effects of manipulating the contours of the natural environment (Giddens 1981a; 1985a).

The type of interplay that this dialectic of control generated in empires can be explained by the fact that social integration tended to predominate over system integration in all non-capitalist societies. The lower surveillance of routine everyday activity at the frontier regions of empires reflected class-divided societies' dialectic of control; walls are an acknowledgement of a lack of information, as well as a physical boundary (see Giddens 1985a, 50). But the dialectic of control straightforwardly resulted from the length of time that movement across space took. In other respects, empires were a qualitative break with earlier and contemporaneous 'social forms'. Empires exhibit the greatest degree of system integration prior to capitalism. This is because violence and the threat of military force were the chief means of administration where governance based on surveillance remained low; hence force is of a far more general significance in defining system integration (Giddens 1985a, 58). Of course, force and surveillance do not stand in a quantitatively inverse relationship to one another. Giddens, however, comes close to implying that they qualitatively do in the history of social formations. He considers that the limited capacity for surveillance in premodern societies is a primary reason why empires 'compose really the only examples of large-scale centralized societies before the advent of capitalism' (Giddens 1981a, 102).

In Giddens's opinion, Marx's 'class reductionist' analysis failed to appreciate the interplay between the different institutions of domination that are constitutive of modernity. The dominance of the capitalist class is historically novel because it is not sustained through 'direct access to the means of violence', but Marx 'does not ask what happens to the means of violence "extruded" from the labour contract' (Giddens 1985a, 159–60). The 'extrusion' of force from the sphere of production and exchange was complementary to the centralizing of the means of violence in the state. The 'professionalized army' correlates with the internal pacification of the nation-state. This double-sided process constituted an unprecedented historical development, given that the possession of the means of violence and the threat of force were the principal mechanism of appropriating surplus in class-divided societies. It is worth mentioning that this is not the only place in which Giddens's historical analysis of the formation of modernity has strong parallels with Norbert Elias's interpretation of the civilizing process.

The discontinuity in how surplus is appropriated meant that class conflict became *intrinsic* to the process of production with capitalism, owing to the 'mutual dependence' of the wage-labourer as immediate producer upon capital for employment in order to labour, and, in turn, the owners of capital's 'dependence' on extracting surplus-value from wage-labour. It is this relationship of 'asymmetrical reciprocity' that principally makes the sphere of economic production into a 'system'. Unlike class-divided systems' authoritative means of organizing allocative resources, the structuration of the capitalist economy is intrinsic to actual processes of production, so that the structures of capitalist production are internally organized towards their reproduction. Giddens's depiction of the 'institutional reflexivity' of capitalism is very much indebted to Marx's argument that the capitalist system reproduces itself as a class structure, because ownership of private property in the means of production is constitutive of the structuration of the social system and a source of the dichotomy between classes (Marx 1976; Giddens 1981a; 1985a).

Giddens believes that the technical division of the labour process was just as much shaped by modes of control as it was by the allocative criteria of efficiency and profit. This domination is veiled however, because the involuntary authoritarian socialization of capitalist production is connected to the commodification of labour-power and the regulation of time (Giddens 1981a). Capitalism transfers the 'dialectic of control' into the process of production, where it is expressed in conflicts over the intensity, duration and direction of work. Unlike all preceding modes of production, control over labour is exercised in capitalist production without the threat of force. It is founded, as Marx claimed, in 'dull economic compulsion'.

The exchange of labour power as a commodity subordinates the worker to the authority of capital. And yet, the structural interdependence of capitalist production means that appropriating surplus is applied to the activity of labour itself and not to the acquisition of the product of labour. The surplus is mediated, as Marx showed, by the transforming of labour-power, that is, the potential for labour, into the actual practice of labour. Commodification turns labour-power into a cost for employers and, consequently, the asymmetrical interdependence operates on capital. There appears to be no disagreement between Giddens and Marx on the fact that the continual extraction of surplus labour-time is a condition of the reproduction of capital (Giddens 1981a). Giddens attributes the systematic surveillance of work and the rise of management to the spatial concentration of labour and the determination of the value of production in relation to time.

Modern forms of surveillance are a major concern of Giddens's analysis, partly because he considers the analysis of surveillance to be essential to understanding the modern potential for totalitarian organization. This does not mean that he regards surveillance to be solely negative and oppressive; Giddens's position concurs with Foucault's analytics of power in considering that surveillance is also generative and productive. Indeed, he implies that its dialectical quality needs to be properly appreciated, but his analysis does demonstrate that there can be no 'value-neutral' technical administration from the standpoint of power (Giddens 1985a; 1981a). Surveillance is an essential part of the radical discontinuity of modernity and capitalism; it is more integral to them than it was to any earlier form of society. This is most strikingly demonstrated by the nation-state coming to replace the city as the chief power container in modernity, something that was largely made possible by the increased surveillance associated with modern communication media's greater time-space distanciation and the overall expansion in administrative control. The growth in modernity of administrative control underpins a broad reorganization of social relations. Even in the Absolutist state, which precedes and prefigures many of modernity's institutions, surveillance capacity was rudimentary compared to the nation-state (Giddens 1985a, 83–121).

Despite Giddens's (1994a) later disavowing the economics of the labour theory of value, he originally endorsed Marx's claim that the extraction of surplus was relative to the socially necessary expenditure of labour time under capitalism (Giddens 1981a). Indeed, he does not depart from Marx in arguing that property has to have become highly alienable for time to supply the measure of the commensurability of commodities. Due to its abstract quality and alienability, the radically different temporal arrangements of commodified property are exhibited in Weber's analysis of money and the rational accounting procedures of double entry bookkeeping (Giddens 1985a; Weber 1978). By its systematic information control, this procedure served as a new storage mechanism quantifying the future. It complements the more intensive surveillance of the labour process in modernity. Giddens (1984) proposes that the key to the quantification of production is the convertibility of the commodity form. Marx described this structural set in the reproductive circuit of money-commodity-money. Hence, Marx's labour theory of value illustrates how capitalism reflexively incorporated time into the regulation of processes of production and how these 'intentional' changes promoted new levels of system integration, that is, the spatial as well as temporal extending of markets and exchange relations with those physically absent. This analysis of the intersecting of 'intentional' and 'extensional' processes is probably the most interesting dimension of Giddens's reinterpretation of Marx's account of the real abstraction of capitalism.

Although they are interdependent moments of structuration, Giddens argues that the 'insulation' of the economy from the sphere of political authority should be understood in terms of the labour contract rather than the market in goods. Giddens criticizes the emphasis on market exchange, rather than the originating structure of production, in Wallerstein's (1974; 1979) conception of the world system. But he agrees with Wallerstein that capitalist accumulation generates globally expanding markets, as well as creating national and an international division of labour (Giddens 1985a; 1990a; 1981a). According to Giddens, the globalizing tendency of capitalist production is reinforced by the development of the nation-state system. The authoritative power of the state expands, as we saw, due to the centralizing of force associated with the pacification of everyday life and the new media enabling greater administrative control of information. Modern communication systems expand the surveillance capacity of the nation-state far beyond those of class-divided systems and these means of administrative integration involve 'disembedding' processes similar to those of the capitalist commodification of property. Information exchange separates from the movement of material phenomena across space and the temporal duration of the transmission of information diminishes towards the point of instantaneous communication. These media promote a dynamic 'reflexive monitoring' of social relations and initiate a new dialectic of control in extending state surveillance (Giddens 1985a).

The dialectic of control does not follow a simple linear pattern in modernity, as some of the media for collating information become means for its dispersal and reappropriation. Whilst this change promotes the democratizing tendencies that Giddens associates with the contemporary stage of reflexive modernization, his initial conception seems to too closely associate the constitution of democracy with the expansion of state-administrative control. He proposes that the same processes that generated the sovereignty of the nation-state and the expansion of surveillance were linked to the constitution of modern civil rights and the political form of modern democracy or polyarchy. Like Lindblom, Giddens defines polyarchy as 'the rule by the many, and involves the continuing responsiveness of the government to the preferences of its citizens considered as political equals' (Giddens 1985a, 199). Although he stresses the basis of polyarchy in modern systems of rights, Giddens consistently argues that civil society is generated through a relationship to the state. In his opinion, civil society is not really a category independent of the state, but 'was bound up with the state and its centralization'. Indeed, he claims that civil society 'was an aspect of that *centralization*, a set of reinvented traditions' (Giddens 1994a, 124, 135).

In Giddens's opinion, modern notions of social association were conditioned by the internal pacification of the nation-state, yet the composition of the system of states was substantially the outcome of the contingencies of military power. This is one of the reasons why it sometimes appears as though he seeks to simply correct the classical sociological theorists' accounts of modern institutions with empirical history (Giddens 1985a). The contingency of the nation-state, he suggests, is disguised by nationalism. Nationalist sentiments respond to the insecurity generated by the new arrangements of time and space, which are produced especially by the commodification of everyday life and the 'created environment' of modern urbanism. These are 'denuded' of moral content and nationalism fabricates a 'cultural homogeneity' that endows the sovereignty of the nation-state with its ideological content (Giddens 1985a, 218–21; 1981a, 191–96).

Modern nation-states differ from class-divided societies in many respects other than the normative cohesion they exhibit. For Giddens, the critical difference consists in the fact that the nation-state is an internally almost completely administratively pacified entity. Rather than this being due to an initial cultural and normative patterning, it is this pacifying that enables the cultural cohesion and normative integration of nation-states. It may be, paradoxically, that Giddens's critique of the normative functionalist assumption that integration is based on deeply internalized values that results in his accentuation of the sense of ontological security that individuals derive from nationalism.

The contrasting potentials of nationalism illustrate in miniature what Giddens (1994a; 1994b) perceives to be the alternate implications of contemporary detraditionalization. On the one hand, the ontological security supplied by nationalist sentiments can, in the context of unsettling change, promote an affective attachment to charismatic leaders. On the other hand, where the sovereignty of the nation-state is anchored in a conception of citizenship rights, nationalism may be a symbolic expression of democratic solidarity. The other side of symbolic expression is the hermeneutic closure of administrative power. Giddens agrees with Foucault that there is a 'sequestration' of experience in modernity, especially the sequestering of phenomena like madness, criminality and sickness (Giddens 1991a, 144–80; Foucault 1977; 1979). As these examples from the work of Foucault attest, sequestration is connected with the increased surveillance in modernity. Further, Giddens assumes 'that the ontological security which modernity has purchased, on the level of day-to-day routines, depends on an institutional exclusion of social life from fundamental existential issues which raise central moral dilemma for human beings' (Giddens 1991a, 156). He argues that the sequestration of these moral dilemmas is generally a consequence of modern social systems' replacement of 'external' criteria by 'internal'. In this way, the 'end of nature' as external to the social has parallels with the processes of detraditionalization and it could be argued that Giddens's is updating Weber's diagnosis of how rationalization in modernity is based on a depersonalizing separation of facts and values, as well as undermining meaningful value commitments (Giddens 1991a).

The modern state is significantly shaped by the alignment of resources. In capitalist society, the dominant class derives its power from the control and ownership of allocative resources; the ruling class does not need to possess the authoritative resources of the modern state to dominate society. At the same time, the state in its capacity for surveillance, administration and violence has sources of power that are not reducible to class relations and these features enable, within certain parameters, autonomous state action (Giddens 1981a; 1985a). Giddens considers that this analysis is critical of the Marxist views of the state as defined by the class antagonism of capitalism, but accepts certain features of recent Neo-Marxist arguments. Like Habermas and Offe, he considers that the modern state largely depends upon processes of capital accumulation that it 'does not control' for its taxation revenue. Unlike the precapitalist state, the power of the modern state to sanction is not directly exercised in the capitalist process of extracting a surplus from immediate producers; rather under the circumstances of the reforms ensuing from class struggle, the state has to varying degrees legally regulated the fundamental structure of the capitalist labour contract. However, this does not alter the insulation of the capitalist economy from the political-administrative state and it is this separation that conditions the class compromise of the welfare state. Giddens claims that 'Offe is certainly right' in pointing to the contradiction involved in the state's reliance on the mobilization and success of privately owned capital and the state's assumption of the 'responsibility for the provision of a range of community services' (Giddens 1981a, 214). In short, the state cannot pursue the latter too strongly as it would require revenue-raising measures, such as through increased taxation, that impinge on the former processes of capital accumulation and business investment.

Giddens draws on T. H. Marshall's notion of citizenship rights to identify how far the welfare state has shifted the parameters of class domination and the 'dialectic of control' connected to each of the institutional dimensions of modernity. Marshall proposed that there are three types of citizenship rights and that they developed in a sequence, so that the prior legal rights to enter into contracts contributes to the development of political rights and these rights to participation in the political process then prepare the ground for social rights (Marshall 1991). Like Habermas's (1987a) account of the successive waves of juridification, Marshall's categories of legal, political and social citizenship rights correspond to different stages in the development of the modern state. Social rights are founded on the institution of the welfare state and they include various income and social security provisions. For Marshall, principles of justice inform social rights and they aim to enable citizens to fully access the other rights. Giddens criticizes the evolutionary logic of Marshall's analysis and he contends that citizenship rights have not remodelled capitalist society in the manner that he believes Marshall suggested. In particular, the conflict intrinsic the labour contract persists as a fundamental organizing feature of capitalism. Similarly, Giddens argued that the dependence of the welfare state upon revenue that is generated outside its control indicates that Marxist arguments about the limitations of state action and its systematic class allegiance have considerable validity.

The extent to which these criticisms dissent from Marshall's analysis is open to dispute. There is arguably an even greater disparity between their emphasis on social conflict and Giddens's later positions in his political policy contributions of 'The Third Way' (Giddens 1998; 2000). These tensions will be considered later, but there can be little doubt that Giddens's interpretation of each of the rights of citizenship as opposing different types of surveillance is more ambivalent than Marshall's view. Although he finds Marshall's interpretation of the universal application of rights important to understanding the character of the class compromise of the welfare state, Giddens proposes that the extension of rights is a product of class conflict, rather than that the rights of citizenship have undermined class conflict.

> In my view, therefore, it is more valid to say that class conflict has been a medium of the extension of citizenship rights than to say that the spread of such rights has blunted class divisions. *All three forms of citizenship right distinguished by Marshall are double-edged.* As aspects of surveillance, they can be mobilized to expand the control other members of the dominant class are able to maintain over those in subordinate positions. But, at the same time, each is a lever of struggle, which can be used to counter that control. In a capitalist society, class domination provides the most important single institutional axis around which these struggles converge and, in that respect, Marx's view is still cogent. But it does not follow from this that surveillance is an epiphenomenon of class, or that the modes of generating power which it provides will disappear with the transcending in the capitalist class system. Conflict centred upon 'bourgeois rights' is not necessarily class conflict, and the level and nature of their realization has to be regarded as altogether more problematic than Marx believed. (Giddens 1985a, 208–9)

Despite the terminological differences, Giddens's analysis of the dialectic of citizenship rights outlines problems similar to those covered by Habermas's thesis of the internal colonization of the lifeworld. Owing to its view of class struggle, Giddens's interpretation is more agonistic and the centrality of power to his analysis means that he does not perceive a linear process of rationalization that leads to the development of the welfare state. Habermas saw this development as paradoxical and the colonization of the lifeworld was a consequence of the displacement of the class conflict of capitalist production. Like Habermas, Giddens's writings attempt to constructively address the contemporary 'obscurity' concerning the future of the welfare state. In this context, he argues that the social preconditions of Marshall's analysis of citizenship have been overtaken by the changes of the phase of reflexive modernization that commenced in the latter decades of the twentieth century (Giddens 1994a; 1996).

Before turning to these themes, I want to underline a feature of the shifts in Giddens's position. I have argued that a change of perspective is involved in his emphasis upon the institutional diversity of modernity over the determination of a fundamental structural principle. The implication of this change is that the question of class as a collective agency takes on a lesser importance. As a consequence, Giddens more broadly delineates the potentials for transformation. He suggests that a corresponding social movement contests the forms of domination associated with each of the institutional clusters of modernity: democratic and free speech movements contest the power of surveillance, the conflicts of capitalist production engender the labour movement, industrialism is opposed by ecological movements, which espouse counter-cultural values, and peace movements seek to limit and resist militarism and violence (Giddens 1985a; 1990). In his opinion, the labour movement 'retains a centrality in capitalist societies because of their inherently class character', but the organizing role of the labour movement in relation to other types of protests does not mean that it is 'inevitably the prime source of opposition' (Giddens 1985a, 314–15).

In moving away from the generative conception of structural principles, Giddens turns toward an explanation of modernity in terms of consequences. The latter could be viewed as inconsistent with some of the precepts of structuration theory. The assessment of consequences seems to be a major reason for Giddens's distinguishing industrialism from capitalism, since it facilitates a greater appreciation of the questions of risk in late modernity. In his view, Marx was a critic of capitalism but not of industrialism. Yet, 'it is evident that some of the most urgent problems facing the world economy are to do with industrialism rather than with the mechanisms of capitalist production as such. That is to say, they lead us to look away from the traditional areas of concentration of Marxist theory – in its more orthodox forms at any rate – towards ecological problems' (Giddens 1985a, 340). Giddens's later political writings attempt to more systematically integrate ecological considerations into the programme of social democracy. Further, they aim to promote the present tendencies of democratization that have already restructured aspects of contemporary social relations. The latter argument is similar to Habermas's conception of the communicative rationalization and it enables Giddens to elaborate a conception of generative processes that is distinct from Marx's production paradigm. At the same time, it is supposedly consistent with the praxis philosophical critique of forms of organization that are detached from the context of life activities and that seek to influence this context through indirect means. In other words, he aims to promote a renewal of participation in civil society.

Giddens's institutional typology of modernity: capitalism, surveillance industrialism, and the military violence of the nation-state, reflects what he considers to be the conjunctural origins of capitalism (1985a; 1990a). Yet, this argument potentially conflicts with his earlier more quasi-Marxian concern with the conflicts and dynamics generated by system contradictions and, as I suggested, the delineating an overall structural principle. Still, a significant implication of Giddens's critique is that modernity and the capitalist dimension of it are epochally different. Marx's suggestion that post-capitalist socialist society would be the radically discontinuous historical formation is qualified by this implication. The practical-political repercussion of this argument seem to be that Marx underestimated the constraining conditions modernity imposed upon the possibility of radical change. That is, he underestimated the unforeseen problems and perniciously risky conditions created in realizing an emancipated and autonomous society. Giddens's arguments for radicalizing the dimensions of change beyond those envisaged by Marx, paradoxically lead to a position justifying his later relatively 'moderate' political programme (Giddens 1994a; 1996; 1998a; 2000). He perceives that the shift to a stress on the institutional diversity of modernity has significant ramifications for progressive politics and that in the case of the institutions of capitalism, industrialism, surveillance and violence:

> None is wholly reducible to any of the others. A concern with the consequences of each moves critical theory away from its concentration upon the transcendence of capitalism by socialism as the sole objective of future social transformations. (Giddens 1985a, 5)

The major categories of Giddens's account of late modernity rework the conception of abstraction and distanciation that has been outlined, like those of institutional reflexivity, the disembedding mechanisms such as abstract systems and symbolic tokens, and the separation of time and space (Giddens 1990a; 1991a). Likewise, the institutional distinction between the social and the natural is constitutive of modernity; as we saw, he claims that the precapitalist forms of relating to nature meant that social relations were not a completely self-structuring principle of their organization. Marx's analysis of the real abstraction of capitalist production is therefore important because it illuminates how the capitalist system is socially structured, the economic system is insulated from the political and social class becomes the structural principle. Giddens's remark that in capitalist society existential contradiction is suppressed by 'structural contradiction' reflects this radical transformation. He contends that it underlies Marx's conception of the fundamental contradiction of capitalist society between private appropriation and socialized production (Giddens 1981a; Marx 1976).

Habermas objects to a notion of social self-structuration because of its analogy to the subject (Habermas 1982; see Habermas 1987b). Giddens's subsequent stress on the institutional diversity of modernity compared to the earlier notions of structural principles and contradiction could be viewed as an attempt to resist the implications of this criticism. Indeed, to a certain extent, Giddens agrees with Habermas that it is not the extension of instrumental reason that is the defining feature of modern social systems but the internal reflexivity of their operations and the type of historicity that this creates in modernity.

> The overall thrust of modern institutions is to create settings of action ordered in terms of modernity's own dynamics and severed from 'external criteria' – factors external to the social systems of modernity. Although there are numerous exceptions and countertrends, day-to-day social life tends to become separated from 'original' nature and from a variety of experiences bearing on existential questions and dilemmas. (Giddens 1991a, 8)

Conclusion

Giddens's theoretical perspective on history was clarified in the process of explicating his critique of historical materialism; and this results in a number of contrasts with Habermas's theory. Giddens's theory focuses on the historical augmentation of power, both in the traditional meaning of the expanding of the institutions and systems of domination and in the more specific structuration theory sense of generative power. The latter represents the infrastructural conditions of forms of social domination and this conceptualization fits the structuration theory interpretation of the conversion between structure as the medium and outcome of action. It likewise leads to Giddens's historical analyses of how power goes together with the enhancement of social capabilities, such as in the power to span time and space, the concentrating of capacities in cities, the relative degree of the intrusion of surveillance into everyday life, and the expansion of power that ensues from the earliest activities of rationalization, like numerical listing and writing. The focus on power means that social conflict appears more prominent in Giddens's historical account of different social orders than in Habermas's reconstruction of historical materialism. Giddens's lesser emphasis on the normative dimension of social relations means that the legitimation of power is less significant for his theory and interpretation of historical formations than it is for Habermas's theory. Habermas considers that normative development and cultural rationalization can advance beyond the existing social order and shape social change.

In the case of Giddens's theory, force and coercion are likewise considered to be major determinants of historical processes. The 'internal pacification' of society is defined by him as one of the distinguishing developments connected to the modern institution of the nation-state. Giddens agrees with Marx and Weber that the commodification of labour is integral to the institution of capitalism and that it is fundamental to the distinction between precapitalist class-divided societies and modern class society. In a sense, these transformations are broadly equivalent to those Habermas described as the separation between lifeworld and system; however, there are two differences that are worth underlining. First, Giddens position implies a greater degree of contingency with respect to both the processes of the institutionalization of this distinction and its reproduction. This partly reflects the greater significance of power in Giddens's approach and a more qualified position on the rationality of social systems, although Giddens does argue that the reflexivity of social systems expands with modernity (Giddens 1981; 1990).

Second, Giddens's perspective sustains a greater sense of the dialectics of control, even though some elements of his formulations concerning these dialectics is open to dispute, such as in its treatment of civil society as largely constituted by the state. It has been argued that contrary to its intentions, Habermas's critical deployment of systems theory undermined the sense of contestation and dialectics of control. Giddens's subsequent work on modernity expands on some of the themes of his original critical theory of history but considerably diverges from aspects of its approach. There is arguably a shift from power as the leading category in Giddens's theorizing of large-scale social processes to that of risk in his work on contemporary modernity, sometimes described by him as late-modernity, high modernity and reflexive modernization. The latter category refers to how the original phase of modernization, that is associated with the transition from premodern feudal society and the institutionalizing of such processes as those of industrialization and rationalization, generates a second phase in which the processes of modernization are now enacted on the already largely modernized society. As we will see, Giddens and Beck argue that the consequences of this process are paradoxical and that modernization is now generating increasing risk and uncertainty (Giddens 1990, 1994b; Beck 1992).

It is worth reiterating that the historical details of the pattern of European modernization that Habermas and Giddens detail contain many similarities, like some version of the separation of the economy from the state, the growth of bureaucratic organization, the modernist displacement of class conflict by way of nationalism and the welfare state, the emergence of more diverse forms of social movements. There is undoubtedly a sense that they broadly recognized that aspects of this modernizing constellation were under strain, but that the Marxist predictions concerning a transition from capitalism to socialism had receded. Further, for each of them the praxis philosophy interpretation of the nexus of history and subject needed to be rethought under these conditions and this had motivated many of the revisions of their respective theories of history and accounts of modernity's institutionalization. At the same time, the difficulties that have been identified point to unresolved problems in Habermas's and Giddens's contrasting perspectives on history and it will become apparent that their later works on the contemporary constellation of modernity are arguably somewhat more delimited in their themes and frameworks.

Before exploring Habermas's and Giddens's work on the contemporary constellation of modernity and the significantly revised approaches that inform these conceptions, this section will conclude with some 'Intermediate Reflections' on the contrasts and divisions that have so far been uncovered and alluded to in my comparative analysis. This analysis draws attention to some of the problems and relative deficiencies of Habermas's and Giddens's social theories. It consequently provides some insight into the motivations that lie behind the revisions outlined in the next section and it clarifies several of the contrasts that have been noted in the explications of the main theoretical frameworks of Habermas and Giddens.

Chapter Five

INTERMEDIATE REFLECTIONS ON SOCIAL THEORY ALTERNATIVES: CONTRASTS AND DIVISIONS

The preceding analysis disclosed how Giddens's aim of sociologically extending the praxis perspective differs from Habermas's (1987b) assessment that the philosophy of praxis has been effectively superseded by the paradigm of understanding. A number of these contrasts warrant specific consideration, because they are relevant to Habermas's and Giddens's contrasting interpretations of the institutionalization of modernity and their broader theoretical conceptions of historical change. These contrasts are similarly related to the immanent difficulties of Habermas's change to the paradigm of understanding and equally the need for Giddens to further develop the presuppositions of his programme. In fact, Habermas and Giddens highlight how the institutionalization of modernity was shaped by similar major developments, particularly the separation of the capitalist economic system from the state. Yet, owing to their different theoretical perspectives, they sometimes characterize these same developments in contrasting ways and present different, as well as well as sometimes complementary, evaluations of their implications.

My discussion here will initially draw attention to the potentials that structuration theory contains for rectifying certain difficulties of Habermas's theory, particularly those limitations that result from his formulation of the intersubjective constitution of identity as a rational mediation of the universal and particular. Habermas's explanation of the historical institutionalization of modernity is based on the theoretical argument that processes of cultural rationalization initially made possible the structural rationalization of the spheres of the capitalist economy and the state administrative system. The latter processes consolidate the separation between the lifeworld and system, with the expansion of the latter developing to a stage where it paradoxically threatens the communicative reproduction of the lifeworld. As expected, Giddens's explanation of the institutional transition to modernity places greater emphasis on the changing complexion of power and the radically new temporal and spatial dynamic of the structuration of institutional systems, particularly capitalism and the mediated transmission of information more generally. The normative changes that Giddens identifies are largely considered in combination with power. The limitations of this approach will become apparent when the perspectives are reversed and the weaknesses of Giddens's theory of structuration and deconstruction of historical materialism are considered in light of Habermas's theoretical standpoint.

First, Giddens's conception of social practices accentuates 'ontological' aspects of human action. Those aspects of action that he explicates arguably have a certain affinity with Marx's understanding of the existential conditions of production, like the process character of social activity and the constitutive significance of human finitude (Marx 1976; Sayer 1987). Habermas, to be sure, recognizes these aspects of Marx's dialectical social theory, but, in my opinion, he subordinates them to the rationality considerations of communication theory (Habermas 1984a, 1987a). This subordination is most evident in Habermas's evaluation of Marx's category of labour and his understanding of subjects' communicative competence. Habermas's notion of communicative competence not only includes subjects' ability to participate in argumentative discourse, but it is specified in light of discourse procedures that are distinct from the actual processes of social action.

I have argued that Habermas's theory of action is primarily concerned with the processes of intersubjective coordination and that this is consistent with his core conception of the constitution of identity. In fact, he acknowledges that the basis of most action is the warrant of the validity claims raised in intersubjective speech or dialogue. The warrant is the presumption that is made that the speaker could provide, if queried, a rational justification for the claims that are made in speech acts, such as through providing rational arguments in defense of them. Habermas claims that to understand a speech act is to know the conditions under which it is acceptable, because often in everyday interaction speakers do not explicitly state those reasons or grounds that would redeem a validity claim in the face of the criticisms.

> Thus a speaker owes the binding (or bonding: *bindende*) force of his illocutionary act not to the validity of what is said but to the coordinating effect of the warranty that he offers: namely to redeem, if necessary, the validity claim raised with his speech act. (Habermas 1984a, 302)

For the most part, the same action sequence follows from the acceptance of the speech act on the presumption of a warrant to redeem a validity claim as would be the case if the speaker provided further reasons that addressed potential criticisms of the validity claim raised in the speech act. This presumption is important for the further reason that Habermas's theory of modernity seeks to disclose the extent to which communicative rationality has penetrated into the lifeworld background. Habermas contends that this is the appropriate measure for evaluating rationalization, rather than the acting process itself (Habermas 1984).

It could be argued that Habermas's category of the lifeworld covers, on the one hand, much of what Giddens conceive of with the notion of practical consciousness. On the other hand, Giddens's activist account of practical consciousness intimates at how much Habermas's notion of communicative rationality refers to conditions when the 'pressures' or constraints of action have to varying extents been suspended. That is, on Giddens's analysis, the provision of reasons is associated with the reflexive moment of action and conditioned by the specific forums of discussion. Indeed, consistent with Giddens's analysis of alternate traditions of action theory, epistemological considerations did influence Habermas's original decision to ground the social sciences in a theory of language (Habermas 1988a). Habermas's theory of action is more innovative in one particular respect than Giddens's theory. It is more consistent and thoroughgoing in its elaboration from an intersubjective standpoint. Giddens seems to alternate between endorsing this intersubjective approach and expressing scepticism about some of its purported implications. Further, by contrast with Habermas theory of intersubjective communication, Giddens's conception of practice is certainly not as strong in its normative grounding as that of the original praxis philosophy conception.

Second, despite Giddens's initial affinities with Marx's standpoint, he develops a 'generic' conception of praxis, rather than extending the philosophical anthropology of labour. Nevertheless, this generic version of social practice is not subject to many of the objections that have been raised against Habermas's early contrast between labour and interaction or the problems of the distinctions that are employed in Habermas's later typologies of action. For example, there is arguably the inconsistency between teleology being considered a common structure of all action and a distinct type of strategic-instrumental action that contrasts with communicative action (Habermas 1984a). Although Habermas's communication theory framework involves a more radical departure from phenomenological and ethnomethodological accounts of action, Giddens's basic conception of action exhibits stronger continuities with these traditions than his criticisms of their overall inadequacies suggests. Nevertheless, consistent with those general criticisms of various theories of action which informs his structuration perspective, Giddens claims not only that Habermas's formulation of the action theory categories of labour and interaction suffers from its emphasis upon epistemological considerations, but also that Habermas has not adequately developed an ontological conception of praxis. As a consequence, Giddens argues that there is an 'absent core' to Habermas's theory owing to its neglect of the production and reproduction of social life (Giddens 1982b, 159).

In this critique, Giddens drew particular attention to the problems of Habermas's fusing Marx's notion of the dialectic of the forces and relations of production with Weber's categories of purposive-rational action and value-rational action (Giddens 1982b). According to Giddens, Habermas, in effect, simplifies the layers of structuration through assimilating the institutional significance of Marx's notion of production to Weber's analytical categories of action (Giddens 1982b). In one sense, Giddens's claim that Habermas neglects the production and reproduction of social life is simply wrong and misleading, given that Habermas's categories of system and lifeworld are both concerned with social reproduction. Similarly, Habermas's adoption of the notion of system appears to have been partly motivated by a need to rectify this identification of action types and institutional spheres. Rather, the validity of Giddens's criticism relates to Habermas's diversion from the praxis philosophy conception of the dynamics involved in social constitution and reproduction.

Third, Giddens's theory potentially rectifies some of the inadequacies of Habermas's conceptualizing power and social conflicts. Since Giddens does not consider power as primarily a media of social systems, he avoids the 'fiction' of a lifeworld arena that is free of power (Honneth 1991). Habermas (1991) has revised his position without necessarily conceding this criticism, but his criticism of George Herbert Mead's 'reflections on social evolution', 'neglect of economics, warfare, and the struggle for political power' could also be applied to the major statement of his own theory (Habermas 1987a, 110). By contrast, Giddens's intent in reformulating the notions of contradiction and exploitation is closer to the suppositions of Marx's interpretation of class conflict than is Habermas's account of contemporary social pathologies due to the inner colonization of the life-world. Habermas's interest in their non-class specific character partly accounts for this difference, but notions of social pathology have had a wider currency in functionalist discourses, especially amongst those influenced by Durkheim's explanation of the con-sequences of the transition from mechanical to organic solidarity (Habermas 1987a). Berger comments that in *The Theory of Communicative Action*

> it is no coincidence that Habermas speaks of 'pathologies' in the Durkheimian tradition and not of 'crises' in the Marxist tradition; crises lead either to a resolution or to destruction; resolu-tion is 'self-purgation' and destruction is 'self-destruction'. Pathologies continue or are stopped from the outside. As faulty developments, pathologies can be corrected. (Berger 1991, 170)

Fourth, starting from its revision of sociological action theory, Giddens's structuration perspective suggests that Habermas's recourse to a functionalist understanding of sys-tems could have been avoided. In particular, Giddens's approach questions those ele-ments of Habermas's conception of systems which were indebted to Parsons's theory of society. It questions both its analytical and historical justification. Structuration theory is probably more consistent in conceptualizing the dialectical interconnection of sys-tem and lifeworld. In his exposition of different theoretical approaches to the lifeworld, Habermas (1987a) did note how important the spatial and temporal conditions of prac-tices were to Schutz and Luckmann's investigations (Schutz 1967; Schutz and Luckmann 1974). Unlike Giddens, he does not then examine the extent to which spatial and tempo-ral processes of social reproduction may be equally constitutive of social systems. System integration need not be juxtaposed to subjects' practices, but neither then is the for-mal definition of systems sufficient to ascertain the dynamics of their reproduction (see Calhoun 1995, 205–12).

These considerations make it an open question regarding how much time and space condition, what Habermas describes as, the systemic steering medias' relieving the com-municative coordination of action, and system integration is less a formally predefined structure than a social process. In my opinion, Giddens develops a sustained critique of the functionalist criteria of complexity, whereas Habermas originally presented the possibility of such a critique but subsequently seemed to adapt this category for his own purposes of delimiting critiques of modernity (Habermas 1987a; 1987b). Hartmut Rosa's interpretation of modernity in terms of social acceleration is indicative of how Giddens's interest in the constitutive significance of temporal and spatial processes can be developed (Rosa 2013). Rosa's contention that social acceleration drives processes of structural differentiation in modernity, rather than the predominant sociological view of the reverse, is anticipated by Giddens. It provides a different perspective on Habermas's distinction between lifeworld and system.

Fifth, Giddens's interpretation of social practice informs a considerably differ-ent account of history and social change to Habermas's reconstruction of historical materialism. In the first instance, Giddens is critical of Habermas's procedure of rational reconstruction; he implies that the logical structure of rational reconstruction precludes a satisfactory approach to the contingency of history.[1] If anything, Giddens reverses the emphasis of Habermas's theory of evolution, in Giddens's writings the dynamics of history are prioritized over the logic of development. Nevertheless, whilst rejecting a phylogenetic logic of evolutionary development is entirely consistent with his greater emphasis upon the constitutive role of power and arguments concerning the contingency of social reproduction relative to the transformative capacity of agency, it also reflects what commentators like Arnason (1984) and Kilminster (1991) describe as Giddens's having forsaken the question of meaning in history and the historical-genetic conception of synthesis of critical theory. In a sense, he attempts to justify this deficiency in his later works by arguing that modernity is characterized by constant change and that the attempts to reflexively employ history to shape the present in the light of the potential future has undermined providential and teleological notions of the direction of history (Giddens 1990a; 1994a).

I have argued that Habermas's theory is organized by the problem of social identity and that this results in his emphasizing the moments of coordination, exchange and distribution, rather the generative moment of production. Despite revising the action theoretical foundations of social practice, Giddens's generative orientation and process conception are closer to some of the suppositions of Marx's theory. The tradition of praxis philosophy adhered to a stronger sense of the objectivity of structure and of how the translation between action and structure has historically increased the independence and power of the latter, such as with respect to capitalist appropriation then increasing the composition of capital and its capacity for the appropriation of labour power. This difference can be demonstrated by reference to some of the influential criticisms of the theory of structuration.

Habermas and Giddens agree on the need to integrate action theory and systems theory, however, Giddens dissents from Habermas's definition of this problem, and hence he disagrees with Habermas's solution in a two-level conception of society. According to Giddens, Habermas's valid criticisms of functionalist reason are not sufficiently far reaching and the final result is an ineffective compromise (Giddens 1987). At the same time, although Margaret Archer's criticism of structuration theory's mistaken conflation of action and structure may be disputed, it can be interpreted as providing indirect support for the intentions behind Habermas's division of lifeworld and system (Archer 1982; 1996). Similarly, William Sewell contention that the two components of Giddens's conception of structure are not equivalent could suggest that Giddens underestimated the objective and external character of the social relations that Habermas attributed to the system (Sewell 1992; 2005). Sewell argues that rules have a virtual existence but resources always exist. Although Sewell's contrast is not equivalent to Habermas's distinction between system and lifeworld, the contrast between the communicative reproduction of

---

1   Although he accepts that an epistemologically diluted version of reconstructive science is representative of 'what sociologists do', see Giddens (1987) for his inaugural lecture on this theme.

the lifeworld and the material reproduction of social systems would appear broadly in line with this contrast.

For his part, Habermas viewed Giddens's intentions as sharing the symptomatic problems of the philosophy of praxis, its derivation from the subject-centred philosophy of consciousness and the complementary conception of teleological action. Habermas stated that

> Giddens wants to distinguish [...] a concept of practice that is supposed to be related to the constitution of action complexes and their reproduction. I do not think that this choice of conceptual strategy is a fortunate one, because the basic epistemological concept of 'constitution', which refers to the formation of object domains causes confusion in social theory. [...] it is advisable, first, to separate clearly concepts of action from those of society, second, to distinguish between society as a symbolically structured lifeworld [...] and society as a system [...] in order, third to develop from this *a two-level concept of society* and corresponding concepts of social reproduction. The latter cannot be reduced, as Giddens proposes, to *Praxis*. The overextension of action concepts in a theory of constitution remains stuck in metaphors; the basic concept of the philosophy of *Praxis* gives us at best an anthropomorphistic concept of society. (Habermas 1982, 269)

Habermas uses the idea of system differentiation in rejecting the perspective of the philosophy of praxis, whereas Giddens was from the outset critical of the functionalist definition of the problem of order and this leads to his later questioning the notion of differentiation. The theory of structuration then involves a simultaneous transformation of the meaning of the problem of order and the understanding of social action. Like Habermas, Giddens believes that it is mistaken to presume that either of these tasks could be pursued independently of the other, and hence they must be conceived together. Yet, Habermas's conception demarcates the legitimate domain of action theory in such a way that it downplays the internal dynamics of formal organizations and subordinates types of action to both the means of action coordination that establish social order and the rationality requirements of communicative action.

Given its commencing from a critique of functionalism, some of the difficulties of functionalism should be unlikely to appear in Giddens's theory of structuration. However, commentators, like Bauman (1989), have suggested that his conception of the basic question in social theory does not sufficiently depart from that of Parsons's approach and others claim that Giddens's attempt to integrate structure and action obscures the real difference between them (Archer 1982; 1990). The problems that these criticisms signal have a wider bearing on the potential of the theory of structuration and it is probably fair to note that Giddens's theory of structuration will always be viewed critically by those committed to the distinction between action and structure, especially when this distinction is taken to refer to not just different domains but opposed epistemological standpoints. For instance, Habermas (1987a) drew attention to the distinction between the 'internal' perspective of the actor in action theory and the 'external' perspective of the observer in theories of the functional reproduction of systems.

In terms of Habermas's distinction between system and lifeworld, it is worth noting that the generative approach of the philosophy of praxis presumes that action theory has precedence. This is continued, as Bernstein (1989, 23) notes, in the structuration theory argument that the 'crucial concept of "unintended consequences" itself presupposes a viable concept of human agency.' Habermas, it may be recalled, initially proposed that a systems theory perspective is necessitated by the unintended consequences of action and he has subsequently revised this position in response to criticisms. By contrast, Giddens recognized the illuminating approach to institutions of approaches like phenomenology, ethnomethodology and symbolic interactionism. Habermas's distinction between lifeworld and system appeared to downplay the insights of these approaches beyond the domain of the lifeworld. As McCarthy (1985) suggests, the insights of these approaches is the exact opposite to that of the conclusions Habermas (1987a) drew in defining systems based on the criteria of formal membership. For they have shown that the actual operation of organizations depends on actors neglecting formal regulations and that authority is negotiated.

Despite recognizing the importance of interpretative and action theoretical perspectives' insights, Giddens argues, like Habermas, that evident problems limited these perspectives from constituting overall theories of society. He points to problems such as weaknesses in the case of comprehending history as conditioning circumstances of interaction and inadequacies in explaining the unintended consequences of action. A failure to satisfactorily address either of these problems simply opened the way for a return of the functionalist solution of the coordinating role of social systems (Giddens 1979, 7). In Giddens's opinion, these approaches would never develop into satisfactory alternatives to functionalist analyses of the institutional structures of society. This constituted the aspiration of his theory. His alternative to functionalism developed from an attempt to elucidate how it is that action and structure logically presuppose one another in the production and reproduction of society.

In pursuing this task, Giddens initially drew inspiration and orientation from Marx's theory of praxis. Marx's theory of praxis represented a general alternative to functionalism and the limitations of sociological action theory, but Giddens considered the practical orientation of Marx's theory had to be extricated from the functionalist arguments of historical materialism and this 'deconstruction' served to clarify many of the features of his own approach (Giddens 1981a; 1984). However, it is possible to consider whether Giddens's theory of structuration formulations actually meet the requirements of the praxis philosophical conception of transformation and mediation, given its critical notions of reification and alienation. It can be queried whether the concepts of structuration theory are really able to account for the translation involved where system reproduction conforms to the logic of processes that are not independent of the practices that constitute them, but are neither simply reducible to these.

In some respects, the concepts that Giddens develops to explain the contemporary phase of modernity do, as we will see, precisely attempt to depict this kind of translation. Yet, these works on late-modernity tend to focus on individual's subjective experience of these social processes, rather than the constitutive interactions that generate them. Indeed, Giddens argues that there are now a range of social processes associated with daily life that are of global extension in late modernity, especially those relating to communication, information, and consumption (Giddens 1991a). The subsequent analysis

will reveal that Giddens's positions on the practical-political implication of the transformations of late-modernity contain significant tensions and possibly even contradistinc-
tions. In some respects, the stronger normative underpinnings of Habermas's theory
may limit its conceptualization of dynamic processes, but it does provide a certain internal consistency.

Giddens may reject the perspective of Habermas's theory of communicative action,
but the normative positions he endorses are still for most part those of the 'project of
modernity'. His emphasis on the dynamics of change leads to an accentuation of the
theme of risk and the supposedly new politics of 'reflexive modernization' (Giddens
1994a, 1998a). The justification that Giddens sometimes presents for the latter in terms
of the fact of change itself is not always convincing, given the deficiency of his approach
to history from a normative standpoint and the oscillations in the emphases of the political content of his historical analyses (Giddens 1998a). Of course, the contrasting intentions of theory of structuration that have been outlined have to be developed and it could
be argued that this potential was never fulfilled. Second, the kind of differences that were
noted at the beginning, such as that Giddens's theory is less developed in terms of its normative foundations and the broader philosophical debates that Habermas engages with.

Similarly, although Giddens's original elaboration of structuration theory identified with the broadly defined orientation of critical theory, the actual practical political
implications of his perspective had yet to be clarified in a detailed manner. This would
change later, of course, with Giddens's writings on *The Third Way* (Giddens 1998, 2000).
However, the next section will clarify how this attempted rethinking of social democracy is based on a diagnosis of a waning of specific understandings and institutionaliza-
tions of the modernist vision of social autonomy, particularly that of state socialism. In
this, Giddens's rethinking of social democracy will be seen to have certain parallels with
Habermas's interpretation of the 'new obscurity' that ensues from the impasse of welfare state mass democracies. Habermas and Giddens remain committed to clarifying the
potentials for social progress that are immanent in the present development of society
and the new section will explicate how they have sought to satisfy this methodological
requirement through the provision of substantial conceptions of contemporary processes
of democratization and cosmopolitanism.

These intermediate reflections have highlighted a number of contrasts and divisions.
In some respects, these contrasts demonstrate why Habermas's and Giddens's interpretations of modernity are conditioned by the general social theory standpoints that they
propose and why, at the same time, for all of their importance, they are limited by the
relative weaknesses and priorities of their theoretical frameworks. In part, the arguments
that Habermas and Giddens subsequently develop in relation to the contemporary constellation of modernity do not resolve these limitations but deviate from some of the
substantial aspects of their theoretical frameworks and interpretations of the historical
institutionalization of modernity. It may be therefore worthwhile mentioning again some
of the parallels that make the points of comparison particularly constructive before proceeding: Habermas and Giddens similarly develop their theories through the synthesis of
various perspectives, they share a common commitment to some version of hermeneutics, they converge in their oppositions to a number of alternate theoretical standpoints,

from positivism through to postmodernism, their interpretations of modernity are deeply founded on critical reinterpretations of classical sociological theory, they have mobilized elements of the theories in critically engaging with pressing contemporary social and political issues, and they have reworked the praxis philosophy intentions of establishing a heightened reflexivity concerning the social conditions that inform their theories and of relating social theory to social practice.

Part III

THE POLITICAL AND
SOCIAL CONSTELLATION OF
CONTEMPORARY MODERNITY

Chapter Six

GLOBALIZATION, THE WELFARE STATE AND SOCIAL DEMOCRACY

Introduction

The presumption that the contemporary period constitutes a transition to a new phase of modernity has always been present in the work of Habermas and Giddens. However, the changes that commenced in the last decades of the twentieth century compelled revisions in their respective interpretations of the modernist vision of the autonomous constitution of society. In particular, while the collapse of state socialism may have confirmed the core elements of their interpretations of the institutionalization of modernity, it appeared to justify substantial reframings of their perspectives on contemporary capitalist society. Habermas and Giddens consider that the breakdown of state socialism reinforced the critical conclusions that their respective reconstructions and deconstructions of historical materialism drew about the Marxist vision of emancipation. Similarly, they consider that the political changes of this period confirmed their assessments of the limitations of the welfare state from the standpoint of the modernist vision of autonomy.

Habermas and Giddens have consequently sought to contribute major rethinkings of social democracy and to define the immanent potentials for democratization. In the case of Giddens, these considerations are articulated in the political project of *The Third Way*, which positions itself between the new right and the old left (Giddens 1998; 2000). Habermas discourse theory of law and democracy likewise seeks to delineate a way of overcoming the impasse of welfare state mass democracies (Habermas 1996a). The discourse theory of democracy and law subsequently forms the basis of Habermas's attempt to establish cosmopolitan justice in relation to the 'postnational constellation' of globalization (Habermas 2001a). There can be no denying that these practical-political articulations of their respective programmes are of considerable significance and that they address major questions concerning the social conditions of autonomy and justice. At the same time, my analysis highlights limitations intrinsic to Giddens's formulation of *The Third Way* and Habermas's discourse theory conceptions of law, democracy, morality and justice.

Habermas's theory originally focussed on developments within national societies and he has admitted that his prior lack of engagement with globalizing processes was a major limitation (Habermas 2000). With its emphasis on social reproduction's temporal and spatial characteristics, Giddens's theory was predisposed towards apprehending globalizing processes. Similarly, his Third Way political programme is based on a more favourable view of contemporary processes of modernization (Giddens 1998; 2000). He acknowledges the negative consequences of these modernizing developments, especially the effects of the ecological crisis, but tends to argue that changes are generally 'double-sided'. However, the double-sided character of change is now seen more as a matter of the combination of risk and opportunity, rather than constraint and enablement. This appears to reflect his view of the extension in late modernity of the value of individual autonomy, the democratizing of social interaction, and the expansion of reflexivity. Habermas similarly seeks to revise the social democratic conception of the means for achieving social justice, but is somewhat more wary of reforms based on the suppositions of the theory of reflexive modernization advanced by Giddens and Ulrich Beck (Beck 1992; 1994; Giddens 1994b). He contests some of the implications of reflexive modernization's theses of individualization and the 'disembedding' of the market (Habermas 1992; 2001a).

The contemporary constellation of modernity appears to entail curtailed expectations concerning collective transformation and historical transition. Habermas believes that the discourse theory of democracy and justice can counteract the contemporary decline in 'utopian energies' and the failings of the welfare state that were specified in the thesis of the colonization of the lifeworld (Habermas 1989: 1996a). Giddens (1994a; 1998) endeavours to incorporate the perspective of 'utopian realism' in his rethinking of social democracy. The public policy proposals based on 'utopian realism' are simultaneously consistent with the generative standpoint of structuration theory and inconsistent with its insights into the reproduction of systems of domination. These policy proposals reflect Giddens's assessment of how the phase of reflexive modernization undermines the social conditions that had given shape to the political projects of socialism and the welfare state. Similarly, Habermas's engagement with the themes of normative political philosophy is a reflection of his view that liberal political institutions and the constitutional state incorporate an unrealized normative potential (Habermas 1996a). The discourse theory of democracy, morality and law, he argues, discloses this immanent potential for radical democracy.

The Welfare State Paradox: Utopian Energies and the Loss of Alternatives

Habermas's endeavour to ascertain the normative possibilities contained in the present and to make these the foundation of a project of social reorganization appears very much contrary to the mood of the times. In order to uphold a progressive notion of directional change, Habermas linked his theory of communicative action to the continuation of the 'project of modernity' (Habermas 1996c; 1984a; 1987a; 1987b). He sought to counter contemporary scepticism about progressive change by demonstrating that not only is there no viable alternative to communicative action in the key areas of identity-formation, socialization, cultural transmission and the moral resolution of questions of justice, but also that an appreciation of its intersubjective format can assist in overcoming the self-misunderstanding of modern thought concerning its orientating ideals, such as those of individual and collective autonomy, rationality, and universal justice (Habermas 1987b). According to Benhabib (1986, 260), 'Habermas's fundamental concern in developing a theory of communicative action and rationality is to warn against the nihilism which may result from this ambivalent relation to the legacy of the moderns'. Habermas claims, in effect, that the ideal of a rational and autonomous organization of society remains binding upon modern subjects.

The contemporary mood that Habermas energetically opposed nonetheless left its traces in his social theory. Habermas's theory of communicative action appears to reinforce the dilemmas that it diagnosed. Its distinction between system and lifeworld arguably renders the 'paradoxical' problems of modernity perennial. The role that it assigns to law in the uncoupling of the system from the lifeworld means that the relationship between these domains can be realigned but not really reconstituted. The conditions for reversing the process of the lifeworld's 'inner colonization' lie in the lifeworld and would presumably be expressed in deliberative discourses and channelled through the law. Yet, the stronger constitutive significance that law has for the systemically integrated domains of the capitalist market and state administration undermines the degree of feasible change. This problem could be foreseen in the proposal that law both institutionally embeds the system in the lifeworld and defines its boundaries from it. Habermas's (1996a) discourse theory clarification of the genesis of law in communicative action partly rectifies this restrictive model; its argument that there is a mutuality of law and democracy is examined in the next chapter.

It is less clear whether the discourse theory of law and democracy addresses the problem of the imbalance concealed in the claim that the distinction between system and lifeworld permits a channelling in either direction. Once the static outline of integration moves to an analysis of the dynamics of social reproduction then it is likely to reveal that system integration prevails over social integration. Habermas had shown how the legal means employed to implement aspects of the social democratic project of the welfare state increased the preponderance of the system over the informal domains of the lifeworld. The extent to which the contemporary mood influenced Habermas's theory is equally apparent in his delineating the conditions for democratizing contemporary societies on the basis of the decline of most of the socio-political movements that aspired to extend the ideals of the French Revolution, particularly the labour movement and socialism. From this assessment of the exhaustion of various alternatives, he seeks to distill the aperture through which progressive contemporary social change should pass (Habermas 1996c).

The various problems surveyed in Habermas's approach to history make themselves felt in his response to postmodernist and neo-conservative critiques of the modernist categories of the subject and reason. By no longer normatively grounding critical theory in a philosophy of history, it may seem inevitable that his theory would exhibit a loss of confidence in the historical process. The constrictions that Habermas places upon historical innovation and his depiction of the closed trajectory of rationalization certainly suggest a certain mistrust concerning the historicity of social change. Nevertheless, the persistence of the anticipatory consciousness that shaped modern culture and social organizations is critical to his response to postmodernism and neo-conservatism. Modern forms of utopian thought, he argues, represented alternatives to existing heteronomy and indignity, they had the practical value of inspiring the action of subjects through their connection to history. A signature feature of the 'project' of modernity is a distinctive fusing of utopian and historical modes of thought (Habermas 1989a, 48–51).

This fusion brought utopian expectations into the horizon of the present, while the structure of historical anticipation reflected the new time consciousness of modernity (Habermas 1987b' 1989a). Modernity's temporal consciousness lent a future historical significance to action and action in the present was justified in the light of the anticipated future. As we saw, Giddens argues that the intensification of this modernist anticipatory consciousness has led to paradoxical inversions. These culminate in the temporal horizon of risk projections displacing utopian visions (Giddens 1990; 1994). It is not surprising then that Gidden argues for the position of 'utopian realism' in this new phase of modernity. He claims that the current potentials for universal justice and collective mobilization often develop in response to the 'negative' capacities for potential global annihilation, such as those of ecological devastation and military power (Giddens 1994a).

There is a marked discrepancy between Habermas's response to critiques of the project of modernity and his counter-utopian restrictions on the conditions of progressive change. This discrepancy is compounded by his claim that postmodernist approaches remain closed to the left-Hegelian insight that the antinomies of the subject and reason can only be resolved through transcending the social-historical conditions that give rise to them (Habermas 1987b). In a manner that is contrary to postmodernism, critical theory combines historical analysis and utopian projections of alternative futures. However, Benhabib persuasively argues that Habermas subordinates the utopian moment of the transfiguration of modernity to that of the project of fulfilling the normative promise of liberal democracy (Benhabib 1986, 342). One consequence of this subordination of 'anticipatory-utopian' critique is that a 'legal-juridical' interpretation of the autonomous subject comes to predominate in Habermas's discourse theory. This completes Habermas's relative omission of those dimensions of the individual subject that were signalled in his original departure from Adorno's critique of identity, like the dimensions of needs, desires, bodily experience, and creative self-expression. Given the relative subordination of these facets of the individual subject, it is probably not surprising that Honneth's revision of Critical Theory commences from the argument that Habermas's theory does not accurately represent the way in which individuals' experience injustice and domination, as well as their motivations for opposing injustice and heteronomy (Honneth 1995b).

Habermas's structural definition of the principles of modern consciousness generates problems for the idea of transformation that are analogous to those ensuing from his mistrust of the historical process. The main problem is not so much his circumspection concerning agency as the decentring entailed by his formal determination of agents. It means that the struggles of collective actors are limited to actualizing principles and it cancels the possibility of innovations arising from the indeterminacy of practices. In part, Habermas's altering critical theory's motif of historical change from that of emancipation to democracy unburdens critical theory of criteria of 'transfiguration', like those of innovation and transfiguration (see Benhabib 1996). It would be hard to consider that this is a determinate negation of praxis philosophy. Rather, it is related to Habermas's rejection of alternative attempts to develop the praxis perspective, like that of Castoriadis and, in a quite different sense, Giddens (Habermas 1987b). These attempts to rework the philosophy of praxis and to draw on its insights into social constitution have arguably led to social creativity becoming a leading concern of current social theory (see Joas 1993; Domingues 1999; 2000; Murphy 2012).

Habermas's refutation of postmodern and neo-conservative arguments is twofold in character. First, it seeks to show that in the paradigm of understanding there is an alternative to their undialectical rejection of reason and, of course, that its intersubjective perspective means that the notion of the autonomous subject can be reconstructed. In this way, his theory of communicative action reinvigorates and redefines the 'normative content' of modernity. From this perspective, the pathologies of modernity are a result of the deficit rather than an excess of reason (Habermas 1987b, 310). Second, he accepts that postmodernist articulations of the contemporary mood do have an objective basis, but argues that the 'thesis of the onset of the postmodern period' is 'unfounded' (Habermas 1989a, 52). Rather, postmodernist scepticism towards notions of progress is symptomatic of the contemporary experience of the welfare state impasse. It is not the normative content of modernity and its horizon of utopian anticipation that is exhausted, but rather a specific variant of it. The 'utopian energies' associated with the project of the transformation of a society founded on social labour have been exhausted. It 'has lost its persuasive power' because 'that utopia has lost its point of reference in reality: the power of abstract labour to create structure and to give form to society' (Habermas 1989a, 53).

In this way, Habermas's refutation of postmodernism intersects with his critique of the philosophy of praxis. He argues that social democrats and conservatives shared the 'productivist vision of progress', but that this image of progress no longer delineates the movements at the forefront of contemporary social and political change. According to Habermas, the welfare state translated the normative aspiration of a just and dignified life grounded in labour and its collective organization into a form appropriate to a complex society. It did not directly embody the original utopian ideal of socialized labour and the fraternal conceptions of early socialism, which includes Marx's image of a 'free association of producers'. These envisaged that emancipation from alienated labour and its external control would transform work into a mode of self-activity and that equality would emerge from the mutual participation of workers in this freedom (Habermas 1989a; Marx and Engels 1977).

The welfare state project, by contrast, did not aim at the revolutionary abolition of the dependent condition of labour. Rather, it was along the lines of the interchange between system and lifeworld that it indirectly pacified class antagonisms. That is, as we saw, for the burdens 'connected with the cushioned status of dependent wage labour, the citizen is compensated in his role as client of the welfare state bureaucracies with legal claims, and in his role as consumer of mass-produced goods, with buying power' (Habermas 1989a, 55). The dissipating of the energies deriving from the imaginings of utopian alternatives results from a peculiar bind that is connected to the consolidation of both the welfare state and its critique. The recognition of the problems and limitations of the welfare state project coincides with the awareness that there is no real alternative to the welfare state. Habermas's description of this impasse restates many of his arguments on the structural limitations of the interventionist-state owing to its dependence upon capital accumulation to obtain sufficient taxation revenue to fund its compensatory measures.

The welfare state can only influence 'private investment activity' 'through interventions that conform to the economic system' and its failure to alter the class structure has made it clear that it 'is not an autonomous "source of prosperity" and cannot guarantee employment as a civil right' (Habermas 1989a, 57). New divisions of social exclusion are overtaking the class compromise of the welfare state and there are strains in its basis of support in the class of social labour. Those disconnected today from the process of production lack any leverage equivalent to that of the withdrawal of labour, because capital is not dependent of this 'impoverished and disenfranchised' minority for its reproduction. Despite ameliorating the business cycle and providing necessary economic organization, the indirect means at the welfare state's disposal predispose it to problems of legitimation. In Habermas's opinion, due to the globalizing of production and technological change, the level of system integration of the capitalist economy had reached a critical threshold: 'developed forms of capitalism can no more live without the welfare state than they can live with its further expansion' (Habermas 1989a, 59).

The thesis of the colonization of the lifeworld concerned a more fundamental problem confronting the social-democratic and utopian impulses of the welfare state. It drew attention to how legally and bureaucratically implemented programmes that are intended to enhance autonomy can undermine it, particularly by transforming citizens into passive clients of institutions. In other words, the colonization of the lifeworld alluded to a basic contradiction between the normative-utopian goals of the welfare state 'project' and its 'methods'. The social democratic version of the utopia of social labour was 'based on the notion that society could act upon itself without risk, using the neutral means of political and administrative power' (Habermas 1989a, 63). Habermas contends that administrative power had been shown to operate according to its own internal logic and regularly distorts the social objectives it is meant to serve. This partly explains why the distinction, or differentiation, between the respective logics of cultural rationalization and societal modernization was so important to his entire theory of modernity. As we saw, he argues that in 'structurally differentiated lifeworlds a potential for reason is marked out that cannot be conceptualized as a heightening of system complexity' (Habermas 1984a, xlii).

Cultural rationalization constitutes a potential for reversing the deleterious consequences of the welfare state impasse and grounds for opposing the growing scepticism about the modern aspirations of enlightened reform and progress. On this point, Habermas perceives a certain convergence between contemporary neo-conservatives and the new social movements' critiques of development. Neo-conservatives trace the failures of the capitalist economic system to provide full employment and restraints on investment to the 'costs of the welfare state'. They blame discontents on cultural modernization, rather than social modernization. New social movements are important in their resistance to the colonizing of systemic steering media and in their promotion of discourse. But, he argues, some new social movements misunderstand the conditions of progressive change and their very own activity when they confuse the rationalization of the system and its pathological side effects with the process of modernization as a whole. The 'new politics' reflects the fact that the medium of administrative power is unable to generate a 'form of life' and this is the final source of the dissipation of the energizing capacity of the welfare state project. Habermas (1989a, 69) claims that 'utopian accents had shifted from production to communication' but the question still remains of discovering a form of institutional expression that could be similarly inventive to that of the welfare state translation of the project of a restructured labour society. McCarthy sketches the initial parameters for such a proposal in the arguments of *The Theory of Communicative Action*:

> There is a type of rationalization proper to the lifeworld, namely an expansion of the areas in which action is coordinated by way of communicatively achieved agreement. A communicatively rationalised lifeworld would have to develop institutions out of itself through which to set limits to the inner dynamic of media-steered subsystems and to subordinate them to decisions arrived at in unconstrained communication. (McCarthy 1984a, xxxvii)

A considerable disparity exists then between the force of Habermas's diagnosis of the exhaustion of utopian energies and his difficulties in depicting a positive alternative. A number of the reasons for Habermas's indecision concerning the institutional shape of a communicative utopia have been explored. His notion of discourse is self-limiting in this respect and it is only with his subsequent clarification of modern law's democratic foundations that its institutional form is properly consolidated. It is fairly clear, though, as commentators like Cohen and Arato suggest, that Habermas's analysis implies that the resolution of the welfare state impasse requires the mutually reinforcing changes of the lifeworld's decolonization and the democratization of the system (Cohen and Arato 1992, 455). A new relationship between the state and a self-organizing civil society is crucial, especially because Habermas accepts the systems theory argument that in highly modernized societies there is no central locus of change. Society had become radically decentred and complex; yet the functionalist suppositions of his distinction between system and lifeworld entailed that democratization could only be effected upon the system from the outside. Habermas describes this as a 'siege' model of democratically influencing the system and the decolonization of the lifeworld had an analogous meaning at that time.[1]

> I have considered state apparatus and economy to be systematically integrated action fields that can no longer be transformed democratically from within, that is, be switched over to a political mode of integration, without damage to their proper systemic logic and therewith their ability to function. The abysmal collapse of state socialism has only confirmed this. Instead, radical democratization now aims for a shifting of forces within 'a separation of powers' that itself is to be maintained in principle. The new equilibrium to be attained is not one between state powers but between different resources for societal integration. The goal

---

1   'Communicative power is exercised in the manner of a siege. It influences the premises of judgement and decision making in the political system without intending to conquer the system itself. It thus aims to assert its imperatives in the only language the besieged fortress understands: it takes responsibility for the pool of reasons that administrative power can handle instrumentally but cannot ignore, given its juridical structure' (Habermas 1996c, 486–87).

is no longer to supersede an economic system having a capitalist life of its own but to erect a democratic dam against the colonializing encroachment of system imperatives on areas of the lifeworld. (Habermas 1992b, 444)

For the most part, Habermas successfully distinguishes those rationality achievements specific to modernity and whose rationalization opens up the possibility for increased democratization from the deformations of reason associated with capitalist modernization. Specifically, his theory of communicative action explicates and reflects the competences of subjects to participate in the intersubjective structures of their lifeworld. It makes a convincing case for perceiving a decentred understanding of the world and post-conventional structures of moral consciousness as embodied in the context forming horizon of the lifeworld, and hence the background to subjects' actions. Whilst the problems of the interplay between competences and development have been explored, it nevertheless constitutes a highly original conception of the social nexus. These contentions underpin Habermas's discourse theory of democratization, which is examined in the next chapter, but it is worth underlining the extent to which he justifies this approach on the basis of the alleged failures of alternative attempts to provide a social translation of practical philosophy, such as he claims that the philosophy of history only identifies a normative content that it speculatively projected and that philosophical anthropology does not satisfy the formal conditions of discursive rationality (see Habermas 1996a).

According to Habermas, the rational internal structure of communicative action, which he identifies through a formal analysis of its basic constituents, takes on a special importance once it is no longer overlain by pre-existing traditions and prior normative contexts. Although communicative action only emerged with increasing purity as an outcome of the rationalization of the lifeworld, Habermas impressively sketches its role in the historically significant restructuring that produced modern society. He does this with particular reference to the formative role of ethical-rational conduct and the increasing achievement of mutual understanding on the basis of the provision of reasons. This account of modernity rectifies some of the lacunae of his earlier evolutionary theory. Yet, this perspective does not really overcome the problem of the distinction between the logic of development and the historical developmental dynamics. Similarly, the initial laying down of the parameters of modernization on the basis of learning achievements that are consistent with the formal structures of communication has fairly restrictive consequences, because in a quasi-functionalist manner it attributes the overall cultural programming of development to the structures of consciousness inherent in the lifeworld. The actual historical dynamics of change then either conform or deviate from the pattern or programme established by the structures of consciousness comprising the lifeworld Arnason notes that this perspective on change equally produces a limited conception of social systems and it partly explains the delimited trajectory of the 'project' of modernity:

The claim to superiority and universality which Habermas reads into the self-understanding of modernity is derived above all from a specific interpretation of its cultural foundations; the obverse of this foundationalist privileging of modern culture is a reductionist conception of economic and political structures which supposedly can therefore develop, achieve a certain degree of independence and give rise to alternative systems only within the scope prescribed by the cultural pattern. (Arnason 1991b, 183)

Habermas proposes that the continued rationalization of the lifeworld would lead to a close approximation to the ahistorically and counterfactually postulated model of communicative action. For Habermas, this model translates into subjects' practical demands for universal and equal opportunities to participate in discourses: the 'procedures of discursive will formation established in the structurally differentiated lifeworld are set up to secure the social bond of all with all precisely through equal consideration of the interests of each individual' (Habermas 1987b, 346–47).

The success of Habermas's theory is partly paid for at the cost of the various difficulties of the distinction between system and lifeworld. But both Habermas's success and failure in this regard are a reflection of the potential and limitations of his interpretation of the constitution of social identity through the intersubjective structure of communicative action. As I have argued, *The Theory of Communicative Action's* contrast between the functionalist logic of social systems and the communicative reproduction severely delimits potential alternatives in modernity. To some extent, this is not surprising, given that part of the motivation behind his 'siege' model was that of an opposition to any notion of the revolutionary conjunction in the state of the subject and history (Habermas 1997, 135).

The differentiation of the system from the lifeworld is far more convincing in its precluding the democratizing of the internal organization of systemically integrated spheres than it is in its claims for the insertion of democratic principles into formal institutions. Habermas's arguments for the assertion of social solidarity against the media of money and power are still underdeveloped at this stage. These types of tensions are evident, on the one hand, in his recognition that social complexity now poses the greatest challenge to the continuation of the emancipatory aspirations of modernity, and, on the other hand, his own adaptation of the category of complexity. For complexity can be deployed as an argument for reducing democratic participation and a justification for replacing rational will-formation through communication by the restricted codes of money and power. Habermas's highly sophisticated critiques of this type of argument are difficult to reconcile with his usage of similar arguments against the philosophy of praxis and new social movements. One could have expected that he would have been aware of the self-fulfilling character of such arguments from his comment that the 'more complex the systems requiring steering become the greater the probability of dysfunctional secondary effect' (Habermas 1989a, 51). In so arguing, he prefigures the analyses of Beck and Giddens of the 'risk society' associated with the contemporary phase of reflexive modernization (Giddens 1994a; 1994b; Beck 1992; 1994).

Habermas's distinction between system and lifeworld is not, to be sure, without considerable analytical merit and the comparison with Giddens's social theory facilitates a better appreciation of the exact dimensions of its validity. Similarly, Habermas's (1996a) major later work on the 'discourse theory of law and democracy' lessens some of the constraints imposed by the theory of communicative action's model of rationalization.

In particular, it retrieves the first-person perspective of critical theory and it develops themes that Habermas had originally explored in his first work on the public sphere (Habermas 1989b). Even so, the direction of change is heavily tied in this later framework to the project of realizing through discourse the constitutional state's normative principles. By extending the application and enriching the meaning of these principles, this project allows for historical innovation. However, consistent with the theory of communicative action, this legal binding and institutional underpinning of change qualifies the envisaging of possible alternatives and the scope of feasible transformation. In fact, it reflects a deep-seated determinant of Habermas's thought, one that constitutes the final grounds of his assessment of all social and political alternatives: 'the anxiety of regression' (Habermas 1994, 119; see Bernstein 1985; Beilharz 1995).

Still, is an opposition to regression the same as an acceptance of the change to the paradigm of understanding? Habermas's estimation of *the theory of communicative action* having replaced the exhausted standpoint of the philosophy of praxis would certainly appear premature. It is premature less because of the possible exaggeration contained in this assessment, and more, ironically, with respect to the important initiatives that his programme provoked. In a survey of the 'immanent critiques' of Habermas's theory, Strydom comments that they usually involve 'a shift away from the architects of the communication theoretical turn in critical theory towards an emphasis on praxis, yet without communication theory being surrendered' (Strydom 1993, 304, 308).[2] Giddens's theory of structuration is by no means the most important inspiration of the critiques that Strydom surveys, but it can be counted among the influences on these revaluations of praxis. On a number of points, Giddens's criticisms of Habermas's theory overlap the arguments of these 'immanent critiques', like those relating to shortcomings with respect to power and its acceptance of functionalist perspective on systems. Giddens's emphases often correspond to the themes that immanent critics have given prominence, like the role of conflict and the less formal sense of rationality present in social interaction (see Honneth 1995b; McCarthy 1991).

The themes of these immanent critiques emerge partly in response to the failings and omissions of Habermas's theory. I have already drawn attention to some of the immanent critiques' arguments, but in turning to the category of praxis they do not, to be sure, aim to restore Marx's original philosophy of praxis conception of the intersection between history and the subject. They have, nevertheless, contested the evolutionary framework of Habermas's theory of development; they often contend that the rationality considerations of Habermas's reconstruction of communicative action have distracted from the practical character of action. The practical character of action is considered to contain potentials for innovation that cannot be entirely equated with communicative rationality. For instance, it has been emphasized how Johann P. Arnason critiques the organizing function of cultural rationalization for the closure that it seems to dictate in relation to social change and it has been highlighted how the manner of Habermas's

---

2   Strydom (1992) lists 'immanent' critics like Arnason, Eder, Honneth, Joas, and McCarthy. See the Bibliography for a selection of some of their relevant works in English.

recourse to systems theory was consistently disputed (Arnason 1991b). These critical arguments mark out some of the praxis philosophical considerations that Giddens sought to encompass in his theory of structuration, although the latter involves something of a dilution of the normative intentions of this tradition. Giddens's programme of the Third Way rethinking of social democracy does, however, largely presuppose the basic validity of Habermas's theses concerning the structural contradictions of the welfare state in capitalist society and the diagnosis of the welfare state project having reached an impasse.

Reflexivity and Globalization

Although Giddens's later writings depart from the original format of his project of a 'contemporary critique of historical materialism', substantial themes from this critique feed into his later theorizing (Giddens 1994a). These continuities include Giddens's explication of tradition from the perspective of recurrent practices, the idea of the socialization of nature, the conceptualizing of globalization as a form of time-space distanciation, and the notion of disembedding mechanisms. The notions of distancing media and disembedding mechanisms are linked to his reinterpreting Marx's conception of the principles and suppositions of the 'real abstraction' of capitalist production (Marx 1976). Giddens attempts to translate structuration theory's incipient perspective on societal change into a new appreciation of the dynamic of late modernity. Likewise, his action-theoretical account of the participatory character of 'generative' politics and his understanding of deliberative democracy are broadly consistent with some elements of the orientation of the philosophy of praxis. In other respects, Giddens's later works diverge decisively from the philosophy of praxis, especially from Marx's conception of the potential for the transfiguration of capitalism. The tensions between these features of Giddens's standpoint serve to indirectly clarify the significance of Habermas's amendments to his theory and its superior proposals for democratization (Giddens 1994a; Habermas 1996a).

It would be an exaggeration to suggest that the critique of orthodox Marxism from the praxis perspective prefigured the political rethinking of democracy and citizenship in the last two decades of the twentieth century (see Cohen and Arato 1992; Benhabib 1996; Bohman and Rehg 1997). However, this perspective's reflection upon how radical emancipatory change requires a reconstituting of the relationship between structure and agency delineates the key question Giddens addresses in contributing to this rethinking. These continuities owe to praxis philosophy's more diffuse normative background and its accentuating Marx's sublating (in the Hegelian sense of preserving in transcending) liberal notions in his conception of socialism. Whether attempts to reformulate praxis philosophy entail a view of the 'future of radical politics' that is convergent with Giddens's proposals is more controversial and would certainly be disputed (Giddens 1994a; see Loyal 2003, Kiely 2005).

One response to this conjecture is that it probably depends on the extent to which the problem of 'self-limitation' is considered the defining feature of present projects for social and political change (Offe 1996). The problem of self-limitation inflects Giddens's (1994a) attempts to incorporate ecological and feminist critiques of Marxist notions of a socialist transformation into his redefinition of radical politics. Habermas similarly introduced a notion of self-limitation to characterize the limits to the action of the welfare state in light of the tendencies for the colonization of the lifeworld and the constraints upon the actions of social movements in civil society. In the case of Giddens, the notion of self-limitation is partly mediated by the ecological critique of production and its sequels in Ulrich Beck's (1992) sociological interpretation of the risk society. Beck argues that in 'advanced modernity the social production of *wealth* is systematically accompanied by the social production of *risks*' (Beck 1992, 19). The risk society is an unintended outcome of industrial society and it inverts the logic of progress that inflects industrial society. For instance, in the risk society the distribution of negative effects of industrialization, like pollution, becomes increasingly significant. These 'bads' vitiate the distribution of the positives of modernization, like the accumulation of wealth and development in general.

These various considerations lead to Giddens's interest in the paradox of circumstances where further developments in forms of material production and the extension of welfare-state interventions into civil society result in outcomes that are counterproductive from the standpoint of the intentions which guide them. Indeed, Giddens applies the notion of paradox quite widely, such as to topics like taxation and family policy; it is slightly less framed by ecological questions than Beck's conception of the paradoxical transition from industrial society to risk society (Beck 1992; Giddens 1994a; 1998a). It should be clear that Giddens's notion of paradox has parallels with Habermas's critique of the colonization of the lifeworld. In particular, Habermas made use of feminist critiques of the ambiguities of welfare-state policies to justify a reformulation of the conditions of democratic legitimation (Habermas 1987a; 1996a). Feminist critiques highlighted how welfare state measures intended to promote autonomy regularly resulted in the institutionalizing of constraining definitions of women's roles and identities.

Giddens similarly proposed the notion of paradoxical contradictions to clarify how progressive changes intended to address an established social problem can result in the reformulation of the problem or even its compounding (Giddens 1984a). The notion of paradox, nonetheless, cannot fully explain the extent to which Giddens's later political programme of the Third Way's arguments concerning the themes and issues surrounding citizenship and democracy are at variance with his earlier critique's position on authoritative sources of domination (Giddens 1998; 1981a). His later political proposals and policy recommendations neglect some of the implications of power and domination that were central to his critical theory of history, like the dynamics of social resistance and ideology.

Giddens notes that the work begun as the last in the trilogy of contemporary critiques of historical materialism, under the working title of 'between capitalism and socialism', transmogrified into the book *Beyond Left and Right*, as his 'interests moved away in somewhat different directions' (Giddens 1994a, viii). This change in title indicates what is most significant about his altered outlook and the socio-political context it addresses. Namely, the notion that socialism supplied a directional orientation, through disclosing the historical transformation immanent in the present, is displaced by the idea that contemporary changes are of such consequence that the preceding political and sociological coordinates have lost their basic orientating power. This latter idea had already informed the project of clarifying the contemporary historical context of critical theory, so that this shift is not so much a rupture as a change in emphasis and a reinterpretation of the implications of the former analysis. The main elements of this shift in outlook are related to the specific themes, but the most consequential disparity is summarized in Giddens's observation that political 'radicalism can no longer insert itself, as socialism did, in the space between a discarded past and a humanly made future' (Giddens 1994a, 10). This change does not reflect a dissolution of the problem of agency, rather it acknowledges the qualifications implied by the less predictable dynamics of late modernity, as well as the consequences of its associated 'dislocation'.

Marx's (1976) argument that the contradictory structuration of capitalist social relations is manifested in the opposition between an increasingly socialized production and private appropriation throws light on what is possibly the most profound theoretical aspect of this change in outlook. Giddens's (1981a) project of a contemporary critique of historical materialism originally aimed to discern equivalent, but also institutionally different, socializing tendencies immanent in the present. Yet, he now conceives these socializing tendencies to be associated with the general reflexivity intrinsic to modernity, rather than to those immanently related to its socialist transfiguration (Giddens 1994a; 1991a). Giddens originally discerned the limits to such a socialist transformation in the forms of administrative control that created many of the preconditions for the socialization of modern institutions (Giddens 1981a; 1984). He later contends that the 'cybernetic' notion of control, typical of modern administrative systems, has been undermined and overtaken by the changes connected to a later phase of 'reflexive modernization' (Giddens 1994a; 1994b; 1998a).

The developments associated with globalization, reflexivity and post-traditional social orders are likewise at the root of the dilemmas forcing a reconstruction of the welfare state. For Giddens, the contemporary phase of modernization has revealed the limits of the 'cybernetic' model of control and organization. In a sense, as Beck (1994) suggests, these developments are at variance with some of the social theoretical analysis that underpinned Horkheimer's and Adorno's (1972) diagnosis of the totally administered society and their critique of instrumental reason. Marx (1976) had anticipated the development of monopoly capitalism in his critique of the contradiction between socialized production and private appropriation. But, as Dubiel (1985) and Postone (1993) have shown, the limitations of the 'socialization' of production in the form of state control was central to Horkheimer and Adorno's critique of the totally administered society and their assessment of the negative outcomes of future progress in the development of the forces of production. Giddens agrees with Habermas that the dynamic of modern social systems is best understood as the development of self-referential organizations and not as the expansion of instrumental reason (Giddens 1991a).

Horkheimer and Adorno's (1972) argument that control over nature is constitutive of the domination over society finds its sequels today, Giddens believes, in the 'socialization of nature' (Giddens 1994a; 1994b). Socialization means that nature is no longer an external environment. For Giddens, this aspect of domination is part of social processes that can no longer be completely controlled by a cybernetic model of central authority and such processes entail a greater degree of risk and unpredictability than those of the

earlier phase of modernization. Socialism had signified the replacement of the irratio-
nality of the market by conscious control and state planning, yet this version of rationality no longer applies. Giddens points to the reflexivity of the market that derives from
information and communication:

> Yet there is no longer a 'road to socialism' via the increasing transcendence of market forces.
> A modern economy, influenced by globalisation and the developed reflexivity of individuals
> and groups making, buying, selling and investment decisions, depends upon constant bottom-
> up information for its effectiveness. Socialism presumes what might be called a cybernetic
> model of economic organisation. The theory underlying the cybernetic model depends upon
> the premise that 'lower order; information can be handled most effectively by a higher-order
> intelligence – a cybernetic governor. Plausible though it is, the cybernetic model doesn't work
> for very complex systems: to the contrary, it tends to produce rigidity and lack of adaptation
> to change. (Giddens 1993b, xiii)

These contentions probably appeared more convincing shortly after the collapse of
state socialism than they do after the early twenty-first century global financial crisis
and economic recession. Interestingly, Giddens claimed that socialism's inadequacies
with respect to the 'significance of 'markets as informational devices' 'only became fully
revealed with intensifying processes of globalization and technological change from the
early 1970s onwards' (Giddens 1998, 5). Indeed, it could be argued that these tendencies
extended reflexivity, but in ways that were highly counter-productive, since they resulted
in increasing concentrations of wealth and higher levels of social disorganization. This
disorganization is associated with the inability of institutions to effectively coordinate
major contemporary changes, including those that they have initiated, such as in the
case of the introduction of the 'Euro'. In any event, such cases of disorganization are
generally consistent with Giddens's vision of the implications of the dynamism of late-
modernity and the phenomenological experience that it creates of being 'on the edge'
(Hutton and Giddens 2001).

Giddens's view of the limits of socialism was not just about the functional limitations
of state planning, it concerned the implications of the normative expectations that were
connected with the unfolding of modernity. He argued that the detraditionalization and
reflexivity actually promote agency and individuation. Under modernity's present social-
historical institution, the structuration theory notion of agency appears to be practically
realized and its process approach to structure finds a wide-ranging application. Yet, this
conception of reflexive modernization reverses some of Giddens's historically grounded
arguments concerning administrative systems of domination. These reversals indicate that
not all of Giddens's arguments can be simultaneously correct. He conceives current social
developments to be dialectical: in the sense of double-edged and depending upon their
location. While this characterization may be one way of explaining social processes as
mediating and constituted relationally, it is not entirely consistent with the structuration
theory orientation that Giddens derived from reworking the perspective of the philosophy
of praxis.

During the last decades of the twentieth century, social theory was obsessed with the
'project' and problems of modernity. The debate over the constitutive characteristics

and potential possibilities of modernity remained largely intractable, even the initial conditions for its resolution appeared intangible. Indeed, the lack of suitable criteria for adjudicating between diverse positions was but one moment of the wider parameters of dispute, and for some judgement had already become an untenable position. Instead of exhausting the contemporary discourse on modernity, this situation had the opposite consequence of its proliferation. In Giddens's opinion, the proliferation of discourses on modernity should not be viewed as at all surprising. Reflexive interrogation is one of the seminal and central aspects of modernity. He argues, however, that reflexivity is today bound to a parallel experience of disorientation, because this reflexive comprehension remains essentially fragile. Knowledge claims can never entirely dissolve this experience, because they are implicated in the processes of renewing modernity's dynamism. In sum, the Enlightenment view of reflection and insight has proven to be inconsistent with the ramifications of the practices that it inspired and modernity's expansion of knowledge.

> Modernity is constituted in and through the reflexively applied knowledge, but the equation of knowledge with certitude has turned out to be misconceived. (Giddens 1990a, 39)

In the book *Reflexive Modernization*, Giddens, Beck and Lash (1994) claim that the then pervasive debate over modernity and postmodernity has 'grown wearisome'. In their opinion, a more institutional or structural approach discloses not just the persistence of modernity, but modernity's simultaneous extension and intensification. Giddens's notions of late modernity or high modernity has parallels with Beck's notions of an emerging risk society and reflexive modernization. Indeed, the parallels extend to the details of Giddens's understanding of modernity and the central notion of reflexivity (Beck 1992; Beck et al. 1994; Giddens 1990a; 1991a; 1994b). Like Beck, Giddens argues that reflexive modernization refers to the 'modernizing of an already modern society'. The transformations connected to this reflexive phase are displacing the earlier stage of 'simple modernization' (Giddens 1994a, 80–87). Simple modernization is primarily a process of linear economic development and the consolidating of a system of political administration based in the nation-state.

Giddens contends that the political-economic principles of socialist organization and the institution of the welfare state were, in varying ways, shaped by features characteristic of simple modernization. The ideals of socialism remain and the welfare state needs to be refashioned but the belief that socialism represents a future stage of historical development has been undermined. Socialism was not solely undermined by the changes connected to the most advanced processes of modernization. Giddens argues that the 'failure of socialism as a means of Third World development has been as much of a hammer-blow for Western Marxism as any of the developments in the more industrialized parts of the world' (Giddens 1994a, 65). He believes that this type of reflection is indicative of a new cultural sense of time and space, although one could argue that the emergence of the alter-globalization or global justice movement may have the opposite consequence in terms of the reinvigoration of socialism. In any event, Giddens claims that cultural changes are breaking down much of the perspective that underpinned notions of Western superiority. 'A reflexive universe of social action, simply put, is one where nobody is outside' (Giddens 1996, 123).

Furthermore, Giddens believes that globalization and the uncertainty of manufactured risk are connected to the expansion of reflexivity in late-modernity. Manufactured risk is a product of human intervention, rather than a threat posed by the external environment. For Giddens, globalization is not just a process of economic integration, but a much broader trend that he defines 'as the intensification of worldwide social relations which link distant localities in such a way that local happenings are shaped by events occurring many miles away and vice versa' (Giddens 1990a, 64). Globalization is a species of time-space distanciation and the basic categories of the theory of structuration are well suited to illuminating the mechanisms of extending social relations. In fact, apart from being one of the first social theorists to offer a theory of globalization, Giddens's perspective distinctively attempted to comprehend globalization as a process of social action as well as a matter of system integration.

The notion of 'disembedding' gives particular representation to this conception of the relations between presence and absence, social integration and system integration, as they concern the organizing of time and space interrelationships. Giddens argues that the concept of 'disembedding' of social relations should replace the notion of differentiation, which derives primarily from functionalism and tends to justify assumptions about social complexity. In Giddens's theory, disembedding refers to the mechanisms and processes facilitating 'the "lifting out" of social relations from local contexts and their restructuring across indefinite spans of time-space' (Giddens 1990a, 21; 1991a, 18). He argues that the mechanisms lifting social relations out of their local contexts, like symbolic media such as money and 'expert systems', are correspondingly media *bringing together* social relations. The binding together of social processes is the precondition for social relations to undergo structural differentiation. This dynamic of intersecting social processes is not effectively captured, Giddens claims, by differentiation. Rather, differentiation is related to visions of social evolution as a process of change from simple to complex social structure.

> Differentiation carries the imagery of the progressive separation of functions, such that modes of activity organised in a diffuse fashion in pre-modern societies become more specialised and precise with the advent of modernity. No doubt this idea has some validity, but it fails to capture an essential element of the nature and impact of modern institutions – the 'lifting out' of social relations from local contexts and their rearticulation across indefinite tracts of time-space. This 'lifting out' is exactly what I mean by disembedding, which is the key to the tremendous acceleration in time-space distanciation which modernity introduces. (Giddens 1991a, 18)

According to Giddens, the developments of manufactured risk, globalization and heightened reflexivity shape the present and have altered the parameters of any project of intended social change (Giddens 1994a; 1994b). These processes converge with several others reshaping the present phase of social developments, especially individualization and detraditionalization. Reflexive modernization presents a new dilemma for modernist conceptions of the nexus between history and subjectivity. This dilemma corresponds to the reasons why intended change's foundations or justifications have to be secured by way of an acceptance of contingency, rather than through the interdiction of contingency.

Reflexive monitoring, Giddens argues, is a fundamental feature of modern organization and it developed in association with a new awareness of historicity, that is, 'the active mobilization of social forms in the pursuit of their own transformation' (Giddens 1979, 221). This key presupposition of modernity represents a 'profound potential' for social life's 'deroutinization' and reconstruction, but its full effects have only been realized with reflexive modernization. The uncertainty that manufactured risk engenders was comparatively limited during the phase of simple modernization. There was a lesser disparity between means and outcomes. This changes during the stage of reflexive modernization and the risks of human activities founded on scientific and technological development are potentially of such 'high consequence' that they persist well beyond the present, for example, the dangers of nuclear contamination have a millennial duration (Giddens 1990a; Beck 1992).

In Giddens's theoretical conception, the dynamic character of modern social systems results not in reflexivity being opposed to unintended consequences but instead in the reflexive acceptance and incorporation of unintended consequences. At the level of the individual's personality system, these dynamics' paradoxical or contradictory effects can be identified. Reflexivity and globalization are, on the one hand, sources of modern forms of life's sense of undiminished possibilities. On the other hand, these possibilities are simultaneously countered by the experience of stress and anxiety that are engendered by major facets of modernity (Giddens 1990a; 1994a). Giddens (1990; 1991; 1999) regularly invokes the image of the profound momentum of forces and events that are apparently 'outside our control'. Notably, he deploys the conceptual metaphors of the 'juggernaut' of modernity and the 'runaway world' of globalization:

> The modern world is a 'runaway world': not only is the pace of social change much faster than any prior system, so also is the *scope*, and the *profoundness* with which it affects pre-existing social practices and modes of behaviour. (Giddens 1991, 16)

The conclusions that Giddens draws from this idea of current social developments that are 'outside our control' are quite unlike Marxist notions of the alienation of the subject and the transcendence of alienation through the activity of the subject. Giddens argues that the condition of modernity is one of constant change and that it is necessary to take this into account, rather than believing that it can be overcome. In his opinion, the notion of a political avant-garde depended on a now refuted teleological view of history and the idea of a central locus of economic planning in the state has similarly been overtaken, particularly with the broad recognition of the 'cybernetic' model's limitations under the conditions of high reflexivity. The dispersal of information means that actors in markets, as well as everyday life, anticipate the intended effects of state intervention. In Giddens's opinion, reflexivity thereby changes, to varying degrees, the outcomes of these actions of the state and those of individuals (Giddens 1994a; 1987). Of course, it could be argued that this position exaggerates the power of individual agency and that it is only relatively highly empowered and the minority of extremely wealthy individuals that can effectively subvert the actions of state intervention.

For Giddens, these increases in knowledge and reflexivity have implications similar to those of the organizational incorporation of unintended consequences; they can lead to outcomes that are paradoxical or inconsistent with the original intentions of state action. It is necessary therefore, Giddens claims, to incorporate this sense of reflexivity into the welfare state (Giddens 1994a; 1987). He argues that state planning does not possess the degree of directing power that it had during the phase of simple modernization and new means of influencing economic decision-making are required in particular. However, it is precisely this type of argument that has provoked scepticism over whether this 'third way' analysis cannot but fall prey to the neo-liberal agenda it criticizes (Giddens 1998a; 2000; see Loyal 2003; Kiely 2005). Even if it is intended to contest neoliberalism, the practical application of the categories that Giddens employed, like reflexivity or flexibility, may have been redefined in a manner that is compatible with the 'new spirit of capitalism' (Boltanski and Chiapello 2005). Indeed, the crystallizing of the new spirit of capitalism through the reflexive adaptation of formerly critical categories may represent a social process that would be better explained on the basis of the theory of structuration, rather than some of Giddens's subsequent conceptions of the dynamics of late-modernity.

The theme of the democratizing of social life is integral to Giddens's vision of reflexive modernity. He links this democratic potential to arguments about the implications of changes in interpersonal relations. Giddens believes that these changes are positive to the degree that they involve a critique of the authoritarian dimensions of culture and social relations. The political sequels of the post-traditional lifestyle connected to these changes are, in his opinion, an extension of the principles of active trust and dialogic democracy. This conceptual development is partly a response to what he regards as the emergence of 'life politics' alongside that of 'emancipatory politics' (Giddens 1990a; 1991a; 1992; 1994b). Emancipatory politics is concerned primarily with improving 'life-chances' and aims 'to reduce or eliminate *exploitation*, *inequality* and *oppression*' (Giddens 1991a, 211). It is not hard to perceive that emancipatory politics has largely defined the objectives of the 'left' politics of social democracy and socialism. According to Giddens, 'life politics' marks a shift from struggles centring on freedom and equality to those oriented by questions of identity, lifestyle and choice. Giddens (1994a) argues that life-politics is promoted by the uncertainties created by the reconfiguring of the division between the social and the natural which was originally constitutive of modernity, hence the significance of ecological considerations and the 'personal' to life politics. To some extent, life politics is an outcome and a means of the democratizing of interpersonal relations and everyday life.

In many respects, Giddens's account of life politics overlaps Habermas's (1987a) analysis of the contemporary forms of protest and new social movements' concern with the 'grammar of forms of life', rather than the themes of distribution and security that defined the class compromise of the welfare state. Indeed, Giddens's conception and evaluation of the democratic potential of post-traditional lifestyles parallels Habermas's account of the communicative rationalization of the lifeworld. It would appear to endorse the projections that Habermas makes on this basis about the future arrangement of the structural components of culture, society and personality, like the sense in which their reproduction is contingent on the communicative agreement of subjects and that they are no longer fixed by traditions but oriented more by a more open historical future. This is an important area of general agreement between the two theorists. Although there are differences in their explanations and categories, they both identify a connection between dialogue and democracy as an organizing principle of post-traditional social relations.

A final aspect of Giddens's altered outlook is a shift from the more abstract questions of social theory to a far more direct type of engagement with contemporary politics. Although it is in no way logically connected to direct intervention into politics, there is evidence of a different conception of critique associated with this shift. The implication of it seems to be that the social transformation that Giddens supports does not privilege the demands for different arrangements over the reform of existing circumstances. Rather, it is as much about improving, that is, modernizing and reorienting, existing institutions. Social transformation is not only to be grounded in the present development of society, but is circumscribed by the immediate practicalities of policy implementation (Giddens 1998a; 2000). Further, Giddens regards a political ethic of 'repair' and limitation as appropriate to the present context of social democracy; hence it can incorporate some of the intentions, though not the substantive positions, of traditional conservatism (Giddens 1994a).

How far this perspective was shaped by immediate political contingencies may explain some of the oscillations in Giddens's arguments and its attempt to hold together the seeming contrary notions of 'radical' and 'centre'. The Third Way programme was heavily conditioned by its reacting to the British neoliberal government of Thatcher and Major, which had already been in power for over a decade and a half by the time of Giddens's attempt to outline 'the future of radical politics' in the book *Beyond Left and Right* (Giddens 1994a). Despite the deficiencies that may be identified, Giddens's contributions to policy debates demonstrated the relevance of sociological conceptions that had been pushed to the periphery by the neo-liberal political agendas and disillusionment with institutional reform. The shifts in Giddens's perspective should equally be seen in light of the weaknesses of his original programme of a critique of historical materialism. However, viewed retrospectively, the later position may be equally, if not more, consequential. The overall value of Giddens's theoretical project may be underestimated if it is too closely associated with the politics of the Third Way. In any event, the various details of this political programme heavily depend on Giddens's conceptualization of late modern globalization and reflexivity.

Democratization and Detraditionalization: Rethinking the Welfare State

Like Habermas, Giddens seeks to interrelate an account of the structural limitations of the welfare state with an explanation of the origins and possibilities of the new forms of 'political' action. A rather different sense of historicity informs his largely complementary diagnosis of the exhaustion of the labourist vision of the social welfare state (Giddens 1994a; 1998a). Giddens believes that it is necessary to move beyond the 'productivist' logic of most modernizing political perspectives and that the structural problems of the welfare state should be analyzed from the standpoint of risk. He argues that because the welfare state developed during the phase of simple modernization, it is based on a notion of external, rather than manufactured, risk. Social welfare represents a type of social insurance against risk and the state provides compensations for misfortunes. The major success of the welfare state has been in 'risk sharing'; it has been unsuccessful, he contends, in redistributing wealth and income. It is actually 'incapable', Giddens claims, of significant wealth redistribution (Giddens 1994a, 149; 1998a, 116). The modern state, he argues, is defined in part by the provision of welfare, precisely because the state was always a system of administration. The different forms of the state regulation of social welfare were associated with the increased surveillance in modernity. It is important to his proposals for rethinking the welfare state that it was not solely the product of social democrats and that in many nation-states social democrats sought to adapt pre-existing institutions for their objectives.

According to Giddens, the typical divisions between left and right are being unsettled. Conservatism has embraced the 'future orientation' formerly associated with the socialist critique of capitalism, but left politics are still distinguished by an opposition to inequality and an adherence to the principle of social justice (Giddens 1994a; 1998a). Due to the rise of neo-conservatism and the collapse of state socialism, socialists became defenders of the welfare state, rather than critics of its class compromise. For Giddens, the socialist recognition of the limitations of the welfare state remains relevant; equally the neo-conservative and neo-liberal programmes represent contradictory and self-defeating responses to developments reshaping capitalist societies, primary amongst these are globalization, reflexivity and detraditionalization. He nevertheless controversially accepts some aspects of right-wing criticisms of the inflexibility and impersonality of welfare bureaucracies' and the existence, under certain structural and then cultural conditions, of welfare dependency (Giddens 1994a, 76, 147–48). Further, Giddens contends that the 'emancipatory political' assumptions that shaped the welfare state mean that it is 'strained or ineffective where life political issues loom increasingly large and where generative political programmes are needed to cope with them' (Giddens 1994a, 153). The positive, or generative, approach that he advocates attempts to deal with life problems 'at source', rather than after the negative consequences of misdevelopments and risk. In this way, 'positive welfare' is preventative; it seeks to redefine the conditions that give rise to life problems, like the conception of age, career changes, and health.

This positive model of welfare is similarly necessary, Giddens argues, due to the different order of risks of reflexive modernization and for which the existing versions of the welfare state are inappropriate. A generative model is needed in order to address 'high consequence' risks, like global warming, and the reflexivity of everyday life, where there is knowledge of such things as high divorce rates. Positive, rather than negative, welfare is appropriate to dealing with the 'manufactured uncertainty' that can be a by-product of better living conditions and the inequalities that ensue from a lack of individual agency or relevant life skills. Of course, the risks of hazards and dangers of living are, in many respects, actually less today; however, risk takes on a greater significance owing to its being integral to modernizing innovation. Following Beck's thesis of the risk society, Giddens argues that the problems of the ecological crisis exemplify a feature of the new risk order: that is, where the further development of previously progressive reforms becomes counterproductive and the existing means are potentially inappropriate (Giddens 1994a; see Beck 1992). This type of contention leads Giddens to suggest that the welfare state may compound some of the problems that it was designed to solve, such as reinforcing the social exclusion of the aged. He highlights research showing that usually the greatest beneficiaries of the welfare state are not necessarily those in greatest need (Giddens 1998a; 1994a).

In a similar vein, Giddens argues that a number of the social conditions that underpinned the type of Keynesian economic management associated with the welfare state have been overtaken. The reasons for this change are similar to those that altered the underpinnings of Marshall's account of citizenship, particularly the reflexivity of the markets and globalization. These exposed the limits of the cybernetic model of planning. Like state socialism, the social democratic project of the welfare state depended on the organizing capacity of the nation state. The cybernetic model of a central directing authority worked reasonably well within the context of a limited range of individual needs and life options. However, many of the features of the period of the welfare state's expansion after the second world war no longer hold and are unlikely to be restored, like male full (full-time) employment and a (mythical) model of the nuclear family. Unlike external risks, manufactured uncertainties are less amenable to the 'insurance principle' of simple modernization. The calculations of risks and consequences of modernizing changes and outcomes are less certain precisely because manufactured uncertainties are a product of human activity and debates between experts are often unresolved. In many cases, the necessary preventative action alters potential outcomes, such as in relation to individual health or the collective effects of reducing toxins in the environment. These actions concern future scenarios and possibilities. In Giddens's opinion, all of this differs from the more fatalistic notion of problems that guided the welfare state protection of individuals across the life cycle (Giddens 1998a, 10, 116; 1994a, 18).

Likewise, the welfare state needs to be rethought in terms of a generative programme, as the parameters of state action are changed by the global flow of information and the appropriation of expert knowledge. According to Giddens, these developments promote tendencies towards democratization and the 'revolutionary changes of our time are not happening so much in the orthodox political domain as along the fault-lines of local and global transformations' (Giddens 1994a, 95). Of course, it is worth noting that much of this analysis would not be convincing to those committed to the older political categories. Moreover, Giddens's proposals have been considered to reflect an underlying commitment of structuration theory to a liberal view of individual agency (see Smith, 1998; Loyal 2003). There is undoubtedly an element of truth to this assessment. Giddens's theory of structuration did, however, contain the possibility of a more complex sociological understanding of autonomy. Whether this understanding is given full expression in his programme of the Third Way is more open to dispute. Much of the Third Way analysis, like the theory of reflexive modernization more generally, depends on the claim that contemporary social structure is individualizing (Beck, Giddens and Lash 1994; Giddens 1998; 1999; 2000).

Although Giddens accepts much of the critique of the welfare state as a class compromise, he asserts that the preceding conditions of class formation and class solidarity have been transformed. He believes that a more fluid polarity of inclusion and exclusion is emerging. A polarity reflected in the experience of class as mediated through individuals encountering constraints and opportunities (Giddens 1994a, 143–144; 1998a, 103–4). 'Class relations simultaneously become more centred on the labour market and refracted through new exclusionary mechanisms' (Giddens 1994a, 188). There is some justification to his argument that the inequality of exclusion tend to have more social and psychological consequences for the individual, but this analysis risks endorsing a policy of simply coping and functional adjustment (Giddens 1994a, 90). The proximity of Giddens's 'Third Way' proposals to New Labour in Britain has meant that his arguments have sometimes been seen as appropriating and repackaging a neo-liberal policy agenda (see Giddens 2000; see Kiely 2005). He has, in principle, set his position apart from neo-liberalism in stating that: 'widening economic inequalities within society are not, certainly not necessarily, the condition of increasing overall prosperity' (Giddens 1994a, 88).

The processes of globalization, reflexivity and detraditionalization are mutually reinforcing and they are related to the other developments that are altering institutions, especially that of individualization (Giddens 1994a; 1994b). Like Beck (1992; 1994), Giddens proposes that the structural changes of reflexive modernization are making individual choices unavoidable and that the regions of a person's life subject to decision are expanding. The self is becoming 'experimental', so that such choices are experienced as individual risk taking. Similarly, the construction of identity has become a reflexive project, entailing individuals' knowing and constant participation in the fabrication of their biographies. The 'family', he claims, is becoming democratized, with an emphasis on the 'pure relationship', so that the family is no longer considered a framework external to the determination of its participant members (Giddens 1992a). Work remains critical to identity but, like other areas of life, it is no longer experienced as 'fate'. For Giddens, this development harbours the opportunity to break with the logic of 'productivism' as a form of compulsory action for the individual, though not with enhanced productivity. At the same time, this opportunity is indissoluble from the uncertainty of risk, especially in the context of global economic competition and technological change. The effects that these have on employment are a major concern of Giddens's social policy arguments. However, it is debatable whether these arguments entirely offset some of the difficulties of his analysis.

Leaving aside the question that Habermas poses later of whether the practical application of these policy proposals may generate contrary and regressive outcomes, there is the conundrum of whether this accentuation of the individual is compatible with the sense of collectivity that has been central to the development of the welfare state and social democracy. In one sense, Giddens's wants to argue that it is necessary to move beyond this earlier conception of collective, but it is not clear that individualism can generate an equivalent sense of justice. He may have underestimated the contradictions involved in spite of his own endeavours to redefine social justice and solidarity. Further, Giddens does not really consider whether the innovations of the new economy may be simply a part of longer-term cyclical processes (see Murphy 2012). The latter view would emphasize the limitations to extrapolating and projecting from current changes in relatively new industrial sectors. Will Hutton makes a parallel criticism. He argues that, at least prior to recent financial crisis and recession, Giddens 'tends to collapse into a Manichean characterization of the stakeholder economies of Europe as bad and the Anglo-Saxon world of flexible labour markets and shareholder value as producing a more creative business civilization – a view I think is oversimplified and wrong' (Hutton 2001, xvii).

Giddens rejects the notion that this 'new individualism' corresponds to the notion of the actor in neo-liberal economic theory and the anti-state political agenda of privatization and unimpeded markets (Giddens 1998a). He believes that the new individualism is connected to the diffusion of post-materialist values, like self-actualization, and that the extension of citizenship rights underpins contemporary individualism.

> The new individualism, in short, is associated with the retreat of tradition and custom from our lives, a phenomenon involved with the impact of globalization widely conceived rather than just the influence of markets. The welfare state has played its part: set up under the aegis of collectivism, welfare institutions have helped liberate individuals from some of the fixity of the past. Rather than seeing ours as an age of moral decay, then, it makes sense to see it as an age of moral transition. (Giddens 1998a, 36)

One of Giddens's major points is that globalization is not a process distinct from action and that it is not outside the lifestyle decisions of individuals. Life-politics is a reflection of how with the extensions of late-modernity forms of social living are becoming post-traditional. This detraditionalization differentiates, in his opinion, the current period from the preceding phase of modernity, which perpetuated as well as opposed tradition. In some ways, the notion of structure as a medium and outcome of practices could readily be applied in a hermeneutic interpretation of tradition. However, tradition is so diffuse and inseparable from every aspect of social systems in premodern civilizations that the specification of tradition and the traditional, in the proper sense, only emerge with modernity and out of the contrast to the modern (Giddens 1994b).

Giddens rejects the functionalist understanding of tradition as serving the latent function of reproducing social solidarity and instead proposes that repetitive conduct is the key to the structuration of tradition. There is an organizing of time distinctive to tradition, which is more complex than the dominance of the past over the present. Tradition 'reaches out to return the future to the past, while drawing on the past to reconstruct the future' (Giddens 1994b, 62). What distinguishes tradition is a claim to authenticity, not longevity. All traditions are in some sense invented but fundamental to the authority of traditions and their legitimation of social structures is how they disguise their invention. Namely, the inventing of tradition is disguised by the very character of how traditions are invoked and by the ritual contexts of actualization.

Giddens insightfully draws together different features from various interpretations of tradition and disaggregates them into the following combination of elements: tradition is a medium of 'collective memory' and is never private; because its authenticity is evoked in rituals, specific rituals preserving the integrity of tradition are shielded from the interference of mundane and purposeful action; and intrinsic to tradition is a 'formulaic notion of truth', that is, truth inheres in the very rites and utterances and not so much in their logical comprehension or external reference. Moreover, traditions have 'guardians' with exclusive control over ritual enactment and interpretation, guardians are more than regulators; guardians are often repositories of tradition and 'mediators of its causal powers'. Lastly, tradition 'unlike custom, has binding force which has a combined moral and emotional content' (Giddens 1994b, 63). This content's binding force provides the psychic underpinnings of social repetition and its reverse, the social underpinnings of psychic repetition. Despite the rational critique of tradition that has always characterized modernity since the Enlightenment, the first phase of simple modernization 'rebuilt' tradition as well as critiqued it. Tradition persisted, not so much as remnants of the premodern that were transmitted and preserved from the past, but rather as cultural symbols and social arrangements that were consolidated during the phase of simple modernization.

The sense in which Giddens considers that the contemporary phase is that of high modernity or 'radicalized modernity' is apparent from detraditionalization and the related tendencies that internally restructure domains that were formerly effected externally by modernization (Giddens 1990). Detraditionalization means, above all, that social identity is known to be constructible and to be a construction. Giddens contrasts the components of tradition with modern expertise and abstract systems; both of which transcend local contexts and are *disembedding* mechanisms' reorganizing time and space. Disembedding mechanisms facilitate globalization and the 'intentional' reconstructing of personal identity that undermines the 'stasis' tradition placed certain social arrangements in. And, by so doing, end the 'collaboration' of modernity with tradition that had served to legitimate authority (Giddens 1994b, 91). This dissolving of the boundaries that tradition preserved against modernization, by its rendering traditions 'external to human activity', is paralleled by the 'socialization of nature' annulling the meaning of environment. Giddens argues that risk is intrinsic to institutional reflexivity, because these processes are determined by projecting into the future the outcomes of human intervention.

The answer that Giddens gives to the question of why, despite its rational disempowering of tradition, 'modernity has rebuilt tradition' is not original. The basis of tradition's continued reproduction resided in its being a mechanism for the displacement of anxiety and the 'ontological security' it provides. From this standpoint, he reads Freud and Weber as elucidating the historical mutation of repetition, from practices authenticated by tradition into modern compulsions (Giddens 1994b). Giddens, gliding over the possibility of his drawing an incompatible analogy, finds compulsions similar to those of the puritan ethic manifested in contemporary addictions. These are repetitive routines that impede autonomy. The literature on addictions, he presumes, can assist in clarifying the post-traditional condition. First, addictions are often seen in this literature as signs of an unmastered past. This perception is illustrative of a general 'disinterring' of behaviour and institutions. Second, this literature is an instance of institutional reflexivity, that is, the regular infiltrating of originally expert knowledge back into daily practices in late-modernity and the reorganizing of practices through its incorporation. The disinterring of the layers connecting future action to the past is then informed by claims to knowledge other than those of tradition; but it differs from earlier detraditionalization in its bearing on affect (Giddens 1994b).

The changing of affective ties is one of the reasons why detraditionalization generates hostile and even violent reactions. Although conceived differently to Habermas's theory of rationality, processes of communication are crucial to Giddens's notion of a post-traditional society. He suggests that fundamentalism is often the alternative today to open communication. Fundamentalism is, Giddens proposes, 'the defence of tradition' in a traditional manner (Giddens 1994a, 85; 1994b). Fundamentalism really only emerged recently in response to the questioning of tradition and the alterations of reflexive modernization. In his opinion, fundamentalism is not exclusive to religious belief-systems. Giddens argues that fundamentalism 'in a world of cosmopolitan communication is always potentially dangerous. For it is a refusal of dialogue in circumstances where such dialogue is the only mode of mutual accommodation' (Giddens 1994a, 48). For these reasons, he argues that where it is not lapsing into fundamentalism, tradition too can be adhered to only by way of post-traditional practices.

The notion of repetition is the linchpin of Giddens's explicating the potential disjuncture between the opening up of choices with an 'evacuating' of tradition in reflexive modernity and actual autonomy. This question is critical to his claim to present an alternative to liberal conceptions of freedom and the sense in which his notion of the transformative capacity of agency is to be understood. The possible meaning of autonomy had initially been negatively indicated in terms of the threats and experiences of its diminution on the part of subjects in 'critical situations' and the idea of contingency remains integral to his model of the agency (Giddens 1984). A routinizing of practices remains essential for ontological security and unless practices are 'geared' to institutional reflexivity they 'become empty' (Giddens 1994b, 71). This gearing, Giddens proposes, depends on 'active trust' and the alternative to it is the 'frozen trust' of compulsions, which block off reengagement (Giddens 1994b, 90). It may lack the assurance of tradition, but active trust is opposed to tradition's authoritarian hold. By being constituted through a dialogical explicating of social relations, active trust is democratizing and presumes a positing of autonomy, in a refusal to violate the integrity of others. The implications of active trust, he believes, are new forms of social association and the tendencies for the 'democratization of democracy' (Giddens 1998a, 69–78) Democratization is either occurring below or cuts across the liberal-democratic state. It extends the democratic dialogic principle of post-traditional social relations to a myriad of deliberative forums.

Like Habermas, Giddens sees the defining feature of democratization as the openness to deliberation and dialogic procedures. Giddens stresses the origination of democratization in trust and reflexivity, rather than the formal pragmatics of communication (Giddens 1994a; 1998a). These democratizing tendencies represent, he argues, a resource for the development of types of solidarity opposed to fundamentalism and neo-nationalism. The latter have arisen in response to contemporary uncertainty and the globalizing processes that have produced a more cosmopolitan social environment, and hence the increased probability of encountering difference within former 'local' contexts.

The centrality of choice and motivation to this analysis may exacerbate the problems some critics have found in Giddens's conceptualization of constraint (see Cohen 1989;

Thompson 1991; Stones 2005). It is by no means as straightforward as Giddens assumes that the ideal of autonomy in self-help literature is the same as that guiding the critique of the heteronomy of systems of domination. Likewise, overcoming compulsions utilizes the dialogical principles of active trust and, although this has important implications for democratization, the injustices of inequality and subordination, as Giddens himself recognizes, have systematic features that transcend individual action.

Despite the various qualifications Giddens presents, the idea of behavioural change may be misleading in relation to the problems of unemployment and poverty. This is one of the serious repercussions of Giddens's subtle change in emphasis from a more social to a personal and individual meaning of the category of intentional. This change is partly veiled by its counter-concept of 'extensional'. Domingues argues that a similar, and to my mind undoubtedly related, shift occurs in Giddens's work from a more social interactive meaning of reflexivity to a more restricted individualistic one (Domingues 2000), Although Giddens's aim is precisely to disclose contemporary liberation without real autonomy, the seeming equation of constraint with compulsion could obscure the more systematic restrictions and modes of domination, including even those he has previously examined. For similar reasons, it is possible to imagine on the basis of his arguments a scenario where moral agencies of the state and civil society apply the arguments for an active citizenry in a way that turns 'mutual obligations' into a type of surveillance. The line of risk in such contexts could appear to be that of least resistance.

Praxis philosophy connected a generative idea of self-determination to the social model of workers' self-management, yet while Giddens's proposals may imply institutional democratization this remains to be elaborated. The new agenda of the intersections between globalization and a restructuring of personal life seems to exacerbate both the voluntarism of individual and the power of the large-scale processes of globalization to require changes in intermediary agencies, including the welfare state. Nowhere does Giddens underestimate the problems of democratic determination as much as in his view of the infiltrating of expertise into everyday life and the control this supposedly endows agents with.[3] Habermas's conception of fragmentation and the cultural impoverishment resulting from the detachment of expertise seem to better define the actual situation. In a similar vein, Habermas's attempt to move beyond the welfare state paradigm of law contains possibilities for rectifying some of the oscillations of Giddens's perspective and Third Way policy proposals (Habermas 1996a). At the same time, Habermas's discourse theory has to be refined in order to take into account the globalizing developments that Giddens considers central to contemporary modernity and that generate variable changes in different contexts.

---

3 Beck (1998, 101), for instance, comments that 'in equating reflexive and *expert-determined* modernization, Giddens underestimates the *pluralization* of rationalities and agents of knowledge and the key role of known and repressed types of *unawareness*, which constitute and establish the discontinuity of "reflexive" modernization in the first place. Giddens thus misunderstands the questioning of the foundations of expert-determined modernization as well as the various efforts to create forms and forums of debate inside and outside of organizations in order at least to tie the contradictory rationality claims into a discursive context and a consensus on procedure.'

There are not only the disparities between Giddens's arguments over systems of domination and the consequences of the expansion of risk, between the disclosure of the discontinuity of the structural principle of capitalist society and the appreciation of the institutional diversity of modernity, but also a peculiar disparity between the claim that certain contemporary developments are virtually irresistible and compel change, and the notion that the freedom of subjects from authoritarian forms of constraint has increased and that the social is being reflexively shaped by action. This basically restates the dilemma contained in the philosophy of praxis' problem of the intersection of the subject and history. Perhaps this disparity is really only a part of a dialectical process and it can be encompassed within the duality of structure as the medium and outcome of practices. My analysis of Giddens's theory has attempted to demonstrate that this cannot be the case, so long as it depends on the advancement of claims that are inconsistent with one another and the standpoint of dialectical reflection undermines itself.

The deficiencies in the normative grounding of Giddens's attempted renewal of social democracy leads us back to Habermas's critical theory. In the next chapter, I consider how Habermas's parallel account of deliberative democracy can enhance Giddens's analyses of an emerging cosmopolitan citizenry and the universalistic perspective which he believes is promoted by a globalizing modernity. On this basis, it will become clear that Habermas's reworkings of discourse theory have clarified some of the potential of his arguments that were previously occluded and that, paradoxically, the contemporary disembedding of social relations, which Giddens has done the most to elucidate, create a context in which Habermas's normative-political proposals accrue greater relevance. The contrasts drawn will reinforce the theoretical and practical advantages and disadvantages that have been pointed out in these two most influential social theories. Habermas's explanation of the exhaustion of some of modernity's utopian energies and interpretation of postmodernist critiques of reason as one of its symptomatic expressions appeared to accurately characterize the situation. Yet, in its inability to explain subsequent modernizing developments this interpretation actually has certain continuities with these positions. Habermas later sketches the implications of the postnational constellation for social democracy and this leads him to argue for a cosmopolitan identity that is based on constitutional patriotism and civil solidarity (Habermas 1998). Giddens's arguments for the democratization of democracy are an extension of those that have just been presented on detraditionalization and welfare state reform. In both cases, democratization would enhance the actuality of the tendency that these conceptions depict.

Conclusion

It has been shown how Habermas and Giddens contend that the contemporary processes of modernization necessitate a rethinking of the social democratic project of the welfare state. Habermas and Giddens likewise consider that while the postmodern scepticism towards future progress is understandable, postmodernism constitutes an inadequate interpretation of the institutional structure of society. In some respects, postmodernism is symptomatic of the decline of modern utopian outlooks and the shift away from praxis philosophical conception of the social as constituted by the subject and history.

Habermas naturally opposes postmodernist perspectives on rationality and morality, yet embraces elements of the notion of post-industrial society in arguing that labour is becoming less significant for the overall structure of society. Giddens incorporates some of the claims about the new economy in his rethinking of social democracy, particularly emphasizing the circulation of information and the connection between knowledge and agency.

One consideration that Habermas's and Giddens's rethinkings of the welfare state have in common is the view that the state's role as the central agency of the reflexive action of society upon itself has to be reconsidered. In their opinions, the sphere of civil society is an important channel of democratization, both as a source of public discourse that shapes state policy and as a domain of democratizing interaction in its own right. The self-organizing potential of civil society appears to be the major domain of potential progressive change, yet Habermas and Giddens emphasize the significance of a politics of self-limitation in the contemporary period. Habermas argues that it is necessary to sustain a division between forms of social integration and that an appropriate balance is required between the 'system' and the 'lifeworld', or more specifically, between the state and civil society. Giddens's notion of utopian realism implies an even broader sense of societal self-limitation, but he agrees with the view that each of the spheres of the state, markets and community should be self-limiting, or, rather, none of them should be either too strong or too weak.

Giddens assessment of the limits of the welfare state reflects his conception of globalization and the implications, in his opinion, of generalized reflexivity. In particular, reflexivity means that market participants anticipate the consequences of state actions. Similarly, globalization is a continuation of the increasing time-space distanciation in modernity; the disembedding of social relations results in local circumstances being increasingly affected by distant events. These developments alter the conditions and means of state action, but they equally generate a potential sense of ontological insecurity on the part of subjects. Although Habermas later elaborated a more extended position on globalization, he did note how the former global pattern of inequality between core and periphery was being somewhat replicated in individual nations states, with the emergence of a segments of the population becoming peripheral to the capitalist labour market. This demonstrates how the resurgence of market capitalism exceeded Habermas's expectations at the time of his formulation of the distinction between lifeworld and system. Similarly, Habermas's formulation of how the lifeworld could democratize the system were unconvincing, partly because demands for democratization are supposed to remain external to the system and because of the way in which law is conceived to anchor the system in the lifeworld. In the next chapter, we will see that Habermas modifies this position and that this alteration enables a greater sense of democratizing interchange between lifeworld and system. Further the prospects of the European Union becomes a much more significant consideration for Habermas and Giddens. It will be suggested that this is indicative of how the project of modernity comes to be articulated in increasingly cosmopolitan terms.

Chapter Seven

DELIBERATIVE POLITICS, THE DEMOCRATIZING OF DEMOCRACY AND EUROPEAN COSMOPOLITANISM

The preceding analyses highlighted how Habermas's general theory of modernity was framed in order to account for the dilemmas of welfare state mass democracies and what he describes as the '*indissoluble* tension' between capitalism and democracy (Habermas 1987a, 345). This broad overall diagnosis is not mistaken but Habermas's theoretical formulation of the institution of modernity did not permit an entirely satisfactory approach to it. In retrospect, Habermas probably overestimated the extent to which the welfare state had altered the logic of the capitalist system and possibly underestimated the continuing significance of social labour. It is clear that the tendencies that Giddens's framework pointed towards, especially that of globalization, were changing the parameters of the tension between capitalism and democracy, even if contemporary developments were not entirely overtaking its earlier forms (Giddens 1990a). Habermas subsequently addresses these changes in a substantial manner. He questions some of the implications of modernizing reforms that are supposedly consistent with the logic of the new phase of modernity (Habermas 2001a). Habermas's and Giddens's distinct and overlapping approaches to the contemporary constellation of modernity strongly accentuate the processes of democratization.

Habermas and Giddens have made significant contributions to democratic theory. In part, this reflects their shared view that democracy is critical to the progressive transformation of contemporary society and that there are immanent tendencies toward the democratization of late-modern societies. The ensuing analysis explicates the ways in which Habermas's conception of communicative action's intersubjective format entails a commitment to democracy and how this leads to his revision of critical theory's notion of emancipation. On his view, individual autonomy is conditional on the autonomy of the other. Habermas is one of the major theorists of deliberative democracy (Habermas 1996a). This facet of discourse theory presupposes the communicative rationalization of the lifeworld, particularly with respect to the dimensions of post-traditional identity and civil society, whilst the institution of constitutional democracy is itself an aspect of this process of communicative rationalization (Habermas 1996a).

Giddens similarly endorses the notion of deliberative or dialogical democracy. He argues for the 'democratising of democracy', considering democracy to be a principle applicable from intimate interpersonal relations through to the global order (Giddens 1994a; 1998). Further, he claims that reflexive modernization compels revisions in the means of achieving the objectives of social democratic and progressive politics, particularly the left's values of equality and social justice. Habermas and Giddens have increasingly come to define the potentials for progressive change in cosmopolitan terms and they have each contributed multiple statements on the project of the European Union (Habermas 2009; 2011; 2015; Giddens 2007; 2014).

In this chapter, I show how some of the divergences in these two theorists' approaches, particularly Habermas's orientation to normative grounding and Giddens's to dynamic processes, can become the basis for intersections that result in a mutually reinforcing position. This mutuality is partly made possible by their shared endorsements of democracy and democratization. Like Giddens's rethinking of social democracy, Habermas's discourse theory of democracy is intended to constitute a constructive means of addressing the welfare state impasse and superseding the existing limitations of socialist organization, with their groundings in models of society based on social labour and distributive justice (Giddens 1994a; 1998a; 2000; Habermas 1996a; 1998). Further, the discourse theory conception of deliberative democracy and law represents another attempt to translate into institutional form Habermas's core conception of the intersubjective constitution of an identity that is both universal and particular. Democratic deliberation evidently depends on the normative principles that Habermas associates with communicative mediation: egalitarian reciprocity and mutual respect. Habermas (1996a) aims to show, above all, how the discursive conditions of justification are constitutive of the legitimacy of modern law and democracy.

These intentions of Habermas's discourse theory are substantial. The difficulties that are highlighted in discourse theory clarify whether its construction actually enables them to be realized. In this respect, there are four difficulties that are underlined in the ensuing analysis. First, Habermas's formulation is somewhat circular, it presupposes what it is meant to achieve. In one sense, this circularity is intrinsic to its critique of the failure of democratic institutions to coincide with their normative justification. Yet, presupposing autonomy is a problem common to theories of democracy and justice. Where other theories of democracy underline the contingency that this creates owing to the dependence on practice (Lefort 1988; Castoriadis 1991), Habermas endeavours to demonstrate grounds that limit contingency. This intention somewhat undermines discourse theory's critique of the contradiction between facts and norms (Habermas 1996a).

Second, then, Habermas's discourse theory is simultaneously anti-utopian in being consistent with the institutional reality of the existing political forms of democracy and the law, and too utopian in its envisaging the potential of existing institutions. The problem is that the discourse theory model is neither entirely satisfactory with respect to either side of this polarity. Habermas's clarification of the normative content within actual social reality is nevertheless significant, but it does not really conform to the process approach of critical theory's methodology of immanent critique. Third, these antinomies of Habermas's discourse theory are partly conditioned by its orientation to debates in normative political philosophy. Honneth is broadly right to contend that Habermas's deliberative model ultimately gives precedence to the political sphere relative to the broader social relations (Honneth 2007; 2014). In this sense, Habermas's discourse theory could be more directly grounded in social practices, even though it is meant to give expression to the normative implications of communicative practices. This represents a substantial limitation that Habermas's discourse theory has not fully overcome and it contrasts with the approach to social practice of the theory of structuration, rather than Giddens's later works intended to rethink social democracy, which share an equivalent, though not identical, deficiency (Giddens 1998a; 2000; 2007).

Fourth, Habermas has to extend and slightly modify the discourse theory conception of law and democracy in order to take into account the emergence of the 'postnational constellation' and to reinforce the European Union's potential for cosmopolitan justice and democracy (Habermas 2001). These alterations are indicative of how the conditions of realizing the intentions of the discourse theory of democracy and law were changing at the point of its formulation. Nevertheless, Habermas's application of discourse theory to cosmopolitanism enables him to address themes that were previously peripheral to his theory. He makes a major contribution, one the one hand, to comprehending how the parameters of democratization have changed, and, on the other hand, how this process of democratization can draw on subjects' existing competences and the normative principles of modern institutions (Habermas 2001a; 2011).

Giddens's proposals concerning the European Union, by contrast, are more continuous with the categories of his general theory of modernity. Even so, the tribulations and strains of the European project during the past decade have induced some subtle shifts in his arguments and their suppositions. Finally, Habermas's and Giddens's arguments concerning democracy, democratization and the postnational constellation represent interpretations of the modernist problem of the relationship of instituting practices to the instituted society. Of particular significance, these accounts of law, democracy, democratization, and cosmopolitanism consolidate the drift away from the nexus of the subject and history in their work. In so doing, Habermas and Giddens overlook some of the potential for reconfiguring this notion of the social and for reassessing its forms of modernity. The reconsidering of the nexus of the subject and history in the most important recent social theory perspectives on modernity will be overviewed in the Conclusion to this work that follows this chapter.

Democratization: Process and Institution

Habermas's and Giddens's perspectives on the potential for democratization are intended to be responses to the disillusionment with the dominant practices and institutions of liberal democratic politics. Yet, Habermas's and Giddens's innovative arguments for democratization are sometimes in tension with their somewhat affirmative perspectives on the institutions of liberal democracy. These tensions are manifest in Habermas's argument that discourse theory's radical democratic implications are consistent with the constitutional state's normative principles, since the existing state seems to either constrain democracy or represent a rather limited expression of it. In a sense, Habermas's perspective is built on the implications of the discrepancy between facts and norms, that is, the difference between institutional reality and the justifying principles (Habermas 1996a). He suggests that democratization involves the practical realization of the constitutional principles of the democratic state, rather than that radical democracy presupposes the generation of new norms and political projects.

There is a considerable contrast between the assumptions underlying this position and those of the praxis philosophical conception of radical democracy. The praxis philosophy conception is based on a projected future transformation of the entire social structure and the corresponding way of life. This projection applied to both the capitalist and state socialist variants of the institution of modernity. It is worth recalling that the praxis philosophy perspective partly originated from the critiques of the constitutional state and the liberal conceptions of freedom (Marx 1977c). Habermas retains aspects of these praxis philosophical intentions in his discourse theory of democracy and law, such as in the conception of communicative power. However, the divergences of his discourse theory from the praxis philosophy understanding of radical democracy and social emancipation are equally pronounced and a key difference is explicitly conveyed in Habermas's statement that:

> The 'emancipated society' is an ideal construction that invites misunderstanding. I'd rather speak of the idea of the undisabled subject. In general, this idea can be derived from the analysis of the necessary conditions for reaching understanding – it describes something like the image of symmetric relations of the freely reciprocal recognition of communicatively interacting subjects. Of course, this idea can't be depicted as the totality of a reconciled form of life and cast into the future as a utopia. [...] I've always said that 'socialism' is useful only if it serves as the idea of the epitome of the necessary conditions for emancipated forms of life, about which the participants *themselves* would have to reach an understanding. (Habermas 1994, 113)

In a similar vein, Giddens has difficulties reconciling democratization's programmatic and transformative potential with arguments conditioned by the vicissitudes of traditional party politics. This tension means, as the experience of the British New Labour government influenced by his Third Way program appears to suggest, that the demands of sustaining parliamentary majorities sets limits to democratic dialogue in the public sphere and the social changes that would ensue from democratization. Of course, this position is never explicitly stated by Giddens, but the very notion of the Third Way implies a basic acceptance of the institutional parameters of capitalist modernity. In the long-term, the contradictory imperatives of arguing for considerable democratization and seeking to sustain parliamentary majorities probably compounds disillusionment with liberal democratic institutions and the political process more generally. Indeed, it would compound the very disillusionment that the arguments for democratization were intended to address and raises questions about whether the conception of democratization has been conceived in a way that enables greater social justice.

Nevertheless, Giddens (1994a) conception of the 'democratizing of democracy' reflects a significant shift away from authoritarian modes of social organization. Like Habermas's argument that there has been a metamorphosis in the 'accent' of utopian aspirations, Giddens's notion of deliberative democracy simultaneously presupposes the change to 'post-traditional' identities and it reinforces the import of 'life-politics' to progressive social change (Giddens 1994a). In a number of ways, Giddens seeks to show how the participatory and discursive features of life-politics can serve the more traditional social democratic objectives of reducing social inequality. This approach could naturally be queried from the perspective of Giddens's earlier notion of structure as constraining and enabling, given the disparities in the allocation of resources that condition power and the complications of processes of structuration. In this sense, a more traditional liberal conception of social action and agency appears to inform Giddens's formulation of the Third Way. Consequently, some of the complications that the theory of structuration illuminated concerning social practices are occluded or neglected in Giddens's later works. It is not hard to suggest, then, that it would have been possible to avoid some of the deficiencies these later works, even though this may have been at the expense of their immediate public impact (Giddens 1998a; 2000).

Habermas and Giddens return, then, to the institution of democracy and rights in order to define the contemporary forms of the modernist vision of an autonomous society; they consider that these institutions of liberal democracy embody principles for resisting the revived politics of unregulated market. Habermas criticized the Frankfurt School critical theory for underestimating the significance of this bourgeois legal and constitutional heritage. Similarly, Giddens considers that citizens' public deliberation is fundamental to the discontinuity of modernity. Although Habermas and Giddens reject the idea of a redemptive politics of revolution, quasi-utopian projections of change remain important to their theories. In their opinion, utopian notions continue to have an orienting function for political practice. A fundamental question is how this potential of utopian projections can be infused into the institutions of democracy and rights. The answers to this question are basic to their ideas concerning how rights and democracy can be more than is suggested by liberal political philosophy's notion of negative liberty and its protection. These answers are critical to addressing the problem, as Habermas defines it, of continuing the welfare state program at a higher level of reflection (Habermas 1989a).

In Giddens's opinion, the welfare state project remains a source of social progress, although it could become an impediment to utopian prospects, like that of a post-scarcity order, if reflexive modernization's historical consequences are not recognized and incorporated into a rethinking (Giddens 1994a; 1998a). Despite the alternative positions hinted at in the contrasting ideas of reflection and reflexivity, Habermas and Giddens believe that the liberal definition of democracy and rights as the protection of 'negative freedoms' is an inadequate approach to current social developments and that changes, like globalization, welfare reforms, manufactured uncertainty, the ecological crisis, and cultural diasporas. These changes require the participatory approach of the 'positive freedoms' to shape institutions (Berlin 1969).

One of the important accomplishments of Habermas's and Giddens's theories are their detailed and original accounts of the social-historical foundations of democracy and citizenship rights. These interpretations of the social-historical foundations of democracy equally determine the way in which they perceive utopian anticipations can be infused into institutions and their explanations of how principles of autonomy extend far beyond the sphere of political institutions. The practical-political value of their interpretations is evident, as we will see, in their contributions to debates over cosmopolitanism and the

European Union. (Giddens 2007; 2014; Habermas 2009; 2012; 2015). There is a basic agreement between them that the questions of continuing the welfare state project has to be addressed at the national and transnational levels, especially in the European context. In the opinion of Habermas and Giddens, what are required are transnational processes of justice and democratization, as well as changes in the structure of collective identity.

In certain respects, Habermas's and Giddens's theorizing of democratization imply that traditional domain of political praxis is no longer necessarily the privileged locus of practices of radical change. The political sphere has to mediate the progressive changes taking place in the lifeworld or everyday life. It would even be fair to suggest that informal interaction most clearly exhibits the democratic and dialogical principles of 'institutional reflexivity' and communicative rationalization. This contention is consistent with these two theorists' accounts of the critical character of post-traditional identities and Habermas's notion of a universalistic moral consciousness formed through unimpeded intersubjective communication (Habermas 1990a). These visions of social interaction as the location of progressive change build upon the turn of praxis philosophy to mundane action and everyday life. This turn commenced with Marx's interpretation of labour and his critique of the abstract character of political freedom in bourgeois society. The 'lifeworld' and 'practical consciousness' are two founding categories concerned with everyday life and they are tailored to its diffuse experience. Habermas's and Giddens's conceptions naturally seek to disclose how the political domain is changed by these alterations in social practices and how political institutions can underpin the democratization that is incipient in these practices and identities.

Habermas's account of making a part of the background horizon of the lifeworld a theme of communication, and hence a subject of explicit evaluation, depicts a spiral of rational and progressive change. One that is similar to Giddens's interpretation of the alterations in practices ensuing from detraditionalization. In the opinion of both theorists, social movements and, especially for Giddens, therapeutic self-help groups are major new agencies of change, unified around the questions of the conditions of identity and ways of living (Giddens 1994b). Of particular significance, the communicative organization of informal social relations takes on considerable importance in its generating types of prepolitical and parapolitical experiments in democracy, such as those of deliberative forums, citizens' juries, and spaces of digital communication (see Browne 2006).

Although Habermas and Giddens recognize that it is countered by other trends, they believe that such democratization introduces more exacting conditions of legitimation and that it substantially undermines traditional legitimations of hierarchical structures of authority. The undermining of traditional hierarchies particularly influences their views on the significance of the dialogical mediation of social relations, as well as the process and procedural character of democratization. The former is evident, for example, in Giddens's view of how the 'pure relationship' of contemporary intimacy reproduces itself through processes of communication, rather than being determined by criteria and institutions that are external to that of the intimate relationship itself; such external criteria were formerly established by the church, the state, and the wider family (Giddens 1992). The interpretation of procedure is central to Habermas's discourse theory and he argues that it has become diffused as a principle of justification or legitimation (Habermas

1996a). As we saw earlier, this is something that he considers contributes to the more fluid and abstract character of post-traditional social identities.

Habermas and Giddens partly accept the validity of communitarian critiques of political liberalism and consider social solidarity to be integral to the reorganization of institutions and the countering the destructive effects of market capitalism. However, they argue that the dialogical and democratizing features of contemporary social interaction enable increasing individual autonomy and that this dynamic of change is inconsistent with some of the emphases of communitarian positions, particularly in its generating critiques of traditional community. According to Habermas, 'solidarity and the orientation to the common good appear as a third source of social integration' alongside the functional coordination of the systemic steering media of money and power in modern societies (Habermas 1996a, 269, 299). Cohen and Arato's definition of solidarity overlaps Habermas's conception and it discloses the links that this conceptualization of solidarity has to Habermas's founding intuition concerning the communicative constitution of identity:

> Solidarity involves a willingness to share the fate of the other, not as the exemplar of a category to which the self belongs but as a unique and different person. Despite this orientation to 'difference,' the resource of solidarity nevertheless presupposes a common membership in some actual or ideal group, and beyond this some common norms, symbols, and memories as well. Solidary individuals are consciously rooted in the same or significantly overlapping lifeworlds, and this guarantees consensus about important matters, even in a modern lifeworld where their content can be discussed and challenged. (Cohen and Arato 1992, 472)

Habermas rectifies some of the difficulties associated with his distinction between system and lifeworld in arguing for the mobilization of solidarity and the actualizing of the legal institution of democratic principles. By contrast, the 'structural pluralism' of Giddens's 'third way' political position leads to the oscillation between the alternatives of the market, state and community (Giddens 2000, 55). Giddens not only argues that solidarity is compatible with 'modernizing' reforms but that social solidarity is a condition of a balanced relation between markets, governments and the 'civil order' (Giddens 2000, 55–56). In his opinion, the parameters of community and trust relations change in a cosmopolitan, globalized and post-traditional society. The principles of autonomy and democracy should apply across a spectrum from personal relations to the global order (Giddens 1994a, 127–28). Given his earlier accounts of power and domination, the extent to which Giddens believes that democratization is continuous with existing institutions and developments is perhaps surprising.

In Giddens's opinion, the phase of reflexive modernization involves the dissolution of certain types of solidarity and the reconstitution of social solidarity, including new forms and revisions of earlier versions (Giddens 1994a; 1998a). Civil commitments are not necessarily in decline, rather an 'increasingly reflexive society is also one marked by high levels of self-organization' (Giddens 1998a, 80). Like Habermas, he nevertheless accepts that there is considerable justification to arguments that social bonds are under strain and that there is widespread disillusionment with the political process. Habermas and Giddens broadly agree that the dissatisfaction with liberal-democratic institutions is connected to the demands for democratization.

Habermas considers that this dissatisfaction supports his position that legitimacy depends on processes of public communication and a principle of democracy grounded in the possibility of discursively achieved agreement (Habermas 1996a). He argues that such dissatisfaction points to the fact that radical democracy is actually required by the normative principles of modern law and the constitutional state. Yet, Habermas's understanding of radical democracy is unusual in its supposition that radical democracy is continuous with the democratic-constitutional state. That is, he suggests that the constitution of the democratic state should be the foundation for a historical project intended to elaborate and fully realize the system of rights it embodies. Radical democracy is not at all a utopian aspiration, but, rather, an immanent principle of modernity. Habermas bases these suggestions on the claim that his discourse theory demonstrates 'that there is a conceptual or internal relation, and not simply a historically contingent association, between the rule of law and democracy' (Habermas 1996a, 449).

In this way, discourse theory gives new vitality to 'the old promise of a self-organizing community of free and equal and citizens' (Habermas 1996a, 7). In Habermas's opinion, the project of realizing through discourse the normative principles of the constitutional state would appropriately actualize the communicative ethic of the post-traditional social identity. It translates into explicit political institutions a procedural conception of democracy that is founded on the structures of communication. Habermas highlights how this discourse theory interpretation of democratic 'self-organization' differs from that of the standard interpretation of socialism:

> At any rate, this concept of democracy no longer has to operate with the notion of a social whole centred in the state and imagined as a goal-oriented subject writ large. (Habermas 1996a, 298)

Habermas nevertheless admits that the cultural transformation founded on communicative practices has not shaped contemporary modernization to a degree comparable to that effected by the structural changes in the capitalist economy and the political system. This assessment does not undermine the desirability and normative validity of democratic communicative practices but it does pose questions about their sufficiency and whether democratizing change actually depends on factors like additional forms of social experience, a more agonistic sense of social struggles, or the supplementary agency of a collective subjectivity (Honneth 1995a; 2014; Domingues 1996; 2000; 2006).

Giddens recognizes current changes similar to those of the communicative rationalization of the lifeworld. But, mainly due to his generic notion of practice, he does not distinguish between the cultural and systemic modernizing developments in the manner of Habermas's theory. This difference is apparent in Giddens's claim (1994a, 22–50) that conservative thought is contradictory, because markets are a major force in the undermining of tradition. The contrast between Giddens's emphasis on historicity of the dynamics of change and Habermas's prioritizing of the logic of development has been extensively underlined in the preceding discussion. I argue that this prioritizing leads to the problems of Habermas's inflexible understanding of social development, owing to his anchoring of social development in principles of social differentiation and the quasi-functionalist implications of his idea of the lifeworld performing the role of cultural programming. I highlighted some of the weaknesses this approach has in explaining the actual dynamics of change. Drawing on the analyses of Arnason (1991) and Joas (1993), I pointed to its difference from the praxis philosophy conception of social creativity. Habermas's framework permits only a rather narrow range of possible future development. This will be shown in the 'Conclusion' to contrast with the subsequent theories of multiple modernities and global modernity (Domingues 2012; Bringel and Domingues 2015; Eisenstadt 1999b; 2000; Arnason 2002; 2005; Wagner 2012).

The weaknesses of such inflexibility could however be considered a strength in the context of my comparative analysis. Habermas's logical grounding of socio-cultural values precludes the types of oscillations that characterize Giddens's writings, like the various meanings of the notion of structural principles and those tensions ensuing from the disparity between his arguments for the necessity of responding to recent modernizing processes and their alleged promotion of agency. In my opinion, Habermas's theory provides a stronger basis for resisting neo-liberal reforms and grounds for ascertaining both the appropriateness of the market and the needs that are not satisfied through exchange. He is able to show that the welfare state has a basis in the intersubjective relations of social solidarity and this enables greater evaluation of the progressive and regressive consequences of modernizing reforms. Further, Habermas proposes democratic procedures by which the project of the welfare state could transcend its limitations in the direction of promoting greater autonomy.

Similar intentions, to be sure, orient Giddens's writings on the welfare state and he notes that different models of the welfare state reflect the 'historical and cultural' background of respective nation-states (Giddens 1998a, 114). This may be an important consideration in relation to the background contexts of Habermas's and Giddens's respective images of a 'third way'. Habermas's theory has sometimes been interpreted as proposing a third way (Pusey 1987). Although they are not reducible to these backgrounds, the differences that the 'varieties of capitalism' and 'worlds' of welfare states classifications make may be relevant to appreciating these differences (Hall and Soskice 2000; Esping-Andersen 1990; Goodin et al. 1999). For example, the German welfare state is considered to be more comprehensive and its variant of capitalism more regulated than the British welfare state, which is seen as relatively less comprehensive and situated in a more liberal form of capitalism, being anchored to a greater extent in 'deregulated markets'. If national backgrounds are relevant then they would suggest that Habermas's and Giddens's conceptions of the parameters of Third Way reform are somewhat different and it may equally explain why Giddens's Third Way arguments for adopting elements of European social democratic policies are regularly overlooked in favour of the more liberal and individualizing positions (see Loyal 2003; Kiely 2005).

Besides its specific public policy proposals and adaptation to immediate political realities, it remains the case that the most consequential sense in which Giddens's Third Way position may be an alternative to Habermas's analysis lies in its making greater concessions to the neo-liberal critiques of the welfare state. This is certainly how one could interpret Habermas's comments on the negative implications of the social and economic reforms that appear consistent with reflexive modernization's values of facilitating individual agency and personal autonomy:

> But these positive aspects all have their flipside: the 'flexibilization' of career paths hides a deregulated labour market and a heightened risk of unemployment; the 'individualization' of life projects conceals a sort of compulsory mobility that is hard to reconcile with durable personal bonds; the 'pluralization' of life forms also reflects the danger of a fragmented society and the loss of social cohesion. Although we should take care not to assume an uncritical view of the achievements of the social welfare state, we must also not blind ourselves to the costs of its 'transformation' or collapse. One can remain sensitive to the normalizing force of social bureaucracies without closing one's eyes to the shocking price that a reckless monetarization of the lifeworld would demand. (Habermas 2001, 87)

Giddens would naturally contest this characterization of the 'flipside' as applying to the Third Way reforms and he would perhaps consider that such outcomes could only derive from the misunderstanding and omission. In fact, some hostile critics of the Third Way argue that what Habermas describes as the 'flipside' is actually the primary consequence of Third Way policies (see Giddens 2000; Callinicos 2002; Kiely 2005). Either way, these critical perspectives suggest that a firm statement of the Third Way's underpinning values and normative commitments might obviate the potential misunderstandings that are incipient in these criticisms. However, this may not be quite so straightforward, as these critical responses may actually reveal deep-seated tensions between the Third Way's normative justification and the actual means that is proposed to achieve them. In other respects, Giddens's positions are basically complementary to Habermas's arguments on citizenship rights and democracy. Indeed, Habermas's grounding of rights in a dual conception of public and provide autonomy could provide Giddens's Third Way policy contributions with a buttress against unwarranted concessions to neo-liberal and conservative agendas (Habermas 1996a).

The comparative analysis with Giddens's proposals reveals further instances of the paradox of substantially flawed aspects of Habermas's theory acquiring a new degree of validity and practical relevance. I argued that Giddens's introduction of time and space as central considerations of his social theory meant that it is particularly well suited to theorizing contemporary globalization. Giddens successfully conceptualizes manifold features of globalization, however, I demonstrated that the theory of structuration contains possibilities for breaking new ground in relation to the topic of globalization, which have not been fully explored. One need not agree with all of Giddens's arguments to appreciate that his analysis offers insights into globalization that go beyond the typical emphases on economic integration. By contrast, Habermas's discussion of all forms of intersocietal relations was fairly limited until relatively recently. Besides more general reflections on the future of European integration, he has sought to clarify the capacity of international law to regulate globalization and he has provided substantial discussions of such transnational phenomena as immigration policies (Habermas 1998a).

Habermas's discourse theory position foregrounds human rights and suggests that political legitimacy derives from their actualization. I have proposed that unlike the

dominant perspective of praxis philosophy, Habermas's approach accentuates the processes of distribution rather than the generative structure of production. This emphasis
underpins his critical rejection of models of workers' self-management and it is consistent
with Habermas's innovative interpretation of the communicative mediation of the universal and the particular. Significantly, the incipient universalism that Giddens (1994a;
1998a; 2000) perceives in diverse processes of globalization need to be channelled through
democratic procedures. Habermas's communicative model of participation and the institutional translation of democratic deliberation are arguably more relevant to this process
than the structuration of workers self-management (Habermas 1996a). In this way, globalization provides a superior justification for Habermas's proposal of a movement away
from praxis philosophy's model of workers' self-organization of production than the one
that he advanced by way of the systems theory informed category of complexity.

Habermas's perspective on identity could become a basis for framing discussions over
the democratic control of production and this could be one way of understanding the
implications of Giddens's account of the limits of cybernetic model of economic control
(Giddens 1994a). If this could be the case, then, Habermas's discourse theory of law and
democracy is potentially complementary to Giddens's argument on the cosmopolitan
polity created by globalization (Habermas 1996a). In other words, the very normative
positions Giddens seeks to uphold could be reinforced through the grounding in discourse theory. Of course, the paradox is that Habermas's approach acquires increased
relevance precisely through the occurrence of processes, like globalization, that it was,
on my analysis, originally incapable of satisfactorily explaining. This argument naturally
presupposes that Habermas's discourse theory is able to overcome some of the serious
internal problems of his social theory, especially those relating to a distancing from practice and its substantial weaknesses with respect to power.

Democratic Law and Communicative Power

Habermas's discourse theory argument that there is an 'internal connection' between
law and democracy reverses the pessimistic conclusions of his original account of the colonization of the lifeworld and some of the limiting practical-political implications of his
binary model of society, notably, the limiting entailed by the claim that democratic communication can only influence the system from the outside (Habermas 1996a; 1987a).
Habermas's general theory of communicative action did not inevitably entail these
conclusions and their restrictions upon democratization. His application of discourse
theory to law and democracy is therefore particularly important because it demonstrates
the practical application of the theory of communicative action and the potential for
expanding mutual autonomy. Discourse theory finesses the relationship between the
functional logic of social systems and the communicative reproduction of the lifeworld
in a way that partly corrects the institutional deficiency of a purely normative theory and
it restores the utopian projection of far-reaching democratization in a compelling manner (Habermas 1996a).

The utopian dimensions of critical theory are now to be found, however, in Habermas's
depiction of the counterfactual premises of everyday communication, rather than in the

historical process itself. The move that was important to Habermas's restoration of the utopian dimensions of critique was his stressing the 'idealization' of validity claims and their context-transcending quality. He did this in order to defend the universality of the reasons justifying a validity claim, in spite of the fact that a validity claim is always raised in the specific context of the here and now (Habermas 1992a; 1996a). In other words, relativist objections are deflected by an argument that speakers and hearers associate their validity claims with a truth that goes beyond the present circumstances.

The notion of the context-transcending character of validity claims fits Habermas's contention that a post-conventional identity presumes that it can justify its positions in front of the idealized projection of an unlimited communication community. Habermas proposes that in modernity a type of 'second level of idealization' is a consequence of social reality being constituted through communicatively achieved agreement. This social reality 'takes as its yardstick the intersubjective recognition of criticizable validity claims' (Habermas 1996a, 20). Significantly, the idealizations of communication point to how the conditions of justification may contradict the factual order of society. At the same time, these conditions of justification are necessary for the existence of society, because they are the counterfactual presuppositions of understanding. In other words, the presumptions of discourse function as a kind of 'regulative ideal', they are practical precondition of engaging in communication. For instance, when individuals engage in communication they have to presume mutual commitments, a preparedness on the part of each other to justify validity claims, and willingness to revise positions on the basis of the provision of reasons and convincing arguments.

According to Habermas (1996a), the duality of 'facticity' and 'validity' that inhabits communication obtains an institutional equivalent in law. On the one hand, compliance can be based simply on the facticity of law. Actors can choose to obey in order to avoid sanction, law having the power to coerce. On the other hand, where actors agree with the law's normative content and principles, acceptance derives from its validity dimension. It is the distinctive capacity of law to translate normative precepts into factual constraints that are sanctioned. Nevertheless, Habermas argues that ultimately the legitimacy of law derives from its validity dimension and not simply from its positivity (Habermas 1996a). Law is unique, he argues, in extending the principles of social coordination through mutual understanding beyond the context of face-to-face interaction. Habermas considers that the normative standards of justice and fairness do not need to be brought to bear upon the law from the outside. Instead, because of the validity requirements of legal legitimation, justice and fairness can be extrapolated from the conditions of reciprocal understanding and the structures of mutual recognition intrinsic to communicative action (Habermas 1996a).

The principles of understanding can then accomplish the social integrating function of regulating abstract forms of interaction between strangers through being translated into the institutional medium of law. While this claim seems to only reiterate the earlier historical analysis of the institutional component of the lifeworld, the practical-political implications of Habermas's later position become clear with his claim that only processes of democratization that enable citizens' participation in public discourses can stabilize the tension between the 'facticity' and 'validity' dimensions of law (Habermas 1996a).

Discourses, he argues, have a constitutive significance in the production of law and this is why they have an 'internal relation' to a central principle of democracy. The reflexivity of discourse enables the addressees of law to understand themselves to be, at the same time, its authors (Habermas 1996a).

Praxis philosophy partly originated from the attempt to extend modern political philosophy's notions of constitution and autonomy beyond the realm of explicit political institutions to the realm of the social. Habermas somewhat reverses this extension in returning the problem of constitution to the political institutionalization of democracy. He seeks to eliminate the image of a self-organizing community that is borrowed in modern political theory from the philosophy of the subject. Rather, his approach is continuous with praxis philosophy in its attempt to reconstruct from principles of discourse the intuitions underlying the constitutional state. The discourse principle is based on an expectation of the 'assent of all': 'Just those action norms are valid to which all possibly affected could agree as participants in rational discourse' (Habermas 1996a, 107). Legitimacy is based on the presumption that communicative processes of justification have been unimpeded and that these discursive procedures produce reasonable, that is, rational results.

Habermas believes that this 'procedural paradigm' supersedes the liberal contract model on account of its intersubjective interpretation of citizenship rights and that its vision of autonomy responds to the limitations of social welfare law. Discourse theory suggests that rights extend mutual recognition and are grounded in the rationality of 'discursively achieved agreement'. It therefore differs from the liberal-contract paradigm's framing of rights in terms of the model of the market relations. In discourse theory, rights are not things possessed, they are relational and subjects mutually accord them to one another. According to Habermas, founding law in the voluntary association of subjects is the 'anarchistic core' within the notion of communicative freedom. From this starting point, he stresses that 'the liberal rights protecting the individual against the state apparatus, with its monopoly on violence, are by no means *originary* but rather emerge from a transformation of individual liberties that were at first *reciprocally* granted' (Habermas 1996a, 457).

Discourse theory's procedural paradigm requires the legal institutionalization of the reciprocity of public and private autonomy to be effective. Habermas argues that the exercise of autonomy in one of these spheres entails its existence in the other. The alloy of these interconnections is a 'basic system of rights' (Habermas 1996a). That is, a procedural interpretation of legitimacy means that rights have to guarantee the private autonomy to enjoy subjective liberties through presupposing the public autonomy to participate in law making. This dual conception of autonomy is particularly significant and it supplies normative criteria that could weigh the implications of proposals like those of Giddens for reforming the welfare state (Giddens 1998a). Further, it discloses how the discourse principle is compatible with rectifying the inequalities of social exclusion. Yet, the important notion of the mutuality of public and private autonomy can be criticized as potentially ineffective owing to a certain circularity. It can only point to the potential losses of legitimacy and justification under the conditions where it is not met, rather than the conditions of its effective practical actualization and, it will be suggested below, that discourse theory imposes constraints on the practical actualization of radical democracy.

The procedural paradigm affirms social welfare rights, but rights are not justified in this social model on the 'productivist' grounds of distributive justice. Rather, welfare rights are institutionalized to counter the inequalities limiting autonomy, because legitimacy requires the self-determination of citizens. However, the precedence that this construction may suggest of participation is slightly deceptive. In actual fact, participation is significantly curtailed. Habermas claims that the discourse principle that operates at the 'horizontal level' of social interaction has to be complemented by institutionalized legal codes so as to be constitutive of the principle of democracy. This means that it is not the participation of subjects that is the primary condition of democracy but it is instead the institutional procedures determining legitimacy. Habermas states this in the following terms:

> The principle of discourse can assume the shape of a principle of democracy through the medium of law only insofar as the discourse principle and the legal medium interpenetrate and *develop* into a system of rights that brings private and public autonomy into a relation of mutual presupposition. (Habermas 1996a, 128)

Although Habermas considers that a capacity to transcend the existing order of society is intrinsic to the legitimating conditions of modern law, the potential for transformation immanent in his model is no less intrinsically limited. The reciprocal relationship of public autonomy and private autonomy facilitates the political participation of citizens and legally circumscribes the possibilities for self-determination. Habermas opposes all utopian ideas of the social that annul the distinction between the private and public spheres. The notion of the social grounded in the problem of the mediation of the universal and the particular can again be seen in Habermas's deriving rights from the mutual recognition and reciprocity of communicative action.

The basically 'counterfactual' quality of the validity conditions of law, and behind this mutual understanding, mean that Habermas's arguments are readily open to empirically informed objections regarding how the facticity dimension of law functions to legitimate and disguise power and domination (Habermas 1996a, 39). In fact, Habermas utilizes criticisms of the failures of welfare state legislation to establish justice and autonomy to initiate the 'procedural' legal paradigm. His arguments for a dual conception of autonomy have parallels with those of Marshall's interpretation of social rights enabling citizens to realize their civil and political rights. However, like Giddens, Habermas considers that Marshall's proposals need to be revised in the light of social and cultural changes (Marshall 1991). Multiculturalism and feminist politics have revealed the paradox that welfare state legislation intended to guarantee equality has often consolidated traditional social roles and stereotypes (Habermas 1996a). Habermas believes that discourse theory's procedural understanding of rights is not 'blind to cultural difference', because, properly understood, the basic system of rights details the conditions under which citizens should understand themselves to be both the authors and the addressees of law. Accordingly, rights require democratic discourses that articulate 'those aspects under which equals should be treated equally and unequals treated unequally' (Habermas 1996a, 426).

Habermas does not see any inconsistency between the need for actors to find and determine for themselves the conditions and limits of autonomy and this privileging of legal institutionalization in his model of democracy. He claims that once the sacred authority of institutions based on a metasocial interpretation has been undermined by rational critique, the principle of democracy is already present at the stage of deciding to form a community of legal consociates and to regulate social relations according to the rule of law. In this way, 'popular sovereignty forms the hinge between the system of rights and the construction of a constitutional democracy' (Habermas 1996a, 169). But Habermas's discourse model of democracy seeks to mediate between the liberal and republican conceptions of citizenship and the state. Since the liberals give priority to human rights and the private interests of individuals, they restrict democratic processes to establishing compromises and regulating state power. Whereas republicans adopt the standpoint of a 'self-organizing' ethical community, they understand the collective action of a political citizenry to be constitutive of society as a whole. As we have seen, Habermas's procedural model divests popular sovereignty of the ties it has to the idea of the community as a self-determining subject and which, he argues, is taken from the philosophy of consciousness.

> According to the discourse-theoretic conception of government by law, popular sovereignty is no longer embodied in a visibly identifiable gathering of autonomous citizens. It pulls back into the, as it were, 'subjectless' forms of communication circulating through forums and legislative bodies. Only in this anonymous form can its communicatively fluid power bind the administrative power of the state apparatus to the will of the citizens. (Habermas 1996a, 135–36)

Habermas would seem to have found in law a means to overcome those elements of the division between system and lifeworld that vitiated his earlier 'siege' model of communicative power. Public discourses and social solidarity transmitted into rational will formation were conceived to encircle the political system and to exert influence upon it from the outside. The later 'sluice' model is more open and does not adhere to the systemic closure of the earlier siege model (Habermas 1996a). The 'sluice' model argues for the partial inclusion of democratic deliberation and will formation inside the political administrative system. Similarly, the sluices 'opening' and the 'flow' of the communicative power generated by the voluntary association of subjects in civil society mean that the legitimacy of legislation depends on far higher levels of public participation.

Habermas's analysis of the exhaustion of utopian energies concluded that the idea of a political programming centre is unable to meet the expectations that were invested in it by social democrats. The parameters of democratization have changed. What occurs in the 'periphery', that is, civil society and informal networks of social relations, is equally – if not more – important as the political core of the 'parliamentary complex', public administration and the courts. Lacking the formal decision-making power of the inner core institutions, the periphery is the variegated associations of civil society, the public sphere of formal and informal networks of communication, and the private sphere. In particular, it is the periphery that is endowed in this model with the capacity to perceive and interpret social problems, as well as the location for actions and innovative projects of social movements (Habermas 1996a).

According to Habermas, a self-organizing public sphere and the constitution of rational will-formation through 'communicative freedom' themselves depend on the 'liberal political culture' and 'enlightened socialization' of a rationalized lifeworld. Habermas strenuously asserts that the project of democratizing complex societies through realizing the system of rights does not contain anything like an 'ideal projection of a concrete form of life'. Rather than presenting a 'utopia', the procedural paradigm of discourse only defines 'formal' conditions. Habermas's vision of democratic change amounts to no more, but actually requires no less, than '*all* the involved actors must form an idea of how the normative content of the democratic state can be effectively and fully exploited within the horizon of existing social structures and perceived developmental tendencies' (Habermas 1996a, 395). Needless to say, there is something elegant and puzzling about this position, it presupposes in large part precisely what needs to be achieved for there to be justice and democracy.

The extent to which the dispersed networks of communicative power are capable of democratically directing the state administrative system in a way that would significantly differ from the liberal determination of legitimacy is not satisfactorily clarified by Habermas. The difficulty resides not so much in Habermas's accepting a basic tenet of the liberal perspective over the richer republican alternative, but rather his coupling liberal reservations with a systems theory inspired notion of the polycentric character of contemporary societies. Bohman comments that Habermas's 'descriptive account of social complexity grants too much to systems theory, many of the "necessary" deviations from radical democratic norms are due to an uncritical acceptance of its theoretical presuppositions rather than to "unavoidable social facts"' (Bohman 1994, 900).

In so doing, Habermas may undercut the associative power of subjects to reshape institutions. A great deal hinges on the capacity of the medium of law to convert communicative power into administrative power, since in Habermas's model the possibilities for democratic self-determination are curtailed by the differentiation of the functionally organized political administrative system. Outhwaite (1994) accurately summarized the potential dilemma that confronts Habermas construction: in order to avoid the abstract utopianism of a discourse ethic without institutional form, there is the possibility of constructing a model of democracy and law that has lost its critical edge, because it identifies too closely with the existing state. Giddens's theory of structuration is relevant to this question of conversion of communicative power into administrative power, especially because Habermas's position depends on the *duality* of the facticity and validity dimensions of law, rather than the juxtaposition of them. Of course, this duality is by no means identical to that of structure and action, but it is the difference between them that makes the contrasts reciprocally illuminating.

Habermas's conceptions of action coordination and the constitution of social identity are founded on the normative reciprocity of the interaction between subjects. This reciprocity is, in turn, grounded in the social necessity of intersubjective agreement. The validity of an agreement depends on the procedure of its being achieved through communicative action oriented to understanding. Even so, the connection between the facticity and the validity dimensions of law holds so long as the analogy with 'institutionally unbound' speech is accurate and insofar as communicative power is not itself subject to systematic distortion. Giddens's notion of structuration, by contrast, was always related to the connection between subjects and institutions, structure is located in practices but action contributes to the reproduction of systems. Giddens better appreciates than Habermas the entwinement of both types of mediation in the structuration of social systems. Nevertheless, the tensions between different strands of Giddens's programme exemplify some of the problems of striking the right balance between communicative power and administrative power.

Habermas originally sought to define institutionalization as an outcome of the synthesis between social struggles and conditions of legitimation anchored in cultural projections of a just social organization (Habermas 1978a). The shifts in his perspective eventuate, however, in his overlaying institutions on a structure of interaction that is tailored to normative discourses and the constitution of a rational social identity. Despite the limitations of this latter approach, I want to suggest that Habermas is entirely consistent with its basic supposition in arguing for the regulation of systems from the outside. *Between Facts and Norms* offers the prospect for democratizing inside part of the system, yet rectifying the earlier institutional deficit may still only displace an underlying problem concerning conflicts and the motivation for actualizing democratic principles (Habermas 1996a; see Honneth 1994).

The response of sympathetic commentators to Habermas's theory of democracy and law have highlighted some of the consequences of displacing problems like those of struggle and conflicts onto the formal structure of discourse procedures. There is, to be sure, a great deal of validity to this construction and Habermas's position does not even attempt to meet the praxis philosophy expectations of reconciling form and content, justice and the good life. The problem is, as Bernstein (1998) demonstrates, whether the distinction that Habermas draws between moral discourses concerned with justice and ethical discourses concerned with the 'good life' corresponding to identity is too artificial from the perspective of actual practices. It is more likely the case that cultural projections of identity inform notions of justice, as well as conceptions of justice define an identity. In one sense, Habermas agrees entirely, implying that he merely distinguishes between discourses and equates democracy with procedures in order to preclude any potential for ethnocentrism and to acknowledge the plurality found in complex societies. Still, this line of argument risks undermining the real significance of Habermas's founding insight, because his discourse theory actually 'relies on, and presupposes, substantial-ethical considerations' (Bernstein 1998, 289).

In the theory of structuration, Giddens's general position starts from an acceptance of the knowledgeability and the transformative capacity of agency. His generative notion of agency and Habermas's conception of communicative power could be regarded as complementary, though they are not equivalent. The structuration approach to the administrative conversion of discourses would imply a recognition of a dialectic of control influencing this process. Indeed, this interpretation of the dialectic of control would be another way of understanding the relationship between facticity and validity, both in terms of intersubjective understandings and law. It would not replace the normative standpoint of discourse theory, but it points to an avenue for rectifying weaknesses in Habermas's model. In particular, it preserves an awareness of the subordinated interests that initiate struggles for change, while accepting that a rational agreement requires the following of procedures. Interestingly, Habermas (1996a; 1998a) actually appreciates the importance of 'struggles for recognition' to realizing the normative principles of institutions and how the limitations of the present embodiment of modern principles of autonomy and equality have been revealed by the projects of transformation that guide these struggles.

Habermas's theory, however, incorporates these dimensions of change only to defuse their potential implications. In his model, the actualizing of popular sovereignty and the implications of realizing the system of rights have to be largely consistent with existing institutions. In a sense, Habermas's difficulties in incorporating conflicts into his model of discursive democracy seem to stem from his belief that an acceptance of the probability of disagreement risks undermining this model's principle of the agreement of all. In his opinion, this problem should not arise at all, precisely because deliberative politics draws its power from the freedom of subjects to resolve disagreements through the communicative processes of rational argument.[1]

The historical analyses of Giddens's critiques of historical materialism, alternatively, support a far more sceptical view of the implications of an administrative conversion of discourses (Giddens 1981a; 1985). They imply that Habermas's conception of law preserves the facticity of authority at the price of diluting the institution of power of its actuality as a mode of control and domination. In these historical analyses, Giddens suggests that the political-administrative pacification of the nation-state is associated with enhanced surveillance and information control (Giddens 1985). Although these analyses of the modern state administration appear to diverge from Habermas's only in their emphases, the conclusion they portend is precisely the interpretation of law that Habermas opposes, that is, that the facticity dimension of law becomes its validity dimension. According to Giddens (1985), modern civil law was fundamental to the institutionalizing of both modern systems of domination and the capitalist mode of production. He considered, at least during that period of his thought, that it was class struggle that promoted citizenship rights. Giddens explicitly opposes the notion of an evolution of democracy, so that change would be a logical elaboration of principles (Giddens 1985; 1996).

Despite revealing a greater ambivalence, these arguments are not really incompatible with Habermas's interpretation of the dialectical development of law. The question they raise is whether Habermas's model adequately depicts the interconnections and relative balance between the different components of modern social formations, like citizenship and class, administration and solidarity. Dews (1995) and Outhwaite (1994) have pointed

---

1 McCarthy (1998) has provided an extensive review of the issues which disagreement poses for Habermas's discourse theory and he correctly points to certain revisions in Habermas's model which I have suggested rectify some problems but do not perhaps resolve them at source.

to the tension between Habermas's view of the erosion of solidarity and the expectations of discourse theory concerning the democratic potential of law. The reinvigorating of solidarity may converge with this potential, but, even so, Outhwaite rightly states that legal 'and political autonomy are at best necessary and not sufficient conditions for this' (Outhwaite 1994, 151).

Of course, recognizing the problems that Habermas neglects in seeking to define the internal connection between law and democracy, need not entail an endorsement of Giddens's position as an alternative. Nevertheless, this comparison reinforces, on the one hand, my contention that on citizenship rights and deliberative democracy, Giddens does not provide a normative position that is a substantial alternative to Habermas's discourse theory. On the other hand, Giddens's historical analyses clarify some of the obstacles to Habermas's carrying through the programme of discourse theory and they highlight just how felicitous and tenuous are Habermas's argument for democratic determination in his dual conception of autonomy. The tenuousness of these claims does not detract in any way from the desirability of seeking to realize the project to which they belong. The tenuousness of the claims does mean, however, that they reiterate some of the problems that inspired the response of the philosophy of praxis and the attempt to define emancipation in social, and not just political, terms. The political ideal of history making subjects arose, as Castoriadis and Habermas have shown, from the conception that there is no extra-social source of the institutions of society. It was subsequently recognized that the modern principles of autonomy – insofar as it derived from the tradition of 'natural law' – was still exclusive in being legal and political without being founded socially (Castoriadis 1991; Habermas 1974a).

I have argued that Habermas does found these principles socially in a theory of inter-subjective communication; but that this conception cannot encompass all of the aspects of the social. The perimeters of its validity are defined by the nexus between the constitution of identity and normative adjudication. Habermas's conception of the mediation of the universal and the particular translates into the democratic ideal of free and equal opportunities for subjects to participate in discourses. It is important, above all, because it offers a means for continuing the programme of critical theory and it shows that a level of democratization that goes beyond that already achieved in capitalist mass democracies is not tied solely to the reorganization of production.

Habermas's procedural model of democracy and deliberative politics constitutes a programme for continuing the welfare-state project at a higher level of reflection. In particular, he has restored the priority of the participant's perspective in critical theory and presented from this angle a formal but still affirmative image of a reorganized contemporary society. The specification of how actors can understand themselves to be the authors of the laws to which they are themselves subject as addressees is probably an unsurpassed clarification of how the normative principles of existing institutions can best be practically realized. The difficulty is that Habermas makes this case at the price of excluding the problems that praxis philosophy locates under its process approach to the social. Giddens far more successfully retains the process approach of praxis philosophy in his theory of structuration and he better captures the *'action at distance'* of contemporary process of mediation (Giddens 1994a, 4).

For Giddens, the time-space distanciation of globalization is one of the dimensions of diverse processes of contemporary socialization and these processes extend beyond Marx's vision of the fundamental contradiction of capitalist society, that of the contradiction between private appropriation and socialized production. A new mediation of the universal and the particular at the level of consciousness is likely to be implicated in the structuration of these processes, like the socialization of nature and 'the transformation of intimacy' (Giddens 1994a; 1992). Habermas's notions of democratic solidarity and the individual, as well as the social, identity deriving from a rationalized lifeworld, are extremely relevant to the shape of this consciousness and the morality of its practices.[2]

Unlike Habermas's (1984a; 1987a) theory of communicative action, Giddens's expansive notion of reflexivity suggests a way of advancing autonomy against complexity, but his conception of a 'critical theory without guarantees' seems to represent a project that can only be validated by its own momentum or is subject to the evident oscillations of a 'utopian realism'. The dilemmas of this position can only be obscured, rather than resolved through understanding structuration theory as a dialectic of different implications. Structuration theory was originally envisaged, instead as an approach that is politically bound to the reorienting of generative processes. Habermas's theory may be even less prospective in terms of the reorienting systemic steering media and cautious in its extrapolating from immanent developments, yet it nevertheless contains convincing normative criteria. Normative criteria that are opposed to the 'disabling' of subjects and that contain the formal outline of the project of democratization. Even though this project is ultimately only guaranteed by the unavoidability of the communication of subjects, it makes an invaluable contribution to the continuation of critical theory in setting itself against some of the pessimistic conclusion that have often been drawn from recent historical developments.

It may be the case, however, that Habermas salvaged this normative standpoint by setting it against the implications of historical reflection in general. Neither Habermas nor Giddens seek to reconcile the subject and history in the manner of Marx's philosophy of praxis; they develop more modest versions of critical theory that endeavour to counteract those contemporary tendencies that are anti-social. Habermas's and Giddens's social theories have arguably given us a clearer delineation of the parameters of praxis today. One could suggest that in their commitment to the modernist vision Habermas's and Giddens's theories have always been cosmopolitan. Nevertheless, cosmopolitanism has become a more explicit theme in their recent work, especially in connection with their contribution to debates over the European Union. In a sense, it might be claimed

2   Benhabib sketches the sorts of questions I have in mind in the following comment, and the reason for Habermas's relevance to addressing them should be clear: 'The challenge to contemporary social and political thought in the new global constellation is the following: can there be coherent accounts of individual and collective identity which do not fall into xenophobia, intolerance, paranoia and aggression toward others? Can we establish justice and solidarity at home without turning in upon ourselves, without closing our borders to the needs and cries of others? What will democratic collective identities look like in the century of globalization?' (Benhabib 1998, 98).

that the perceived need for some conception of the postnational form of collective self-determination represents a reconfiguration of the problem of the nexus of history and the subject. The rethinkings of this nexus that have been undertaken over the course of Habermas's and Giddens's work make possible new conceptions that are relevant to the changing circumstances.

European Cosmopolitanism

The preceding analysis compared how Giddens's theory was originally at the forefront of discussions of globalization with Habermas's somewhat later engagement with this theme. This difference reflected the contrasting theoretical approaches to the social, particularly the importance of temporal and spatial dynamics to Giddens's theory and the impediments that Habermas's formulation of the distinction between lifeworld and system may have posed to effectively theorizing globalizing processes. Habermas has, however, subsequently adapted important dimensions of his theoretical perspective to the analysis of globalization (Habermas 2001a; 2006a; 2006b; 2011). There are three interrelated dimensions of this theoretical modification that are particularly important to the comparison of Habermas's and Giddens's interpretations of the contemporary constellation of modernity.

The first is the position that Habermas provides on revising social democracy and the greater sense that he has of globalization's undermining of democracy. This has already been touched on and Habermas proposes a contrast between the respective phases of the 'opening' and 'closing' of modernizing lifeworlds. He argues that the 'disembedding of the market' differs from the political and cultural 'opening' and 'closing' of lifeworlds (Habermas 2001a). The second is how Habermas clarifies the characteristics of cosmopolitan citizenship and the transnational public sphere. The former is related to his notions of 'constitutional patriotism', which contrasts with ethnic definitions of the nation, and it reflects his view that 'civil solidarity' is a necessary underlying principle of a transnational public sphere, that is, the 'solidarity of strangers' (Habermas 1998a). The third dimension is the discourse theory conceptualization of cosmopolitan law (Habermas 1996a; 2006b; 2012). Habermas here engages with the themes of force and violence that Giddens had given greater priority to in his theory of history (Habermas 2012; 2015).

Habermas's perspective on cosmopolitan law is one that is intended to enable an increased sense of justice; it seeks to meet the justificatory and legitimacy conditions of discourse theory. Habermas's analyses and advocacy of the European Union give concrete shape to these themes. He treats the European Union as an 'exemplary' case that illustrates the considerations that shape a cosmopolitan democratic order (Habermas 2009; 2012; 2015). For similar reasons, the European Union has been a major theme of Giddens's later works. He has, like Habermas, sought to promote European integration, while counteracting those tendencies of European institutions that lead to increasing inequality and the disregarding of democracy (Giddens 2007; 2014). The European project might be considered to give new forms to many of the dilemmas of the institutional realization of the modernist vision of the autonomous constitution of society.

Habermas's central intuition concerning identity underpins his conception of how globalizing processes can be reoriented. Its sense of the communicative mediation of the universal and the particular is inherent in such categories as those of cosmopolitan law, civil solidarity and the transnational public sphere. According to Habermas, the processes associated with globalization restate the problem of 'collective self-determination' but the required cosmopolitan standpoint is not that of a 'world citizenship' (Habermas 2006b; 2012). Rather, in the concrete case of the European Union, Habermas argues for a type of federated community of democratic states. He considers that this would be the most feasible democratic institutional form in the European context. In short, this is because such an institution of the European Union and nation states would be founded on a sense of identity that considers itself to be capable of collective self-determination:

> Any political community that wants to understand itself as a democracy must at least distinguish between members and non-members. The self-referential concept of collective self-determination demarcates a logical space for democratically united citizens who are members of a particular political community. Even if such a community is grounded in the universalist principles of a democratic constitutional state, it still forms a collective identity, in the sense that it interprets and realizes these principles in light of its own history and in the context of its own particular form of life. The ethical-political self-understanding of citizens of a particular democratic life is missing in the inclusive community of world citizens. (Habermas 2001a, 107)

Habermas argues that the postnational constellation presents contrasting alternatives, but that it has been dominated by the neoliberal project of the deregulating and the 'disembedding', in Polanyi's sense, of market capitalism (Habermas 2001a: Polanyi 1957). This development constitutes a threat to the social democratic project of the welfare state and to the very notion of the institution of society as founded on the actions of its members (Habermas 2001a). In this case, disembedding means that the market system, that seemingly operates outside of society, is restructuring institutions and undermining the social rights of citizenship, the conditions of labour, and the sovereignty of the territorially defined national state. The ensuing social divisions can lead to the erosion of social solidarity. This has significant additional consequences, given that the sense of community that derives from social solidarity served to justify the redistributions of wealth and resources in welfare state mass democracies (Habermas 1996a; 1998a; 2001a).

The boundaries and complexion of the social are being transformed by the various processes associated with globalization. These changes imply that the creation of conditions equivalent to those that facilitated the consolidation of the welfare state's institution depend on the extension and reinvention of solidarity. Habermas contends that the postnational constellation requires new forms of 'democratic steering' (Habermas 2001a, 88). In his opinion, there is currently a lack of effective coordination and regulation of transnational processes. It would be hard to disagree with this assessment and much of it is shared by Giddens (2014). Although Giddens's Third Way perspective arguably presumes that the disembedding of markets is already so advanced that earlier forms of collective control had become less effective (Giddens 1998a; 2000). The imbalance in power that this presumption creates is one of the reasons why Giddens's proposals concerning the new forms of reflexively influencing and regulating markets are either often overlooked or are simply considered to be ineffective and even serve to extend the liberalizing of markets (see Kiely 2005; Loyal 2003).

It has been suggested that globalization exacerbates the structural contradictions of the welfare state that Habermas diagnosed (Habermas 1979; 1987a). In short, the end of Keynesianism has resulted in the depletion of the resources of the welfare state and the shrinking tax base is producing a crisis in state budgets (Habermas 2001a, 77). In fact, Habermas commented that the recent banking and debt crisis means that: 'Today we are not (yet) experiencing a legitimation crisis, but we are witnessing a palpable economic crisis' (Habermas 2015, 85). Like his earlier analyses, Habermas questions the notion that modernizing reforms consistent with neoliberal economic globalization are irresistible and that there is no alternative to them (Habermas 2001a; 2015). He criticizes the notion of 'locational competition' that informs neoliberal globalization, especially on a the grounds of its simplifying assumptions concerning social action, its inconsistency with the normative principles of the discourse theory of justice, its contributing to increasing material inequality, and its suppression of democratic determination (Habermas 2001a). Habermas argues that the task is not to institute politically and culturally regressive forms of national closure in response to globalization, rather, it is to bring global economic networks under political control; this depends on the action of transnational institutions, as well as nation states (Habermas 2001a; 2009).

There is a further implication of the neoliberal project of the market society that limits democratic control. Habermas points to difference between the two subsystem steering media and the shift that neoliberal globalization makes from administrative power to money. 'The regulatory power of collectively binding decisions operates according to a different logic than the regulatory mechanism of the market. Power can be democratized; money cannot' (Habermas 2001a, 78). The distinction that Habermas draws between the opening and closing of lifeworlds has some parallels with the earlier contrast between structural and cultural modernization, but it differs in its appreciation of how changes are related to exogenous or 'external' tendencies. In this sense, it is closer to Giddens's perspective on social integration and system integration (Giddens 1979; 1985). It likewise appears to be founded less on functionalist suppositions concerning social reproduction than the earlier theory of communicative action, although this may simply reflect the fact that the distinction between the opening and closing of the lifeworld has not been as extensively developed.

Habermas's depiction of the opening and closing of the lifeworld through the networks of markets and communication tracks a process of change that leads to increasing contingency. 'With each new impulse toward modernization, intersubjectively shared lifeworlds open, so that they can reorganize, and then close once more' (Habermas 2001a, 83). The new openings lead to expanded horizons, but equally generate conditions that require new institutional regulation and organization. This is how Habermas interprets Polanyi's notion of the 'double movement' of nineteenth-century market liberalization and the subsequent movement by society against the deleterious consequences of the liberalizing of markets, especially against that of the social disorganization caused by the market in international finance during the early decades of the twentieth century

(Polanyi 1957). Polanyi highlighted the social disintegration that ensued from the chaos and crises of financial markets. The 'double movement' of society against the 'disembedded' market system culminated in higher levels of state regulation and controls relating especially to finance and trade (Polanyi 1957).

The changes associated with the regulation of liberal market capitalism can be described, Habermas argues following Peter Wagner, as generating the form of 'organised modernity' (Habermas 2001a; Wagner 1994). Consequently, contemporary processes of globalization are part of the 'opening' and dismantling of the institutional structures of the phase of organized modernity. The destructive consequences of the current changes and their independence from the lifeworld demand new form of control or closure. In this sense, the opening towards a cosmopolitan lifeworld presumes the equivalent constitution of democratic institutions. It is worth reiterating that this perspective incorporates a strong sense of the dynamics of modernization, but that there is little potential for internally altering economic globalization. Instead, Habermas's proposals concerning the regulating of changes centre on the potential of law, human rights, and political democracy (Habermas 1998a; 2001a; 2006b; 2008).

The limitations of this approach to globalization will be considered later, but the difficulties identified in Habermas's discourse theory of law and democracy impinge on these proposals (Habermas 1996a). For instance, an enormous amount turns on the identification of radical democracy with the normative principles of the constitutional state and the question of whether the institution of law can effectively transmit the communicative power of subjects. Although the question of whether Habermas overestimates the degree to which existing institutions are open to progressive demands and the genuine realization of the conditions for the active participation by citizens is still unresolved, there are certainly strong grounds for suspecting that his proposals contain elements of utopian projection concerning these institutions. In other respects, Habermas's conception of the conditions for the progressive reform and regulation of globalization is certainly less than utopian, since supranational organization's and the transnational agencies of civil society's capacities for mobilization are still relatively low and major problems are addressed through indirect negotiations (Habermas 2001a).

The expansion of the lifeworld's horizons that Habermas details broadly fits with the pattern previously outlined of normative progress and the extension of consciousness towards a more universalistic perspective (Habermas 2001a). Habermas's opposition to retrogressive nationalist reactions to globalization is reflected in his notions of 'constitutional patriotism' and civil solidarity. It is important to emphasize that the legitimacy conditions that have been sketched concerning democratic law and basic rights remain the basis for action in this model under globalization (Habermas 2001a, 77). The democratization of globalization depends on a postnational civil society. In Habermas's conception, a postnational civil society cannot be separated from the institution of cosmopolitan law. However, cosmopolitan law equally depends on an effective transnational public sphere and the extension of the sense of civil solidarity that enabled the nation state to address the injustices of capitalist society. Civil solidarity implies the mutual recognition of the 'rights of strangers' and an orientation to some notion of the common good (Habermas 1998a). Civil solidarity historically generated commitments to subordinate individual 'self-interest' in order that the vulnerable and disadvantaged of a community have their basic needs met and that they can lead a dignified form of life (Habermas 1996a; 1998a).

This modern sense of civil solidarity is the product of a long historical process, since it is founded upon an abstract and general commitment to others. The corresponding modifications in forms of identity constitute adaptations to changes in the structure of society and the broad alterations in social relations in modernity. National identity, Habermas (1998a; 2001a) contends, involved a more abstract form of social integration than premodern modes of integration, such as the premodern estate based integration of feudal orders and the corporate forms of early modernity. Nationalism generated a sense of 'imagined community', to use Benedict Anderson's term, and the solidarity of common citizenship justified the redistributive measures of the welfare state (Anderson 1983). According to Habermas, a postnational identity would be a further application of the same logic of abstraction and, at the same time, it is a form of identity that is being reinforced by concrete developments, like the formation of transnational institutions (Habermas 2001a; 2008). This postnational or cosmopolitan identity constitutes another mode of giving expression to the mediation of the universal and the particular. This may partly explain why Habermas considers that nationally founded 'constitutional patriotism' is consistent with a commitment to postnational cosmopolitanism, rather than in contradiction with it.

The notions of civil solidarity and 'constitutional patriotism' are significant extrapolations from Habermas's theory of modernity. Discourse theory, he contends, implies the more abstract national identity of constitutional patriotism (Habermas 1998a). In short, constitutional patriotism endorses the constitutional state's universalistic principles, and hence the equal treatment of all citizens. It contrasts with more genealogical view of the nation as a distinct ethnic community. Interpretations of the nation in terms of ethnicity accentuate features of the pre-political community, believing these to be the ultimate basis of solidarity. In Habermas's opinion, this genealogical version of nationalism is not intrinsically democratic. Constitutional patriotism, by contrast, is based on a belief in the legitimacy of democratic procedures and the constitutional elaboration of the rights of citizenship. In this sense, constitutional patriotism entails subjects' identification with abstract principles and formal procedures. According to Habermas, constitutional patriotism's principle of the equal treatment of all is relevant to the diversity of multicultural societies and the integration of different national societies into a single union or federation. It enables the same legal principles to be 'interpreted from the perspective of different national traditions and histories' (Habermas 1996b, 500).

For this reason, a transnational public sphere is critical to the development of a sense of civil solidarity, so that the members of the currently different national communities can have a shared sense of the right to equal treatment and a shared commitment to the well-being of members of another national community. Of course, the actual functioning of the existing public sphere only partially satisfies these conditions, but there are nevertheless instances in which the barriers of language, private media ownership and the regressive nationalism are transcended, such as in relation to ecological concerns or opposition to military interventions. In a sense, cosmopolitan solidarity can only exist in being realized and it is complemented by the constitution of the broader transnational institutions and civil society, such as international courts and parliaments. For all these reasons, Habermas's interpretation of cosmopolitanism presupposes a strong commitment to social justice and the enacting of the principles of discourse. That is, it depends on the fulfillment of the democratic procedures of discourse and the instantiation of redistributive mechanisms in order to counter material inequalities (see McCarthy 2002). Nevertheless, cosmopolitanism implies a more indirect and mediated realization of the democratic principle of subjects being the authors of the laws that they are the addressees.

The obvious criticism of Habermas's interpretation of cosmopolitanism is that it is largely counterfactual. For the cosmopolitan expression of constitutional patriotism to be practically effective it has to extend the 'solidarity amongst strangers' that was consolidated by national consciousness (Habermas 1998). Yet, national identification implied stronger socially grounded bonds than Habermas's vision of civil solidarity deriving from constitutional patriotism. The fact that Habermas demonstrates that civil solidarity does not need to be based on strong nationalist commitments is a major strength of his conceptualization, yet the counterfactual quality of cosmopolitanism is reflected in the extent to which Habermas attempts to define its legal form, rather than more fully grounding cosmopolitanism in general practices. In this way, some of the dilemmas of Habermas's discourse theory of justice at the national level are replicated at the level of transnational citizenship, with its reliance on ethical commitments that have no place in its formal conception of justice and democracy. Robert Fine and Will Smith argue that Habermas's position overlooks the potential tensions between constitutional patriotism and cosmopolitanism:

> The problem for Habermas is that constitutional patriotism is either too strong or too weak to serve his purpose. In its strong form, it binds the people of a particular nation around their own distinctive interpretations of abstract constitutional principles, but at the cost of closing them off from effective participation in or identification with cosmopolitan institutions. In its weak form, it constitutes a simple adherence to formal procedures for the realization of constitutional principles and fails to establish the ethic of solidarity necessary to facilitate democratic deliberation and decisions. (Fine and Smith 2003, 473)

In fact, the abstraction from ethical commitments is probably more plausible at the level of transnational relations, since abstracting from some of the contextual background is generally the condition of transnational interaction. Naturally, this supposition means that Habermas's proposal is plausible precisely because of its limitations with respect to the prospects of democratization of globalizing processes and institutions. Despite these critical limitations, Habermas's interpretation of cosmopolitanism is a major alternative to reactionary nationalism. It is debatable, however, whether it actually signifies normative standards of justice and autonomy that are in advance of those currently institutionalized. This evaluation seems to be a virtual reiteration of the dilemma previously sketched in relation to Habermas's position on the constitutional state, that is, of its being too utopian with respect to the extant institution of the constitutional state's emancipatory potential and insufficiently utopian with respect to the changes required to realize justice and democracy.

The preceding discussion highlighted the extent to which Giddens's social theory attempted to incorporate the theme of violence and coercion and how these themes were relatively marginal concerns of Habermas's theory. In fact, one of the criticisms of Giddens's theorizing of late-modernity was precisely that, compared to his earlier work, the central theme of domination and its expression in forms of coercion became subordinated to the theme of risk. The salience of violence was by no means ignored, yet it is perhaps not be chance that it became less central. Giddens's public policy proposals are framed in a way that downplays domination and heteronomy. For this reason, there is a kind of reversal in perspective that occurs in relation to the recent discussions of cosmopolitanism and globalization. At least this is the case insofar as Habermas's work on international law has given greater prominence to the 'civilizing' of violence (Habermas 2012).

Habermas remarked that the recent Gulf Wars and military interventions provoked his interest in the relationship of law to violence (Habermas 2015). In other respects, Habermas's work on cosmopolitan law represents a continuation of his discourse theory of law and democracy. The notion of cosmopolitan law reflects the influence of Kant and the adoption of a normative perspective on international relations, as opposed to the more instrumental and realist frameworks. Habermas likewise develops a communicative perspective in opposition to the work of Carl Schmitt (Schmitt 2007). Schmitt proposed a contrary perspective on the intersubjective relations of politics and international relations, one based on the binary distinction between friend and foe.

Habermas's argument is that cosmopolitan law 'civilizes' violence through its subjecting force and coercion to the normative demands of justification. Yet, it is hard to perceive how cosmopolitan law can generate effective change without the existence of broadly shared social practices and moral orientations. It is possible that without these social practices the intentions of Habermas's theory of cosmopolitan law cannot be realized (see Blokker 2010). Further, the situation is more complicated, precisely because the current organization of law serves to coordinate market relations and it thereby undermines solidarity. The problem is not so much Habermas's arguments with respect to the cosmopolitan potential of law, but rather the sufficiency of the institution of law, even where there is an effective transnational public sphere. In short, there is the question of whether there is a misplaced confidence in the law and the constitutional format to generate alterations in the existing organization of globalizing processes.

It would nonetheless be hard to disagree with Habermas's arguments for the civilizing character of the 'constitutionalization' of force and violence, as well as those for democratic law and human rights. Rather, the problem is the one that has been underlined throughout this work and that appears to apply to Habermas's interpretation of cosmopolitan law. That is, that the praxis philosophy perspective on the social partly emerged from the critique of the limitations of the legal-political interpretation of citizenship rights. Habermas simultaneously recalls this standpoint and somewhat subordinates it to that of the formal procedures of discourse and the existing function of law in establishing the legitimacy of constitutional democracy (Habermas 2006b' 2012). Habermas's orientation to law reflects his basic intuitions concerning social identity and the ensuing prioritizing in his theory of the problem of coordination.

Giddens's position on cosmopolitanism is similar in its commitment to transnational justice. However, his arguments justifying cosmopolitanism have tended to be elaborated in the context of related themes, particularly those of the European Union, the post-traditional practices of reflexive modernization and, to some extent, the politics of climate change (Giddens 1994b; 2007; 2009). In all these cases, it is evident that Giddens considers that a cosmopolitan practical disposition is the appropriate counterpart to globalization. This is because the principles of reflexive individual agency are deployed in the enacting of cosmopolitanism. Cosmopolitanism represents the openness that is necessary for the encountering of differences on a regular basis in contemporary multi-cultural societies (Giddens 1994b; 2007; 2014).

Giddens agrees with Habermas that global capitalism has expanded beyond the former constraints that were imposed upon it by state regulation and that this development has various deleterious consequences, including those of the detachment of elites from national communities and the disorganization caused by the ineffective regulation of global finance (Hutton and Giddens 2000). At the same time, Giddens's position is somewhat more positive with respect to globalization. This can be seen in how the normative ideal of cosmopolitanism is deployed by him to justify the revisions to political programmes and public policy positions (Giddens 1998a; 2000) Similarly, Giddens argues that the transitions to liberal democracy in former State socialist societies and authoritarian nation states are associated with some of the major changes that have influenced globalization, particularly the influence of satellite communication and the 'abstract systems' of 'disembedded' expertise (Giddens 1994a).

This naturally raises the question that was previously posed of whether the arguments that Giddens makes are consistent with the ideals of social democracy that he is supposedly rethinking. In the case of cosmopolitanism, while his position is certainly normative, it is primarily analytical. He argues that globalization is creating a context in which individuals combine multiple identities. It is necessary, Giddens argues, for institutions to represent this more intense intercultural form of diversity (Giddens 2014). In another sense, this claim reflects a position on globalization that Giddens and Habermas share, that is, that modernity can no longer be singularly identified with Western societies and the diffusion of social processes from them (Habermas 2009, 95; Giddens 1990a). Rather, modernity is now being advanced in various regional and national contexts. Cosmopolitanism implies a recognition of how contexts are being be shaped by interdependencies and the dynamics of global processes.

The general implications of these positions on cosmopolitanism for the nexus of the subject and history will be returned to after the explication of Habermas's and Giddens's proposals regarding the European Union. In line with the cosmopolitan standpoint that was just suggested, Giddens (2007; 2014) argues that the question of the future of Europe must be addressed from a perspective that takes into account global developments. Similarly, one of the other motivations for Habermas's interest in transnational law has been the debate over the institution of a constitution of the European Union (Habermas 2006b; 2009). The European constitution represents some of the dilemmas that the theorizing of cosmopolitanism confronts: the process of constitutionalization should result in an enhancement of democracy but the negative responses to the proposed European constitution suggest that it was viewed as actually reducing democracy and popular sovereignty.

It is worthwhile outlining some of the reasons for the emergence of Europe as a theme in social theory discourses before turning to Habermas's and Giddens's positions. First, the consolidation of the European Union would seem to be an exemplar of the immanent tendency of globalization. Second, the European Union appears to be a novel process of institutional development but its origination from an international trade agreements means that it is a process that has yet to achieve full self-consciousness. In other words, the European Union has to achieve democratic self-determination in order for it to be consistent with the modernist vision of the autonomous constitution of society. Third, despite its bureaucratic organization and the institution of a parliamentary assembly, the institutional architecture of the European Union is still relatively open. This is evident from the debates over a constitution; however, how amenable European institutions are to democratization is another question.

Fourth, there are a variety of competing political interpretations of Europe. The social model of continental European nation-states and its regulated capitalism appear, in principle at least, as an alternative to neoliberal Anglo-American capitalism. The European Union can be seen as a site of struggle between these alternatives. Fifth, the European Union has played a part in overcoming the history of violent conflicts that beset the continent. This may be indicative of a shift to the normative commitment to peace in international relations, something tested particularly by the second Iraq war. Sixth, the extension of these trends and others connected to the European Union are suggestive of a transition from the national to the cosmopolitan. The European Union might be an instance of a nascent cosmopolitanism, although this possibility is currently constrained by existing divisions in power and the cultural identifications with the nation. Further, the actions of institutions associated with the European Union in the imposing of austerity regimes have undoubtedly undermined some of the legitimacy of transnational political commitments.

Habermas and Giddens broadly agree that the European project can be a means of furthering the modernist vision of an autonomous constitution of society but that the existing institutionalization of this project contains serious impediments to meeting this objective. In fact, the recent economic crisis and the strains and tensions ensuing from the subsequent implementation of austerity programmes give expression to the problems of this institutionalization. Further, there is a need to contest conflicting interpretations of the European project, particularly the neoliberal interpretation that serves to justify austerity regimes. Habermas and Giddens highlight the disparity between growing European integration and the limited means of coordination, which is most notably evident in the difficulties of the monetary union. Similarly, Habermas and Giddens have sought to address the problem of the European Union's 'democratic deficit' and they argue that it is through the democratizing of European institutions that the coordination problems need to be overcome. This position means that they oppose the 'technocratic' vision of European modernization, although they recognize that it has significantly determined the extant form of the European Union (see Habermas 2015; Giddens 2014). Their arguments for democratization are intended to increase social justice and to counteract the increasing inequalities in European societies. The latter is partly an effect of the erosion of the so-called European social model based on a comprehensive welfare state (see Giddens 2007).

In a general sense, Habermas and Giddens have sought to delineate and reinforce the progressive dimensions of the European project, while presenting critical diagnoses of the evident problems and sources of discontent. The period of economic recession and the enactment of austerity regimes may have intensified discontent with European institutions, but substantial discontent was apparent before this in the debates over a European constitution and the results of national referendums that led to the constitution's abandonment. The entire process of the formation and operation of the European Union can be seen to involve a conflict between capitalist globalization and democracy. The European Union does, however, partly represent an attempt to transcend politically and socially the restricted form of an economic community. It could be regarded as an attempt to preserve and extend the civilizing achievements of European nation states and to apply, at least to citizens of the European Union, the principles of equal treatment and respect.

The progressive developments that Habermas and Giddens interpret as attempts to institutionalize these principles include the remnants of the European social model, although it is subject to the contradictions of the welfare state, the tangible sense of cosmopolitanism that the European Union has instilled, despite the regressive and xenophobic reactions that have emerged in response to cultural diversity and shifting sovereignty, the fact that European integration has enabled the overcoming of historical enmities and preceding histories of violent conflict, and the universalistic standpoint that can be seen in the general European recognition of the ecological crisis and the appreciation of the common commitment that is required to address it. For these reasons, there are integral features of the European project that are worth preserving and they represent resources for enacting progressive change.

Despite the considerable overlaps concerning the objectives of the European project, the approaches of Habermas and Giddens to the European Union exemplify leading dimensions of their respective theoretical perspectives and assessments of the current constellation of capitalist modernity. Habermas's approach is notable for its elaboration from the perspective of intersubjective identity and the centrality that it attributes to cosmopolitan law. Giddens is concerned with the structuring processes and how the European Union can deal with various contingencies of modernity and globalization, although this perspective is now framed more by the Third Way political programme and the specification of policy prescriptions and less by the elaborated social theory of structuration. Habermas's main argument is that the European Union's economic integration has to be matched by political integration and the democratic organization of the European project. He is critical of how the current formation of the European Union and related transnational institutions have enabled the implementation of neoliberal policy regimes and how the sources of the recent financial crisis have transferred the costs onto citizens and national states (Habermas 2009; 2012; 2015).

Given his discourse theory perspective on the integrity of the rule of law and democracy, it is probably not surprising that Habermas endorses the notion of a European constitution. He argues that the three components that were aligned at the national level enter into a new configuration at the European level: 'first, the democratic association of free and equal legal persons, second, the organization of collective decision-making powers and, finally, the medium of integration of civic solidarity among strangers' (Habermas 2011, 13).

In Habermas's opinion, the process of the constitutionalization of law can underpin the democratization of the European Union and it enables the transnational mediation of the will of free and equal persons. He points to two significant developments of the European Union that are representative of the changes in relation to sovereignty: the prioritizing of European law in relation to specific national laws and the acceptance of sovereignty as shared between the national state and the citizen (Habermas 2011, 54). Habermas argues against the juxtaposition of the 'collective decision making powers' of the nation state and the European Union, but neither is the European Union, in his opinion, a standard version of a federation, such as the United States, nor is it a precursor of a cosmopolitan world government. Similarly, the formation of a transnational public sphere does not mean, according to Habermas, the creation of a single domain, but rather a context in which different national public spheres 'take an interest in each other'. It is possible to consider that instances of this mutual interest already exists, such as in the European opposition to the second Iraq War. This instance of collective mobilization did not necessarily depend on a common identity, but it did make reference to some shared normative commitments. Habermas's reflections on the opposition to the second Iraq War's relationship to the values of a 'core Europe' imply that the foundations exist for a strong sense of a shared European identity, one that is open to different national and cultural expressions (Habermas 2006).

Similarly, Habermas has sought to demonstrate that the core value of solidarity is not just a moral orientation. Solidarity is a form of commitment to the other that is not equivalent to the universalistic notion of justice. Solidarity pertains to the right of others that are in a relatively proximate relationship to make demands upon one another. In the context of the European Union, this is critical to the acceptance of financial interdependence and the contribution that one member state may make to the financial well-being of another state. These implications of solidarity can extend to other spheres, such as in relation to citizenship and policies on asylum. The European Union remains, on this view, a necessary but imperfect expression of the movement towards cosmopolitan justice and democracy. It might be possible to argue that European Union is for Habermas like modernity more generally in 'being at variance' with itself and that it is beset by a one-sided rationalization. In short, this position implies that the European Union suffers from a lack of legitimacy, but that the core European values can be mobilized in relation to its current institutionalization.

Giddens's contributions to debates over the future of the European Union are broadly consistent with his Third Way rethinking of social democracy. This is most evident in his book *Europe in a Global Age*, which as the title suggests contends that European developments need to be seen in the context of globalization (Giddens 2007). The policy prescriptions that are proposed there, like that of 'positive welfare' and 'innovation', are defined by the contemporary changes that have shaped Giddens's analyses of 'late-modernity', like reflexive modernization, individualization, and detraditionalization (Giddens 1991a; 1994b). In particular, there is a strong commitment to 'life politics' and democratization. One of Giddens's key claims is that European institutions have to be responsive to the 'everyday democratization' that is occurring outside of the established political arena. The European Social Model is under strain, he argues, given that it is meant to represent a comprehensive system of social welfare. Although there are significant variations between European nation states with respect to the comprehensiveness of the institution of the welfare state and this reflects significant historical differences in state formations. European nation states have to come to terms, Giddens argues, not just with the effects of globalization, but also the internal 'blockages' that limit, in different ways, these nation state's capacities for undertaking modernizing reforms that will enhance growth, expand employment, transition to the new economy, and address both the entrenched inequalities and the new forms of social exclusion that ensue from changes. The latter change includes the decline of manufacturing industries, the marginalizing of some categories of migrants, and the paradox of 'passive welfare' often compounding individuals' diminished ability to actively participate in the labour market and civil society (Giddens 2007).

These difficulties of the welfare state foundations of the European Social Model should be addressed, Giddens (2007) argues, at the source, such as through increasing labour market participation of the aged and other marginalized groups. Although there is undoubtedly the emergence of the new inequalities, he underlines the potential for the modernization of the European project and identifies resources within European societies for change, especially that of the resource of human capital (Giddens and Diamond 2005; Giddens 2007). Like Habermas's analysis, the seemingly limited capacity of the European Union to generate commitment to the European project is seen to be a major impediment to progressive change.

Giddens's later work *Turbulent and Mighty Continent – What Future for Europe* engages with the effects of the financial crisis and austerity programmes (Giddens 2014). The potential fraying of the monetary union is taken into consideration and Giddens proposes measures in order to counteract future scenarios, like the widely discussed possibility of Greece's exit from the Euro and the introduction of Euro bonds. In short, Giddens believes that unless measures to enhance growth are taken the European Union will remain at an impasse. In other words, the fractures in the European Union will persist whilst the required policy measures are deferred. Giddens argues that the Euro has created an increased interdependency within the European Union and the financial crises of member states has exposed the limitations of the current institutional means to support it. There is a need consequently to build institutional mechanisms to properly enable the coordination of interdependency (Giddens 2014).

The main contention that Giddens develops is that democratization has to occur at all of the levels of the institutions of the European Union. Democratization, based on higher levels of public involvement, is required to avoid deepening disillusionment and to reverse the quite justified sense that the European Union is an elite project. The European Union needs to 'get closer to its citizens and vice versa'. He argues that the level of inequality resulting from austerity regimes must be reduced and reversed. Broadly in agreement with Habermas, he believes that this depends on enhanced regulation of global financial capital. At the same time, Giddens continues his earlier approach in arguing for the harnessing of the potentials for economic innovation that are present in the 'new' information economy. In his opinion, there is no alternative in a global age to a cosmopolitan and multicultural, or rather 'interculturalist', Europe. Similarly, the European Union should act collaboratively to address climate change, although this actually means more action on policy implementation, as there has been considerable work done on policy formulation. Like the analysis of his book *The Politics of Climate Change*, Giddens foregrounds the relationship between climate change and the energy policy 'trilemma' of emissions, economic prosperity, and resource security (Giddens 2014, 20; 2009).

Without going further into the substantive details of these policy proposals, it is clear that Giddens is making the case for continued and closer European integration. Indeed, he now argues that many of the attributes of a state are necessary to address the problems of European Union, since this is the condition for overcoming the existing limitations, whether it be the problems of effective policy implementation, the power to more effectively coordinate economic policy, simply to achieve the full benefits of the process of integration, and for the European Union to be 'relevant' in a global context (Giddens 2014). It would be possible to argue that what is at stake in these debates is the meaning of the European project and the sense in which the European Union's enlargement has meant that it has to transcend its current limitations. One could question the specific details of these proposals but the overall vision that Habermas and Giddens present is of a European Union that fulfills the normative commitments that underpin it and that it approximates to its inclusive social ideal.

Whether in their overall outlook or policy details, the positions of Habermas and Giddens are intended to heighten democratic participation and lessen the inequalities that have expanded with the implementation of austerity programmes. One can see the importance of principles of self-organization to this complex democratic form and the need that they identify for a reflexive subjectivity. There is a considerable tension between the strong claims for democratization that they have proposed and the sense that changes are unlikely to generate situations that are superior to welfare state. In this respect, the modernist vision of an autonomous constitution of society is no longer primarily a projection that is dependent on historical transition; rather it has become more a condition for sustaining the existing institution of democracy and social justice. In Giddens's case, some of the problems of his position derive from attempting to reconcile the 'everyday democratization' that is occurring outside the established political arena with a focus on the matrix of traditional representative politics. Similarly, Habermas and Giddens's scrutinizing of the currents limitations of the European Union make some of their proposal appear rather counterfactual. It's quite possible to argue that the normative underpinnings of the European project continue to be rather threadbare and that the actual practices of European institutions, such as in enabling austerity regimes and the consolidation of market capitalism, reveal that their priorities diverge from Habermas's and Giddens's proposals.

The fact that Habermas and Giddens have defended European Union on the basis of its potential for becoming more democratic gives some insight into their general views of cosmopolitanism. If we take into account the long-term historical view of

Habermas and Giddens then it is possible to perceive that they argue that the creation of greater social interdependencies produces a widening of the horizons of the potentials or possibilities for social autonomy. In this sense, they suggest that cosmopolitanism is a development immanent within history and that its meanings have expanded and consolidated through its increasing integrity with the conditions of social practices. In recent discussions, it is sometimes noted that the notion of cosmopolitanism preceded the institutionalization of modernity and a case could made that it has become a kind of normative 'pacemaker', to return to Habermas's theory of historical development, in relation to questions of justice, especially those associated with globalizing processes (Benhabib 2004; 2006; Fine 2007; Delanty 2009). Cosmopolitanism is suggestive of an enlarged sense of responsibility and active engagement, as distinct from the more disengaged position of the tolerance of cultural difference. This positive sense of cosmopolitanism nevertheless appears in many respects counterfactual. It is not difficult to question whether cosmopolitan discourses veil the degree to which social justice and social practices are dependent on the agency of nation state institutions (Calhoun 2007).

There are many categories of Giddens's theory that are concerned with the forms of the mediation of social relations that are relevant to ascertaining the cosmopolitan potential of globalizing processes, including the notion of structuration itself. Similarly, the notion that the creation of interdependencies widens the horizons of potentials and meanings of autonomy is conveyed by Habermas's conception of the 'opening' of the lifeworld and its implication of the progressive altering of lifeworld perspectives beyond their former limits. It would be wrong, however, to presume that the creation of connections, such as through the market exchange of trade, generates a cosmopolitan perspective, especially because interdependencies of this type rarely commence on the basis of egalitarian reciprocity. Likewise, many political and economic interdependencies are corrosive of subordinated cultures and undermine the reproduction of elements of their social structure, such as through distorting the systems of material production. For these reasons, the expansion of the potential for cosmopolitanism is bound up with the dynamics of the dialectics of control and the modifications in the conditions of interdependency. It is this dialectic, in my opinion, that precipitates the shift towards mutual understanding and egalitarian reciprocity. Cosmopolitanism would be the enlargement of the perspective of all of those involved in the social relations and a shift towards an awareness of how their particularity derives from a universalism.

Although the cosmopolitan potential of the European Union reposes the question of dimensions of the modernist vision of an autonomous constitution of society and the conditions of its realization, the progressive features of this aspect of the contemporary constellation confront the tendencies of economic globalization that have undermined the social capacities for collective self-determination and aspects of the welfare state. Habermas and Giddens have been led to reformulate the nexus between history and the subject as primarily a problem of democracy and democratization. In this respect, they have been able to reveal some of the immanent practices of democratization and their strong connection to the communicative construction of post-traditional identities. In some respects, Habermas and Giddens present democratization as a means of rectifying institutional failures and the condition for sustaining the European project. This is an appealing position, although it probably amounts to a self-limiting version of the modernist vision of social autonomy.

CONCLUSION

In this work, it has been argued that the social theories of Habermas and Giddens are framed by the modernist vision of an autonomous constitution of society and that they seek to explain the contemporary impediments to the realization of social autonomy. The relationships that the social theories of Habermas and Giddens have to the philosophy of praxis conception of the social as constituted by the nexus between the subject and history has been taken as central to comprehending their theories' significant and constructive contributions to understanding modernity. The praxis philosophy conception of the social equally served to delineate some of the major limitations of their respective theoretical perspectives and potential alternatives to the positions that they develop on modernity. Modernity is simultaneously the object of Habermas's and Giddens's work and the interpretative horizon that shapes their perspectives. For this reason, modifications in modernity have significant consequences for their arguments and conceptual frameworks. Besides drawing some of the threads of my analysis together and underlining the conclusions that should be drawn from it, the present discussion will detail the most important strand of contemporary theoretical work on modernity. It sketches how the perspectives of multiple modernities and global modernity reconsider aspects of the nexus between history and the subject.

My analysis has sought to demonstrate how the mediation of the universal and the particular is the organizing problematic of Habermas's social theory. The conception that Habermas proposes of the communicative mediation of the universal and the particular is critical to his overall characterization of modernity and his argument for a change in the paradigm of Critical Theory. Habermas contests various facets of the Frankfurt School's critical conception of modernity. He believes that the demarcation of communicative rationality from that of instrumental reason discloses an alternative dimension of progressive development (Habermas 1984a; 1987a; 1987b). Similarly, Habermas reinterprets Adorno's critique of identity thinking and contends, instead, that intersubjective communication enables the formation of a rational social identity (Habermas 1974b; 1992a). This reinterpretation of the problem of identity is undoubtedly of considerable significance and it enables a reframing of Critical Theory. Nevertheless, I drew attention to the theoretical sequels of the limitations of Habermas's notion of social identity with respect to power, time-space, agency, creativity, social conflict, and the process perspective of praxis philosophy. Giddens developed an alternative approach to these themes in his theory of structuration and many of them are constitutive of its distinctive theoretical orientation. The theory of structuration likewise endeavours to reformulate some of the intentions of the philosophy of praxis. However, I argued that its constructive extension of elements of the praxis philosophy approach is not always matched by the retention of its normative commitments and critical orientation. The relative deficiencies in Giddens's theory that ensue from this selectivity are apparent in the inconsistencies that his theory exhibits and some of these limitations will be reviewed in the current discussion.

Habermas (1987b) contends that his paradigm change constitutes a determinate negation of praxis philosophy. In actual fact, to some extent, this shift comes at the cost of developing the nexus between history and the subject. Habermas's negation of praxis philosophy was overdetermined by his own response to the perceived critical limitations of his original attempt to reformulate the nexus between the subject and history in the programme of knowledge constitutive interests (Habermas 1978a). The major strengths of Habermas's change to the paradigm of communication are clearly those of its intersubjective conception of identity and, from this, the provision then of normative grounds for theorizing justice and discursive democracy (Habermas 1984a; 1987a; 1996a).

By contrast, Giddens's theory of structuration is far more oriented by the praxis philosophy position on the dynamic and dialectical character of social processes. This leads to a social ontology that seeks to clarify the elemental processes involved in the production and reproduction of social life, as well as to a greater appreciation of contingency and power (Giddens 1979; 1985). In Giddens's theory, power is considered to be both an expression of the constitutive character of social action and the most significant determinant of the historical forms of society or social systems. Giddens attempted, I argued, to explain the historical development of social reflexivity in a manner that is neither evolutionary nor functionalist. Yet, the ultimate consequences of this perspective on reflexivity are probably inconsistent with the intentions that originally informed it. In short, the conclusions that Giddens subsequently drew from this interpretation of increasing social reflexivity imply an undermining of the nexus between the subject and history, rather than a reinforcement of it.

While Habermas and Giddens oppose the notion of postmodernity, they broadly agree that the contemporary period has seen the emergence of a new phase of modernity. Although this new phase involves changes that they anticipated, like the strains of the welfare state compromise and the democratizing of interpersonal relations, some significant dimensions of contemporary transformations appear inconsistent with aspects of their preceding conceptions. The most notable contemporary changes that diverge from their expectations are the resurgence of neoliberal capitalism and the entrenching of inequality, since these tendencies have endured longer than they anticipated and their works on the contemporary constellation of modernity represent responses to the ensuing dilemmas for progressive transformation (Habermas 2001a; 2015; Giddens 2007; 2009; 2014). The difficulties of these responses are themselves a reflection of how current processes of modernization do not amount to linear processes of progressive change. Indeed, there have been forms of social regression that Habermas and Giddens had not originally anticipated, like the renewal of populist nationalism in capitalist democracies. Habermas and Giddens have made important interventions to counteract these tendencies and their work continues to delineate what they perceive to be the conditions and direction for progressive change, such as with respect to the European Union (Habermas 2011; 2015; Giddens 2014). This does not mean, of course, that their proposals concerning progressive change have been undisputed.

The relationship of the instituted form of society to the constitutive instituting practices is a central concern of the modernist vision of social autonomy. Habermas and Giddens have sought to reinterpret this relationship in their general theories of society. The methodological approaches that they outline constitute interpretations of the interchanges between the instituted society and instituting practices, for instance, Giddens's theory of structuration is founded on the notion of the conversion between structure and action, so that structure is a medium and outcome of practices. As a consequence, the social theories of Habermas and Giddens provide important insights into the potential of human freedom and the constraints upon its realization, such as those associated with the institutionalized injustices that are revealed by the discourse principle and the discord between public autonomy and private autonomy, whereby the limiting of one comes to undermine the other (Habermas 1996a). The preceding analysis implies that there is an increasing disparity between the original conditions that Habermas and Giddens delineate for realizing autonomy and the current institutional order of capitalist society. The institutional order of contemporary constellation of capitalist modernity appears increasingly separate from the instituting practices, owing to factors like the growing global extension of institutions and the new patterns of inequality. The ecological crisis, as Giddens's book *The Politics of Climate Change* details, could be readily added to these examples of the negative implications of a separation between the originating practices and their outcomes (Giddens 2009).

In some respects, this disparity from the original conditions that Habermas and Giddens specified as necessary for autonomous instituting is concealed in their later works. It is veiled, on the one hand, by the continuity that their later perspectives have with existing institutions, such as is evident in the assumptions of Habermas's discourse theory approach to law and Giddens's Third Way public policy proposals (Habermas 1996a; Giddens 1998a). On the other hand, the disparity is concealed by the shift in the discourse of institutions to that of espousing the values of participation, consultation and dialogue, even though the actual organization of institutions usually contradicts these values (see Boltanski and Chiapello 2005). Further, consistent with Habermas's and Giddens's arguments, interpersonal relations and everyday life in the majority of capitalist societies have become less authoritarian and post-traditional. Of course, conservative mobilizations in opposition to these changes, especially insofar as they are associated with the emancipation of women and the challenging of belief systems formerly immune to criticism, have developed in these societies. These mobilizations are one of the justifications for the emergence of the perspective of multiple modernities that will be overviewed in this conclusion (see Eisenstadt 1999b).

The problem is that these democratizing developments have not resulted in an equivalent institutional transformation and there has been a 'hollowing out', to use Honneth's phrase, of the objective conditions that underpin the autonomous constitution of society, such as with the curtailing of social rights, the deregulation of working conditions, and the mass media manipulation of the public sphere (Honneth 2014). At the same time, there has been considerable progress in terms of the rights of citizens and the extension of these rights to those categories of persons that were formerly excluded from them, such as exclusions based on ethnicity or sexual orientation. The progressive extensions of citizenship rights does not mean that substantive equality has been equally consolidated. Habermas and Giddens have each offered significant interpretations of the 'paradoxes' of progressive welfare state reforms and how these reforms can sometimes give rise to unintended consequences, whether it be prescriptive categorizations of gender or where positive measures have 'perverse' effects, like incremental improvements in a welfare benefit undermining access to them because of the ensuing recategorization of recipients. The latter paradoxical contradictions ensue, according to Giddens and Habermas, from the tensions in capitalist modernity between the 'decommodification' of the welfare state and the market principle of commodification (see Giddens 1984, 316–17; Habermas 1987a; see Offe 1984; 1985).

The difference between Habermas's belief that modernity is an 'incomplete' project and Giddens's position that there are a multitude of human projects has been highlighted. Giddens's position means that the modernist vision can, nonetheless, be assumed as a 'project', but, from his perspective, it is less binding or encompassing. Giddens broadly agrees with the values that Habermas identifies with the project of modernity; however, he does not subscribe to a teleological conception of the modernist project. The implications of Giddens's arguments would seem to be that the attempts to realize the modernist project changes it.

Habermas similarly highlights the project of modernity's openness in terms of the communicative logic of the rational reconstruction of its forms. Yet, Habermas's contention that modernity is 'at variance with itself' may not convey the sense of contingency or – if we take up Castoriadis's view of social imaginaries – radical indeterminacy of the project that conditions its alterations (Castoriadis 1987). In one sense, Habermas's core intuition concerning identity implies that the dialogical reconstitution of the modernist project does not contradict it. This position is actually similar to the functionalist view of the lifeworld as a programming centre or cultural pattern. It would appear that Giddens does not accept Habermas's defense of this project in terms of the distinction between cultural and structural modernization. He does not dispute this analytical distinction in itself but is more concerned with the intertwinement of structural and cultural modernization (Giddens 1996). Giddens explicitly rejects aspects of the functionalist view of differentiation and substitutes the notion of 'disembedding' to characterize equivalent social processes (Giddens 1991a).

The comparative analysis that has been presented develops a number of immanent or internal criticisms of the social theories of Habermas and Giddens. That is, it accepts many of the intentions of Habermas's and Giddens's respective theoretical projects and criticizes the conceptions and arguments that they elaborate which do not satisfy these intentions. Indeed, it has been shown that sometimes the theoretical elaborations serve to undermine the intentions. In the case of Habermas, my analysis accepted the intentions of his change to the paradigm of communication and his revising critical theory in light of historical changes and evident theoretical problems. Habermas attempted to explain the contradictory imperatives of modernity on the basis of this new paradigm. Nevertheless, it has been argued that the manner in which Habermas formulated this theoretical perspective was inconsistent with its objectives. In particular, Habermas's theory of communicative action is intended as a critique of functionalist reason, yet it is reliant on functionalist forms of explanation (Habermas 1984a; 1987a). Similarly, it has been argued that Habermas proposes a theory of action that is less about the processes of acting and more concerned with social coordination, interpretation and justification. Habermas's theory of communicative action addresses a range of questions in a complex and brilliant manner, yet its synthetic conception of 'the social' does not succeed in the conversion of the perspectives of social action and social systems into one another. Rather, the outcome of Habermas's theory of communicative action is closer to what Joas described as 'the unhappy marriage of functionalism and hermeneutics' (Joas 1993; see McCarthy 1985).

These immanent deficiencies of Habermas's theory are to some extent the other side of its most significant and innovative components, particularly the intersubjective conception of identity and its communicative notion of democratization. Following Honneth (1991), I claim that Habermas's conception of the internal colonization of the lifeworld was overdetermined by the technocracy thesis and Habermas's equation of this technocratic perspective with that of systems theory. On this view, the functionalist reason that determines the reproduction of systems constitutes a threat to the moral-practical basis of social and individual identity. The alternative that Habermas proposes to this imbalanced institution of modernity depends on communicative rationality and the lifeworld (Habermas 1987a; 1987b). This position contains an undoubted antinomy and it suffers from a specific substitution of theoretical categories. Despite Habermas's claims about rethinking the category of practice, the lifeworld in not an equivalent for the praxis philosophy conception of the history constituting subjectivity (Habermas 1987b). In any event, the political sphere's 'channelling' of the communicative power exercised in civil society and the public sphere is the precondition for the lifeworld to actually determine the conditions of a balanced institutionalization of modernity (Habermas 1996a).

Given that this channelling would entail the regulation and restructuring of capitalist dynamics, it will encounter considerable resistance and inevitably involve social conflicts. Habermas's accounts of the colonization of the lifeworld and legitimation crisis appreciate the social conflict involved in such a transformation (Habermas 1987a; 1976c). Similarly, Habermas's interpretation of the postnational constellation consolidates these insights into the 'unresolved tension between capitalism and democracy' (Habermas 1987a; 2001a). At the same time, the normative orientation of the discourse theory of law and democracy tends to subordinate these conflicts. The major limitation of Habermas's discourse theory conception of democratic law is that it presupposes precisely the conditions of equal autonomy that it is meant to achieve (Habermas 1996a). In this sense, it has more in common with the format of normative political philosophy and its mode of criticism. Further, it assumes that liberal democratic institutions are open to demands for democratization and the rectifying of the negative consequences of capitalist deregulation. Even if this is the case, there are strong grounds for considering that democratization involves higher levels of social contestation concerning the orientation of these institutions than is implied by Habermas's discourse theory of law and democracy (Habermas 1996a).

Although the major suppositions of the discourse theory of democracy and law can be rightly criticized as rather counterfactual, Habermas's position is justified to the extent that there is no real alternative to public deliberation. The critical question is whether this deliberation can effectively function without an underpinning transformation of the conditions of social reproduction and the prior creation of the requisite practical orientations on the part of subjects (see Susen 2007). Habermas's distinctive model of lifeworld and system seemed to reflect the period of the post-war consolidation of the welfare state and its suppositions of a balanced institutionalization of these spheres appeared difficult to reconcile with globalization. Even so, it is possible, surprisingly, to contend that globalizing processes lend a certain relevance to Habermas's otherwise problematic conception of the detachment of the market and administrative systems from the lifeworld. Likewise, the somewhat underdeveloped notion of the 'opening' and 'closing' of the lifeworld that Habermas introduces in his work on the postnational constellation implies a less functionalist conception of these interchange between spheres (Habermas 2001a).

In the case of Giddens's theory, it is possible to develop an internal critique that highlights some of the discrepancies and inconsistencies in its conceptualizations, as well as between these conceptions and Giddens's analyses of the substantive social conditions. The latter critique was, for instance, proposed in relation to the central category of structural principles. However, the formulation of an immanent critique, in the proper sense, would have to draw on the normative principles of Giddens's theory. Leaving aside the straightforward discrepancies in conceptualization, the changes in Giddens's emphases make these normative principles actually open to considerable interpretation. It is certainly the case that the political position of the Third Way and its underlying 'structural pluralism' with respect to the state, market and community seem to represent a shift towards the individual and away from the prior social democratic commitment to the collective as the basis of social justice (Giddens 1998a; 2000).

The difficulties of the structuration theory synthesis of action and structure is evident in Giddens's alternating between stronger and weaker notions of domination and constraint, agency and action. The latter explications of action sometimes underline the knowledgeability and creativity of action and, at other times, the repetitive and habitual qualities of action (Giddens 1984). It is certainly the case that the arguments of some critics of structuration theory that these alternations reflect the fact that action and structure are intrinsically different and that they should not be 'conflated' are external to the intentions of structuration theory and a misrepresentation of its basic conception (Archer 1982; 1990; see Stones 2001; 2005). The philosophy of praxis, by contrast, can provide a more immanent explanation of the weaknesses of Giddens's conception and, to some extent, this perspective can encompass some of the implications of the more external critiques' positions. Praxis philosophy contends that the alternating between structure and action is primarily due to the dialectical condition of individuals constituting society without actually being the subjects of this historical process. Marx's theory of value, which as we saw provided some of the inspiration of structuration theory's intentions, sought to demonstrate this claim in relation to the injustices inherent in the cycle of capitalist production (Marx 1976).

In one sense, the sociological programme of the theory of structuration is to transform into explicit knowledge the implicit practical knowledge and capacities of subjects, thereby making it a variant of reconstructive science (Giddens 1987; Habermas

1990a). In another sense, the normative perspective of structuration theory is one of a genuine and conscious reconciliation between the individual and society, since it implies that individuals make the social structures that make them. In fact, this conception is very close to how Giddens describes the democratic structure of contemporary intimate relations, although the notion of structure generally has a more encompassing collective meaning than that of the intersubjective format of intimate relations (Giddens 1992). Moreover, it is possible to perceive the normative intention of Giddens's theory as originally that of disclosing the contradictions inherent in the present development of society. In this sense, it sat 'between capitalism and socialism', to use the original title of Giddens's intended final volume of the 'contemporary critique of historical materialism' (Giddens 1981a; 1994a).

It would appear that Giddens's intention of showing the increasing reflexivity in history was connected to revealing immanent contradictions, but that over the course of his critiques of historical materialism and work on late-modernity the implications drawn from this analysis change (Giddens 1981a; 1990a; 1994a). The increasing reflexivity is shown to generate an awareness of the fallibility of knowledge and contributes to the increasing sense of individuals' participating in social processes that empower their agency but that are outside of their control (Giddens 1991a). Under these conditions the notion of the reconciliation of action and structure is simply a methodological dimension of structuration theory, because the sense in which projects elude their creators has intensified with globalization, especially in the case of the ecological crisis (Giddens 1999). Reflexive modernization reverts or rebounds back upon the subjects of the historical process and, as noted, Giddens describes similar tendencies as the 'perverse contradictions' of the welfare state in capitalist society (Giddens 1984). In Giddens's view, contemporary processes of socialization contradict traditional socialism (Giddens 1994a). The increasing social reflexivity of modernity reveals the limits of the rationality of centralized planning. Consequently, he argues that socialism incorporated suppositions derived from an earlier phase of modernization (Giddens 1993a; 1994a). The corollary of this position is that another type of subjectivity emerges with the historical changes of modernity (Giddens 1990; 1991a). Giddens now argues that socialism represents only a normative commitment to social justice and equality, rather than a systematic programme of the institutional reorganization of society (Giddens 1998; 2000).

Giddens's view of the contemporary constellation of modernity represents a different perspective on the contradictions inherent in the development of capitalist society. It arguably entails a reconsideration of the modernist problem of the relationship of the instituted society to instituting practices. In the period of reflexive modernization, the anticipated future comes to have increasing significance on present actions compared to the former weight of the past (Giddens 1994b; Beck 1992; Marx 1977d). Of course, this change has implications for the praxis philosophy problem of changing the objects of the historical process into that of its subjects. However, the possibility and necessity of reflexive illumination remain. This problem is apparent in a more diffuse and general way in Giddens's description of the paradox that he believes is at the core of the politics of climate change: that action will be taken when the consequences are visible and by then it will already be too late to effect the required change (Giddens 2009, 2).

The relative disappearance of one theme may be important for assessing the shift from Giddens's earlier critiques of historical materialism to the later accounts of modernity that inform his Third Way rethinking of social democracy, the politics of climate change, and the prospects of the European Union in the age of global modernity (Giddens 1994a; 1998a; 2007; 2009; 2014). The notion of the dialectic of control is a major category of the theory of structuration and it originally formed a key part of Giddens's historical analyses of capitalism, the nation state and pre-capitalist social formations (Giddens 1979; 1981a; 1984). However the dialectic of control does not play a significant part in Giddens's Third Way proposals (Giddens 1998a; 2000). This is probably because it would complicate the Third Way policy perspective. The notion of the dialectic of control implies the likelihood of resistance and contestation. In a general sense, Giddens's conceptualization of the dialectic of control incorporated some of the typical characteristics of the earlier phase of modernization, such as the centrality of class relations, the institution of bureaucratic management, and the redistributive framework of the Keynesian welfare state (Giddens 1977; 1979; 1981a; 1982a).

It is possible to evaluate the relative disappearance of the notion of the dialectic of control in Giddens's theory in light of Boltanski and Chiapello's argument that the 'new spirit of capitalism' claims to overturn these features of the earlier phase of modernization. Boltanski and Chiapello, however, clearly consider that this shift is a product of contestation and that the new capitalist spirit is an ideology that conceals persisting conflict (Boltanski and Chiapello 2005). Giddens, rather, largely accepts this self-characterization of the contemporary phase of modernity and the idea that these preceding conditions of class relations and bureaucratic structures do not apply in the 'new economy' and the 'new individualism'. Or, at least, he considers that the preceding conditions of class relations and bureaucratic hierarchy should not apply (Giddens 1991a; 1994a; 1998a; 2000). Indeed, it could be claimed that Giddens's work on late-modernity contributed to the self-characterization of contemporary ideology, even though it was highly critical in a number respects of flexible and financial capitalism. The point, however, is that the shift in capitalism and modernity was not explained by Giddens in terms of the struggles of the dialectic of control, despite the centrality of this notion to his explanation of the dynamics of earlier systems of production and his espousal of the view that capitalism is a distinctively class society (Giddens 1981a).

Giddens previously argued that there develops specific social movements in relation to each of the four institutional dimensions of modernity and that these movements constitute part of the dialectics of control that pertain to these institutions. The peace movement contests militarized violence, the labour movement contests capitalism, the ecology movement contest industrialism, and movements concerned with rights and freedoms contest surveillance (Giddens 1985a; 1990a). Although this approach draws attention to conflicts present in modernity, it tends to be focussed on the overtly politicized dialectics of control and it is important not to neglect the more latent struggles. It may be the case that the notion of the dialectic of control was originally closely connected in the theory of structuration and Giddens's historical analyses to the concept structural principles, since the structural principles of social formations can be readily to seen to condition the unfolding and outcomes of dialectics of control. The problems of Giddens's theoretical formulation of structural principles and the ultimate divergence of his work on modernity from such a conception has been disclosed in the preceding analysis.

It has likewise been argued that the leading theme of Giddens's analysis of modernity shifts from that of domination and power to that of risk. Although it is relevant to the analysis of risk and dangers, the dialectic of control is less integral to Giddens's interpretation of these features of late-modernity. In fact, different characteristics of control are foregrounded in relation to risks, such as the importance of prevention in relation to ecological risk. It is likewise possible to consider that aspects of globalization are a product of the surpassing of some of the framing of dialectics of control, like that of the national frame to use Nancy Fraser's term (Fraser 2009). Be that as it may, there are clearly considerable theoretical and practical benefits to reconsidering the concept of dialectic of control. In my opinion, the concept of the dialectical of control should be integral to any attempted renewal of the theory of structuration and the potential that structuration theory contains for enhancing the explanatory framework of critical theory.

These comments on the trajectories of the social theories of Habermas and Giddens draw attention to the modifications that ensued as a result of historical changes in the complexion of modernity and how the overall perspectives that they apply in their later works are arguably less expansive. Indeed, Habermas became increasingly preoccupied with the problems of normative political philosophy and Giddens's contributions were conditioned by the exigencies of immediate political contexts. In other words, they do not engage in reworking their social theories and this leaves some considerations unresolved. Of course, it may be the case that they do not feel the need to reiterate their former statements. The more restricted approaches does not mean that they have not addressed large scale themes, like future of the European Union and climate change. Rather, the refocussing of their approaches correlates with a diminution in their visions of transformation, since the change that they propose has greater continuities with existing developments, even where it is the case that they argue that current developments should be reversed or regulated. The diminished visions of transformation probably reflects the recent ascendancy of neoliberalism and the lesser prominence of Marxism, which had foregrounded the theme of historical transition.

Habermas and Giddens had originally sought to develop longer-term historical perspectives on change, but they largely adhered to linear conceptions that did not consider the potential range of variation in the forms of modernity. In this respect, the division between capitalism and socialism was consequential for their arguments. Although neither Habermas nor Giddens developed a fully satisfying approach to the socialist variant of modernity, it undoubtedly influenced their original views of the range of potential alternatives of modernity (see Giddens 1993b). In some respects, Giddens's theory does have a range of concepts relevant to comprehending globalizing developments and a greater diversity of modernities, whereas Habermas treated socialism as prioritizing the system steering media of administrative power (Habermas 1987b). The later interpretation is not entirely wrong, but rather narrow with respect to the overall context of the historical institution of socialist nation states (see Arnason 1991b; 1993).

While its themes may not be at the forefront of current social theory discussions, Habermas's theory of the broad lines of historical development offers a reconstruction of directional change. That is, it contains a theoretical interpretation of the cumulative and directional progress in normative structures and the increases in the complexity of the social systems of material production and administrative organization. Habermas's reconstruction of historical development is limited by its generality and broad parameters. These are characteristics that he attributes to a theory of social evolution, rather than to explanations and narratives of historical change (Habermas 1979b). Habermas's theoretical reconstruction of historical materialism and modern rationality provide, in effect, some orientation for approaching the question of historical progress and for evaluating the historical development of social formations. The weaknesses of this theory of development means that it is more of a heuristic guide, since it remains conditional on the depiction of rationality and it simply does not adequately account for historical dynamics and the creativity of social transformations. In a similar vein, Habermas's theory of historical development does not satisfactorily grasp the radical alterity of different social imaginaries or cultural understandings (see Castoriadis 1987). It rather treats these in a structuralist manner; that is, in terms of the formal structures of cognition and the modes of reasoning. These structures are compatible with the competences of the socialized individuals and the 'forms of understanding' of historical formations in different phases of development (Habermas 1987a).

These structuralist and evolutionary assumptions of Habermas's theory of historical development are some of the main reasons why criticisms equivalent to those that praxis philosophy made of orthodox historical materialism were applied to Habermas's reconstruction, such as its subordination of the creativity and transformative power of social agency, and its establishment of a constraining pattern of historical change. In other respects, Habermas's theory of historical development is a radical departure from the Marxian paradigm of production and a comprehensive interpretation of the logical development of cultural forms of understanding and normative structures. Habermas's interpretation of modernity is thoroughly based on the assumptions of this theory of historical development and it represents a major application of this framework. This is evident from Habermas's characterization of the modern decentred understanding of the world and the universalistic moral perspective that is considered to underpin the legitimacy of modern institutions (Habermas 1984a). In another sense, the historical formats of Habermas's and Giddens's early works come to have less significance for their later work and it appears less central to their justifications. Modernity is still founded, of course, in their opinions, on a distinctive 'historical time consciousness' and the 'use of history to make history'.

Social Theory Revisions and Enlarged Perspectives on Modernity

Although it is not possible to provide a complete survey of the developments in social theory that are relevant to the themes covered in this comparative analysis, it is worth noting several of the most salient developments and the implications that they hold for the social theories of Habermas and Giddens. For the sake of brevity, these comments will be framed around the following themes: the contemporary state of the philosophy of praxis, Honneth's theoretical extension and revision of the programme of critical theory, and the perspectives of multiple modernities and global modernity. Given the synthetic approaches of Habermas and Giddens, it is not surprising that there are considerable intersections between these themes and that arguments about one are based on suppositions concerning the other. It is important to reiterate that these observations are selective and indicative of a larger argument about contemporary social theory. For instance, I have discussed in other contexts some of the subsequent refinements that have been proposed in structuration theory, especially noting that of Rob Stones's strong programme of structuration theory, innovative developments in action theory, particularly those associated with Luc Boltanski's linking of action and justification, and Hans Joas's pragmatist theory of the creativity of action (Browne 2016; 2014; 2009).

The philosophy of praxis has been central to defining the modernist vision of an autonomous constitution of society. Habermas's earlier endeavour to reconstruct praxis philosophy gave way to claims to have superseded this tradition with his theory of communicative action (Habermas 1987b). Although Giddens formulated a critical deconstruction of historical materialism, he drew inspiration from Marx's original turn to social practices and he sought to generalize elements of the praxis approach (Giddens 1979; 1981a). The social theories of Habermas and Giddens involve the provision of alternatives to the praxis philosophy conception of the social as derived from the nexus between history and the subject. The preceding analysis explicated the suppositions of these alternatives, like the connection between competences and development in Habermas's theory of history and the interpretation of different temporal and spatial layers of structuration in Giddens's theory. It highlighted various strengths and weaknesses. Given the current state of the philosophy of praxis, Habermas's and Giddens's assessments of their social theories' relationships to this tradition of thought are broadly correct. Even so, these positions do not exhaust the contemporary significance of praxis philosophy. It has been argued that aspects of the themes and orientation of praxis philosophy could still rectify some of the limitations and oversights in Habermas's and Giddens's theories, such as those with respect to the constitutive significance of social action and the meaning of social autonomy.

The distinctive neo-Marxist schools of praxis philosophy have largely waned and it would be hard to identify this perspective as a collective project. In part, this is a reflection of the changed sociopolitical context, the dispersal of its former schools, and realignments in theoretical perspectives (see Browne 2017). Habermas's and Giddens's theoretical proposals are informed by these realignments and, to some extent, contributed to them. In other respects, Habermas and Giddens responded to the more hostile challenges to the praxis philosophical interpretations of the modernist vision, such as those from the perspectives of neoliberalism and postmodernism.

From a different angle, the perception of the dissipating of the philosophy of praxis is misleading and some of its intentions have become diffused throughout contemporary social theory and sociology. As we saw, the orientation of praxis philosophy informs the perspectives of attempts in critical theory to revise Habermas's synthesis of formal pragmatics and systems theory, such as those of Klaus Eder and Axel Honneth (Strydom 1993). The diffusion of some of praxis philosophy's intentions are apparent in the so-called 'practical turn' in social theory (Schatzki et al. 2001). Giddens and Bourdieu are the two most important sociological contributors to this turn to practice as the 'elementary' unit of social analysis (Reckwitz 2002). It is fairly clear, though, that the sociology of practice does not currently possess the normative depth and political interest of the philosophy of praxis (Browne 2017). Similarly, it does not have the long-term historical perspective that has shaped praxis philosophy and that has been somewhat reworked, as will be outlined below, in the contemporary perspectives of global modernity and multiple modernities. Despite significant differences, these two perspectives on modernity are like the philosophy of praxis in their concern with the historical relationships of instituting practices to the instituted form of society.

There are various components of the praxis philosophy *problematique* that remain relevant to the modernist vision of the autonomous constitution of society. Despite Habermas's and Giddens's assimilating the category of labour to more general categories of social action, it remains of continuing relevance to the prospects of modern society. Notably, the growing insecurity of work in many advanced capitalist societies has generated a renewed interest in the conditions of labour and instances of contestation (Smith and Deranty 2012). The category of alienation has likewise undergone an international revival and its applications have been extended beyond the domain of production. The image of the 'new economy' that Giddens largely embraced has been questioned and alienation is perceived in the discrepancy between the claim and reality of 'network' capitalism (Boltanski and Chiapello 2005; Sennett 2006). The notion of the dialectic of control, as already indicated, is another praxis philosophical category that warrants further development. It is certainly connected to the notion of alienation but it can be explored independently of it. The dialectic of control always sustains a link to practical interaction, even in the cases of its displacement and attempted subversion. The concept of the dialectic of control can rectify some of the deficiencies in Habermas's theory with respect to the conflicts of social interaction and the interchange relation of system and lifeworld, while its absence from Giddens's later political contributions explains some of their deficiencies and the dialectic of control enables a more intricate appreciation of the processes of structuration.

With its origins in the philosophy of Hegel, the notion of the dialectic of control may be seen as critical to the development of Honneth's theory of the struggle recognition in response to the limitations of Habermas's theory (Honneth 1995a). Honneth's major criticism of Habermas's theory of communicative action was that it could not account for the actual experience of suffering and the motivation for the resistance to injustice and domination (Honneth 1995b; 2007). The theory of communicative action's critical diagnosis was based on the social pathologies of capitalist modernity being manifested in deformations and distortions of the formal structures of communication. Honneth argues, instead, that individuals' experiences of injustice and oppression take the form of denied recognition and disrespect (Honneth 1995a; 1995b; 2007). It is this experience that motivates resistance and Honneth argues that demands for recognition have a moral content. The continuities that Honneth's theory of recognition has with Habermas's original intuition concerning the intersubjective constitution of identity are not difficult to perceive. Given its concern with experience and motivation, Honneth's interpretation of the dynamics of mutual recognition encompasses aspects of the subject that

Habermas's theory marginalized, like those of affective and bodily experience. For these reasons, Honneth's philosophical anthropology of recognition represents an alternative elaboration of the paradigm of communication in critical theory. Indeed, it has been criticized by Nancy Fraser for equating the problem of justice with that of the formation of identity (Fraser 2003a; 2003b).

Honneth's critique of Habermas's theory overlaps many of the themes that have been covered, like those relating to the problems of the distinction between system and life-world, the overestimation of the legal component of democratization and social justice, and the simplification of the action theoretical perspective of the philosophy of praxis (Honneth 1991; 2014). Similarly, the theme of history is more central to Honneth's arguments than it is for Habermas's later theory, although Honneth's approach sometimes fall prey to a simplifying teleological perspective (see Honneth 2014). The greater orientation to conflict is apparent in Honneth's claim that Habermas's theory tended to bracket the inequalities between speakers and is a central dimension of his alternate intersubjective theory of the struggle for recognition (Honneth 1991; 1995a). The problem of rationality, which is fundamental to Habermas's entire theory of modernity, is certainly less integral to the format of Honneth's theory of recognition. This lesser concern with rationality entails both strengths and weaknesses. It means that it is less restrained by rationality considerations and can better explore the types of experiences that fall outside of Habermas's vision of communicative rationality. It is a weakness because Honneth tends to rely upon Habermas's discourse theory to provide criteria for adjudicating between warranted and unjustified demands for recognition (Honneth 1995a; 1995b).

The differences between Habermas and Honneth on rationality are therefore more a matter of degree than one of contradictory standpoints, but there is one significant contrast that ensues from it. Honneth argues that critical theory has typically pointed to the systematic restraints that impede the full realization of rationality (Honneth and Hartmann 2012). However, this has changed in the context of contemporary capitalist modernization. The emancipatory intentions that were formerly presumed by critical theory to contradict the capitalist order have now supposedly become aspects of its systematic reproduction. This does not mean that these emancipatory intentions have been truly realized, but rather that there are particular capitalist forms of their articulation. For example, the notion of the liberation of desire that originally seemed to contradict bourgeois rationality has proven to be compatible with capitalist commodification and network capitalism claims to have dissolved some of the former authoritarian modes of work organization. For this reason, the earlier critical theory model of rationalization does not apply in the way that it previously did, but the capitalist articulations of formerly critical conceptions are not really emancipatory. The consequent distortions amount to pathologies of reason (Honneth 2009).

The contradictions of contemporary capitalist modernization, Honneth argues, play out in a more paradoxical manner (Honneth and Hartmann 2012). The latter notion is partly informed by Giddens's conception of 'perverse contradictions' (Giddens 1984). A paradoxical contradiction is where the practical instantiating of progressive change contradicts its intentions and can even compound the original social problem that it was intended to address. In a sense, this argument was anticipated in Habermas's characterization of the 'new obscurity' of the welfare state and the contradiction between the objectives of social democracy and its reliance on the means of state administrative power (Habermas 1989). Further, Honneth's conception of paradoxical contradictions is particularly influenced by Boltanski and Chiapello's characterization of the new spirit of capitalism and their argument concerning how capitalism came to incorporate elements of its critique, whilst modifying the meaning of the former critical conceptions and the enacting of justifications (Boltanski and Chiapello 2005). For instance, they argue that the notion of flexibility metamorphosizes from a term that referred critically to the rigidity of capitalist work organization into a category that reflects demands for market deregulation and the growth in intermittent, insecure and casual forms of employment (Boltanski and Chiapello 2005; see Browne 2014).

Honneth's theory of recognition contains the nucleus for rethinking the relation between subject and history, especially in its taking into account intersubjectivity (Honneth 1995a; 2014). It represents a strong corrective to the specific difficulties of Habermas's theory that resulted from its reliance on perspectives that are external to the orientation of critical theory, such as systems theory and liberal normative political philosophy (Habermas 1987a; 1996a). At the same time, it may be most productive to treat Honneth's theory of recognition as being in a continuous dialogue with Habermas's theory. In this way, it can be seen to clarify the conditions and potential for realizing Habermas's interpretation of the modernist vision of social autonomy. Honneth's theory of the struggle for recognition constitutes a more socially grounded version of communicative action (Honneth 1995a).

Honneth's later theory of social freedom is indisputably a major contribution to the modernist vision of social autonomy, although it is limited by the fact that it is largely detailed in the form of a 'normative reconstruction' (Honneth 2014). In my opinion, a case could be readily made that a fuller conception of social freedom depends on an account of the processes of structuration, one that particularly highlights the dynamics of the dialectic of control. In this respect, the synthesis of the normative intentions of Honneth's intersubjective conception of social freedom with elements of Giddens's theory of structuration could lead to a more complex and compelling theory of democratic ethical life. However, such a conception would be something of a corrective to some of the tendencies and emphases of Giddens's programme of the Third Way, especially with respect to this programme's embracing the 'new individualism' and, more equivocally, the reflexivity of the market (Giddens 1998).

Although Honneth's theory of modernity is extremely comprehensive, it would be fair to claim that it is not as expansive as either that of Habermas or Giddens. In some respects, this is actually a strength, since it does not have to engage with many of the complications of these larger theoretical syntheses. Honneth's theory is remarkably consistent and coherent, although it has undergone revisions. One could argue that there is a shift from his earlier prioritizing of instituting practices in the struggle for recognition to the later social freedom position of giving precedence to the instituted form of society (Honneth 2014). The slightly less expansive perspective of Honneth's theory means that it less concerned with the larger cultural background horizon of meaning that conditions the modernist vision. This is a consideration that has been central, as we will see, to the emergence of the multiple modernities perspective and its explorations of equivalents of the nexus between history and the subject. Similarly, while Honneth's theory of struggles for recognition is, to my mind, open to a diversity of applications, it has been criticized from the standpoint of the perspective of global modernity for treating the concept of recognition 'as a key to grasp any phenomenon in the world' and as indicative of a more generally shared 'limited view of the world, centred exclusively on Western Europe and the United States' (Domingues 2012, 13, 14).

The major historical changes during the past decades have compelled sociologists to revise elements of their interpretations of modernity. It has led to attempts to theorize the variations in modernity and the implications of modernity's global consolidation. The global scale of modernity and its diverse institution are apparent from changes like the industrialization of China and East Asian societies, the Iranian Revolution, the democratization of Latin American nation states that had been subject to authoritarian regimes, and the integration of some former state socialist societies into the European Union. These transformative processes were preceded by the period of decolonization and the formation of new nation-states. The outcome of the Iranian Revolution is distinctive in its ideological departure from modernity, but these transformations point to potentially divergent trajectories of the institution of modernity. It had been previously presumed that modernization would lead all societies or nation states to share a common pattern of institutions and cultural values. Change would, in effect, lead to a convergence in the form of modern societies and underpinning this assumption was the equating of modernization with other notions, especially those of progress, rationalization and development. The interpretations of the diversity of modern societies that was evident in the division between the first, second and third world did not necessarily represent a departure from this view (see Wagner 2012).

Habermas and Giddens perceived that these interpretations of modernization were not entirely satisfactory and that this standpoint was becoming increasingly untenable. Habermas's proposals, in response, were more methodological complex distinctions, such as that between formal structures of rationality and the rationality of substantive forms of life (Habermas 1984). It was in this way that he dealt with the questions of divergent cultural understandings. In any event, the modernization of non-European societies was a rather peripheral consideration of his theory of modernity. Giddens's critical theory of historical change is more open-ended and it can more readily encompass different historical trajectories. A number of the categories of Giddens's theory of historical change are intended to illuminate contextual variations and the effects of intersecting processes. Yet, in several respects this conceptual framework contradicts Giddens's subsequent analyses of modernity. This is possibly because of his assuming that modernity is becoming a global condition, rather than in spite of it. The main theses of Giddens's analyses of 'late-modernity', like detraditionalization and individualization, are presented in a general manner and with limited reference to the relative variations of them (Giddens 1990a; 1991b). It can be argued that the social theorists associated with the perspective of global modernity, especially José Maurício Domingues and Peter Wagner, drew inspiration from Giddens's original critical theory of history in opposition to his later approach to modernity (Domingues 1996; 2000; Wagner 1994).

The perspectives of global modernity and multiple modernities are concerned with relations that are broadly equivalent to that of the subject and history. In particular, they explore the different cultural and political configurings of the relations between the institutional order and social agency. Since it is only possible to illustrate here some dimensions of these approaches, it is worthwhile noting the general questions that make them particularly salient. Multiple modernities and global modernity are substantial current social theory perspectives on modernity, although these categories are being used to cover the work of theorists that define their proposals in more precise terms, such as Wagner's world sociology of modernity (Wagner 2012). These perspectives' connections to praxis philosophy have sometimes, though not always, been overlooked. Rather, the continuities that the multiple modernities standpoint has with Weber's comparative historical sociology has justifiably been emphasized (Weber 1958a; 1958b; 1978; 1988; Spohn 2001). To varying degrees, the frameworks of multiple modernities and global modernity have been shaped by critical reflection on Habermas's and Giddens's social theories. In some respects, multiple modernities and global modernity insinuate at new understandings of the conditions of the realization of the modernist vision of an autonomous constitution of society. Notably, these perspectives provide insights into the emancipatory potentials of social innovations associated with modernizing processes outside of Europe and North American, such as the democratizing initiatives to be found in Latin American and African societies that have undergone transitions from authoritarian regimes (Wagner 2012; Domingues 2012).

The global modernity approach can provide insights into the historical effects of colonization and decolonization in ways that have not been explored by Habermas and Giddens. In a similar vein, multiple modernities and global modernity are relevant to addressing the intercultural relations and understandings that are expanding with globalization. One of the strengths of these approaches is that of making cross-cultural comparisons of the institution of modernity. However, this consideration equally points to one line of criticism of them. That is, that multiple modernities really reiterates the comparative sociological approach of modernization theory, such as in tracing the nation building projects of different societies. For these critics, multiple modernities is within the existing framework of modernization theory, which never denied that there would be relative differences and variations in how modern social structure emerge and develop (Schmidt 2010). This critique arguably underestimates the potential of the multiple modernities approach, the implications of the weightings it gives to different spheres of society, and it is probably more relevant to less theoretically informed notions of multiple modernities than those of S. N. Eisenstadt and J. P. Arnason. It is the case, though, that the multiple modernities perspectives has to assume that there are some common defining features of variant modernities. These features do not have to be substantive institutions or structures, like the state's political administrative system or the nuclear family, but they can be general cultural orientations that are open to different instantiations, such as those of critique and reflexivity.

Multiple modernities commences from the questioning of the notion of historical convergence of modern societies. It emphasizes instead the variations in the constitution of modernity due to the background cultural context and the historical period of modernization. For example, East Asian modernization occurred during a period when most European societies had already undergone several phases of industrial modernization. For this perspective, modernity is considered to accentuate human agency and this is manifested in the mobilizing of significant political and religious movements, such as nationalist, communist and fundamentalist movements (Eisenstadt 1999a). Multiple modernities contends that the tensions and conflicts intrinsic to modern social formations generate diverging outcomes and alternative configurations of institutions. In this sense, it highlights the conflict in modernity between the tendency for the rationalization of institutions and the creative enacting of meanings that are antithetical to the logic of rationality. Likewise, multiple modernities' comparative historical sociology elucidates the variations ensuing from the encounter between the programmes that shape the mobilizations for change and the extant institutional patterns, such variations include that between heterodox religious groups and traditional orthodoxy, the difference between European and North American democratizing movements on the basis of their background sociocultural interpretations of the state, and how the Soviet model of modernization was conditioned by the synthesis between revolutionary movement and imperial background (Arnason 1993, 1998, 2002, 2005; Eisenstadt 1999a, 2000).

The multiple modernities perspective traces differing trajectories of modernization and institutional configurations to the influence upon modernizing initiatives of prior cultural meaning systems, especially religious, and preceding structures of political authority, such as the power of the centre compared to the periphery, the social complexion of elites, and judicial authority, all of which have resulted in kinds of path dependencies that effect change. These religious-cultural meaning systems generally have civilizational dimensions, owing to the scope of the world religious background and the internal variations of a common cultural framework, such as results from conflicts over theological authority and the formation of different religious denominations and sects (Eisenstadt 1999). The 'world-images' of different civilizations provide responses to profound questions, like the nature of authority, the basis of justice, the purpose of living, and the difference between immanence and transcendence. Eisenstadt expands on Karl Jasper's interpretation of how the Axial Age instituted the distinction between immanence and transcendence (Eisenstadt 1986; Jaspers 1953). The Axial Age is the period of the formation of the belief systems of major world religions and philosophy, including those of Judaism, Buddhism, Ancient Greek philosophy, Confucianism, and it encompasses later antecedents like Christianity and Islam. The cultural transformation of the Axial Age coincided with changes in the structure of social organization, most notably with the consolidation of religious elites and with the rationalization of political authority.

Eisenstadt's perspective on multiple modernities accepts Weber's general thesis that modernity presupposes a disenchanted view of the world, but the transformative practices mobilized on this basis involve strong elements of creativity and are not reducible to rationality and rationalization. Eisenstadt emphasizes the antinomian strands of the major world religious and the role that they have played in initiating major transformations of social orders. In some respects, these tensions represent the background or progenitor of the modernist conceptions of the need to overcome the alienated nexus between the subject and history. Similarly, Eisenstadt identifies parallels between the totalizing or Jacobin objectives of a radical social reordering of modern political and religious movements (Eisenstadt 1999a). In this way, there are divergent and competing attempts to shape and enact the modernist supposition of the constitution of society on the basis on collective and individual agency. Multiple modernities highlights the modernist suppositions of contemporary movements, such as religious fundamentalist or communal religious movements, that explicitly contest the modern notion of the exclusion of 'extra-social' explanations, to use Castoriadis's term, of social processes (Castoriadis 1991; Eisenstadt 1999a). These counter-modernizing movements are naturally shaped by their conflict with the modernizing tendencies that Habermas and Giddens have highlighted, like the communicative rationalization of the lifeworld and 'everyday democratization' (Habermas 1984a; Giddens 2007). Eisenstadt argues that these fundamentalist religious and politically conservative movements have been mobilized by their conflicts with contemporary emancipatory movements, most notably with feminism, that seek to realize the universalistic norms of the modernist ideals of equal liberty (Eisenstadt 1999a).

For the multiple modernities perspective the conflicts between movements is indicative of attempts to control 'historicity', in Touraine's sense, that is, the making of history and its framing in terms of a cultural model (Touraine 1977; 1981). Of course, many of these movements, including authoritarian nationalist and religious fundamentalist, do not adhere to the modernist vision of the autonomous constitution of society. Eisenstadt's multiple modernities' argument about the struggle between movements is one that Habermas and Giddens appreciate. Giddens (1981a; 1985a) originally considered that the conflicts of movements, organizations and the structuring of dialectics of control, were part of the institutional definition of modernity. However, multiple modernities contends that 'tradition' and traditional identities are more significant influences on the present than Giddens and Habermas had originally presumed. Eisenstadt accentuates the persistence of inherited cultural assumptions in institutionally modified forms, such as in the variant realizations of the distinction between order-maintaining and order-transforming visions (Eisenstadt 1995, 306–327).

One of the ways in which Eisenstadt's framework diverges significantly from the normative standpoint of praxis philosophy is in its emphasizing the role of elites as sources of social and cultural innovation. The critique of social hierarchy and its justifications is a basic consideration of the entire orientation of the philosophy of praxis. The agency of elites, whether they be political, cultural or economic, is considered by praxis philosophy as generally a distortion of the nexus between the subject and history, being inconsistent with the normative standpoint of the general interest and ideological in claiming that elite actions are in the interest of the general interest. It is worthwhile noting, again, that some strands of the philosophy of praxis developed out of an opposition to the oversight and direction of Communist party elites. Marx's critiques of alienation and the division of labour similarly initiated a process of challenging hierarchical forms of social organization and its bases in the distinction between theory and practice.

In some respects, Habermas's and Giddens's positions are more evaluative of social and political movements than that of Eisenstadt and they arguably have a stronger sense of how change results in the surpassing of traditional modes of justification. The implications of this quite different standpoint are, for instance, apparent in Giddens's argument that democratic institutions may not require a long-standing cultural background in order for democracy to be consolidated in societies undergoing transition, such as in the case of state socialist societies (Giddens 1994a). In this regard, the perspective of global modernity has more in common with Habermas's and Giddens's position, but it is closer to that of multiple modernities in its engagement with a diversity of regional contexts. The global modernity standpoint tends to diverge from aspects of the 'civilizational' perspective of Eisenstadt. Eisenstadt (2001; 1999b; 2000) proposes that modernity constitutes a new civilization, with its own distinctive attributes and a clear differentiation from preceding civilizational forms. Like earlier civilizations that were founded on particular orientations to the world and different forms of collective agency, modernity has generated variations in its elaborations and institution. In other words, this implies that the multiplicity of the forms of modernity has been generated out of the civilizational 'programme' of modernity, such as the critique that draws on the antinomic relation to existing institutions, the social imaginary of the rational domination of nature, a distinctive form of the self-relation of subjectivity, and the commitment to the vision of autonomy (Eisenstadt 1999a; 1999b; 2000; 2001).

It is undoubtedly the case that there are various tensions in Eisenstadt's theorizing of multiple modernities and civilizational analysis, for instance, there are tensions concerning the weighting that should be given to the impact on modernizing trajectories of cultural understandings that originate prior to modernity, especially compared to those of the civilization of modernity, which should exhibit significant discontinuity with them. Similarly, the civilizational understandings of modernity are open to the extent of permitting alternate programmes intended to realize them. But Eisenstadt's conception does not give sufficient consideration to the possibility of the transformation of these cultural understanding on the basis of changes ensuing from either the processes of enacting them or the 'external' influence of formerly non-modern societies, that is, non-Western societies and cultures, upon the meaning system of modernity (see Bhambra 2007). Of course, it is no doubt difficult to formulate a civilizational framework that satisfactorily addresses the sociological problem of the relation of structure and action. Eisenstadt sometimes appears to endorse the notion that action is heavily structured by cultural patterns, but often appears to foreground action or agency in a way that is inadequate with respect to the possible structural determinants and constraints upon historical change (see Joas and Knöbl 2009). In my opinion, these tensions within Eisenstadt's theorizing are both a source of weakness and strength. It is a strength to the extent that multiple modernities perspective can claim that the tensions, such as those over the degree of agency and the openness to cultural alternatives, actually derive from the modernist conception of the social order as a construction.

There are likewise differences within the multiple modernities and civilizational analysis approach to the questions of continuity and change. These differences are relevant to its transfiguring of the praxis philosophy conception of the linkage of the subject and history. At various junctures during the preceding analysis, Johann P. Arnason's incisive criticisms of Habermas's and Giddens's theories have been endorsed. These criticisms gestured at the positions that Arnason would subsequently develop into a version of the multiple modernities and civilizational analysis. In this context, Castoriadis's elucidation of the social imaginary informs Arnason's perspective, particularly with respect to the significance of cultural meaning and social creativity (Castoriadis 1987). The latter was a central consideration of the praxis philosophical perspective on modernity and Castoriadis's elucidation of the imaginary opens the way for a more expansive perspective on the social-historical institution. Despite presenting a sustained critique of Castoriadis's theoretical framework, Habermas acknowledged that it represented the most substantial and original attempt to rethink the problem of the creative institution of society and history (Habermas 1987b).

For Castoriadis, the creativity of the social imaginary is that of ontological genesis, it brings meanings into being that are founded on the social imaginary. Social imaginary significations are not reducible to the determination by the existing material reality, nor can they be derived from the rationality of logical combination, as is presumed by the structuralist approach to meaning (Castoriadis 1987). It is worth noting that this work has drawn on Castoriadis's posing of the question of the relationship of instituted society to instituting society, however, Castoriadis contends that the imaginary institution of society is the social-historical work of society as an anonymous collective (Castoriadis 1987). Arnason takes this 'world making' character of the social imaginary into account in developing a hermeneutic-phenomenological approach to the relationship between meaning and historical contexts. He considers that there was a significant shift during the twentieth century from the problem of knowledge to that of meaning. This interpretative turn leads to Arnason's concern with the cultural orientations of institutions, for instance, he underlines the centrality of the imaginary signification of unlimited accumulation to capitalism and the different civilizational endowments of the world with meaning (Arnason 2005).

Arnason (1991b) argues that Habermas's theory of rationalization undermined a conception of modernity as a 'field of tensions', including the tensions between the various institutional components of the social order, as well as those deriving from collective struggles. Similarly, cultural understandings or social imaginaries are complex combinations of meanings and significations, which are open to alternate articulations and the associated significations can be mobilized at different social and historical junctures. Arnason highlights the tension in modernity between the logic of rationalization, including Habermas's communicative version of rationalization, and the values expounded by Romanticism, such as those of creative self-expression, nature and community (Arnason 1991b). However, where Eisenstadt considers that history is shaped by cultural 'programmes', Arnason rather refers to civilizational 'problematics'. The latter notion of problematics permits a greater latitude of responses and subsequent modifications. Wolfgang Knöbl (2011) rightly underlines how Arnason's version of civilizational analysis has a greater sense of contingency than that of Eisenstadt. Eisenstadt's relative occlusion of contingency is evident in his explicit – and implicit – deployment of such notions as those of unfolding cultural patterns and the path dependent tracks of development. Significantly, Eisenstadt subsequently revised some of his formulations in light of Arnason's criticisms (see Knöbl 2011).

Arnason proposes that there are different layers of institutionalization and he emphasizes the mutually constitutive significance of the interaction between them. The broad horizons of meaning that are the concern of civilizational problematics generate different world orientations and cultural 'premises' (Arnason 2005). Arnason's macro-phenomenological interpretation of the cultural consolidation of these worlds takes the form of a historical anthropology of civilizations. He argues that cultural horizons of meanings are crystallized in the institutional constellations of power, meaning, and material production. Modernizing processes draw upon the potentialities that are present in world orientations. Arnason considers cultural worlds to be multiform complexes of meaning, hence with scope for different historical activations. The resulting interplay of institutions produces variations in the historical forms of modernity. For instance, the Soviet variant of modernity represented an institutional fusion of the conflicting interpretative tendencies of a revolutionary programme and the imperial background (Arnason 1993). Arnason recognizes that it is necessary to explicate the common features of modernity, but argues that 'we can no longer impose a general definition prior to historical and comparative exploration' (Arnason 2002,132).

According to Arnason, the culture of modernity is strongly shaped by self-critical and self-questioning traits; it is likewise defined by its opposition to the limits embodied in existing institutions and those inherited from the past. In a sense, Arnason's work on multiple modernities and civilizational analysis can be considered to disclose the broader cultural sources and political backgrounds that shape the praxis philosophy conception of the nexus between history and the subject. Arnason has foregrounded the hermeneutic or interpretative component of social practices; the sense in which practice deploys meanings that are historically consolidated and contributes to the creation of worlds of meaning that transcends them. The actual format and outcomes of practical relations are conditioned by the world orientations and institutional constellations. Although these comments are insufficient with respect to depth and originality of Arnason's work, they are indicative of how his social theory is shaped by the internal critique of the Marxian philosophy of praxis and the endeavour to rethink some of the intentions of this perspective. The historical sociological approach of multiple modernities is shared by the perspective of global modernity, but global modernity is primarily concerned with the dynamic relations within modernity. My discussion here will be basically limited to reflecting on two major articulations of the global modernity perspective, those of Peter Wagner and José Maurício Domingues.

While endorsing multiple modernities' orientation to cultural meanings and extending the contexts of investigation beyond Europe and North America, Peter Wagner (2012) makes two main criticisms of this approach. First, he argues that the multiple modernities perspective's accentuation of the cultural patterns of civilizations may obscure the extent to which moments of crisis and conflict result in radical breaks with prior cultural meanings and institutions. Second, he points to the risk of cultural relativism ensuing from the multiple modernities explication of plurality and diversity. In this respect, Wagner seeks to sustain the modernist commitment to a notion of social progress, however qualified and self-critical may be this view (Wagner 2016). Wagner's conception of 'successive modernities' has already been indirectly encountered, such as in the context of Habermas's reference to it in characterizing the institutional form of the nationally regulated capitalism that was being overtaken by the postnational forms of globalization.

Wagner (1994) argues that in the first few decades of the twentieth century the first liberal phase of modernity gave way in the face of economic and political crises to another phase of 'organized modernity'. Organized modernity entailed a greater degree of state coordination, the expansion of bureaucratic capitalist organization, the development of social policy and mass consumption based on standardized production. Although there is a sense in which these institutional changes are part of the developmental progression in modernity, there are significant elements of discontinuity to the successive phases of modernity.

The successive phases of modernity result from the loss of legitimacy of formerly dominant understandings and the diffusion across major social institutions of another set of common principles and practical orientations, as well as the creation of new social organizations (Wagner 1994). Wagner emphasizes how shifts ensue from the changes in the rules and conventions of social practices, especially insofar as this relates to the application of knowledge to generic problems, like those of political power, economic allocation, and legitimate knowledge. Besides the details of this interpretation of successive modernities, Wagner's framing is of interest for its creative reworking of some themes of structuration theory and the links it makes between them and important developments in current social theory, especially the pragmatic sociology of justification, morality and conventions that is most associated with the work of Luc Boltanski and Laurent Thévenot (2006). It leads to a synthesis that enables Wagner to propose a distinctive conception of the relationship between the reflexivity of modernity and history constituting social practices:

> Practices have to be constantly renewed to make them form institutions. If we see institutions as relatively stable sets of social conventions, then we may regard the building of such institutions as a process of conventionalization, and a crisis as marked by tendencies toward de-conventionalization, followed by the creation of new sets of conventions. The chains of interaction that link human beings may be reoriented or extended and the kinds of linkages that are used may be altered, and so societies change their shape and extension. Crises will then be understood as periods when individuals and groups change their social practices to such an extent that major social institutions and, with them, the prevailing configuration of institutions undergo a transformation. (Wagner 1994, 31)

Wagner claims that two broad notions have shaped modernity, those of liberty and discipline. Liberty and discipline form the points of reference for modern endeavours to modify society and to control processes of change. In part, the dynamic of modernity can be traced to the institutional and everyday practical attempts to make liberty and discipline mutually reinforcing and the changes that ensue from the persistent tension or conflict between autonomy and control. The intersections that this position has with the perspective on modernity deployed in this work should be readily apparent. Wagner argues that the third phase of modernity, which he terms that of 'extended liberal modernity', involves an expansion of contingency and tendencies similar to those Giddens and Habermas associate with individualization and the shift to post-traditional social relations (Wagner 1994). Wagner claims that around 1970 the phase of organized modernity entered into crisis and that it is in the process of being succeeded. The crisis of organized modernity is evident in challenges to its core framing dimensions of the state, the nation and class, the related tendency of individuals constructing a more differentiated relationship to collective categories, like class and citizenship, as well as the more general redefining of social identities, the emergence of post-Fordist discourses of deregulation and flexibility, and the questioning of the ability of the social sciences to make predictions and to produce an accurate representation of the world (Wagner 1994; 2001a; 2001b).

The notion of successive modernities does, nevertheless, imply significant continuity; change remains a matter of the different institutional articulations of the core orienting notions of autonomy and control. Although Wagner's conception of the transition from organized to 'extended liberal modernity' is founded on several distinctive theoretical assumption, the method of demarcating and contrasting the contemporary period and its types of dominant institutions with earlier phases of modernity is shared by a number of perspectives, such as Beck and Giddens's distinction between simple and reflexive modernization (Beck 1992; Beck, Giddens and Lash 1994). Like the multiple modernities perspective, Wagner argues for an interpretative approach that can account for variations in modernity's institution and the corresponding forms of subjective experience (Wagner 2008; 2012). Wagner seeks to explain how different experiences of modernity derive from variant responses to circumstances that are structured by commonly shared 'problematiques'. Wagner proposes that modernity is configured in relation to three problematiques: the economic problematique of the 'satisfaction of needs', the political problematique of the 'question of the rules for life in common', and the epistemic problematique that is concerned with the question of 'valid knowledge' (Wagner 2008, 4). These three problematiques elicit different societal responses depending on the historical circumstances of modernization, such as the phase of modernity to which it belongs and the particular historical constraints that have limited the modern significations of autonomy and equality. The latter is evident, for instance, in the South African case of the dismantling of the apartheid system and the implications of its legacy in the present (Wagner 2012).

The term problematique derives from the work of Michel Foucault and refers to the self-problematizing character of discourses (Wagner 2008; Foucault 1985). It is a notion that reinforces modernity's tendencies for self-questioning and self-critique, something which Arnason had likewise underlined in his explications of modern culture. Wagner points to the dynamic in modernity of undermining and exceeding the particular framings of problematiques. He argues that individualist notions of freedom and rational choice became influential during the latter half of the twentieth century as a consequence of major social and political conflicts having weakened confidence in collective categories (Wagner 2008). Wagner maintains that individualist notions significantly inform how the political, epistemic, and economic problematiques are framed and addressed in the current period. However, liberal individualism, rational choice theory, and similar, all represent, in his view, rather limited conceptions of modernity's signification of autonomy and they displace the key concern with 'collective self-determination' (Wagner 2008). This displacement of collective self-determination clearly bears upon perceptions of the nexus between history and the subject, as well as the displacement is a cause and consequence of rather limited and constrained perceptions of the potential contemporary forms of the autonomous constitution of society.

It is worth noting that even though the versions of individualism associated with rational choice theory and liberal notions of private right differ from Giddens's conception of the 'new individualism', Wagner's interpretation provides important insights into the implicit assumptions of Giddens's arguments for rethinking social democracy. It reinforces not just the limitations of these arguments that have been previously identified, but also the sense in which Giddens's rethinking of social democracy did not meet some of the epistemic requirements of structuration theory, such as with respect to how individuals are 'contextually located' and the 'position-practices' that incorporate the constraining, as well as enabling, property of social structure (Giddens 1984). Similarly, Wagner's argument clarifies the difficulties that ensue from Habermas's discourse theory of justice and democracy being significantly shaped by its engagement with normative political philosophy and political liberalism (Wagner 2008). It means that even though Habermas's discourse theory contests the liberal understanding of individual autonomy, it has difficulties, as we have seen, overcoming assumptions that work against notions of collective self-determination.

Wagner differentiates his approach to modernity from those focused primarily on either 'process' or institution (Wagner 2015). The latter approaches, he argues, underpin the contention that the major contemporary tendencies are those of globalization and individualization, such as was expressed by proponents of reflexive modernization, like Giddens, and a range of sociological perspectives. Wagner argues that an interpretative approach to modernity differs from institutional and process approaches in its comprehension of how modernist orientations are manifested in forms of 'collective self-understanding' (Wagner 2008). It is possible to perceive certain parallels between the interpretative approach Wagner is proposing and Arnason's hermeneutical revision of the praxis philosophy problematic of the nexus between the subject and history. These significant developments in social theory cannot be assessed in the present context, but it is worth noting that some alternative versions of the interpretative 'epistemic mode' appear to lack much of the explanatory and practical-political intentions of Habermas's and Giddens's endeavours to revise the philosophy of praxis (see Browne 2013; Reed 2011).

Wagner's version of global modernity is concerned with the 'world' in two senses. The first is that of a 'world sociology of modernity'; in the sense of a more encompassing exploration of the global manifestations of modernity and the rectifying of those omissions that ensue from an exclusive identification of modernity with Europe and North America. The second sense of the notion of 'world' is that of 'world making', that is, of the world as an interpretative horizon of understanding. The world, in this sense, is distinguished from the geographical and empirical descriptive meaning of the category of the global or, what Hannah Arendt termed, the earth (see Wagner 2015b; Arendt 1958). It is these latter empirical-descriptive meanings of the category of world that generally inflect discussions of globalization. Drawing on Arendt's alternative usage of the notion of the 'world', Wagner suggests that the 'world' creates a sense of the 'worldliness' of being.

> Earth is the planet on which we live, the ground of our existence; world, in turn, is the social space that human beings create between each other. There is only one earth, but the political

imagination of human beings can institute different worlds – worlds that can coexist with each other, and worlds that can be the imaginary points of reference for action. (Wagner 2015b, 23).

Wagner appreciates that the aspirations of the modernist vision are no longer specific to western modernity. He considers that discussions of modernity have developed far beyond its European origins and that it is necessary to take into consideration the different trajectories of modernity (Wagner 2008; 2012). The notion of trajectory implies a strong sense of dynamic processes and some uncertainty concerning outcomes. In this sense, modernity involves trying to achieve a reflexive understanding of the present and to facilitate the reflexive agency of society. The latter is something that, for example, nation states in decolonized societies have recently attempted to come to terms with in relation to their past histories, although the weight of the past upon the present modernity remains considerable and inflects the institutions of these nation states (Wagner 2015). In another respect, the problem of collective self-determination that Wagner details is central to the dynamic relationship between capitalism and democracy. This relationship is, of course, a dilemma in Europe as well as in non-European societies, especially given the consequences of the dissolution of organized modernity. This does not mean that this formative conflict is the same globally; even in Europe there are 'varieties' of capitalism and welfare states (Wagner 2008; 2012). Nevertheless, Wagner argues that the contemporary period of intensifying economic globalization has generally extended the independence of capitalism from democratic control (Wagner 2012).

Despite this critical characterization, Wagner argues that the view that capitalism and democracy are intrinsically antithetical does not do justice to the complex historical forms of their relationship and this relationship's distinctive contemporary articulation (Wagner 2012). Castoriadis's juxtaposition of the modern imaginary of the project of autonomy and the capitalist imaginary of unlimited rational – but properly pseudo-rational in Castoriadis's opinion – domination and control of nature and society is one such conception of a fundamental incommensurability (Castoriadis 1991; Browne 2016). Wagner accepts the centrality of these two social imaginary significations to modernity, but proposes that it is important to appreciate their historical mediations and the alternate forms that the conflict between capitalism and democracy has taken. In particular, Wagner notes that capitalism and democracy have in common a modern historical emergence in opposition to the *Ancien Regime* and that each has some connection to the Enlightenment image of rationality (Wagner 2008; 2012). In Wagner's opinion, it is a mistake to presume that there is a stable pattern that determines the trajectory of their relationship. Rather, there have been shifts that reflect the originally limited institution of democracy and the consolidation of capitalism.

These shifts include those of the periods of the reversal of liberal democracy in Europe during the early twentieth century, the subsequent establishment of more inclusive democratic institution that channelled demands for justice, and then the late twentieth-century crisis of the welfare state democratic capitalism, and which has culminated in the current phase of a global market capitalism that is increasingly decoupled from the prior modes of democratic coordination and regulation (Wagner 2012). Further, Wagner contends that while the contemporary non-European forms of the relationship of capitalism and democracy may in many respect overlap with the predominant tendencies that have just been outlined, these relationships of capitalism and democracy should not be viewed as bound to reiterate the European pattern. This contention is not just based on a negative assessment of the failings of preceding sociological theories of modernization and their commitment to a uniform pattern of modernization and institution of modernity. Wagner's contention is partly based on the view that the current mobilizing for 'inclusive democracy' may have greater intensity in formerly authoritarian nation states like Brazil and South Africa (Wagner 2012).

In his *Zeitdiagnosen*, Wagner takes up Arendt's critical account of the possible 'worldlessness' or the 'deworlding' loss of world-making capacity of humans (Wagner 2008; 2012). Arendt (1958) traced this 'deworlding' to the consolidating of the perspective of an instrumental mastery of external reality and the loss of the horizon of meaning that takes into account the relations to others, oneself and to the natural environment. Since the meanings of these relations are present in the 'world', the objectivating of external reality produces a loss of this wider horizon of meaningful relations. Wagner suggests that it is the very processes that are generating a sense of the global, such as the media of instantaneous communication and transportation systems, which may be inducing this loss of the world-making capacity (Wagner 2012).

In a sense, this view would imply that the arguments of Habermas and Giddens that globalization could reflect an expanding of the horizons of the lifeworld is countered and possibly negated by the instrumental domination that produces globalization. Wagner somewhat reframes the praxis philosophy problem of the alienated nexus between history and the subject with this notion of 'worldlessness' or 'deworlding'. He does not dispute that the transformation of this nexus is bound up with modernity, but rather considers that it should not be reduced to the processes of modernization. Instead, he suggests that modernity is present wherever the demand for autonomy emerges and that this creation of a self-determining collective can occur in a variety of historical contexts. In this way, Wagner retrieves the modernist vision whilst elucidating the potentially diverse conditions of its emergence in the relationship of instituting practices to an instituted social order.

The questions of the nexus between history and the subject are explicit concerns of the work of José Maurício Domingues. Domingues's connection to the philosophy of praxis is apparent in the centrality to his social theory of the categories of collective subjectivity and social creativity (Domingues 1996; 2000). These conceptions are intended to explicate the generative social processes involved in the constitution and reproduction of modernity. Domingues's theoretical conception of global modernity has likewise been clarified through reflection on the perspective of multiple modernities, standard theories of modernization, and debates over post-colonialism (Domingues 2006; 2012). One feature that makes his work genuinely global is its historical sociological comparison of non-European forms of modernity, specifically China, India and Latin America (Domingues 2012). Domingues notes that this comparison contrasts with the predominant tendency to compare non-European modernization with either the advanced Western form of modernity or the most 'successful' case of non-Western modernization, such as Japan or

South Korea. The result is a limiting view of the historical dynamics of modernity and the complications of transformation, since the potentials for creative innovation in the periphery are downplayed. The established approaches to modernity regularly fail to do justice to the divergent tendencies of regional or nation-state institutions of modernity. The perspective of global modernity is a corrective to this position, whilst Domingues argues that interpretations from the standpoint of non-Western modernities have to demonstrate the general or universal significance of the tendencies that they identify (Domingues 2012).

In certain respects, Domingues formulates the notion of collective subjectivity in response to the limitations of Habermas's conception of social systems and the inconsistencies of Giddens's theorizing of structuration. For this reason, there are considerable parallels with the critical analysis presented in this work and his conceptions are similarly motivated by a need to clarify the cyclical processes by which the actions of subjects come to condition their future actions, as well as the altering of this relationship as means of enabling freedom and giving expression to freedom. The praxis philosophy problem of the transformation of the condition of being the objects of the historical process into that of its subjects informs his theory, but he underlines the sense in which this problem is conditioned by the contexts of modernization and development. Notably, the relations of the periphery to the centre have reinforced the significance of the problems of agency and transformation, whilst imparting additional considerations and dimensions to these core problems, such as with respect to the variations in the temporal horizons of programmes of development and extending the sense in which autonomy presupposes contesting the hierarchical relations within the global capitalist system. In Domingues's opinion, the modern imaginary's central values remain those of freedom and solidarity (Domingues 2006).

Domingues explicitly distinguishes the notion of collective subjectivity from the more common sense notion of individual subjectivity. He contends that collective subjectivity is 'decentred' in a manner that is somewhat equivalent to Giddens's original conception of structure and that it discloses how contexts of social interaction generate forms of collective causality. Collective subjectivity is what produces 'movement in social life' and it is the 'intentionality' that is present in the mobilization of movements and the coordination of organizations (Domingues 1996; 2000). Given the causal effects of the intentionality and creativity of types of collective subjectivity, the variations in the extent of 'centring' is a key consideration of Domingues's reflections and analyses of forms of collective subjectivity. Centring primarily refers to the internally generated coherence and reflexivity of a collective subjectivity, although interaction with other collective subjectivities conditions agency. In a similar vein, collective subjectivity differs from the systems theory conception of self-referential systems through the dynamic character of centring and by its grounding social systems in interaction. The self-referential conception does not sufficiently take into account how social systems' regulating of their relations to external environments is conditioned by interactions, especially those of social struggles and social conflicts (Domingues 2000).

The notion of collective subjectivity is continuous, Domingues claims, with the intentions of Mead's and Habermas's interpretations of the relational and practical character of social constitution. Drawing on these two frameworks, he emphasizes the inherent dynamics that collective subjectivity contains for collective learning and social creativity through reflexive communication (Domingues 2000). The degree of coherence and centring exhibited by a collective subjectivity, whether it be that of movements, classes, organizations, systems, institutions, or public expressions of collective will, are relevant to the determination of the intended outcomes and unintended consequences of social agency and mobilization. This does not necessarily mean that the greater the centring the more that a coherent project of modernization can be pursued. Domingues distinguishes between coherent modernizing projects and more 'dispersed' and even contradictory types of *modernizing offensives* (Domingues 2012).

'Modernizing moves' refers to specific embodiments of collective subjectivity. Modernizing moves are initiatives that seek to bring about some features of modernity and they can extend to an entire societal transformation to modernity or the reorganization of modernity (Domingues 2009). Modernizing moves can be pursued in different social spheres, like those of politics, economics and culture, and they can be initiated by elites from the 'top' or they can be generated 'from below' by the working class or the masses. Moreover, it is possible to perceive that aspects of modernizing moves can be imported and exported, such as in the case of programmes of state-directed development or the neoliberal agenda of market liberalization.

Domingues's conception of collective subjectivity assists in illuminating the historical forms and different configurations of programmes of modernization and the relative limitations upon their realization. It does this through interrelating the externally given constraints, such as the existing level of development, the effects of the different 'routes to' modernity, to use Goran Therborn's term, and the 'internal' capacities of social agencies. Therborn distinguishes between four main 'routes' to modernity: the original western path to modernity, the reactive route to modernity that is typified by Japan, the colonial pathway and the 'settler colonial' formation of modernity (Therborn 1995). It is not hard to perceive how Domingues's categories are intended to reconstruct the nexus between history and the subject. Like the multiple modernities perspective on the relationship between institutional orders and social agencies, Domingues elaborates a framework that permits an appreciation of the diverse forms that that this nexus can assume and the different institutional realizations of collective subjectivity. Similarly, for Therborn, the intersections of the different routes to modernity generate entangled modernities (Therborn 2003).

The forms of modernity, Domingues argues, are shaped by the practical expressions of social creativity. Social creativity is defined by him in a manner that is influenced by praxis philosophy and philosophical pragmatism. It is the genesis of innovations and modifications that derive from the confrontation with the existing social order and inherited understandings. These understandings are consolidated in memories and traditions, which constitute enabling conditions and constraints upon action. Broadly, social creativity is manifested in the projections of the future that are reflexively incorporated into practices and that generate changes or mobilize actions. Domingues understands the modernist vision of autonomy to be relational and bound to collective practices. Memory is structuring in the sense that Giddens proposed; it is manifested in institutional forms and practices draw upon it. Yet, there is always some degree of indeterminacy or contingency involved in the transmission of memory to situations in the present, since these situations are oriented to the future. This means that there is an element of social creativity in the enacting of practices and interaction (Domingues 2000; 2006).

Social creativity implies that there is some scope for individuals to influence contexts of interaction and social institutions, as well as for collective subjectivities to modify systems through the interaction between collective subjectivities. In Domingues's view, this interactive relationship between socially creative practices and systems represents the general condition of the 'dialectic of control' (Domingues 2000; 2012). The relational formations of modern systems and institutions, particularly that of the political order of the state in its relation to citizenship and civil society, constitute dynamic configurations of the dialectic of control. In this context, the configuration of the dialectic of control derives from the institutionalizing of the democratic incorporation of subjects and the ensuing possession of greater agency on the part of citizens (Domingues 1995; 2012).

The praxis philosophical orientation is likewise apparent in Domingues's interpretation of the contemporary tendencies of the disembedding of social relations, reification and real abstractions (Domingues 2006; 2012). His critical diagnoses point to how these tendencies can result in the loss of capacity of agents and the need for effective forms of solidarity to counteract the dislocation of social relations and the negative aspects of increasing social complexity. Domingues draws on Wagner's conception of successive modernities and its notion of the current third phase of modernity (Wagner 1994; Domingues 2012). Domingues argues that the market and network forms of coordination have, to varying degrees, replaced the second phase of modernity's more state-organized coordination through principles of hierarchy and command. Although modernity's third phase is actually a 'mixed articulation' of these different modes of coordination, the elements of earlier phases of modernity are not so much 'erased' in a process of succession as rearranged and realigned in a more layered and complex pattern (Domingues 2012: 26). From the perspective of global modernity, the third phase of modernity amounts to a more flexible and polarizing mode of accumulation. Its global consequences are evident in nation states like Brazil moving away from the second phase of modernity's policy of 'import substitution' and reversion to the primary production of export commodities in line with the market determination of global competition (Domingues 2009; 2012).

It should be clear that Domingues's version of global modernity more strongly foregrounds political economy than the multiple modernities perspective, though it is not limited to this dimension and proposes that there are complex relations between the cultural, political and economic. Domingues considers that multiple modernities' accentuation of culture is a potential limitation. He argues instead that civilizations are more 'fragile' and contingent than civilizational theory suggests (Domingues 2012, 23). Domingues disputes the implied coherence and persistence of civilizations and prefers to speak of 'civilizational elements and constellations'. His position on global modernity is broadly framed in terms of the problem of 'combined and uneven' development. There are contradictory tendencies, Domingues argues, both between and within national and regional forms of modernization. For instance, the democratization of Latin American societies in recent decades contrasts with the regression in democracy in European and North

American societies, whereas Chinese industrial modernization has had various para-doxical regional consequences, such as simultaneously producing regional expansions and contractions in educational institutions and achievement (Domingues 2015; 2012). In Domingues's view, global modernity takes into account both distinctive modernizing trajectories and the variant relations of interchange between regions and national societ-ies. In short, global modernity is concerned with the scale, dynamics, and processes of modernity (Bringel and Domingues 2015).

The works on global modernity importantly considers the large-scale forms and con-ditions of the praxis philosophy problem of the nexus between history and the sub-ject, or the relationship of instituted to instituting practices. Domingues shows how even where there are shared general intentions the globally different starting points – or what Therborn (1995) described as 'routes to modernity' – and the contexts that are encoun-tered, produce significant variations in the institution of modernity and the practices of its instantiation. Similarly, contradictory tendencies within global modernity result from the different social spheres of modernization, such as one can perceive in strong democ-ratizing tendencies in Latin America during the third phase of modernity (Domingues 2012). Yet, at the same time, there are more ambiguous processes of economic develop-ment in Latin America, such as with the regression in some areas of economic mod-ernization and a return to a reliance on the primary sector of the economy with the relative decline in manufacturing and industry. The notions of modernizing moves and collective subjectivities are meant to convey the strains between different spheres. For Domingues, the institutional arrangements of global modernity result from inherited conditions, struggles, contestation, unfolding processes and the imaginative projects that underpin social creativity.

In many respects, Domingues and Wagner's interpretations of global modernity are a corrective to some of the tendencies of recent social theory discourse. Notably, global modernity restores the interest of theories of modernity in social conflict and social contestation. Similarly, the category of the collective is an integral component of their approaches; Domingues is concerned with collective subjectivity and collective causality, whereas Wagner deploys the concepts of collective self-determination and col-lective understandings. In this regard, the perspective of global modernity runs counter to the discourse of individualization and the retreat of sociology into the present (see Inglis 2013). Significantly, the collective is a form of agency in these theories of global modernity and, in this respect, there are certain overlaps with the multiple modernities approach. The global modernity perspective incorporates a questioning of the notion of system and offers a means for reinterpreting social systems. The work of Wagner and Domingues can, then, be seen as attempting to rectify the limitations of Habermas's theory of modernity that result from the distinction between lifeworld and system, on the one hand, and, on the other hand, as pursuing the innovative aspects of the approach to systems that Giddens's set out in the theory of structuration, but without fully consolidat-ing them in either his theoretical conceptualization of structuration theory or his critical theory of history.

The global modernity perspective likewise renews the analysis of capitalism by emphasizing the 'economic' problematique and forms of accumulation (see Browne

2016). In other words, the perspective of global modernity takes up some of the challenges that Habermas and Giddens let slide in their later work on modernity, or, rather, that they only later gesture towards. As we have seen, their work becomes less historical in its focus and justification. The approaches to Europe that Habermas and Giddens develop are certainly cosmopolitan, yet, as they themselves basically admit, the proper complement for such a perspective is that of global modernity.

In terms of the praxis philosophy problematic, there are questions that can be raised regarding the positions of Wagner and Domingues. Domingues's conception of collective causality is consistent with his interpretation of collective subjectivity, but there could be grounds for arguing that these two notions come into potential tension (Domingues 2000). That is, collective causality may undermine collective subjectivity under certain conditions, rather than being an expression of it. Perhaps, this would amount to a context shaped by the interaction of different forms of collective subjectivity. Wagner's reflexive perspective means that he has interrogated some of the potential antinomies of interpretations of modernity. Notably, there is probably a greater emphasis on the contingency that is generated by modernity in some of his initial theorizing of modernity compared to his more recent underlining of historical resistance to progressive transformation (Wagner 2001a; 2012). These positions are not necessarily inconsistent, but they do reflect some potential tensions over the axes of continuity and discontinuity in his conception of successive modernities. Wagner has noted the valuable applications of this conception of phases of modernity beyond its original European and North American points of reference and expressed some warranted caution about whether there is a genuine equivalence of the dimensions of these phases across different contexts of modernization (Wagner 2015).

It is not a criticism to suggest that Wagner has sometimes more forcefully diagnosed the dilemmas of the current phase of modernity than presented a theoretical resolution of them, as he has shown how modernist problems emerge from the posing of the question of autonomy. He argues that reflexive awareness has enabled modernist understandings to advance beyond extant misunderstandings, such as with respect to overly substantive visions of collective self-determination bound to the nation or class (Wagner 2016). Indeed, probably because Wagner's work is intimately tied to the discourse of modernity, it reprises some of the issues that have arisen in our analysis of Habermas's and Giddens's theories of modernity. For instance, Wagner has presented a qualified defense of progress in the present on the basis of countering tendencies towards regression and he has sought to develop an alternate hermeneutic in order to comprehend the modifications that shape the contemporary constellation of modernity (Wagner 2016; 2015).

Concluding Remarks

The dynamic character of modernity and its propensity for change are apparent in the distance between the later statements of the social theories of Habermas and Giddens and the original starting points of their projects. The works of Habermas and Giddens were originally driven by the modernist impulse of transcending the limitations of inherited social theory perspectives. Habermas and Giddens sought to develop conceptions appropriate to the newly emerging phase of modernity and which would clarify the conditions for the practical realization of modernity's normative potential for justice and autonomy. This modernist orientation is certainly true in the case of Habermas, even though his early work was intended to extend and revise the established programme of critical social theory. In the case of Giddens, his theory of structuration challenged the modernized sociological approaches of functionalism and positivism. These were subject to the modernist critique of constituting an 'orthodox consensus' in sociology and as providing methodological justifications of the *status quo*.

In some respects, the trajectories of the social theories of Habermas and Giddens map, but also manifest, the contradictory tendencies of the period of contemporary modernity. It is clear that some of the legitimations and justifications of the extant social order that derive from earlier phases of modernity persist, but that these legitimations and justifications have lost some of their validity and that contexts have altered in ways that make them seem less appropriate. This change is evident in many dimensions of contemporary modernity, such as with respect to former justifications of social exclusion on the basis of gender and ethnic identity. Of course, this does not mean that the achievements in formal equality that follow from these social learning processes amount to substantive equality. Moreover, it is clear that in many contexts the disorientation that ensues from dissolving prior justifications and understandings has generated various regressive reactionary responses and countermodernizing tendencies, such as ethnonationalist and religious fundamentalist mobilizations.

The progress that Habermas and Giddens have detailed in democratic communication is surpassed today by developments that undermine its emancipatory implications. The contemporary period appears one in which the social capacities for the control and coordination of the major modernizing dynamics and the capitalist system have declined. This amounts to a significant diminishing of the potential for social autonomy and this is evident in how progressive arguments for social justice are often framed in the present period in terms of discourses of human rights that actually lack the social grounding to generate effective social change (see Wagner 2015). The recent historical period has witnessed an ideological resurgence of the capitalist imaginary and this has meant that heteronomy is extensively reproduced through the anonymous mechanism of market exchange. Habermas and Giddens have offered strong critical assessments of the limitations of state administrative systems' capacity for collective coordination and the disorganizing effects of unregulated markets, especially that of global financial markets. Despite their respective oppositions to the increasing inequalities ensuing from neoliberal globalization, it is not difficult to perceive that Habermas's and Giddens's later attempts to counteract this development on the basis of the modernist vision of social autonomy lack some of the emancipatory connotations of their earlier proposals. This undoubtedly reflects something of a more general cultural shift in historical consciousness and a change in the 'horizon of anticipation' (Koselleck 1999).

Habermas and Giddens have shown how modernity entails individuals' deployment of particular capacities and competences. These competences, or knowledgeability, of individuals serve the reproduction of the instituted social order of modern societies, however, they contain a critical potential in relationship to its current institution. Habermas has sought to demonstrate how subjects' capacities for rational agreement, social interaction and moral universalism imply the discourse principle of justice. Similarly, Giddens has sought to disclose the constitutive power of social practices and how orientations to the democratic structuring of social relations enhance mutual autonomy. These components of their social theories represent specifications of the nexus of the subject and history in terms of intersubjective relations. The emerging social theory perspectives of multiple modernities and global modernity have, by contrast, sought to more strongly elucidate the variant contemporary forms of collective self-determination and the configurings that these forms of collective agency make, or attempt to make, in the relationship of instituting practices to the instituted social order.

The comparison of the social theories of Habermas and Giddens has resulted in a series of highly significant contentions of general importance to social theory. It has demonstrated, first, that against the tendencies of much contemporary sociology, a historical perspective on the present development of society remains necessary and is a condition of a valid understanding of modernity. Second, that the shift to the framework of intersubjectivity in social theory is of profound significance. It does not overturn earlier theoretical and practical problems but it does enable them to be reposed in a way that is relevant to clarifying the prospects of democracy and the processes of democratization. Third, that despite their shared commitment to the priority of action theory, Habermas and Giddens diverge in their explications of action. Broadly, Giddens prioritizes the action process whereas Habermas gives precedence to communicative coordination. Both provide substantial insights into the dynamics of social practice but the corresponding conceptions of the constitution of social institutions that they propose reflect their respective greater orientations towards either power or morality.

At various times it has been shown, fourth, that both Habermas and Giddens overlook or disregard categories within their own work that would enable a deeper comprehension of modernity and its unfolding dynamics. The notion of the dialectic of control was particularly highlighted in this regard, as a central category of structuration theory that was subsequently subordinated. Fifth, partly reinforced by the collapse of state socialism and the decline of notions of modernity implying a historical transition beyond the constraints of capitalism (see Wagner 2012), Habermas and Giddens came to consider the relationship of instituting practices to the instituted social order in terms of their respective rethinkings of social democracy, the contradictions of the welfare state, and the cosmopolitan potential of the project of the European Union. Despite the practical relevance of these analyses and proposals, there are limitations that these considerations impose on the modernist vision of social autonomy. The welfare state and social democracy have attenuated some of the negative effects of capitalist modernity, but the complications of these mediations of the tensions intrinsic to the instituted social order of capitalist society have actually intensified with contemporary globalization. Nevertheless, my analysis pointed to how Habermas's discourse theory and its specific conception of the mutuality of public and private autonomy could provide the stronger normative grounding that Giddens's Third Way rethinking of social democracy requires. Further, this supplementation could preclude misunderstandings concerning social democratic policy proposals.

Sixth, I have similarly drawn attention to how some of the ideas of Habermas's and Giddens's theory have been taken up in ways that are critical of their more recent elaborations of them. This was noted with respect to the contemporary standpoints of the theories of the struggle for recognition and global modernity. Seventh, the basic disparity that critique discloses between the instituted social order and instituting practices persists. My analysis explored how Habermas and Giddens attempted to reframe critique in a manner that is consistent with their respective social theory perspectives. It showed that whilst this should be recognized as a considerable achievement, they have difficulties effectively balancing the normative and the analytical components of critique. At times, this resulted in the paradoxes of a peculiar utopianism on their part concerning existing institutions, especially those of the democratic constitutional state and therapeutic practices. Moreover, this immanent utopianism is apparent in how Habermas's and Giddens's depictions of emancipatory change or radical democracy sometimes presuppose the conditions of autonomy that they actually consider needs to be established.

One of the founding aspirations of modernist social theory was that of situating the theoretical perspective in the historical process itself. In this way, social theory was meant to provide a reflexive clarification of its own social preconditions and it should give rise to forms of understanding that would enable the liberation of subjects from persisting injustices. The modernist underpinning of social theory was to reveal that the social circumstances emanate from the actions of subjects, even though this was veiled and remained unrecognized. Further, social theory disclosed that the conditions enabling subjects to be self-determining were not equally distributed and that the extant structure of modern society limited individual and social autonomy. Indeed, the philosophy of praxis argued that subjects were still more the objects of historical processes than its actual subjects. In some respects, the modernist vision of the autonomous constitution of society has been recognized to be beset by complications. It has even been seen to involve some duplicity, insofar as its promise of autonomy has been open to distortion and served to conceal existing heteronomy. Despite the problems that have been identified, the social theories of Habermas and Giddens have sought to delineate how the modernist vision of the autonomous constitution of society has been historically consolidated. The work of Habermas and Giddens enables us to grasp how some of the limitations of the existing institution of social autonomy can be transcended through subjects' reflexive, deliberative and dialogical practices.

BIBLIOGRAPHY

Aboulafia, M. 1995. 'Habermas and Mead: On Universality and Individuality', *Constellations* 2: 94–113.

Abraham, D. 1994. 'Persistent Facts and Compelling Norms: Liberal Capitalism, Democratic Socialism and the Law', *Law and Society Review* 28: 939–46.

Adorno, T. 1967. 'Sociology and Psychology', *New Left Review* 46: 67–80.

_____. 1968. 'Sociology and Psychology-II', *New Left Review* 47: 79–97.

_____. 1973. *The Jargon of Authenticity*. Evanston, IL: Northwestern University Press.

_____. 1974. *Minima Moralia: Reflections from Damaged Life*. London: New Left Books.

_____. 1976a. 'Introduction', in D. Frisby (ed.) *The Positivist Dispute in German Sociology*. London: Heinemann, 1–67.

_____. 1976b. 'Sociology and Empirical Research', in D. Frisby (ed.) *The Positivist Dispute in German Sociology*. London: Heinemann, 68–86.

_____. 1978. 'Subject and Object', in A. Arato and E. Gebhardt (eds) *The Essential Frankfurt School Reader*. Oxford: Basil Blackwell, 497–511.

_____. 1979. *Negative Dialectics*. New York: Seabury Press.

_____. 1981. *Prisms*. Cambridge, MA: MIT Press.

_____. 1982. *Against Epistemology: A Metacritique: Studies in Husserl and the Phenomenological Antinomies*. Oxford: Blackwell.

_____. 1984. *Aesthetic Theory*. London: Routledge and Kegan Paul.

_____. 1987. *Philosophy of Modern Music*. London: Sheed and Ward.

_____. 1989. 'Society', in S. Bronner and D. Kellner (eds) *Critical Theory and Society: A Reader*. New York: Routledge, 267–75.

_____. 1991. *The Culture Industry: Selected Essays on Mass Culture*, J. M. Bernstein (ed.) London: Routledge.

_____. 1993. *Hegel: Three Studies*. Cambridge, MA: MIT Press.

_____. 1994. *S. Adorno: The Stars Down to Earth and Other Essays on the Irrational in Culture*, S. Crook (ed.) London: Routledge.

Alexander, J. 1983. *Theoretical Logic in Sociology*, vol. 4, *The Modern Reconstruction of Classical Thought: Talcott Parsons*. Berkeley: University of California Press.

_____. 1985. 'The Parsons Revival in German Sociology', *Sociological Theory* 2: 394–411.

_____. 1986. *Twenty Lectures on Sociological Thought: Talcott Parsons and His Critics in the Postwar Period*. New York: Columbia University Press.

_____. 1991. 'Habermas and Critical Theory: Beyond the Marxian Dilemma?', in A. Honneth and H. Joas (eds) *Communicative Action*. Cambridge: Polity, 49–73.

_____. 1992. 'Durkheim's Problem and Differentiation Theory Today', in H. Haferkamp and N. Smelser (eds) *Social Change and Modernity*. Berkeley: University of California Press, 179–204.

_____. 1996. 'Critical Reflections on "Reflexive Modernization"', *Theory, Culture and Society* 13: 133–38.

_____. 1998. *Neo-Functionalism and After*. Oxford: Blackwell.

Alford, F. C. 1979. 'Review of *Communication and the Evolution of Society*, by Jürgen Habermas', *New German Critique* 18: 176–80.

_____. 1985. *Science and the Revenge of Nature: Marcuse and Habermas*. Tampa: University of Florida Press.

Althusscr, L. 1969. *For Marx*. London: Allen Lane.

_____. 1971. *Lenin and Philosophy and Other Essays*. London: New Left Books.

Alway, J. 1995. *Critical Theory and Political Possibilities: Conceptions of Emancipatory Politics in the Works of Horkheimer, Adorno, Marcuse, and Habermas.* Westport, CT: Greenwood Press.

Anderson B. 1983. *Imagined Communities.* London: Verso.

Anderson, P. 1974a. *Passages from Antiquity to Feudalism.* London: New Left Books.

_____. 1974b. *Lineages of the Absolutist State.* London: New Left Books.

_____. 1983. *In the Tracks of Historical Materialism.* London: Verso.

Apel, K. O. 1972. 'The A. priori of Communication and the Foundation of the Humanities', *Man and World* 5 (1): 3–37.

_____. 1984. *Understanding and Explanation: A Transcendental-Pragmatic Perspective.* Cambridge, MA: MIT Press.

Arato, A. and Gebhardt E. (eds) 1978. *The Essential Frankfurt School Reader.* Oxford: Basil Blackwell.

Arato, A. and Breines, P. 1979. *The Young Lukács and the Origins of Western Marxism.* New York: Seabury Press.

Arato, A. 1982. 'Critical Sociology and Authoritarian Socialism', in J. B. Thompson and D. Held (eds) *Habermas: Critical Debates.* London: Macmillan Press, 196–218.

Archer, M. 1982. 'Morphogenesis versus Structuration: On Combining Structure and Action', *British Journal of Sociology* 33 (4): 455–83.

_____. 1990. 'Human Agency and Social Structure: A Critique of Giddens', in J. Clark, C. Mogdil and S. Mogdil (eds) *Consensus and Controversy: Anthony Giddens.* London: Falmer Press, 73–84.

_____. 1996. 'Social Integration and System Integration: Developing the Distinction', *Sociology* 30 (4): 679–99.

Arendt, H. 1951. *The Origins of Totalitarianism.* New York: Harcourt Brace.

_____. 1958. *The Human Condition.* Chicago: University of Chicago Press.

_____. 1961. *Between Past and Future.* New York: Viking Press.

_____. 1963. *On Revolution.* Harmondsworth: Penguin.

_____. 1982. *Lectures on Kant's Political Philosophy.* R. Beiner (ed.) Chicago: University of Chicago Press.

Aristotle. 1976. *The Nicomachean Ethics.* London: Penguin Books.

Arnason, J. P. 1979. 'Review of *Zur Rekonstruktion Des Historischen Materialismus*, by J. Habermas', *Telos* 39: 201–18.

_____. 1980. 'Reflections on the Crisis of Marxism', *Thesis Eleven* 1: 29–42.

_____. 1982. 'Universal Pragmatics and Historical Materialism', *Acta Sociologica* 25: 219–33.

_____. 1984. 'Contemporary Approaches to Marx, Reconstruction and Deconstruction', *Thesis Eleven* 9: 52–73.

_____. 1989. 'The Imaginary Constitution of Modernity', *Revue Européenne des Sciences Sociales* 86: 323–237.

_____. 1990. 'Nationalism, Globalization and Modernity', *Theory, Culture and Society* 7: 207–36.

_____. 1991a. 'Praxis and Action – Mainstream Theories and Marxian Correctives', *Thesis Eleven* 29: 63–81.

_____. 1991b. 'Modernity as Project and as Field of Tensions', in A. Honneth and H. Joas (eds) *Communicative Action.* Cambridge: Polity, 181–213.

_____. 1992. 'World Interpretation and Mutual Understanding', in A. Honneth, T. McCarthy, C. Offe and A. Wellmer (eds) *Cultural-Political Interventions in the Unfinished Project of Enlightenment.* Cambridge, MA: MIT Press, 247–68.

_____. 1993. *The Future That Failed: Origins and Destinies of the Soviet Model.* London: Routledge.

_____. 1994. 'Reason, Imagination, Interpretation', in G. Robinson and J. Rundell (eds) *Rethinking Imagination.* Routledge: London, 156–70.

_____. 1998. *Social Theory and Japanese Experience.* London: Kegan Paul.

_____. 2001. 'Capitalism in Context: Sources, Trajectories and Alternatives', *Thesis Eleven* 66: 99–125.

_____. 2002. 'The Multiplication of Modernity', in E. Ben-Rafael (ed.) *Identity, Culture and Globalization,* Leiden: Brill, 130–54.

_____. 2005a. *Civilizations in Dispute*, Leiden: Brill.

_____. 2005b. 'The Varieties of Accumulation: Civilizational Perspectives on Capitalism', in C Joerges, B Sträth and P Wagner (eds) *The Economy as a Polity – the Political Constitution of Contemporary Capitalism*, London: UCL Press, 17–36.

_____. 2015a 'Theorizing Capitalism: Classical Foundations and Contemporary Innovations' *European Journal of Social Theory* 18 (4): 351–67.

_____. 2015b 'The Imaginary Dimension of Modernity' *Social Imaginaries* 1 (1): 135–50.

Aronowitz, S. 1996. 'Review of *Beyond Left and Right: The Future of Radical Politics*, by Anthony Giddens', *American Journal of Sociology* 101: 1464–66.

Ashley, D. 1982. 'Historical Materialism and Social Evolution', *Theory, Culture and Society* 1: 89–92.

Avineri, S. 1968. *The Social and Political Thought of Karl Marx*. London: Cambridge University Press.

_____. 1972. *Hegel's Theory of the Modern State*. London: Cambridge University Press.

Barnes, J. 1982. *Aristotle*. Oxford: Oxford University Press.

Bauman, Z. 1989. 'Hermeneutics and Modern Social Theory', in D. Held and J. B. Thompson (eds) *Social Theory of Modern Societies: Anthony Giddens and His Critics*. Cambridge: Cambridge University Press, 34–55.

_____. 1997. 'Review of *In Defence of Sociology: Essays, Interpretations and Rejoinders*, by Anthony Giddens', *Thesis Eleven* 51: 132–37.

Baxter, H. 1987. 'System and Lifeworld in Habermas's Theory of Communicative Action', *Theory and Society* 16: 39–86.

Baynes, K. 1992. *The Normative Grounds of Social Criticism: Kant, Rawls, and Habermas*. Albany: State University of New York Press.

_____. 1995. 'Democracy and the Rechtsstaat: Habermas's Faktizitat und Geltung', in S. K. White (ed.) *The Cambridge Companion to Habermas*. Cambridge: Cambridge University Press, 201–32.

_____. 1996. 'Public Reason and Personal Autonomy', in D. Rasmussen (ed.) *The Handbook of Critical Theory*. Oxford: Blackwell, 243–42.

Beck, U. 1992a. *Risk Society: Towards a New Modernity*. London: Sage.

_____. 1992b. 'How Modern Is Modern Society?', *Theory, Culture and Society* 9: 163–69.

_____. 1994 'The Reinvention of Politics: Towards a Theory of Reflexive Modernization.' U. Beck, A. Giddens and S. Lash *Reflexive Modernization: Politics, Tradition and Aesthetics in the Modern Social Order*. Cambridge: Polity Press, 1–55.

_____. 1995. *Ecological Enlightenment: Essays on the Politics of the Risk Society*. New Jersey: Humanities Press.

_____. 1998. *Democracy Without Enemies*. Cambridge: Polity Press.

Beck, U., Giddens, A. and Lash, S. 1994. *Reflexive Modernization: Politics, Tradition and Aesthetics in the Modern Social Order* Cambridge: Polity Press.

Beilharz, P. 1994. *Postmodern Socialism: Romanticism, City and State*. Victoria: Melbourne University Press.

_____. 1995. 'Critical Theory – Jürgen Habermas', in D. Roberts (ed.) *Reconstructing Theory: Gadamer, Habermas, Luhmann*. Victoria: Melbourne University Press, 39–64.

Benhabib, S. 1981. 'Modernity and the Aporias of Critical Theory', *Telos* 49: 39–59.

_____. 1982. 'The Development of Marx's Thought and the Hermeneutics of Critique: Some Comments on George Markus' 'Four Forms of Critical Theory – Some Theses on Marx's Development', *Thesis Eleven* 5/6: 289–97.

_____. 1984. 'Epistemologies of Postmodernism: A Rejoinder to Jean-Francois Lyotard', *New German Critique* 33: 103–27.

_____. 1985. 'The Utopian Dimension in Communicative Ethics', *New German Critique* 35: 83–96.

_____. 1986. *Critique, Norm, and Utopia: a Study of the Foundations of Critical Theory*. New York: Columbia University Press.

_____. 1992. *Situating the Self: Gender, Community and Postmodernism in Contemporary Ethics*. Cambridge: Polity Press.

_____. 1994. 'In Defense of Universalism – Yet Again! A Response to Critics of Situating the Self', *New German Critique* 62: 173–89.

Benhabib, S. (ed.) 1995. *Feminist Contentions: a Philosophical Exchange*. New York: Routledge.

_____. (ed.) 1996a. *Democracy and Difference: Contesting the Boundaries of the Political*. Princeton: Princeton University Press.

Benhabib, S. 1996b. 'Critical Theory and Postmodernism: On the Interplay of Ethics, Aesthetics, and Utopia in Critical Theory', in D. Rasmussen (ed.) *The Handbook of Critical Theory*. Oxford: Blackwell, 327–39.

_____. 1996c. *The Reluctant Modernism of Hannah Arendt*. Thousand Oaks, CA: Sage Publications.

_____. 1998. 'Democracy and Identity' *Philosophy and Social Criticism* 24 (2/3): 85–100.

_____. 2004. *The Rights of Others* Cambridge: Cambridge University Press.

_____. 2006. *Another Cosmopolitanism*. Cambridge: Cambridge University Press.

Benhabib, S., and Cornell, D. (eds) 1987. *Feminism as Critique: On the Politics of Gender*. Minneapolis: University of Minnesota Press.

Benhabib, S., and Dallmayr, F. R. (eds) 1990. *The Communicative Ethics Controversy*. Cambridge, MA: MIT Press.

Benhabib, S., Bonss, W. and McCole, J. (eds) 1993. *On Max Horkheimer: New Perspectives*. Cambridge, MA: MIT Press.

Benjamin, W. 1968. *Illuminations* H. Arendt. (ed.) New York: Harcourt Brace & World.

Benjamin, J. 1977. 'The End of Internalization: Adorno's Social Psychology', *Telos* 32: 42–64.

_____. 1994. 'The Shadow of the Other (Subject): Intersubjectivity and Feminist Theory', *Constellations* 1: 231–54.

Berger, P., and Luckmann, T. 1967. *The Social Construction of Reality*. London: Penguin.

Berger, J. 1991. 'The Linguistification of the Sacred and the Delinguistification of the Sacred', in A. Honneth and H. Joas (eds) *Communicative Action*, Cambridge: Polity Press, 165–80.

Berman, M. 1988. *All That Is Solid Melts Into Air: the Experience of Modernity*. New York: Viking Penguin.

Bernstein, R. J. 1971. *Praxis and Action*. London: Duckworth.

_____. 1976. *The Restructuring of Social and Political Theory*. Oxford: Basil Blackwell.

_____. 1980. 'Comment on The Relationship of Habermas's Views to Hegel', in D. P. Verene (ed.) *Hegel's Social and Political Thought*. New Jersey: Humanities Press, 233–39.

_____. 1983. *Beyond Objectivism and Relativism*. Philadelphia: University of Pennsylvania Press.

_____. 1985. 'Introduction', in R. J. Bernstein (ed.) *Habermas and Modernity* Cambridge, MA: MIT Press, 1–32.

_____. 1986. *Philosophical Profiles: Essays in a Pragmatic Mode*. Cambridge: Polity Press.

_____. 1987. 'Agnes Heller: Philosophy, Rational Utopia and Praxis', *Thesis Eleven* 16: 22–39.

_____. 1989. 'Social Theory as Critique', D. Held and J. B. Thompson (eds) *Social Theory of Modern Societies: Anthony Giddens and His Critics* Cambridge: Cambridge University Press, 19–33.

_____. 1992. *The New Constellation: the Ethical-Political Horizons of Modernity / Postmodernity*. Cambridge: Polity Press.

_____. 1998. 'The Retrieval of the Democratic Ethos', in M. Rosenfeld and A. Arato (eds) 1998. *Habermas on Law and Democracy: Critical Exchanges*. Berkeley: University of California Press, 287–305.

Bernstein, J. M. (ed.) 1994. *The Frankfurt School: Critical Assessments*. London: Routledge.

Bernstein, J. M. 1995. *Recovering Ethical Life: Jürgen Habermas and the Future of Critical Theory*. London: Routledge.

Best, S. 1995. *The Politics of Historical Vision: Marx, Foucault, Habermas*. New York: Guilford Press.

Bhambra, G. 2007. *Rethinking Modernity*. London: Palgrave Macmillan.

Birnbaum, N. 1968. 'The Crisis in Marxist Sociology', *Social Research* 35: 348–80.

Blaug, R. 1999. *Democracy, Real and Ideal: Discourse Ethics and Radical Politics*. Albany: State University of New York Press.

Bleichner, J. 1980. *Contemporary Hermeneutics*. London: Routledge.

Blokker, P. 2010. *Multiple Democracies in Europe: Political Culture in New Member States*. London: Routledge.

Bohman, J. 1989. "'System' and 'Lifeworld': Habermas and the Problem of Holism', *Philosophy and Social Criticism* 15: 377–401.

_____. 1994. 'Complexity, Pluralism, and the Constitutional State: On Habermas's Faktizitat und Geltung', *Law and Society Review* 28: 897–930.

_____. 1996a. 'Two Versions of the Linguistic Turn: Habermas and Poststructuralism', in M. Passerin d'Entrèves and S. Benhabib (eds) *Habermas and the Unfinished Project of Modernity: Critical Essays on The Philosophical Discourse of Modernity*. Cambridge: Polity Press, 197–220.

_____. 1996b. 'Critical Theory and Democracy', in D. Rasmussen (ed.) *The Handbook of Critical Theory*. Oxford: Blackwell, 190–215.

_____. 1999. 'Habermas, Marxism and Social Theory: the Case for Pluralism in Critical Social Science', in P. Dews (ed.) *Habermas: a Critical Reader* Oxford: Blackwell, 53–86.

Bohman, J., and Rehg, W. (eds) 1997. *Deliberative Democracy: Essays on Reason and Politics*. Cambridge, MA: MIT Press.

Boltanski, L., and Chiapello, E. 2005. *The New Spirit of Capitalism*. London: Verso.

Boltanski, L., and Thevénot, L. 2006. *On Justification*. Princeton: Princeton University Press.

Bookchin, M. 1982. 'Finding the Subject: Notes on Whitebook and Habermas, L.T.D.' *Telos* 52: 79–98.

Bottomore, T., Harris, L., Kiernan, V. G. and Miliband, R. (eds) 1983. *A Dictionary of Marxist Thought*. Oxford: Blackwell.

Bottomore, T. B. 1984. *The Frankfurt School*. London: Tavistock.

_____. 1990. 'Giddens' View of Historical Materialism', in J. Clark, C. Mogdil and S. Mogdil (eds) *Consensus and Controversy: Anthony Giddens*. London: Falmer Press, 205–13.

Bourdieu, P. 1977. *Outline of a Theory of Practice*. Cambridge: Cambridge University Press.

_____. 1984. *Distinction: A Social Critique of the Judgement of Taste*. Cambridge, MA: Harvard University Press.

_____. 1990. *The Logic of Practice*. Cambridge: Polity Press.

_____. 1991. *The Political Ontology of Martin Heidegger*. Stanford, CA: Stanford University Press.

_____. 1998. *Practical Reason: on the Theory of Action*. Cambridge: Polity Press.

Boyne, R. 1991. 'Power-knowledge and Social Theory: the Systematic Misrepresentation of Contemporary French Social Theory in the Work of Anthony Giddens', C. G. A. Bryant and D. Jary (eds) *Giddens' Theory of Structuration: a Critical Appreciation*. London: Routledge, 52–73.

Braaten, J. 1991. *Habermas's Critical Theory of Society*. Albany: State University of New York Press.

Brand, A. 1986. 'The 'Colonisation of the Lifeworld' and the Disappearance of Politics – Arendt and Habermas', *Thesis Eleven* 13: 39–53.

_____. 1990. *The Force of Reason: An Introduction to Habermas' Theory of Communicative Action*. Sydney: Allen and Unwin.

Breuilly, J. 1990. 'The Nation-State and Violence: a Critique of Giddens', in J. Clark, C. Mogdil and S. Mogdil (eds) *Consensus and Controversy: Anthony Giddens*. London: Falmer Press, 271–88.

Brewster, P., and Buchner, C. H. 1979. 'Language and Critique: Jürgen Habermas on Walter Benjamin', *New German Critique* 17: 15–29.

Bringel, B., and Domingues, J. M. (ed.) 2015. *Global Modernity and Social Contestation*. London: Sage.

Bronner, S. E., and Kellner, D. (eds) 1989. *Critical Theory and Society: A Reader* New York: Routledge.

Browne, C. 1993. 'Central Dilemmas in Giddens' Theory of Structuration', *Thesis Eleven* 36: 138–50.

_____. 1996. 'Review: Reflexive Modernization: Politics, Tradition and Aesthetics in the Modern Social Order', *Thesis Eleven* 45: 131–37.

_____. 2006. 'Democratic Paradigms and the Horizons of Democratisation' *Contretemps: An Online Journal of Philosophy* 6 January: 43–58.

_____. 2008. 'The End of Immanent Critique?' *European Journal of Social Theory* 11 (1): 5–24.

_____. 2009. 'Pragmatism and Radical Democracy', *Critical Horizons* 10 (1): 54–75.

_____. 2014. 'The Institution of Critique and the Critique of Institutions', *Thesis Eleven* 124 (1): 20–52.

_____. 2016. 'Critiques of Identity and the Permutations of the Capitalist Imaginary', *Social Imaginaries* 2 (1): 95–118.

_____. 2016. 'Anthony Giddens', in R. Stones (ed.) *Key Sociological Thinkers*, 3rd ed. Houndsmill: Palgrave Macmillan.

_____. 2017. 'From the Philosophy of Praxis to the Sociology of Practice', in M. Jonas and B. Littig (eds) *Praxeological Political Analysis*. London: Routledge.

Brunkhorst, H. 1992. 'Culture and Bourgeois Society: The Unity of Reason in a Divided Society', in A. Honneth, T. McCarthy, C. Offe and A. Wellmer (eds) *Cultural-Political Interventions in the Unfinished Project of Enlightenment* Cambridge, MA: MIT Press, 145–69.

_____. 1996a. 'Critical Theory and Empirical Research', in D. Rasmussen (ed.) *The Handbook of Critical Theory*. Oxford: Blackwell, 78–118.

_____. 1996b. 'Theodor W. Adorno: Aesthetic Constructivism and a Negative Ethic of the Non-Forfeited Life', in D. Rasmussen (ed.) *The Handbook of Critical Theory*. Oxford: Blackwell, 305–39.

Bryant, C. G. A. 1991. 'The Dialogic Model of Applied Sociology', in C. G. A. Bryant and D. Jary (eds) *Giddens' Theory of Structuration: A Critical Appreciation*. London: Routledge, 176–200.

Bryant, C. G. A., and Jary, D. 1991. 'Introduction: Coming to terms with Anthony Giddens', in C. G. A. Bryant and D. Jary (eds) *Giddens' Theory of Structuration: A Critical Appreciation*. London: Routledge, 1–31.

Bubner, R. 'Habermas's Concept of Critical Theory', in J. B. Thompson and D. Held (eds) *Habermas: Critical Debates*. London: Macmillan, 42–56.

Burg van der, W. 1990. 'Jürgen Habermas on Law and Morality: Some Critical Comments', *Theory, Culture and Society* 7: 105–11.

Burger, P. 1981. 'The Significance of the Avant-Garde for Contemporary Aesthetics: A Reply to Jürgen Habermas', *New German Critique* 22: 19–22.

Calhoun, C. 1992a. 'Introduction: Habermas and the Public Sphere', in C. Calhoun (ed.) *Habermas and the Public Sphere*. Cambridge, MA: MIT Press, 1–48.

Calhoun, C. (ed.) 1992b. *Habermas and the Public Sphere*. Cambridge, MA: MIT Press.

Calhoun, C. 1995. *Critical Social Theory: Culture, History, and the Challenge of Difference*. Cambridge, MA: Blackwell.

_____. 2003. 'The Class Consciousness of Frequent Travellers: Towards a Critique of Actually Existing Cosmopolitanism', in D. Archibugi (ed.) *Debating Cosmopolitics*. London: Verso, 86–116.

Calhoun, Craig. 2007. *Nations Matter: Culture, History and the Cosmopolitan Dream*. London: Routledge.

Callinicos, A. 1985. 'Anthony Giddens – a Contemporary Critique', *Theory and Society* 14: 133–66.

_____. 1987. *Making History: Agency Structure and Change in Social Theory*. Cambridge: Polity Press.

_____. 2002. *Against the Third Way*. Cambridge: Polity Press.

Casebeer, K. 1994. 'Paris Is Closer than Frankfurt: The nth American Exceptionalism', *Law and Society Review* 28: 931–37.

Castoriadis, C. 1974a. *Modern Capitalism and Revolution*. London: Solidarity.

_____. 1974b. *Redefining Revolution*. London: Solidarity.

_____. 1984. *Crossroads in the Labyrinth*. Sussex: Harvester Press.

_____. 1987. *The Imaginary Institution of Society*. Cambridge: Polity Press.

_____. 1988. *Cornelius Castoriadis, Political and Social Writings*. Minneapolis: University of Minnesota Press.

_____. 1990. 'Does the Idea of Revolution Still Make Sense?', *Thesis Eleven* 26: 123–38.

_____. 1991. *Philosophy, Politics, Autonomy* D. A. Curtis(ed.) Oxford: Oxford University Press.

_____. 1997a. *World in Fragments: Writings on Politics, Society, Psychoanalysis, and the Imagination* D. A. Curtis (ed.) Stanford, CA: Stanford University Press.

_____. 1997b. *The Castoriadis Reader* D. A. Curtis (ed.) Cambridge, MA: Blackwell.

Chambers, S. 1995. 'Discourse and Democratic Practices', S. K. White (ed.) *The Cambridge Companion to Habermas*. Cambridge: Cambridge University Press, 233–59.

_____. 1996. *Reasonable Democracy: Jürgen Habermas and the Politics of Discourse*. Ithaca, NY: Cornell University Press.

Chernilo D. 2014. 'The Idea of Philosophical Sociology' *British Journal of Sociology* 65 (2): 338–57.

Clark, J. 1990. 'Anthony Giddens, Sociology and Modern Social Theory', in J. Clark, C. Mogdil and S. Mogdil (eds) *Consensus and Controversy: Anthony Giddens*. London: Falmer Press, 21–27.

Clark, J., Modgil, S. and Modgil, C. (eds) 1990. *Anthony Giddens: Consensus and Controversy*. London: Falmer Press.

Clastres, P. 1987. *Society Against the State*. New York: Zone Books.

Cohen, G. A. 1978. *Karl Marx's Theory of History: A Defence*. Oxford : Oxford University Press, New York: Clarendon Press.

Cohen, I. 1986 'The Status of Structuration Theory: A Reply to McLennan', *Theory, Culture and Society* 3: 123–33.

_____. 1987 'Structuration Theory and Social Praxis', in A. Giddens and H. Turner (eds) *Social Theory Today*. Cambridge: Polity Press, 273–308.

_____. 1989. *Structuration Theory – Anthony Giddens and the Constitution of Social Life*. London: Macmillan.

_____. 1990 'Structuration Theory and Social Order: Five Issues in Brief', in J. Clark, C. Mogdil and S. Mogdil (eds) *Consensus and Controversy: Anthony Giddens*. London: Falmer Press, 33–46.

Cohen, J. L., and Arato, A. 1992. *Civil Society and Political Theory*. Cambridge, MA: MIT Press.

Coles, R. 1995. 'Identity and Difference in the Ethical Positions of Adorno and Habermas', S. K. White (ed.) *The Cambridge Companion to Habermas*. Cambridge: Cambridge University Press, 19–45.

Cooke, M. 1992. 'Habermas, Autonomy and the Identity of the Self', *Philosophy and Social Criticism* 18: 269–91.

_____. 1994. *Language and Reason: A Study of Habermas's Pragmatics*. Cambridge, MA: MIT Press.

_____. 1995. 'Selfhood and Solidarity', *Constellations* 1: 337–57.

Coole, D. 1996. 'Habermas and the Question of Alterity', in M. Passerin d'Entrèves and S. Benhabib (eds) *Habermas and the Unfinished Project of Modernity: Critical Essays on The Philosophical Discourse of Modernity*. Cambridge: Polity Press, 221–24.

Coser, L. 1990. 'Giddens on Historical Materialism', in J. Clark, C. Mogdil and S. Mogdil (eds) *Consensus and Controversy: Anthony Giddens*. London: Falmer Press, 195–204.

Couture, T. 1995. 'Feminist Criticisms of Habermas's Ethics and Politics', *Dialogue* 34: 259–79.

Craib, I. 1992a. *Anthony Giddens*. London: Routledge.

_____. 1992b. 'Review: Ira Cohen, Structuration Theory, Held and Thompson (eds), Social Theory of Modern Societies', *Theory, Culture and Society* 9 (2): 175–78.

_____. 1998. *Experiencing Identity*. London: Sage.

Critchley, S., and Dews, P. 1996. *Deconstructive Subjectivities*. Albany: State University of New York Press.

Culler, J. 1985. 'Communicative Competence and Normative Force', *New German Critique* 35: 133–45.

Dallmayr, F. R. 1972. 'Critical Theory Criticised: Habermas's Knowledge and Human Interests and its Aftermath', *Philosophy of the Social Sciences* 2: 211–29.

_____. 1982. 'The Theory of Structuration', in A. Giddens, *Profiles and Critiques in Social Theory*. London: Macmillan, 18–27.

_____. 1984. *Polis and Praxis: Exercises in Contemporary Political Theory*. Cambridge, MA: MIT Press.

_____. 1996. 'The Discourse of Modernity: Hegel, Nietzsche, Heidegger and Habermas', in M. Passerin d'Entrèves and S. Benhabib (eds) *Habermas and the Unfinished Project of Modernity: Critical Essays on the Philosophical Discourse of Modernity*. Cambridge: Polity, 59–96.

Dallmayr, F. R., and McCarthy, T. A. (eds) 1977. *Understanding and Social Inquiry*. Notre Dame, IN: University of Notre Dame Press.

Dean, J. 1996. 'Civil Society: Beyond the Public Sphere', in D. Rasmussen (ed.) *The Handbook of Critical Theory.* Oxford: Blackwell, 220–42.

Deflem, M. (ed.) 1996. *Habermas, Modernity, and Law.* London: Sage.

Delanty, G. (2009) *The Cosmopolitan Imagination.* Cambridge: Cambridge University Press.

Derrida, J. 1976. *Of Grammatology.* Baltimore: Johns Hopkins University Press.

_____. 1978. *Writing and Difference.* Chicago: University of Chicago Press.

_____. 1982. *Margins of Philosophy.* Chicago: University of Chicago Press.

_____. 1990 'Some Statements and Truisms about Neologisms, Newisms, Postisms, Parasitisms, and other Small Seisms', in D. Caroll (ed.) *The States of 'Theory'.* Stanford: Stanford University Press, 63–94.

Descombes, V. 1980. *Modern French Philosophy.* Cambridge: Cambridge University Press.

_____. 1993. *The Barometer of Reason.* Oxford: Oxford University Press.

Dews, P. 1986. 'Introduction', in P. Dews (ed.) *Habermas: Autonomy and Solidarity.* London: Verso, 1–34.

_____. 1987. *Logics of Disintegration: Post-Structuralist Thought and the Claims of Critical Theory.* London: Verso.

_____. 1995. *The Limits of Disenchantment: Essays on Contemporary European Philosophy.* London: Verso.

Dews, P. (ed.) 1999. *Habermas: A Critical Reader.* Oxford: Blackwell.

Dickie-Clark, H. 1990. 'Hermeneutics and Giddens' Theory of Structuration', in J. Clark, C. Mogdil and S. Mogdil (eds) *Consensus and Controversy: Anthony Giddens.* London: Falmer Press.

Doeleman, W. 1990. 'Theories of Communicative Action and Psychoanalysis', *Theory, Culture and Society* 7: 113–15.

Domingues, J. M. 1995. *Sociological Theory and Collective Subjectivity,* London: Macmillan.

_____. 1999. 'Evolution, History and Collective Subjectivity', *Current Sociology* 47.

_____. 2000. *Social Creativity, Collective Subjectivity and Contemporary Modernity.* Houndsmills: Macmillan.

_____. 2006. *Modernity Reconstructed.* Cardiff: University of Wales Press.

_____. 2009. 'Modernity and Modernizing Moves – Latin America in Comparative Perspective', *Theory, Culture and Society* 26 (7–8): 208–27.

_____. 2012. *Global Modernity, Development and Contemporary Civilization.* London: Routledge.

_____. 2014. 'Global Modernity: Levels of Analysis and Conceptual Strategies', *Social Science Information* 54 (2): 180–96.

_____. 2015. 'Vicissitudes in Critical Theory', in B. Bringel and J. M. Domingues (eds) *Global Modernity and Social Contestation.* London: Sage, 86–101.

Dove, K. 1980. 'Comment on the Relationship of Habermas's Views to Hegel', D. P. Verene (ed.) *Hegel's Social and Political Thought.* New Jersey: Humanities Press, 240–46.

Dreyfus, H. L., and Rabinow, P. 1982. *Michel Foucault: Beyond Structuralism and Hermeneutics.* New York: Harvester Wheatsheaf.

Dryzek, J. S. 1995. 'Critical Theory as a Research Program', S. K. White (ed.) *The Cambridge Companion to Habermas.* Cambridge: Cambridge University Press, 97–119.

Dubiel, H. 1985. *Theory and Politics: Studies in the Development of Critical Theory.* Cambridge, MA: MIT Press.

_____. 1992. 'Domination or Emancipation? The Debate over the Heritage of Critical Theory', in A. Honneth, T. McCarthy, C. Offe and A. Wellmer (eds) *Cultural-Political Interventions in the Unfinished Project of Enlightenment.* Cambridge, MA: MIT Press, 3–16.

Dunn, R. G. 1998. *Identity Crises: A Social Critique of Postmodernity.* Minneapolis: University of Minnesota Press.

Durkheim, E. 1964a. *The Rules of Sociological.* New York: Free Press.

_____. 1964b. *The Division of Labor in Society.* New York: Free Press.

_____. 1974. *Sociology and Philosophy.* New York: Free Press.

_____. 1976. *The Elementary Forms of the Religious Life.* London: Allen and Unwin.

_____. 1986. *Durkheim on Politics and the State* A. Giddens (ed.) Cambridge: Polity Press.

Dux, G. 1991. 'Communicative Reason and Interest: On the Reconstruction of the Normative Order in Societies Structured by Egalitarianism or Domination', in A. Honneth and H. Joas (eds) *Communicative Action*. Cambridge: Polity Press, 74–96.

Eder, K. 1987. 'The Origin of Class Societies: A Systems Analysis', in V. Meja, D. Misgeld and N. Stehr (eds) *Modern German Sociology*. New York: Columbia University Press, 324–39.

_____. 1988. 'Critique of Habermas's Contribution to the Sociology of Law', *Law and Society Review* 22: 931–44.

_____. 1992. 'Contradictions and Social Evolution: A Theory of the Social Evolution of Modernity', in H. Haferkamp and N. Smelser (eds) *Social Change and Modernity*. Berkeley: University of California Press, 320–49.

_____. 1996. *The Social Construction of Nature*. London: Sage.

Eisenstadt, S. N., 1986. 'Introduction: The Axial Age Breakthroughs – Their Characteristics and Origins', in S. N. Eisenstadt (ed.) *The Origins and Diversity of Axial Age Civilizations*. Albany: State University of New York Press.

Eisenstadt, S. N. 1996. *Power, Trust and Meaning – Essays in Sociological Theory and Analysis*. Chicago: University of Chicago Press.

_____. 1999. *Fundamentalism, Sectarianism, and Revolution*. Cambridge: Cambridge University Press.

_____. 2000. 'Multiple Modernities', *Daedalus* 129 (1): 1–29.

_____. 1999b. 'Multiple Modernities in the Age of Globalization', *Canadian Journal of Sociology* 24 (2): 283–95.

_____. 1999c. *Paradoxes of Democracy*. Baltimore: Johns Hopkins University Press.

Eisenstadt, Shmuel. N. 2000. 'Multiple Modernities', *Daedalus* 129 (1): 1–29.

Eisenstadt, S. N. 2001 'The Civilizational Dynamic of Modernity: Modernity as a Distinct Civilization' *International Sociology* 16: 320–40.

Eisenstadt, S. N. (2007) 'The Reconstruction of Collective Identities and Inter-Civilizational Relations in the Age of Globalization', *Canadian Journal of Sociology* 32 (1): 113–26.

Elias, N. 1978. *The Civilizing Process*. Oxford: Blackwell.

Engels, F. 1954. *Dialectics of Nature*. Moscow: Progress Publishers.

Esping-Andersen, G. 1990. *The Three Worlds of Welfare Capitalism*. Cambridge: Polity Press.

Feenberg, A. 1981. *Lukács, Marx, and the Sources of Critical Theory*. Oxford: Martin Robertson.

Fehér, F., Heller, A. and Márkus, G. 1983. *Dictatorship Over Needs*. Oxford: Blackwell.

Ferrara, A. 1996. 'The Communicative Paradigm in Moral Theory', in D. Rasmussen (ed.) *The Handbook of Critical Theory*. Oxford: Blackwell, 119–37.

Fine, R. 2007. *Cosmopolitanism*. London: Routledge.

Fine, R., and Smith, W. 2003. 'Jürgen Habermas's Theory of Cosmopolitanism', *Constellations* 10 (4): 469–407.

Forst, R. 'Justice, Reason, and Critique: Basic Concepts of Critical Theory', in D. Rasmussen (ed.) *The Handbook of Critical Theory*. Oxford: Blackwell, 138–62.

Fichte, J. G. 1982. *Science of Knowledge; with the First and Second Introductions*. Cambridge: Cambridge University Press.

Foucault, M. 1970. *The Order of Things: An Archaeology of the Human Sciences*. London: Tavistock Publications.

_____. 1972. *The Archaeology of Knowledge and the Discourse on Language*. New York: Pantheon Books.

_____. 1977a. *Discipline and Punish: The Birth of the Prison*. New York: Pantheon Books.

_____. 1977b. *Language, Counter-Memory, Practice: Selected Essays and Interviews*. Ithaca, NY: Cornell University Press.

_____. 1979. *The History of Sexuality: Volume One*. London: Allen Lane.

_____. 1980. *Power / Knowledge: Selected Interviews and Other Writings, 1972–1977*. C. Gordon (ed.) New York: Harvester Wheatsheaf.

_____. 1982. 'Afterword: the Subject and Power', H. Dreyfus and P. Rabinow *Michel Foucault: Beyond Structuralism and Hermeneutics*. Sussex: Harvester, , 208–26.

_____. 1985 *History of Sexuality: Vol. 2. The Use of Pleasure*. New York: Pantheon Books.

_____. 1998. 'Structuralism and Post-Structuralism', in J. D. Faubion (ed.) *Michel Foucault: Aesthetics, Methods and Epistemology*. London: Allen Lane, 433–58.

Franklin, J. (ed.) 1998. *The Politics of Risk Society*. Cambridge: Polity Press.

Fraser, N. 1981. 'Foucault on Modern Power: Empirical Insights and Normative Confusions', *Praxis International* 3: 272–87.

_____. 1985. 'What's Critical about Critical Theory? The Case of Habermas and Gender', *New German Critique* 35: 97–132.

_____. 1986. 'Toward a Discourse Ethic of Solidarity', *Praxis International* 5.

_____. 1992 'Rethinking the Public Sphere: A Contribution to the Critique of Actually Existing Democracy', in C. Calhoun (ed.) *Habermas and the Public Sphere*. Cambridge, MA: MIT Press, 109–42.

_____. 2009. *Scales of Justice*. London: Verso.

_____. 2003a. 'Social Justice in the Age of Identity Politics: Redistribution, Recognition, and Participation', in N. Fraser and A. Honneth, *Redistribution or Recognition? A Political-Philosophical Exchange*. London: Verso, 7–109.

_____. 2003b. 'Distorted Beyond All Recognition', in N. Fraser and A. Honneth, *Redistribution or Recognition? A Political-Philosophical Exchange*. London: Verso, 198–236.

Fraser, N., and Honneth, A. 2003 *Redistribution or Recognition? A Political-Philosophical Exchange*. London: Verso.

Fraser, N. 2009. *Scales of Justice*. London: Verso.

Freud, S. 1984. 'Beyond the Pleasure Principal', A. Richards (ed.) *Freud on Metapsychology: The Theory of Psychoanalysis*. London: Penguin, 271–338.

Frisby, D. 1976. 'Introduction to the English Translation', in D. Frisby (ed.) *The Positivist Dispute in German Sociology*. London: Heinemann.

_____. 1984. *Georg Simmel*. London: Tavistock Publications.

_____. 1985. *Fragments of Modernity: Theories of Modernity in the Work of Simmel, Kracauer and Benjamin*. Cambridge: Polity Press.

Frisby, D., and Sayer, D. 1986. *Society*. London: Tavistock Publications.

Gadamer, H. G. 1970. 'On the Scope and Function of Hermeneutical Reflection', *Continum* 8: 77–95.

_____. 1972. *Truth and Historicity*. The Hague: M. Nijhoff.

_____. 1976. *Philosophical Hermeneutics*. Berkeley: University of California Press.

_____. 1979. *Truth and Method*. London: Sheed and Ward.

Garfinkel, H. 1967. *Studies in Ethnomethodology*. Englewoods Cliffs, NJ: Prentice Hall.

Geuss, R. 1981. *The Idea of a Critical Theory: Habermas and the Frankfurt School*. Cambridge: Cambridge University Press.

Giddens, A. 1971a. *Capitalism and Modern Social Theory: An Analysis of the Writings of Marx, Durkheim and Max Weber*. Cambridge: Cambridge University Press.

_____. 1972. *Politics and Sociology in the Thought of Max Weber*. London: Macmillan.

_____. 1973. *The Class Structure of the Advanced Societies*. London: Hutchinson.

Giddens, A. (ed.) 1974. *Positivism and Sociology*. London: Heinemann.

Giddens, A. 1976. *New Rules of Sociological Method: A Positive Critique of Interpretative Sociologies*. London: Hutchinson.

_____. 1977. *Studies in Social and Political Theory*. London: Hutchinson.

_____. 1978. *Durkheim*. London: Fontana.

_____. 1979. *Central Problems in Social Theory: Action, Structure and Contradiction in Social Analysis*. London: Macmillan.

_____. 1981a. *A Contemporary Critique of Historical Materialism: Power, Property and the State*. London: Macmillan.

_____. 1981b. 'Modernism and Post-Modernism', *New German Critique* 22: 15–18.

_____. 1982a. *Profiles and Critiques in Social Theory*. London: Macmillan.

_____. 1982b. 'Labour and Interaction', in J. B. Thompson and D. Held (eds) *Habermas: Critical Debates*. London: Macmillan, 149–61.

_____. 1982c. 'Historical Materialism Today: An Interview with Anthony Giddens', *Theory, Culture and Society* 1: 63–77.

_____. 1982d. 'A Reply to My Critics', *Theory, Culture and Society* 1: 107–13.

_____. 1982e. 'Commentary on the Debate', *Theory and Society* 11: 527–39.

_____. 1982f. *Sociology: A Brief But Critical Introduction*. London: Macmillan.

_____. 1983. 'Four Theses on Ideology', *Canadian Journal of Political and Social Theory* 7: 18–21.

_____. 1984. *The Constitution of Society: Outline of the Theory of Structuration*. Cambridge: Polity Press.

_____. 1985a. *The Nation-State and Violence*. Cambridge: Polity Press.

_____. 1985b. 'Marx's Correct Views On Everything With Apologies to L. Kolokowski', *Theory and Society* 14: 167–74.

_____. 1986. 'Action, subjectivity and the Constitution of Meaning', *Social Research* 53: 529–45.

_____. 1987. *Social Theory and Modern Sociology*. Cambridge: Polity Press.

_____. 1989. 'A Reply to My Critics', in D. Held and J. B. Thompson (eds) 1989. *Social Theory of Modern Societies: Anthony Giddens and His Critics*. Cambridge: Cambridge University Press, 249–301.

_____. 1990a. *The Consequences of Modernity*. Cambridge: Polity Press.

_____. 1990b. 'Structuration Theory and Sociological Analysis', *Anthony Giddens, Consensus and Controversy* J. Clark, C. Mogdil and F. Mogdil (eds) Brighton: Falmer, 297–315.

_____. 1991a. *Modernity and Self-Identity: Self and Society in the Late Modern Age*. Stanford, CA: Stanford University Press.

_____. 1991b. 'Structuration Theory: Past, Present and Future', in C. G. A. Bryant and D. Jary (eds) *Giddens' Theory of Structuration: A Critical Appreciation*. London: Routledge, 201–21.

_____. 1992a. *The Transformation of Intimacy: Sexuality, Love and Eroticism in Modern Societies*. Cambridge: Polity Press.

_____. 1992b. 'Commentary on the Reviews', *Theory, Culture and Society* 9: 171–74.

_____. 1993a. 'Modernity, History, Democracy', *Theory and Society* 22: 289–92.

_____. 1993b. 'Preface to the Second Edition', *A Contemporary Critique of Historical Materialism*. London: Macmillan, ix–xix.

_____. 1993c. *The Giddens Reader*. P. Cassell (ed.) London: Macmillan.

_____. 1994a. *Beyond Left and Right: the Future of Radical Politics*. Cambridge: Polity Press.

_____. 1994b. 'Living in a Post-Traditional Society', in U. Beck, A. Giddens and S. Lash (eds) *Reflexive Modernisation*. Cambridge: Polity Press, 56–109.

_____. 1995. *Politics, Sociology and Social Theory: Encounters with Classical and Contemporary Social Thought*. Stanford, CA: Stanford University Press.

_____. 1996. *In Defence of Sociology: Essays, Interpretations, and Rejoinders*. Cambridge, Polity Press.

_____. 1998a. *The Third Way: The Renewal of Social Democracy*. Cambridge, Polity Press.

_____. 1998b. 'The Transition to Late Modern Society: A Conversation with Anthony Giddens', *International Sociology* 13: 117–33.

_____. 2000. *The Third Way and its Critics*. Polity Press: Cambridge, Polity Press.

Giddens, A. (ed.) 2003. *The Progressive Manifesto*. Cambridge: Polity Press.

Giddens, A. 2007. *Europe in the Global Age*. Cambridge: Polity Press.

_____. 2009. *The Politics of Climate Change*. Cambridge: Polity Press.

_____. 2014. *Turbulent and Mighty Continent*. Cambridge: Polity Press.

Giddens, A., and Turner J. H. (eds) 1987. *Social Theory Today*. Cambridge: Polity Press.

Giddens, A., and Pierson, C. (eds) 1998. *Conversations with Anthony Giddens: Making Sense of Modernity*. Cambridge: Polity Press.

Giddens, A, and Diamond, P. (eds) 2005. *The New Egalitarianism*. Cambridge: Polity Press.

Goodin, R. Hedey, B. Muffcs, R and Dirven, H.-J. 1999. *The Real Worlds of Welfare Capitalism*. Cambridge: Cambridge University Press.

Goffman, E. 1971. *The Presentation of Self in Everyday Life*. London: Penguin.

Goldblatt, D. 1996. *Social Theory and the Environment*. Boulder: Westview Press.

Goldmann, L. 1977. *Lukács and Heidegger: Towards a New Philosophy*. London: Routledge and Kegan Paul.

Gottlieb, R. 1986. 'Three Contemporary Critiques of Historical Materialism', *Philosophy and Social Criticism* 11: 87–101.

Gouldner, A. W. 1970. *The Coming Crisis of Western Sociology*. New York: Basic Books.

Gramsci, A. 1971. *Selections From the Prison Notebooks*. Q. Hoare and G. Nowell-Smith (eds) London: Lawrence & Wishart.

_____. 1994. *Antonio Gramsci: Pre-Prison Writings*. R. Bellamy and V. Cox (eds) New York: Cambridge University Press.

Gregory, D. 1989. 'Presences and Absences: Time-Space Relations and Structuration Theory', in D. Held and J. B. Thompson (eds) *Social Theory of Modern Societies: Anthony Giddens and His Critics*. Cambridge: Cambridge University Press, 185–214.

_____. 1990. 'Grand Maps of History: Structuration Theory and Social Change', in J. Clark, C. Mogdil and S. Mogdil (eds) *Consensus and Controversy: Anthony Giddens*. London: Falmer Press, 217–33.

Gregson, N. 1989. 'On the (Ir)relevance of Structuration Theory to Empirical Research', in D. Held and J. B. Thompson (eds) *Social Theory of Modern Societies: Anthony Giddens and His Critics*. Cambridge: Cambridge University Press, 235–48.

Gross, D. 1982. 'Time-Space Relations in Giddens' Social Theory', *Theory, Culture and Society* 1 (2): 83–88.

Grumley, J. 1989. *History and Totality: Radical Historicism from Hegel to Foucault*. London: Routledge.

_____. 1991. 'Marx and the Philosophy of the Subject: Markus contra Habermas', *Thesis Eleven* 28: 52–69.

_____. 1992. 'Two Views of the Paradigm of Production', *Praxis International* 12: 181–204.

Habermas, J. 1970a. 'On Systematically Distorted Communication', *Inquiry* 13: 205–18.

_____. 1970b. 'Toward a Theory of Communicative Competence', in H. P. Dreitzal (ed.) *Recent Sociology*. New York: Macmillan, 114–48.

_____. 1971. *Toward a Rational Society: Student Protest, Science and Politics*. London: Heinemann Educational.

_____. 1973. 'What does a Crisis Mean Today, Legitimation Problems in Late-Capitalism', *Social Research* 40: 643–67.

_____. 1974a. *Theory and Practice*. London: Heinemann.

_____. 1974b. 'On Social Identity', *Telos* 19: 91–103.

_____. 1974c. 'The Public Sphere: An Encyclopedia Article', *New German Critique* 3: 49–55.

_____. 1974d. 'Habermas Talking: An Interview', *Theory and Society* 1: 37–58.

_____. 1975. 'The Place of Philosophy in Marxism', *Insurgent Sociologist* 5: 41–48.

_____. 1976a. 'The Analytical Theory of Science and Dialectics', in D. Frisby (ed.) *The Positivist Dispute in German Sociology*. London: Heinemann, 131–62.

_____. 1976b. 'A Positivistically Bisected Rationalism', in D. Frisby (ed.) *The Positivist Dispute in German Sociology*. London: Heinemann, 198–225.

_____. 1976c. *Legitimation Crisis*. London: Heinemann Educational.

_____. 1977. 'A Test for Popular Justice', *New German Critique* 12: 11–13.

_____. 1978a. *Knowledge and Human Interests*. London: Heinemann Educational.

Habermas, Jürgen. 1978b. 'Knowledge and Human Interests: a General Perspective', in *Knowledge and Human Interests*. London: Heinemann, 303–17.

Habermas, J. 1978c. 'A Postscript to Knowledge and Human Interests', in *Knowledge and Human Interests*. London: Heinemann, 351–86.

_____. 1979a. *Communication and the Evolution of Society*. Boston: Beacon Press.

_____. 1979b. 'History and Evolution', *Telos* 39: 5–44.

_____. 1979c. 'Aspects of the Rationality of Action', in T. F. Geraets (ed.) *Rationality Today*. Ottawa: University of Ottawa Press, 185–212.

_____. 1980a. 'Response to the Commentary of Bernstein and Dove', in D. P. Verene (ed.) *Hegel's Social and Political Thought*. New Jersey: Humanities Press, 247–50.

_____. 1980b. 'On the German-Jewish Heritage', *Telos* 44: 127–31.

_____. 1982. 'A Reply to My Critics', in J. B. Thompson and D. Held (eds) *Habermas: Critical Debates*. London: Macmillan, 219–83.

_____. 1983. *Philosophical-Political Profiles*. Cambridge, MA: MIT Press.

_____. 1984a. *The Theory of Communicative Action*. Boston: Beacon Press.

_____. 1984b. 'Questions and Counter-Questions', *Praxis International* 4 (3): 229–49.

Habermas, J. (ed.)1984c. *Observations on 'The Spiritual Situation of the Age': Contemporary German Perspectives*. Cambridge, MA: MIT Press.

Habermas, J. 1985a. 'Psychic Thermidor and the Rebirth of Rebellious Subjectivity', in R. J. Bernstein (ed.) *Habermas and Modernity*. Cambridge, MA: MIT Press, 67–77.

_____. 1985b. 'Neoconservative Culture Criticism in the United States and West Germany: An Intellectual Movement in Two Political Cultures', in R. J. Bernstein (ed.) *Habermas and Modernity*. Cambridge, MA: MIT Press, 78–94.

_____. 1985c. 'Talcott Parsons: Problems of Theory Construction', *Sociological Inquiry* 51: 173–96.

_____. 1985d. 'Civil Disobedience: Litmus Test for the Democratic Constitutional State', *Berkeley Journal of Sociology 30:* 95–116.

_____. 1985e. 'Reply to Skjei', *Inquiry* 28: 105–13.

_____. 1986. *Autonomy and Solidarity: Interviews* P. Dews (ed.). London: Verso.

_____. 1987a. *The Theory of Communicative Action, Volume 2: Lifeworld and System*. Cambridge: Polity Press.

_____. 1987b. *The Philosophical Discourse of Modernity: Twelve Lectures*. Cambridge, MA: MIT Press.

_____. 1988a. *On the Logic of the Social Sciences*. Cambridge, MA: MIT Press.

_____. 1988b. 'On Hermeneutics' Claim to Universality', in K. Muller-Vollmer (ed.) *The Hermeneutics Reader*. New York: Continuum.

_____. 1989a. *The New Conservatism: Cultural Criticism and the Historian's Debate*. Cambridge: Polity Press.

_____. 1989b. *The Structural Transformation of the Public Sphere: An Inquiry into a Category of Bourgeois Society*. Cambridge, MA: MIT Press.

_____. 1990a. *Moral Consciousness and Communicative Action*. Cambridge, MA: MIT Press.

_____. 1990b. 'What Does Socialism Mean Today? The Rectifying Revolution and the Need for New Thinking on the Left', *New Left Review* 183: 3–21.

_____. 1990c. 'Remarks on the Discussion', *Theory, Culture and Society* 7.

_____. 1991. 'A Reply', in A. Honneth and H. Joas (eds) *Communicative Action*. Cambridge: Polity Press, 214–64.

_____. 1992a. *Postmetaphysical Thinking: Philosophical Essays*. Cambridge, MA: MIT Press.

_____. 1992b. 'Further Reflections on the Public Sphere', in C. Calhoun (ed.) *Habermas and the Public Sphere*. Cambridge, MA: MIT Press, 421–61.

_____. 1992c. 'Concluding Remarks', in C. Calhoun (ed.) *Habermas and the Public Sphere*. Cambridge, MA: MIT Press, 462–79.

_____. 1992d. 'Jürgen Habermas, A Generation apart from Adorno (an Interview)', *Philosophy and Social Criticism* 18: 119–24.

_____. 1993a. *Justification and Application: Remarks on Discourse Ethics*. Cambridge, MA: MIT Press.

_____. 1993b. 'Notes on the Developmental History of Horkheimer's Work', *Theory, Culture and Society* 10: 61–77.

_____. 1994. *The Past as Future*. Lincoln: University of Nebraska Press.

_____. 1996a. *Between Facts and Norms: Contributions to a Discourse Theory of Law and Democracy*. Cambridge, MA: MIT Press.

_____. 1996b. 'An Interview with Jurgen Habermas', *Theory, Culture and Society* 13: 1–17.

_____. 1996c. 'Popular Sovereignty as Procedure', in J. Habermas, *Between Facts and Norms*. Cambridge, MA: MIT Press, 463–90.

_____. 1996d. 'Modernity: An Unfinished Project', in M. Passerin d'Entrèves and S. Benhabib (eds) *Habermas and the Unfinished Project of Modernity: Critical Essays on The Philosophical Discourse of Modernity*. Cambridge: Polity Press, 38–55.

_____. 1997. *A Berlin Republic: Writings on Germany*. Lincoln: University of Nebraska Press.

_____. 1998a. *The Inclusion of the Other: Studies in Political Theory*. Cambridge, MA: MIT Press.

_____. 1998b. *On the Pragmatics of Communication* M. Cooke (ed.) Cambridge, MA: MIT Press.

_____. 1998c. 'Learning by Disaster? A Diagnostic Look Back on the Short 20th Century', *Constellations* 5: 307–20.

_____. 1998d. 'Remarks on Legitimation through Human Rights', *Philosophy and Social Criticism* 24: 157–71.

_____. 2000. 'Globalism, Ideology and Traditions – Interview with Jürgen Habermas' *Thesis Eleven* 63: 1–10.

_____. 2001a. *The Postnational Constellation*. Cambridge: Polity Press.

_____. 2001b. 'From Kant's "Ideas" of Pure Reason to the "Idealizing" Presuppositions of Communicative Action: Reflections on the Detranscendentalized "Use of Reason"', in W. Rehg and J. Bohman (eds) *Pluralism and the Pragmatic Turn*, Cambridge, MA: MIT Press, 11–39.

_____. 2003. 'Toward a Cosmopolitan Europe', *Journal of Democracy* 14 (4): 86–100.

_____. 2006b. *Time of Transitions*. Cambridge: Polity Press.

_____. 2006b. *The Divided West*. Cambridge: Polity Press.

_____. 2008. *Between Naturalism and Religion*. Cambridge: Polity Press.

_____. 2009. *Europe – the Faltering Project*. Cambridge: Polity Press.

_____. 2012. *The Crisis of the European Union*. Cambridge: Polity Press.

_____. 2015. *The Lure of Technocracy*. Cambridge: Polity Press.

Hall, P. A., and Soskice, D. eds. 2000. *Varieties of Capitalism*. Oxford: Oxford University Press.

Harrison, P. R. 1995. 'Niklas Luhmann and the Theory of Social Systems', in D. Roberts (ed.) *Reconstructing Theory: Gadamer, Habermas, Luhmann*. Melbourne University: Carlton Press, 65–90.

Hegel, G. W. F. 1956. *The Philosophy of History*. New York: Dover Publications.

_____. 1967. *Philosophy of Right*. Oxford: Oxford University Press.

_____. 1975. *Logic (Part One of the Encyclopaedia of the Philosophical Sciences 1830)*. Oxford: Oxford University Press.

_____. 1977. *Phenomenology of Spirit*. Oxford: Oxford University Press.

_____. 1979. *System of Ethical Life (1802/3) and First Philosophy of Spirit (part III of the System of Speculative Philosophy 1803/4)* H. S. Harris and T. M. Knox (eds). Albany: State University of New York Press.

_____. 1986. *The Jena System, 1804–5: Logic and Metaphysics* G. Di Giovanni, H. S. Harris and J. W. Burbidge (eds) Kingston: McGill-Queen's University Press.

Heidegger, M. 1959. *An Introduction to Metaphysics*. New Haven, CT: Yale University Press.

_____. 1962. *Being and Time*. Oxford: B. Blackwell.

_____. 1968. *What Is Called Thinking?* New York: Harper & Row.

_____. 1969. *The Essence of Reasons*. Evanston, IL: Northwestern University Press.

_____. 1971. *Poetry, Language, Thought*. New York: Harper & Row.

_____. 1974. *Identity and Difference*. New York: Harper & Row.

_____. 1975. *The End of Philosophy*. London: Souvenir Press.

_____. 1977. *The Question Concerning Technology and Other Essays*. New York: Harper & Row.

_____. 1985. *History of the Concept of Time: Prolegomena*. Bloomington: Indiana University Press.

_____. 1992. *The Concept of Time*. Cambridge: Basil Blackwell.

_____. 1993a. *Basic Writings: From Being and Time (1927) to The Task of Thinking (1964)* D. F. Krell (ed.) San Francisco: Harper and Row.

_____. 1993b. *Basic Concepts*. Bloomington: Indiana University Press.

Hekman, S. 1990. 'Hermeneutics and the Crisis of Social Theory: A Critique of Giddens' Epistemology', in J. Clark, C. Mogdil and S. Mogdil (eds) *Consensus and Controversy: Anthony Giddens*. London: Falmer Press, 155–65.

Held, D. 1980. *Introduction to Critical Theory: Horkheimer to Habermas*, London: Hutchinson.

———. 1982. 'Crisis Tendencies, Legitimation, and the State', in J. B. Thompson and D. Held (eds) *Habermas: Critical Debates*. London: Macmillan, 181–95.

———. 1987. *Models of Democracy*. Cambridge: Polity Press.

———. 1989a. *Political Theory and the Modern State*. Cambridge: Polity Press.

———. 1989b. 'Citizenship and Autonomy', in D. Held and J. B. Thompson (eds) *Social Theory of Modern Societies: Anthony Giddens and His Critics*. Cambridge: Cambridge University Press, 162–84.

Held, D. and Thompson, J. B. (eds) 1989a. *Social Theory of Modern Societies: Anthony Giddens and His Critics*. Cambridge: Cambridge University Press.

Held, D. and Thompson, J. B. 1989b. 'Editors' Introduction', in D. Held and J. B. Thompson (eds) *Social Theory of Modern Societies: Anthony Giddens and His Critics*. Cambridge: Cambridge University Press, 1–18.

Held, D., McGrew, A., Goldblatt, D. and Perraton, J. 1999. *Global Transformations*. Cambridge: Polity Press.

Heller, A. 1976. *The Theory of Need in Marx*. London: Allison & Busby.

———. 1978. 'The Positivist Dispute as a Turning Point in German Post-War Theory', *New German Critique* 15: 49–56.

———. 1982. 'Habermas and Marxism', in J. B. Thompson and D. Held (eds) *Habermas: Critical Debates*. London: Macmillan, 21–41.

———. 1984a. *A Radical Philosophy*. New York: Basil Blackwell.

———. 1984b. *Everyday Life*. London: Routledge & Kegan Paul.

———. 1984c. 'Marx and Modernity', *Thesis Eleven* 8: 44–58.

———. 1985. *The Power of Shame: A Rational Perspective*. London: Routledge & Kegan Paul.

Heller, A., and Feher, F. (1988) *The Postmodern Political Condition*. Cambridge: Polity Press.

Hennis, W. 1988. *Max Weber: Essays in Reconstruction*. London: Allen and Unwin.

Henrich, D. 1992. 'The Origins of the Theory of the Subject', in A. Honneth, T. McCarthy, C. Offe and A. Wellmer (eds) *Philosophical Interventions in the Unfinished Project of Enlightenment*. Cambridge, MA: MIT Press, 29–87.

Heritage, J. 1984. *Garfinkel and Ethnomethodology*. Cambridge: Polity Press.

———. 1987. 'Ethnomethodology', A. Giddens and J. H. Turner (ed.) *Social Theory Today*. Cambridge: Polity Press, 224–72.

Hesse, M. 1982. 'Science and Objectivity', in J. B. Thompson and D. Held (eds) *Habermas: Critical Debates*. London: Macmillan, 98–115.

Hirst, P. 1982. 'The Social Theory of Anthony Giddens: a New Syncretism.' *Theory, Culture and Society* 1 (2): 78–82.

Hohendahl, P. U. 1979 'Critical Theory, Public Sphere and Culture. Jürgen Habermas and His Critics' *New German Critique* 16: 89–118.

———. 1985. 'The Dialectic of the Enlightenment Revisited: Habermas' Critique of the Frankfurt School', *New German Critique* 35: 3–26.

———. 1991. *Reappraisals, Shifting Alignments in Postwar Critical Theory*. Ithaca, NY: Cornell University Press.

Holub, R. C. 1991. *Jürgen Habermas: Critic in the Public Sphere*. London: Routledge.

Honneth, A. 1985. 'An Aversion Against the Universal: A Commentary on Lyotard's Postmodern Condition', *Theory, Culture and Society* 2 (3): 147–57.

———. 1991. *The Critique of Power: Reflective Stages in a Critical Social Theory*. Cambridge, MA: MIT Press.

———. 1993. 'Conceptions of 'Civil Society', *Radical Philosophy* 64: 19–22.

———. 1994. 'The Social Dynamics of Disrespect: On the Location of Critical Theory Today', *Constellations* 1: 255–69.

_____. 1995a. *The Struggle for Recognition: The Moral Grammar of Social Conflicts.* Cambridge: Polity Press.

_____. 1995b. *The Fragmented World of the Social: Essays in Social and Political Philosophy* C. W. Wright (ed.) Albany: State University of New York Press.

_____. 1995c. 'The Other of Justice: Habermas and the Ethical Challenge of Postmodernism', in S. K. White (ed.) *The Cambridge Companion to Habermas.* Cambridge: Cambridge University Press, 289–323.

_____. 1996. 'Pathologies of the Social: The Past and Present of Social Philosophy', in D. Rasmussen (ed.) *The Handbook of Critical Theory.* Oxford: Blackwell, 369–96.

_____. 2007. *Disrespect.* Cambridge: Polity Press.

_____. 2008. *Reification: A New Look at an Old Idea.* Oxford: Oxford University Press.

_____. 2009. *Pathologies of Reason,* New York: Columbia University Press.

_____. 2012. *The I in We.* Cambridge: Polity Press.

_____. 2014. *Freedom's Right – the Social Foundations of Democratic Life.* Cambridge: Polity Press.

Honneth, A., and Joas, H. 1988. *Social Action and Human Nature.* New York: Cambridge University Press.

Honneth, A., McCarthy, T., Offe, C., Wellmer, A. (eds) 1992a. *Cultural-Political Interventions in the Unfinished Project of Enlightenment.* Cambridge, MA: MIT Press.

_____. (eds) 1992b. *Philosophical Interventions in the Unfinished Project of Enlightenment.* Cambridge, MA: MIT Press.

Honneth, A., and Hartman, M. 2012 'Paradoxes of Capitalist Modernization', in A. Honneth, *The I in We.* Cambridge: Polity Press, 169–90.

Horkheimer, M. 1972. *Critical Theory; Selected Essays.* New York: Herder and Herder.

_____. 1978. 'The End of Reason', in A. Arato and E. Gebhardt (eds) *The Essential Frankfurt School Reader.* Oxford: Basil Blackwell, 26–48.

_____. 1985a. *Critique of Instrumental Reason: Lectures and Essays Since the End of World War II.* New York: Continuum.

_____. 1985b. *Eclipse of Reason.* New York: Continuum.

_____. 1993. *Between Philosophy and Social Science: Selected Early Writings.* Cambridge, MA: MIT Press.

Horkheimer, M., and Adorno, T. 1972. *Dialectic of Enlightenment.* New York: Herder and Herder.

How, A. 1995. *The Habermas-Gadamer Debate and the Nature of the Social: Back to Bedrock.* Brookfield: Avebury.

Howard, D. 1988. *The Marxian Legacy.* Basingstoke: Macmillan.

Hoy, D. C. 1996. 'Splitting the Difference: Habermas's Critique of Derrida', in M. Passerin d'Entrèves and S. Benhabib (eds) *Habermas and the Unfinished Project of Modernity: Critical Essays on The Philosophical Discourse of Modernity.* Cambridge: Polity Press, 124–46.

Hoy, D. C., and McCarthy, T. 1994. *Critical Theory.* Cambridge, MA: Blackwell.

Husserl, E. 1960. *Cartesian Meditations.* The Hague: Nijhof.

_____. 1964. *The Phenomenology of Internal Time Consciousness.* The Hague: Nijhof.

_____. 1970. *The Crisis of European Science and Transcendental Phenomenology.* Evanston, IL: Northwestern University.

Hutton, W., and Giddens, A. (eds) (2000) *On the Edge – Living with Global Capitalism.* London: Vintage.

Ingram, D. 1987. *Habermas and the Dialectic of Reason.* New Haven, CT: Yale University Press.

_____. 1990. *Critical Theory and Philosophy.* New York: Paragon House.

_____. 1994. 'Foucault and Habermas on the Subject of Reason', G. Gutting (ed.) *The Cambridge Companion to Foucault.* Cambridge: Cambridge University Press: 215–61.

_____. 1996. 'The Subject of Justice in Postmodern Discourse: Aesthetic Judgement and Political Rationality', in M. Passerin d'Entrèves and S. Benhabib (eds) *Habermas and the Unfinished Project of Modernity: Critical Essays on The Philosophical Discourse of Modernity.* Cambridge: Polity Press, 269–302.

Jacoby, R. 1981. *Dialectic of Defeat: Contours of Western Marxism.* Cambridge: Cambridge University Press.

Jamieson, L. 1999. 'Intimacy Transformed? A Critical Look at the "Pure Relationship"' *Sociology* 33: 477–94.

Jaspers, K. 1953. *The Origin and Goal of History*. London: Routledge and Kegan Paul.

Jay, M. 1973. *The Dialectical Imagination: A History of the Frankfurt School and the Institute of Social Research, 1923–1950*. London: Heinemann Educational.

_____. 1984a. *Marxism and Totality: The Adventures of a Concept from Lukács to Habermas*. Berkeley: University of California Press.

_____. 1984b. *Adorno*. London: Fontana.

_____. 1984c. 'Habermas and Modernism' *Praxis International* 4: 1–14.

_____. 1985. *Permanent Exiles: Essays on the Intellectual Migration from Germany to America*. New York: Columbia University Press.

_____. 1988. *Fin-de-siècle Socialism and Other Essays*. New York: Routledge.

_____. 1993a. *Downcast Eyes: The Denigration of Vision in Twentieth-Century French Thought*. Berkeley: University of California Press.

_____. 1993b. *Force Fields: Between Intellectual History and Cultural Critique*. New York: Routledge.

_____. 1996. 'Urban Flights: The Institute of Social Research between Frankfurt and New York', in D. Rasmussen (ed.) *The Handbook of Critical Theory*. Oxford: Blackwell, 39–56.

_____. 1998. *Cultural Semantics: Keywords of Our Time*. Amherst: University of Massachusetts Press.

Jenkins, R. 1996. *Social Identity*. London: Routledge.

Jessop, B. 1989 'Capitalism, Nation-States and Surveillance', in D. Held and J. B. Thompson (eds) *Social Theory of Modern Societies: Anthony Giddens and His Critics*. Cambridge: Cambridge University Press, 103–28.

Joas, H. 1985. *G. H. Mead, A Contemporary Re-examination of His Thought*. Cambridge: Polity Press.

_____. 1990. 'Giddens' Critique of Functionalism', in J. Clark, C. Mogdil and S. Mogdil (eds) *Consensus and Controversy: Anthony Giddens*. London: Falmer Press, 91–102.

_____. 1993. *Pragmatism and Social Theory*. Chicago: University of Chicago Press.

_____. 1996. *The Creativity of Action*. Chicago: University of Chicago Press.

Joas, H., and Honneth, A. (eds) 1991. *Communicative Action: Essays on Jürgen Habermas's The Theory of Communicative Action*. Cambridge, MA: MIT Press.

Joas, H., and Knöbl, W. 2009. *Social Theory: Twenty Introductory Lectures*, Cambridge: Cambridge University Press.

Kant, I. 1956. *Critique of Pure Reason*. London: Macmillan.

_____. 1987. *Critique of Judgment*. Indianapolis, IN: Hackett.

_____. 1993. *Groundwork of the Metaphysics of Morals*. Indianapolis, IN: Hackett.

_____. 1997. *Critique of Practical Reason*. Cambridge: Cambridge University Press.

Keane, J. 1975. 'On Tools and Language: Habermas on Work and Interaction', *New German Critique* 6: 82–100.

Kearney, R. 1999. *Poetics of Imagining: Modern and Postmodern*. New York: Fordham University Press.

Keat, R. 1981. *The Politics of Social Theory: Habermas, Freud and the Critique of Positivism*. Oxford: Basil Blackwell.

Kellner, D., and Roderick, R. 1981. 'Recent Literature on Critical Theory', *New German Critique* 23: 141–70.

Kellner, D. 1989. *Critical Theory, Marxism, and Modernity*. Baltimore: Johns Hopkins University Press.

Kiely, R. 2005. *The Clash of Globalisations: Neo-liberalism, the Third Way, and Anti-Globalisation*. Leiden: Brill.

Kilminster, R. 1979. *Praxis and Method: A Sociological Dialogue with Lukács, Gramsci and the Early Frankfurt School*. London: Routledge and Kegan Paul.

_____. 1991. 'Structuration Theory as a World-View', in C. G. A. Bryant and D. Jary (eds) *Giddens' Theory of Structuration: A Critical Appreciation*, London: Routledge, 74–115.

Knöbl, W. 2011 'Contingency and Modernity in the Thought of J. P. Arnason', *European Journal of Social Theory* 14 (1): 9–22.

Knodt, E. M. 1994. 'Toward a Non-Foundationalist Epistemology: The Habermas/Luhmann Controversy Revisited', *New German Critique* 61: 77–100.

Kohlberg, L. 1981. *The Philosophy of Moral Development: Moral Stages and the Idea of Justice*. San Fransisco: Harper and Row.

Kompridis, N. 1994. 'On World Disclosure: Heidegger, Habermas and Dewey', *Thesis Eleven* 37: 29–45.

Korsch, K. 1970. *Marxism and Philosophy*. London: New Left Books.

Kortian, G. 1980. *Metacritique: The Philosophical Argument of Jürgen Habermas*. Cambridge: Cambridge University Press.

Kosik, K. 1967. 'The Individual and History', in N. Lobkowicz (ed.) *Marx and the Western World*. Indianapolis, IN: Notre Dame Press, 177–90.

———. 1976. *Dialectics of the Concrete*. Dordrecht: D. Reidel.

Krüger, H-P. 1991. 'Communicative Action or the Model of Communication for Society as a Whole', in A. Honneth and H. Joas (eds) *Communicative Action*, Cambridge: Polity Press, 140–64.

Kuhn, T. 1970. *The Structure of Scientific Revolutions*. Chicago: University of Chicago Press.

Kunneman, H. 1990. 'Some Critical Remarks on Habermas's Analysis of Science and Technology', *Theory, Culture and Society* 7: 117–25.

Laing, R. D. 1965. *The Divided Self.* Harmondsworth: Pelican Books.

Larrain, J. 1986. *A Reconstruction of Historical Materialism*. London: Allen & Unwin.

Lash, S. 'Reflexivity and its Doubles: Structure, Aesthetics, Community', U. Beck, A. Giddens and S. Lash. 1994. *Reflexive Modernization: Politics, Tradition and Aesthetics in the Modern Social Order.* Cambridge: Polity Press, 110–73.

Lefebvre, H. 1968. *The Sociology of Marx*. Harmondsworth: Penguin.

Lefort, C. 1978. 'From One Vision of History to Another', *Social Research* 45: 615–66.

———. 1986. *The Political Forms of Modern Society: Bureaucracy, Democracy, Totalitarianism*. Cambridge: Polity Press.

———. 1988. *Democracy and Political Theory:* Cambridge: Polity Press.

Lepenies, W. 1971. 'Anthropology and Social Criticism: A View on the Controversy between Arnold Gehlen and Jürgen Habermas', *The Human Context* 3: 205–25.

Livesay, J. 1985a. 'Normative Grounding and Praxis: Habermas, Giddens, and a Contradiction within Critical Theory', *Sociological Theory* 3: 66–76.

———. 1985b. 'Habermas, Narcissism, and Status', *Telos* 64: 75–90.

———. 1989. 'Structuration Theory and the Unacknowledged Conditions of Action', *Theory, Culture and Society* 6: 263–92.

Lobkowicz, N. 1967. *Theory and Practice: History of a Concept from Aristotle to Marx*. Notre Dame: University of Notre Dame Press.

Lockwood, D. 'Social Integration and System Integration', in G. Z. Zollachan and W. Hirst (eds) *Explorations in Social Change*. London: Routledge, 244–56.

Love, N. S. 1995. 'What's Left of Marx?', in S. K. White (ed.) *The Cambridge Companion to Habermas*. Cambridge: Cambridge University Press, 46–66.

Löwith, K. 1982. *Max Weber and Karl Marx*. London: George Allen & Unwin.

Loyal, S. 2003 *The Sociology of Anthony Giddens*. London: Pluto Press.

Luhmann, N. 1979. *Trust and Power*. Chichester: Wiley.

———. 1982. *The Differentiation of Society*. New York: Columbia University Press.

———. 1985. *A Sociological Theory of Law*. London: Routledge and Kegan Paul.

———. 1986. *Love as Passion: The Codification of Intimacy*. Cambridge: Polity Press.

———. 1989. *Ecological Communication*. Cambridge: Polity Press.

———. 1992. 'The Direction of Evolution', in H. Haferkamp and N. Smelser (eds) *Social Change and Modernity*. Berkeley: University of California Press, 279–93.

———. 1993. *Risk: a Sociological Theory*. New York: A. de Gruyter.

———. 1995. *Social Systems*. Standford, CA: Stanford University Press.

Lukács, G. 1971. *History and Class Consciousness*. London: Merlin.

_____. 1975. *The Young Hegel: Studies in the Relations between Dialectics and Economics*. London: Merlin.

_____. 1978. *The Ontology of Social Being*. London: Merlin.

Lukes, S. 1973. *Emile Durkheim*. Harmondsworth: Penguin Books.

_____. 1974, *Power: A Radical View*. London: Macmillan.

_____. 1982. 'Of Gods and Demons: Habermas and Practical Reason', in J. B. Thompson and D. Held (eds) *Habermas: Critical Debates*. London: Macmillan, 134–48.

Lyotard, J. F. 1984. *The Postmodern Condition: A Report on Knowledge*. Minneapolis: University of Minnesota Press.

Mann, M. 1986. *The Sources of Social Power, Vol. 1*. Cambridge: Cambridge University Press.

Marcuse, H. 1958. *Soviet Marxism a Critical Analysis*. Harmondsworth: Penguin.

_____. 1964. *One-Dimensional Man*. London: Routledge and Kegan Paul.

_____. 1966. *Eros and Civilization: A Philosophical Inquiry into Freud*. Boston: Beacon Press.

_____. 1967. *Reason and Revolution*. London: Routledge and Kegan Paul.

_____. 1968. *Negations: Essays in Critical Theory*. Boston: Beacon Press.

_____. 1969a. *An Essay on Liberation*. Boston: Beacon Press.

_____. 1969b. 'Contributions to a Phenomenology of Historical Materialism (1928)', *Telos* 4: 3–34

_____. 1970. *Five Lectures: Psychoanalysis, Politics and Utopia*. Allen Lane: London.

_____. 1973. 'On the Philosophical Foundations of the Concept of Labour in Economics', *Telos* 16.

_____. 1976. 'On the Problem of the Dialectic', *Telos* 27: 12–39.

_____. 1978. *The Aesthetic Dimension: Toward a Critique of Marxist Aesthetics*. Boston: Beacon Press.

_____. 1983. *From Luther to Popper*. London: Verso.

_____. 1987. *Hegel's Ontology and the Theory of Historicity*. Cambridge, MA: MIT Press.

_____. 1998. *Technology, War, and Fascism* D. Kellner (ed.). London: Routledge.

Márkus, G. 1978. *Marxism and Anthropology: The Concept of 'Human Essence' in the Philosophy of Marx*. Assen: Van Gorcum.

_____. 1980. 'Four Forms of Critical Theory – Some Theses on Marx's Development', *Thesis Eleven* 1: 78–93.

_____. 1982. 'Alienation and Reification in Marx and Lukács', *Thesis Eleven* 5/6: 139–61.

_____. 1986a. *Language and Production a Critique of the Paradigms*. Dordrecht: Reidel.

_____. 1986b. 'Praxis and Poiesis: Beyond the Dichotomy', *Thesis Eleven* 15: 30–47.

_____. 1993. 'György Markus interviewed by Anthony Uhlmann', *Active: Reactive*, March, 38–44.

Marshall, T. H. 1991. *Citizenship and Social Class and Other Essays*. London: Pluto Press.

Marx, K. 1970. *A Contribution to the Critique of Political Economy*. Moscow: Progress Publishers.

_____. 1973. *Grundrisse: Foundations of the Critique of Political Economy (Rough Draft)*. Harmondsworth: Penguin Books.

_____. 1976. *Capital: A Critique of Political Economy, Volume One*. Harmondsworth: Penguin Books.

_____. 1977a. *Economic and Philosophical Manuscripts of 1844*. Moscow: Progress Publishers.

_____. 1977b. 'Theses on Feuerbach', in D. McLellan (ed.) *Karl Marx: Selected Writings*. Oxford: Oxford University Press, 156–58

_____. 1977c. 'On the Jewish Question', in D. McLellan (ed.) *Karl Marx: Selected Writings*. Oxford: Oxford University Press, 39–62

_____. 1977d. 'The Eighteenth Brumaire of Louis Bonaparte', in D. McLellan (ed.) *Karl Marx: Selected Writings*. Oxford: Oxford University Press, 300–25.

Marx, K., and Engels, F. 1976. *The German Ideology*. Moscow: Progress Publishers.

_____. 1977. 'The Communist Manifesto', in D. McLellan (ed.) *Karl Marx: Selected Writings*. Oxford: Oxford University Press, 221–47.

Matustik, M. J. 1990. 'Jürgen Habermas at 60', *Philosophy and Social Criticism* 16: 61–80.

Matustík, M. J. 1993a. *Postnational Identity: Critical Theory and Existential Philosophy in Habermas, Kierkegaard, and Havel*. New York: Guilford Press.

Matustik, M. J. 1993b. 'Post-National Identity: Habermas, Kierkegaard and Havel', *Thesis Eleven* 34: 89–103.

_____. 1995. 'Derrida and Habermas on the Aporia of the Politics of Identity and Difference: Towards Radical Democratic Multiculturalism', *Constellations* 1: 383–98.

McCarthy, T. 1978. *The Critical Theory of Jürgen Habermas*. London: Hutchinson.

_____. 1982. 'Rationality and Relativism: Habermas's 'Overcoming' of Hermeneutics', in J. B. Thompson and D. Held (eds) *Habermas: Critical Debates*. London: Macmillan, 57–78.

_____. 1984a. 'Translator's Introduction', in Habermas, J. *The Theory of Communicative Action*. Boston: Beacon Press, v–xxxvii.

_____. 1984b. 'Reflections on Rationalization in the Theory of Communicative Action', *Praxis International* 4: 177–91.

_____. 1985. 'Complexity and Democracy, or the Seducements of Systems Theory', *New German Critique* 45: 27–53.

_____. 1991. *Ideals and Illusions: On Reconstruction and Deconstruction in Contemporary Critical Theory*. Cambridge, MA: MIT Press.

_____. 1998. 'Legitimacy and Diversity: Dialectical Reflections on Analytical Distinctions', in M. Rosenfeld and A. Arato (eds) 1998. *Habermas on Law and Democracy: Critical Exchanges*. Berkeley: University of California Press, 115–53.

_____. 2002 'On Reconciling Cosmopolitan Unity and National Diversity', in P. de Greiff and C. Cronin (eds) *Global Justice and Transnational Politics*. Cambridge, MA: MIT Press, 235–74.

McIntosh, D. 1994. 'Language, Self, and Lifeworld in Habermas's Theory of Communicative Action', *Theory and Society* 23: 1–33.

McLennan, G. 1984 'Critical or Positive Theory? A Comment on the Status of Anthony Giddens' Social Theory', *Theory, Culture and Society* 2 (2): 123–29.

_____. 1990. 'The Temporal and the Temporizing in Structuration Theory', in J. Clark, C. Mogdil and S. Mogdil (eds) *Consensus and Controversy: Anthony Giddens*. London: Falmer Press, 131–39.

_____. 1999. 'The Ways Ahead.' *History of the Human Sciences* 12: 147–55.

Mead, G. H. 1932. *The Philosophy of the Present*. Chicago: University of Chicago Press.

_____. 1934. *Mind, Self and Society*. Chicago: University of Chicago Press.

_____. 1938. *The Philosophy of the Act*. Chicago: University of Chicago Press.

Meehan, J. 1994. 'Autonomy, Recognition and Respect: Habermas, Benjamin and Honneth', *Constellations* 1: 270–85.

Meehan, J. (ed.) 1995. *Feminists Read Habermas: Gendering the Subject of Discourse*. New York: Routledge.

Menke, C. 1996. 'Critical Theory and Tragic Knowledge', in D. Rasmussen (ed.) *The Handbook of Critical Theory*. Oxford: Blackwell, 57–73.

Merleau-Ponty, M. 1963. *The Structure of Behaviour*. Boston: Beacon Press.

_____. 1964. *Signs*. Evanston, IL: Northwestern University Press.

_____. 1968. *The Visible and the Invisible: Followed by Working Notes* C. Lefort (ed.) Evanston, IL: Northwestern University Press.

_____. 1969. *Humanism and Terror: An Essay on the Communist Problem*. Boston: Beacon Press.

_____. 1973. *Adventures of the Dialectic*. Evanston, IL: Northwestern University Press.

Mestrovic, S. G. 1998. *Anthony Giddens: The Last Modernist*. London; New York: Routledge.

Misgeld, D. 1976. 'Critical Theory and Hermeneutics: The Debate between Habermas and Gadamer', in J. O'Neill (ed.) *On Critical Theory*. New York: Seabury Press, 164–83.

_____. 1985. 'Critical Hermeneutics versus NeoParsonianism?', *New German Critique* 35: 55–82.

Moon, D. J. 1995. 'Practical Discourse and Communicative Ethics', in S. K. White (ed.) *The Cambridge Companion to Habermas*. Cambridge: Cambridge University Press, 143–64.

Morris, M. 1998. 'Capitalist Society and Its Real Abstractions: The Critique of Reification in Habermas's Social Theory', *Rethinking Marxism* 10: 27–50.

Mouzelis, N. 1992. 'Social and System Integration: Habermas' View', *The British Journal of Sociology* 43: 267–88.

_____. 1997. 'Social and System Integration: Lockwood, Habermas, Giddens', *Sociology* 31: 119.

Muellner-Vollner, K. (ed.) 1985. *The Hermeneutics Reader.* Oxford: Basil Blackwell.

Münch, R. 'Parsonian Theory Today: In Search of a New Synthesis', in A. Giddens and J. H. Turner (eds) 1987. *Social Theory Today.* Cambridge: Polity Press, 116–55.

Murgatoyd, L. 1989. 'Only Half the Story: Some Blinkering Effects of "Malestream" Sociology', in D. Held and J. B. Thompson (eds) *Social Theory of Modern Societies: Anthony Giddens and His Critics.* Cambridge: Cambridge University Press, 147–61.

Murphy, P. 2012. *The Collective Imagination – the Creative Spirit of Free Societies.* Ashgate: Farnham.

Neocleous, M. 1999. 'Radical Conservatism, or, the Conservatism of Radicals: Giddens, Blair and the Politics of Reaction', *Radical Philosophy* 93: 24–34.

Nielsen, K. 1994. 'How to Proceed in Philosophy: Remarks after Habermas', *Thesis Eleven* 37: 10–28.

Norris, C. 1996. 'Deconstruction, Postmodernism and Philosophy: Habermas on Derrida', in M. Passerin d'Entrèves and S. Benhabib (eds) *Habermas and the Unfinished Project of Modernity: Critical Essays on The Philosophical Discourse of Modernity.* Cambridge: Polity Press, 97–123.

Offe, C. 1984. *Contradictions of the Welfare State.* Cambridge, MA: MIT Press.

_____. 1985. *Disorganized Capitalism: Contemporary Transformations of Work and Politics.* Cambridge: Polity Press.

_____. 1996. *Modernity and the State: East, West.* Cambridge: Polity Press.

O'Neill, J. (ed.) 1976. *On Critical Theory.* New York: Seabury Press.

_____. (ed.) 1996. *Hegel's Dialectic of Desire and Recognition: Texts and Commentary.* Albany: State University of New York Press.

Ottmann, H. 1982. 'Cognitive Interests and Self-Reflection', J. B. Thompson and D. Held (eds) *Habermas: Critical Debates.* London: Macmillan, 79–97.

Outhwaite, W. 1975. *Understanding Social Life.* London: George Allen and Unwin.

_____. 1983. *Concept Formation in Social Science.* London: Routledge and Kegan Paul.

_____. 1987. *New Philosophies of Social Sciences.* New York: St. Martin's Press.

_____. 1990. 'Agency and Structure', in J. Clark, C. Mogdil and S. Mogdil (eds) *Consensus and Controversy: Anthony Giddens.* London: Falmer Press, 63–72.

_____. 1994. *Habermas: A Critical Introduction.* Cambridge: Polity Press.

_____. 1996. 'General Introduction', in W. Outhwaite (ed.) *The Habermas Reader.* Cambridge: Polity Press, 1–22.

Owen, D., and Ashenden, S. 1999. *Foucault Contra Habermas: Recasting the Dialogue between Genealogy and Critical Theory.* London: Sage.

Parsons, T. 1949. *The Structure of Social Action Writers.* New York: Free Press.

_____. 1951. *The Social System.* Glencoe, IL: Free Press.

Parsons, T., and Shils, E. A. 1951. *Toward a General Theory of Action.* Cambridge, MA: Harvard University Press.

Parsons, T., Bales, R. F., and Shils, E. A. 1953. *Working Papers in the Theory of Action.* Glencoe, IL: Free Press.

Parsons, T. 1960. *Structure and Process in Modern Societies.* Glencoe, IL: Free Press.

_____. 1966. *Societies: Evolutionary and Comparative Perspectives.* Englewood Cliffs, NJ: Prentice-Hall.

_____. 1971. *The System of Modern Societies.* Englewood Cliffs, NJ: Prentice-Hall.

_____. 1991. *The Early Essays* C. Camic (ed.). Chicago: University of Chicago Press.

Passerin d'Entrèves, M. and Benhabib, S. (eds) 1996. *Habermas and the Unfinished Project of Modernity: Critical Essays on the Philosophical Discourse of Modernity.* Cambridge: Polity Press.

Pensky, M. 1995. 'Universalism and the Situated Critic', in S. K. White (ed.) *The Cambridge Companion to Habermas.* Cambridge: Cambridge University Press, 67–94.

Petrovic, G. 1967. *Marx in the Mid-Twentieth Century.* New York: Anchor Books.

Piaget, J. 1985. *The Equilibration of Cognitive Structures: The Central Problem of Intellectual Development.* Chicago: University of Chicago.

Piccone, P. 1983. *Italian Marxism*. Berkeley: University of California Press.

Poggi, G. 1990. 'Anthony Giddens and "The Classics" ', in J. Clark, C. Mogdil and S. Mogdil (eds) *Consensus and Controversy: Anthony Giddens*. London: Falmer Press, 11–20.

Polanyi, K. 1957. *The Great Transformation*. Boston: Beacon Press.

Popper, K. R. 1976A. 'The Logic of the Social Sciences', in D. Frisby (ed.) *The Positivist Dispute in German Sociology*. London: Heinemann, 87–104.

_____. 1976b. 'Reason or Revolution?', in D. Frisby (ed.) *The Positivist Dispute in German Sociology*. London: Heinemann, 288–300.

Poster, M. 1984. *Foucault, Marxism and History*. Cambridge: Polity Press.

Postone, M. 1992. 'Political Theory and Historical Analysis', in C. Calhoun (ed.) *Habermas and the Public Sphere*. Cambridge, MA: MIT Press, 164–77.

_____. 1993. *Time, Labor, and Social Domination: A Reinterpretation of Marx's Critical Theory*. Cambridge: Cambridge University Press.

Pred, A. 1990. 'Context and Bodies in Flux: Some Comments on Space and Time in the Writings of A. Giddens', in J. Clark, C. Mogdil and S. Mogdil (eds) *Consensus and Controversy: Anthony Giddens*. London: Falmer Press, 117–29.

Pusey, M. 1987. *Jürgen Habermas*. London: Tavistock Publications.

Raffel, S. 1992. *Habermas, Lyotard and the Concept of Justice*. Basingstoke, Hampshire: Macmillan Press.

Rakovski, M. 1978. *Towards an East European Marxism*. New York: St. Martins Press.

Rasmussen, D. M. 1990. *Reading Habermas*. Cambridge, MA: Blackwell.

_____. 1996a. 'How Is Valid Law Possible? A Review of Faktizitat und Geltung by Jurgen Habermas', in M. Deflem (ed.) *Habermas, Modernity, and Law*. London: Sage Publications, 21–44.

_____. 1996b. 'Critical Theory and Philosophy', in D. Rasmussen (ed.) *The Handbook of Critical Theory*. Oxford: Blackwell, 11–38.

Reckwitz, A. 2002. 'Towards a Theory of Social Practice: A Development in Culturalist Studies', *European Journal of Social Theory* 5: 243–63.

Rehg, W. 1994. *Insight and Solidarity: A Study in the Discourse Ethics of Jürgen Habermas*. Berkeley: University of California Press.

Reid, H. G., and Yanarella, E. I. 1977. 'Critical Political Theory and Moral Development: On Kohlberg, Hampden-Turner, and Habermas', *Theory and Society* 4: 505–41.

Reijen, W. van. 1990. 'Philosophical-Political Polytheism: Habermas versus Lyotard', *Theory, Culture and Society* 7: 95–103.

Richters, A. 1988. 'Modernity-Postmodernity Controversies: Habermas and Foucault', *Theory, Culture and Society* 5: 611–43.

Rigby, S. 1987. *Marxism and History*. Manchester: Manchester University Press.

Roberts, J. 1988. *German Philosophy*. Cambridge: Polity Press.

Robertson, R. 1992. 'Globality and Modernity', *Theory, Culture and Society* 9: 153–61.

Rockmore, T. 1989. *Habermas on Historical Materialism*. Bloomington: Indiana University Press.

Roderick, R. 1986. *Habermas and the Foundations of Critical Theory*. New York: St. Martin's Press.

Rorty, R. 1984. 'Habermas and Lyotard on Post-Modernity', *Praxis International* 4: 32–44.

Rosa, H. 2013. *Social Acceleration: A New Theory of Modernity*. New York: Columbia University Press.

Rose, G. 1978. *The Melancholy Science: An Introduction to the Thought of Theodor W. Adorno*. London: Macmillan.

Rose, N. 1999. 'Inventiveness in Politics', *Economy and Society* 28: 467–93.

Rosenfeld, M., and Arato, A. (eds) 1998. *Habermas on Law and Democracy: Critical Exchanges*. Berkeley: University of California Press.

Rundell, J. F. 1987. *Origins of Modernity: The Origins of Modern Social Theory from Kant to Hegel to Marx*. Cambridge: Polity Press.

Rundell, J. 1989. 'From the Shores of Reason to the Horizon of Meaning: Some Remarks on Habermas' and Castoriadis' Theories of Culture', *Thesis Eleven* 22: 5–24.

_____. 1995. 'Gadamer and the Circles of Hermeneutics', in D. Roberts (ed.) *Reconstructing Theory: Gadamer, Habermas, Luhmann*. Carlton: Melbourne University Press, 10–38.

Rustin, M. 1995. 'The Future of Post-Socialism', *Radical Philosophy* 74: 17–27.

Sanderson, S. 1990. *Social Evolutionism: A Critical History*. Cambridge, MA: Blackwell.

Sartre, J. P. 1963. *The Problem of Method*. London: Methuen.

_____. 1976. *Critique of Dialectical Reason*. London: New Left Books.

Sayer, D. 1987. *The Violence of Abstraction: The Analytic Foundations of Historical Materialism*. Oxford: Basil Blackwell.

Sayer. D. 1990. 'Reinventing the Wheel: A. Giddens, Karl Marx and Social Change', in J. Clark, C. Mogdil and S. Mogdil (eds) *Consensus and Controversy: Anthony Giddens*. London: Falmer Press, 235–50.

Sayer, D. 1991. *Capitalism and Modernity: An Excursus on Marx and Weber*. London; New York: Routledge.

Saunders, P. 'Space, Urbanism and the Created Environment', in D. Held and J. B. Thompson (eds) 1989b. *Social Theory of Modern Societies: Anthony Giddens and His Critics*. Cambridge: Cambridge University Press, 215–34.

Schatzki, T. R. 1997. 'Practices and Actions: A Wittgensteinian Critique of Bourdieu and Giddens', *Philosophy of the Social Sciences* 27: 283–308.

_____. 2001 'Introduction: Practice Theory', in T. Schatzki, K Knorr Cetina and E. von Savigny (eds) *The Practice Turn in Contemporary Theory*. London: Routledge, 1–14.

Scheuerman, W. E. 1999. 'Between Radicalism and Resignation: Democratic Theory in Habermas's *Between Facts and Norms*', in P. Dews (ed.) *Habermas: A Critical Reader*. Oxford: Blackwell, 153–77.

Schluchter, W. 1981 *The Rise of Western Rationalism*. Berkeley: University of California Press.

Schmid, M. 1982. 'Habermas' Theory of Social Evolution', in J. B. Thompson and D. Held (eds) *Habermas: Critical Debates*. London: Macmillan Press, 162–80.

Schmidt, A. 1973. *The Concept of Nature in Marx*. London: New Left Books.

_____. 1983. *History and Structure: An Essay on Hegelian Marxist and Structuralist Theories of History*. Cambridge, MA: MIT Press.

Schmidt, J. 1979. 'Offensive Critical Theory? Reply to Honneth', *Telos* 39: 62–76.

Schmidt, V. 2010. 'Modernity and Diversity: Reflections on the Controversy between Modernization Theory and Multiple Modernities', *Social Science Information* 49 (4): 511–38.

Schmitt, C. 2007. *The Concept of the Political: Expanded Edition*. Chicago: University of Chicago Press.

Schnädelbach, H. 1991. 'The Transformation of Critical Theory', in A. Honneth and H. Joas (eds) *Communicative Action*. Cambridge: Polity Press, 7–22.

Schutz, A. 1967. *The Phenomenology of the Social World*. Evanston, IL: Northwestern University Press.

Schutz, A., and Luckmann, T. 1974. *The Structure of the Lifeworld*. London: Heinemann.

Schwinn, T. 1998. 'False Connections: Systems and Action Theories in Neofunctionalism and in Jurgen Habermas', *Sociological Theory* 16: 75–95.

Seel, M. 1991. 'The Two Meanings of "Communicative" Rationality: Remarks on Habermas's Critique of a Plural Concept of Reason', in A. Honneth and H. Joas (eds) *Communicative Action*. Cambridge: Polity Press, 36–48.

Seidman, S. 1983. *Liberalism and the Origins of European Social Theory*. Oxford: Blackwell.

_____. 1994. *Contested Knowledge: Social Theory in the Postmodern Era*. Oxford: Blackwell.

Sennett, R. 2006 *The Culture of the New Capitalism*. New Haven, CT: Yale University Press.

Sensat, J. 1979. *Habermas and Marxism: An Appraisal*. California: Sage Publications.

Sewell, W. H. 1992. 'A Theory of Structure: Duality, Agency and Transformation', *American Journal of Sociology* 98: 1–29.

_____. 2005. *Logics of History: Social Theory and Social Transformation*. Chicago: Chicago University Press.

Shaw, M. 'War and the Nation-State in Social Theory', in D. Held and J. B. Thompson (eds) 1989b. *Social Theory of Modern Societies: Anthony Giddens and His Critics*. Cambridge: Cambridge University Press, 129–46.

Shaw, W. H. 1978. *Marx's Theory of History*. London: Hutchinson.

Shelly, R. 1993. 'Habermas and the Normative Foundations of a Radical Politics', *Thesis Eleven* 35: 62–83.

Sica, A. 1991. 'The California-Massachusetts Strain in Structuration Theory', in C. G. A Bryant and Jary D. (eds) *Giddens' Theory of Structuration: A Critical Appreciation*. London: Routledge, 1–31.

Simmel, G. 1950. 'The Metropolis and Mental Life', in K. Wolff (ed.) *The Sociology of Georg Simmel*. New York: The Free Press, 409–24.

_____. 1990. *The Philosophy of Money*. London: Routledge.

Simon, J. 1994. 'Between Power and Knowledge: Habermas, Foucault and the Future of Legal Studies', *Law and Society Review* 28: 947.

Sitton, J. F. 1998. 'Disembodied Capitalism: Habermas's Conception of the Economy', *Sociological Forum* 13: 61–83.

Sixel, F. W. 1976. 'The Problem of Sense: Habermas v. Luhmann', in J. O'Neill (ed.) *On Critical Theory*. New York: Seabury Press, 184–204.

Smith, A. 1984. 'Two Theories of Historical Materialism', *Theory and Society* 13: 513–40.

Smith, D. 1982. '"Put Not Your Trust in Princes" – a Commentary upon Anthony Giddens and the Absolute State', *Theory, Culture and Society* 1: 93–99.

_____. 1998. 'Anthony Giddens and the Liberal Tradition', *The British Journal of Sociology* 49: 661–69.

Smith, N. H., and Deranty, J. P. (eds) 2012 *New Philosophies of Labour: Work and the Social Bond*. Leiden: Brill.

Smith, T. 1991. *The Role of Ethics in Social Theory: Essays from a Habermasian Perspective*. Albany: State University of New York Press.

Sohn-Rethel, A. 1978. *Intellectual and Manual Labour: A Critique of Epistemology*. London: Macmillan.

Soja, E. 1989. *Postmodern Geographies: The Reassertion of Space in Critical Social Theory*. London: Verso.

Spohn, W. 2001. 'Eisenstadt on Civilizations and Multiple Modernities', *European Journal of Social Theory* 4 (4): 499–508.

Stinchcombe, A. 1990. 'Milieu and Structure Updated: A Critique of the Theory of Structuration', in J. Clark, C. Mogdil and S. Mogdil (eds) *Consensus and Controversy: Anthony Giddens*. London: Falmer Press, 47–56.

Stones, R. 2001. 'Refusing the Realism-Structuration Divide', *European Journal of Social Theory*, 4 (2): 177–97.

_____. 2005. *Structuration Theory*. Houndsmills: Macmillan.

Strong, T. B., and Sposito, F. A. 1995. 'Habermas's Significant Other', in S. K. White (ed.) *The Cambridge Companion to Habermas*. Cambridge: Cambridge University Press, 263–88.

Strydom, P. 1987. 'Collective Learning: Habermas's Concessions and Their Theoretical Implications', *Philosophy and Social Criticism* 13: 265–81.

_____. 1990. 'Habermas and New Social Movements', *Telos* 85: 156–64.

_____. 1992. 'The Ontogenetic Fallacy: The Immanent Critique of Habermas's Developmental Logical Theory of Evolution', *Theory, Culture and Society* 9: 65–93.

_____. 1993. 'Sociocultural Evolution or the Social Evolution of Practical Reason?: Eder's Critique of Habermas', *Praxis International* 13: 304–22.

Susen, S. 2007. *The Foundations of the Social – between Critical Theory and Reflexive Sociology*. Oxford: Bardwell Press.

Swanson, G. E. 1992. 'Modernity and the Postmodern', *Theory, Culture and Society* 9: 147–51.

Taylor, C. 1975. *Hegel*. Cambridge: Cambridge University Press.

_____. 1989. *Sources of the Self: The Making of Modern Identity*. Cambridge: Cambridge University Press.

_____. 1991. 'Language and Society', in A. J. Honneth and H. Joas (eds) *Communicative Action*. Cambridge: Polity Press, 23–35.

_____. 1992. 'Inwardness and the Culture of Modernity', in A. Honneth, T. McCarthy, C. Offe and A. Wellmer (eds) *Philosophical Interventions in the Unfinished Project of Enlightenment*. Cambridge, MA: MIT Press, 88–112.

Taylor, Charles. 2004. *Modern Social Imaginaries*. Durham: Duke University Press.

Tejera, V. 1996 'Has Habermas Understood Peirce?', *Transactions of the Charles S. Peirce Society* 32 (1): 107–25.

Therborn, G. 1971. 'Habermas: A New Eclectic', *New Left Review* 67: 69–85.

_____. 1976. *Science, Class, and Society: On the Formation of Sociology and Historical Materialism*. London: New Left Books.

_____. 1995. 'Routes to/through Modernity', in M. Featherstone, R. Robertson and S. Lash (eds) *Global Modernities*. London: Sage.

_____. 2003. 'Entangled Modernities', *European Journal of Social Theory*, 6 (3): 293–305.

Theunissen, M. 1999. 'Society and History: A Critique of Critical Theory', in P. Dews (ed.) *Habermas: A Critical Reader*. Oxford: Blackwell, 241–70.

Thompson, J. B. 1981. *Critical Hermeneutics: A Study in the Thought of Paul Ricoeur and Jürgen Habermas*. Cambridge; New York: Cambridge University Press.

_____. 1982. 'Universal Pragmatics', in J. B. Thompson and D. Held (eds) *Habermas: Critical Debates*. London: Macmillan, 116–33.

_____. 1984. *Studies in the Theory of Ideology*. Cambridge: Polity Press.

_____. 1989. 'The Theory of Structuration', D. Held and J. B. Thompson (eds) *Social Theory of Modern Societies: Anthony Giddens and His Critics*. Cambridge: Cambridge University Press, 56–76.

_____. 1990. *Ideology and Modern Culture: Critical Social Theory in the Era of Mass Communication*. Cambridge: Polity Press.

Thompson, J. B., and Held, D. (eds) 1982. *Habermas: Critical Debates*. London: Macmillan.

Touraine, A. 1971. *The Post-industrial Society: Tomorrow's Social History: Classes, Conflicts and Culture in the Programmed Society*. New York: Random House.

_____. 1977. *The Self-Production of Society*. Chicago: University of Chicago Press.

_____. 1981. *The Voice and the Eye: An Analysis of Social Movements*. Cambridge: Cambridge University Press.

_____. 1988. *Return of the Actor: Social Theory in Postindustrial Society*. Minneapolis: University of Minnesota Press.

_____. 1995. *Critique of Modernity*. Cambridge, MA: Blackwell.

Touraine, A., Wieviorka, M. and Dubet, F. 1987. *The Workers' Movement*. Cambridge: Cambridge University Press.

Tredennick, H. 1976 'Appendices', in H. Tredennick (ed.) *The Ethics of Aristotle: The Nichomachean Ethics*. Harmondsworth: Penguin.

Tucker, K. H. 1993. 'Aesthetics, Play, and Cultural Memory: Giddens and Habermas on the Postmodern Challenge', *Sociological Theory* 11: 194–211.

_____. 1998. *Anthony Giddens and Modern Social Theory*. London: Sage.

Turner, B. S. 1992. 'Weber, Giddens and Modernity', *Theory, Culture and Society* 9: 141–46.

_____. 1996. *The Blackwell Companion to Social Theory*. Blackwell: Cambridge, MA.

Turner, J. H. 1990. 'Giddens' Analysis of Functionalism: A Critique', in J. Clark, C. Mogdil and S. Mogdil (eds) *Consensus and Controversy: Anthony Giddens*. London: Falmer Press, 103–10.

Urry, J. 1982. 'Duality of Structure: Some Critical Issues', *Theory, Culture and Society* 1: 100–106.

_____. 1990. 'Giddens on Social Class: A Critique', in J. Clark, C. Mogdil and S. Mogdil (eds) *Consensus and Controversy: Anthony Giddens*. London: Falmer Press, 179–89.

Wagner, P. 1994. *Sociology of Modernity*. London: Routledge.

_____. 2001a. *Theorizing Modernity*. London: Sage.

Wagner, Peter. 2001b. *A History of the Social Sciences: Not All That Is Solid Melts into Air*. London: Sage.

Wagner, P. 2001c 'Modernity, Capitalism and Critique', *Thesis Eleven* 66: 1–31.

_____. 2005. 'The *Problematique* of Economic Modernity: Critical Theory, Political Philosophy and the Analysis of Capitalism', in C. Joerges, B. Sträth and P. Wagner (eds) *The Economy as a Polity – the Political Constitution of Contemporary Capitalism*. London: UCL Press, 37–56.

_____. 2008. *Modernity as Experience and Interpretation*. Cambridge: Polity Press.

_____. 2012. *Modernity – Understanding the Present*. Cambridge: Polity Press.

Wallerstein, I. 1974. *The Modern World System*. New York: Academic Press.

_____. 1979. *The Capitalist World Economy*. Cambridge: Cambridge University Press.

Warnke, G. 1995. 'Communicative Rationality and Cultural Values', in S. K. White (ed.) *The Cambridge Companion to Habermas*. Cambridge: Cambridge University Press, 120–42.

Warren, M. E. 1995. 'The Self in Discursive Democracy', in S. K. White (ed.) *The Cambridge Companion to Habermas*. Cambridge: Cambridge University Press, 167–200.

Weber, M. 1930. *The Protestant Ethic and the Spirit of Capitalism* (Trans) Parsons, T. London: Allen and Unwin.

_____. 1958a. 'Science as a Vocation', in *From Max Weber* H. Gerth and C. W. Mills (eds). London: Routledge and Kegan Paul, 129–56.

_____. 1958b. 'Religious Rejections of the World and Their Directions', in *From Max Weber* H. Gerth and C. W. Mills (eds). London: Routledge and Kegan Paul, 323–59.

_____. 1958c. 'The Social Psychology of the World Religions', in *From Max Weber* H. Gerth and C. W. Mills (eds). London: Routledge and Kegan Paul, 267–301.

_____. 1978. *Economy and Society: An Outline of Interpretive Sociology*. G. Roth and C. Wittich (eds). Berkeley: University of California Press.

_____. 1988. *The Agrarian Sociology of Ancient Civilizations*. London; New York: Verso.

Wellmer, A. 1971. *Critical Theory of Society*. New York: Continuum.

_____. 1976. 'Communication and Emancipation: Reflections on the Linguistic Turn in Critical Theory', in J. O'Neill (ed.) *On Critical Theory*. New York: Seabury Press, 231–63.

_____. 1985. 'Reason, Utopia and the Dialectic of Enlightenment', in R. J. Bernstein (ed.) *Habermas and Modernity*. Cambridge, MA: MIT Press, 35–66.

_____. 1991. *The Persistence of Modernity: Essays on Aesthetics, Ethics and Postmodernism*. Oxford: Polity Press.

_____. 1998. *Endgames: the Irreconcilable Nature of Modernity: Essays and Lectures*. Cambridge, MA: MIT Press.

White, S. K. 1988. *The Recent Work of Jürgen Habermas: Reason, Justice, and Modernity*. Cambridge: Cambridge University Press.

_____. 1995a. 'Reason, Modernity, and Democracy', in S. K. White (ed.) *The Cambridge Companion to Habermas*. Cambridge: Cambridge University Press, 3–16.

White, S. K. (ed.) 1995b. *The Cambridge Companion to Habermas*. Cambridge: Cambridge University Press.

Whitebook, J. 1979. 'The Problem of Nature in Habermas', *Telos* 40: 41–69.

_____. 1981–1982. 'Saving the Subject: Modernity and the Problem of the Autonomous Individual', *Telos* 50: 79–102.

_____. 1984. 'Reason and Happiness: Some Psychoanalytic Themes in Critical Theory', *Praxis International* 4: 15–31.

_____. 1992. 'Reflections on the Autonomous Individual and the Decentred Subject', *American Imago* 49: 97–116.

_____. 1995. *Perversion and Utopia: a Study in Psychoanalysis and Critical Theory*. Cambridge, MA: MIT Press.

Wiggershaus, R. 1994. *The Frankfurt School: Its History, Theories, and Political Significance*. Cambridge: Polity Press.

Winnicott, D. 1971. *Playing and Reality*. London: Tavistock.

Wolin, R. (ed.) 1991. *The Heidegger Controversy: A Critical Reader*. New York: Columbia University Press.

Wood, A. W. 1985. 'Habermas' Defense of Rationalism', *New German Critique* 35: 145–64.

Wren, T. E., Edelstein, W. and Nunner-Winkler, G. (eds) 1990. *The Moral Domain: Essays in the Ongoing Discussion between Philosophy and the Social Sciences*. Cambridge, MA: MIT Press.

Wright, E. O. 1989. 'Models of Historical Trajectory: An Assessment of Giddens's Critique of Marxism', in D. Held and J. B. Thompson (eds) *Social Theory of Modern Societies: Anthony Giddens and His Critics*. Cambridge: Cambridge University Press, 77–102.

Wrong, D. 1961. 'The Over-Socialised Conception of Man in Modern Sociology', *American Sociological Review* 26: 183–93.

———. 1990. 'Giddens on Classes and Class Structure', in J. Clark, C. Mogdil and S. Mogdil (eds) *Consensus and Controversy: Anthony Giddens*. London: Falmer Press, 171–77.

Zimmermann, R. 1984. 'Emancipation and Rationality Foundational Problems in the Theories of Marx and Habermas', *Ratio* 36: 143–65.

INDEX

CPSIA information can be obtained
at www.ICGtesting.com
Printed in the USA
FFHW021312191118
49516585-53866FF